D1221215

John Tolan was educated at Yale and
Chicago. He has taught at universities in
North America and Europe and is currently
Professor of Medieval History at the University
of Nantes. He has published widely in both
French and English, including most recently
*Saracens: Islam in the Medieval European
Imagination* (2002).

SAINT FRANCIS AND THE SULTAN

SAINT FRANCIS AND THE SULTAN

THE CURIOUS HISTORY OF A CHRISTIAN-MUSLIM ENCOUNTER

JOHN TOLAN

OXFORD

UNIVERSITY PRESS

JKM Library
1100 East 55th Street
Chicago, IL 60615

OXFORD
UNIVERSITY PRESS

Great Clarendon Street, Oxford OX2 6DP

Oxford University Press is a department of the University of Oxford.
It furthers the University's objective of excellence in research, scholarship,
and education by publishing worldwide in

Oxford New York

Auckland Cape Town Dar es Salaam Hong Kong Karachi
Kuala Lumpur Madrid Melbourne Mexico City Nairobi
New Delhi Shanghai Taipei Toronto

With offices in

Argentina Austria Brazil Chile Czech Republic France Greece
Guatemala Hungary Italy Japan Poland Portugal Singapore
South Korea Switzerland Thailand Turkey Ukraine Vietnam

Oxford is a registered trade mark of Oxford University Press
in the UK and in certain other countries

Published in the United States
by Oxford University Press Inc., New York

© John Tolan 2009

The moral rights of the author have been asserted
Database right Oxford University Press (maker)

First published 2009

All rights reserved. No part of this publication may be reproduced,
stored in a retrieval system, or transmitted, in any form or by any means,
without the prior permission in writing of Oxford University Press,
or as expressly permitted by law, or under terms agreed with the appropriate
reprographics rights organization. Enquiries concerning reproduction
outside the scope of the above should be sent to the Rights Department,
Oxford University Press, at the address above

You must not circulate this book in any other binding or cover
and you must impose the same condition on any acquirer

British Library Cataloguing in Publication Data

Data available

Library of Congress Cataloging in Publication Data

Tolan, John Victor, 1959–
Saint Francis and the sultan: the curious history of a Christian-Muslim encounter/John Tolan.
p.cm.
Includes bibliographical references (p.) and index.
ISBN 978-0-19-923972-6
1. Francis, of Assisi, Saint, 1182–1226. 2. Malik al-Kamil Muhammad, Sultan of Egypt and Syria,
1180?–1238. 3. Missions to Muslims—Egypt—Historiography. 4. Christian hagiography.
5. Francis, of Assisi, Saint, 1182–1226—Art. 6. Christian art and symbolism. I. Title.
BX4700.F6T56 2009   261.2'709022—dc22
2008053082

Typeset by Laserwords Private Ltd, Chennai, India
Printed in Great Britain
on acid-free paper by
CPI Antony Rowe, Chippenham, Wiltshire

ISBN 978–0–19–923972–6

1 3 5 7 9 10 8 6 4 2

For my mother, Sally Tolan, a woman
of peace and of dialogue.

E poi che, per la sete del martiro,
       nella presenza del Soldan superba
       predicò Cristo e li altri che 'l seguiro,

e per trovare a conversione acerba
       troppo la gente, per son stare indarno,
       reddissi al frutto dell'italica erba,

nel crudo sasso intra Tevero e Arno
       da Cristo prese l'ultimo sigillo,
       che le sue membra due anni portarno.

(Dante Alighieri, *Paradiso,* XI. 100–8)

L'histoire est habitée par l'étrangeté qu'elle cherche, et elle impose sa loi aux régions lointaines qu'elle conquiert en croyant leur rendre la vie.

(Michel de Certeau, *Écrire l'histoire,* 58)

Acknowledgements

It would have been impossible for me to complete this book without the help of the National Endowment for the Humanities, which accorded me a fellowship in 2005. Much of the book was written at the Center for the Humanities at Oregon State University, where I was a visiting research fellow from January to June, 2005; my thanks to the staff and members of the Center for their interest and support of my work, and for creating an atmosphere propitious for reflection and research. Particular thanks to the director of the Center, David Robinson. My thanks also to the personnel of the various libraries I used while researching this book: the Bibliothèque Nationale de France, the Vatican Libary, the Biblioteca Nazionale of Rome, the Biblioteca Communale of Assisi, the libraries of the American Academy of Rome and the Ecole Française de Rome, and those of Oregon State University and the Université de Nantes.

Various parts of this book have been presented at conferences and seminars: to the conference 'Between Empires: Orientalism before 1600', at Trinity College, Cambridge; to the Dublin Medieval Society; to the Séminaire Commun des Médiévistes de l'Université Lyon II; to the medieval seminar of the University of California-Riverside; to the Maison des Sciences de l'Homme Ange Guépin in Nantes; to the Medieval Studies Workshop of the University of California-Santa Cruz; to the History Seminar of Santa Clara University; to Brown University's Medieval Workshop. My thanks to all those who invited me to these events and who shared their comments and suggestions, in particular to Alfred Hiatt, Ananya Kabir, Nicole Bériou, Jacques Berlioz, Piotr Gorecki, Sharon Kinoshita, Fabio Lopez Lázaro, and Amy Remensnyder.

For information concerning paintings by Paolo Gaidano at the Holy Saviour Convent in Jerusalem, my thanks to Brother Peter Vasko of the Terra Sancta College in Jerusalem and to Brother Michele Piccirillo of the Studium Biblicum Francescanum of Jerusalem. I received helpful advice from David Burr, Andrew Jotischky, Samantha Kelly, and Steven McMichael. During research trips to Italy, I was welcomed and assisted by Brother Pasquale Magro, director of the Communal Library of Assisi. And I had the good fortune to have the hospitality and advice of Rand Burkert and Manuela Ciri in Spello. Special thanks to Paraska Tolan for tracking down some of the quotations in Boston area libraries. Special thanks also to Nicholas Drocourt for tracking down the mysterious 'Place St. Joseph' in a Cairene taxi and for taking photos of Arnoldo Zocchi's sculptures.

Illustration 24 was taken from Andreas de Puttis, *S. Francisci historia cum iconibus in aere excusis ad Illm. et Rm. D. Dominum Constantium S.R.E. Presb. Cardin. Sarnanum* (Rome, 1594). Permission for the use of illustrations was granted by the following: The Bridgeman Art Library (images 1, 7), Bibliothèque Royale de Belgique (2), AKG Images (3, 4, 5, 6, 21), Artothek (8, 9), Rome, Biblioteca Nazionale (10), Rome, Museo dei Cappuccini (11, 12, 13), Niedersächsischen Landesmuseum Hanover (14), London, National Gallery (15), Széchényi National Libary, Budapest (16), Scala Archives (17, 19, 20, 23), Ludwig Reichert Verlag (18, 25, 28), Diocese di Bergamo (22), Istituto Bancario San Paolo di Torino (26, 27), Studium Biblicum Franciscanum (29), Nicolas Drocourt (30, 31), Amsterdam City Archives (32), Robert Lentz Courtesy of Trinity Stores, www.trinitystores.com (33).

Anne-Marie Eddé and Gerhardt Stenger read and corrected chapters of this book. Finally, I especially thank those who have read the entire manuscript and have offered me their corrections and suggestions: Jacques Dalarun, Isabelle Heullant-Donat, Jean-Claude Schmitt, and Michelle Szkilnik.

Contents

List of Illustrations

Abbreviations

Works attributed to Francis of Assisi

RB	*Regula bullata*
RNB	*Regula non bullata*

Other Franciscan Texts

1C	Thomas de Celano, *Vita prima*
2C	Thomas de Celano, *Vita secunda*
L3C	*Legend of Three Companions*
LM	Bonaventure, *Legenda maior*

Collections and Periodicals

AASS	*Acta Sanctorum*
AF	*Annales Franciscanorum*
AFH	*Archivum Franciscanorum Historicum*
BF	*Bullarium Franciscanum*: Sbahralea (Sbaraglis), *Bullarium Franciscanum* (1219–1302) (4 vols., Rome, 1759–68), continued by Eubel, *Bullarium Franciscanum* (1303–1431), v–vii (Rome, 1898, 1902, 1904); Eubel, *Bullarii Franciscani Epitome addito Supplemento* (Karachi, 1908); Da Latera, *Supplementum ad Bullarium Franciscanum* (Rome, 1780)
CCCM	*Corpus Christianorum, Continuatio Medievalis* (many volumes; Turnhout: Brepols)
DHGE	*Dictionnaire d'histoire et géographie ecclésiastique* (Paris: Letouzey & Ané, 1912–)

ED   *Francis of Assisi, Early Documents*, ed. Regis Armstrong, Wayne Hellman, and William Short (4 vols. New York: New City Press, 1999–2003)

EI²   *Encyclopaedia of Islam* (2nd edn. Leiden: Brill, 1960–).

FF   *Fontes Franciscani*, ed. Enrico Menstò and Stefano Brufani (Assisi: Edizioni Porziuncula, 1995)

Golubovich   Girolamo Golubovich, *Biblioteca bio-bibliografica della terra santa e dell' oriente francescano* (5 vols. Karachi: Collegio de S. Bonaventura, 1906–27)

MGH   Monumenta Germaniae Historiae

RHC occ.   *Recueil des historiens des croisades: Historiens occidentaux* (5 vols. Paris, 1841–1906)

Introduction

A Moorish palace that looks like the Alhambra, its walls carved in geometric relief and arabesques. A reception hall where, on a divan draped in rich cloth, the sultan is enthroned, richly dressed, head wrapped in a turban, a golden ring in his ear. Before the sultan stands Francis of Assisi: standing straight, he holds his left hand over his heart and points with his right hand towards heaven. He speaks to the sultan and looks him squarely in the face. Behind Francis, two turbaned men whisper to each other as they look in from the doorway. The sultan, swarthy, bearded, turns his head towards Francis, but his gaze is lowered: instead of looking the saint in the face, he seems to look blankly and distractedly, without giving the slightest sign of interest or emotion. Francis dominates the solitary sultan, who, seated on a cushioned divan and gazing blankly, incarnates passivity rather than power. The saint of Assisi embodies the virtues of Europe: confidence, eloquence, authority, even audacity—audacity which drove him to this foreign land to preach the Gospel to the most powerful leader of the infidels. These are the qualities that Gustave Doré emphasizes in this etching which dramatizes the encounter. He does not suggest the ascetic rigours of the saint, who here seems well nourished and whose clean bare feet do not seem to have walked far. The saint, in a white habit, bathed in light, bears the brilliance of the true religion back to its cradle, where the shadows of infidelity have reigned for centuries, where doubt and passivity lurk.

Such is the portrait that Gustave Doré sketches of this strange encounter between Francis of Assisi and the sultan of Egypt, Malik al-Kâmil, a meeting which took place, most probably, in September 1219 (Fig. 1). This etching is one of a hundred illustrations that Doré drew for the deluxe edition of the

Fig. 1. Gustave Doré. 'François devant le Sultan', in Joseph-François Michaud, *Histoire des croisades, illustré de 100 grandes compositions par Gustave Doré* (Paris, 1826), gravure 50, i. 402.

Histoire des croisades by Joseph-François Michaud, an international best-seller in the nineteenth century. What historians call the fifth crusade, directed against the Egyptian port of Damietta, gave Francis the opportunity to meet the sultan of Egypt. For Michaud, 'Francis was drawn to Egypt by the rumour of the crusade and by the hope of making a spectacular conversion.'[1] Francis did not succeed in bending the hard heart of the sultan, which proves to the French historian the necessity of waging military crusades against the Muslims. These crusades, though at times marred by excessive violence, sought to bear the fruits of European civilization to the Orient, just like the French conquests in Algeria in Michaud's own day. Francis's voyage was not in vain, for Michaud; it inaugurated Franciscan mission to 'savage peoples', a heroic and colossal effort to deliver these people from their ignorance and misery.

For Michaud, Doré, and other Europeans of the nineteenth and early twentieth centuries, Francis of Assisi's mission to the sultan of Egypt was an act of naïve audacity, yet a noble and admirable act which exemplified Europeans' good intentions towards the Muslims, who needed evangelizing and civilizing. Military crusade and preaching missions, far from being antithetical, were complementary: without European armies, the preachers could never bring their load of light and civilization to these hordes cringing in the shadows.

At the end of the twentieth century and the beginning of the twenty-first, this encounter takes on a quite different hue. One no longer celebrates the crusades; one denounces them as nefarious manifestations of violence, rapacity, and fanaticism. As a result, one cannot imagine that Francis of Assisi, the gentle saint who spoke with birds and who tamed the wolf of Gubbio, could have approved of these wars. On the contrary, it is supposed that he must have been opposed to them and, if one cannot find any textual basis for this anti-war sentiment, one can always affirm that the saint's contemporaries, blinded by the spirit of the crusades, refused to admit that the saint opposed them. Some authors even imagined that Francis went to Egypt in order to attempt to put an end to the bloodshed, to negotiate peace, or even to initiate himself to Sufism! If the crusades lend themselves to the paradigm of the 'clash of civilizations', the peaceful encounter of Francis and al-Kâmil offers, on the contrary, a gleam of hope. Even in the Middle Ages, an age of crusade and jihad, some had cool heads and large hearts and were ready to engage in dialogue instead of war. This is how, for example, Italian journalist Tiziano Terzani presents the encounter, shortly after 11 September 2001, as a model of peaceful dialogue in the midst of war, in opposition to those (from Osama bin Laden to Orianna Falacci) who preach hatred. This singular encounter also has become a model of ecumenical dialogue for various Christian authors, especially Franciscans. In January 2002, Cardinal Joseph Ratzinger, future pope Benedict XVI, affirmed that Francis had understood that the crusades were not the solution to the differences between Islam and Christianity and that he convinced the sultan of this. This peaceful dialogue is a model for today's church: 'let us walk down the path towards peace, following the example of Saint Francis', exhorts Ratzinger.[2] On Christmas day 2006, in the *New York Times*, writer Thomas Cahill lauds Francis as a 'peaceful crusader' who sought to initiate a dialogue which should be a model for us today, to avoid a clash of civilizations.[3]

This unique meeting of two men, in a tent in an armed camp on the banks of the Nile, during a truce in the midst of a bloody war, has fascinated and surprised writers and artists for almost eight centuries. What provoked Francis to cross the sea to Egypt to join the crusader camp, then to cross the enemy lines? If, as seems probable, he indeed met al-Kâmil, nephew of Saladin and sultan of Egypt, what did the two men say to each other? What were the consequences of their discussion, for each of them? How did this encounter influence the lives of these two men? How did it influence the crusade? What impact did it have on the ways European Christians perceived Islam, on Franciscan mission? These questions are difficult or impossible to answer, since the sources, from thirteenth century onwards, are both incomplete and partisan.

What do we actually know about this encounter? It was probably in September 1219 that Francis of Assisi, 37-year-old founder of the Friars Minor, left the crusader camp to meet the sultan of Egypt, al-Malik al-Kâmil.[4] The troops of the fifth crusade had already been camped for over a year in the sand between the Mediterranean and a branch of the Nile delta, before the city of Damietta. The crusaders had been able neither to capture the city nor to rout al-Kâmil and his army, who had come to protect the city. Francis probably arrived in the crusader camp in August 1219, at a time when discouragement and despair were rife on both sides. On 29 August, the crusaders launched a major attack against al-Kâmil's camp. The Egyptians feigned retreat and then cut off a large contingent of crusaders from the rest of their army. The result was a major defeat for the crusaders, which reinforced the morosity in their camp. According to Francis's hagiographer Thomas of Celano, in his *Vita secunda* (1246–7), Francis had predicted this defeat.[5] After this victory, al-Kâmil sent back a prisoner to the crusader camp with a proposal to negotiate peace. The sultan offered to give the crusaders Jerusalem, along with money to reconstruct it and a series of castles in the vicinity; in exchange, the crusaders would leave Egypt. The Holy City was not actually in al-Kâmil's hands, but in those of his brother, al-Mu'azzam, who was undoubtedly party in this proposal. Al-Mu'azzam had recently razed Jerusalem's defensive walls, perhaps in preparation for this proposal. The offer provoked discord in the crusader camp. According to chronicler Oliver of Paderborn, John of Brienne (titular king of Jerusalem), the barons of the kingdom of Jerusalem, and the German crusaders wanted to accept the sultan's offer. But others were opposed, wanting rather to complete the conquest of Egypt: the Italians (for whom Damietta was economically more attractive than Jerusalem), the pontifical legate Pelagius, most of the clergy, the Templars, and the Hospitallers.[6] It was probably during this period of truce and peace negotiations that Francis of Assisi crossed over the enemy lines and spoke with the sultan: an act of daring or folly which would cost him his life—so thought a number of those in the crusader camp. But Francis apparently arrived safely before the sultan and, a few days later, returned unharmed to the crusader camp. Such are the probable facts that we find in the thirteenth-century sources: crusade chroniclers and hagiographical narratives.

No contemporary Arab author mentions this encounter. That should come as no surprise: the chroniclers in the sultan's entourage probably did not imagine that the arrival in the Egyptian camp of a barefoot Italian ascetic, a sort of Christian Sufi who sought an audience with the sultan, could be worthy of mention in their chronicles. Christian religions were of course nothing new to them: there was a large and thriving Christian community in Egypt. Christians and Jews there, as elsewhere in the Muslim world, were considered *dhimmi*, 'protected'. They had to pay specific taxes, the *jizya* (poll tax) and the *kharaj* (land tax), but were otherwise free to practise their religion, to use their synagogues, churches, and monasteries. It was prohibited, however, for them to proselytize Muslims, and certain public displays of a religious nature (putting crosses on the outside of their churches, for example) were forbidden. Each community was granted a fairly large autonomy.[7] There were in fact two major Christian communities: the Monophysites (often called 'Copts') were more numerous; the Melkites (who subscribed to the duophysite Chalcedonian doctrine) were closer to the Byzantine church. Monophysite and Melkite chronicles more often speak about the rivalries between these two communities or within each of them than about their relations with the Muslim majority.

Al-Kâmil was not opposed to religious debate: he apparently presided over a debate between Muslims and Christians in which both Christian patriarchs of Egypt, the Monophysite Cyril III (also known as Ibn Laqlaq) and the Melkite Nicholas, took part; it is unclear whether this was before or after his meeting with Francis.[8] After the crusade, two Christian authors wrote to al-Kâmil to invite him to convert to Christianity: Theodore I Lascaris, emperor of Nicaea, and Oliver of Paderborn, crusader and chronicler who had been taken prisoner at the end of the crusade and who praised the sultan who, he said, proved himself to be more a benefactor than a jailer.[9] It should come as no surprise, then, that al-Kâmil received Francis politely and respectfully, as most of the sources affirm.

Francis probably thought of his mission as part of his quest to live the *vita apostolica,* the life of the Apostles. Son of a rich cloth merchant of Assisi, Francis had renounced his riches and his heritage to pursue a life of poverty and preaching modelled on that of the Apostles. He had inspired the conversion of other citizens of Assisi who had joined him in the small fraternity which (according to his hagiographers) was approved by Pope Innocent III in 1209 or 1210. The Friars, like the Apostles, lived in poverty and travelled the world two by two to preach the Gospel. This desire to preach the Gospel to the world brought Francis to Egypt.

Mission to Muslims was important to Francis and his friars. On 16 January 1220, while Francis was probably still in the East, five friars minor were put to death in Marrakech by the Almohad caliph. The story of these first Franciscan martyrs is related (and no doubt embellished) in a number of Franciscan chronicles and hagiographic texts from the fourteenth century.[10] The five friars went first to Almohad Seville, where they preached the Gospel and said 'many bad things about Muhammad and his damnable law'. The friars were imprisoned, then sent to Marrakech, the capital of the Almohad caliph Abû Ya'qub Yûsuf al-Mustansir (1213–24). The caliph attempted to send them back to Europe, but the friars, not easily dissuaded, returned to Marrakech, where they began to preach anew. Finally the caliph had them arrested and brought before him. As they persisted in insulting Muhammad, he had them submitted to a series of tortures that the hagiographical sources describe in macabre detail. He offered them the standard enticements (women, money, and worldly honours), if they would convert to Islam; when they refused, he beheaded them with his own sword. The king's arm shrivelled to a gnarled stump. The saints' bodies were taken to Portugal, where they duly performed miracles.

These texts reproduce the standard *topoi* of hagiography: the choice between worldly wealth and honours and the much more valuable crown of martyrdom, the blindness and cruelty of the 'infidel' persecutor (who is duly punished by God), the patience and serenity with which the saints undergo torture and execution, the miracles, etc. Yet whilst making allowances for hagiographical excess, there is no reason to doubt the veracity of the narrative. The five friars, close associates of Francis, wished to lead their apostolic life to its logical, glorious conclusion: martyrdom at the hands of the infidel. It took them quite an effort to obtain it: despite repeated affronts to Muslim law (entering a mosque, preaching apostasy, insulting the prophet and the Qur'ân), the Almohad authorities of Seville and Marrakech respond mildly: imprisonment, banishment. Only after repeated and deliberate provocation does the caliph finally give them what they are looking for, the crown of martyrdom. This indeed corresponds to hagiography's need to flesh out the legend of the saints tribulations, prolonging the tortures and showing the friars' determination. The five brothers, through their determination, succeeded in obtaining the martyr's palm that had escaped Francis. According to the fourteenth-century *Chronica XXIV Generalium*, when Francis received the news that the five friars had been martyred in Marrakech, he responded, 'Now I can truly say that I have five brothers!'[11] But Giordano di Giano, a Franciscan contemporary of Francis, affirms that when the story of the passion of the five martyrs was read to the assembled friars, Francis, 'who had a great disdain for praise and who disdained glory, pushed away the *Legend* and prohibited that it be read, saying: "let everyone be glorified by his own martyrdom and not by that of others!" '[12] As this text and others show, the martyrs inspired mixed or ambivalent feelings in the order: some look askance at this active embrace of death, yet others (including Anthony of Padua and Claire of Assisi, apparently) profess a great admiration for this active quest of martyrdom.[13]

The following year, 1221, the order approved the *Regula non bullata* (so called because it was never ratified by a papal bull), the first extant Franciscan rule. The rule establishes the basis of the friars' communal life. Mission to the infidels is an integral part of this life: the sixteenth chapter in the rule is devoted to 'those going among the Saracens and other nonbelievers':

The Lord says: 'Behold, I am sending you as lambs in the midst of wolves. Therefore, be prudent as serpents and simple as doves' [Matt. 10: 16]. Let any

brother, then, who desires by divine inspiration to go among the Saracens
and other nonbelievers, go with the permission of his minister and servant.
If he sees they are fit to be sent, the minister may give them permission and
not oppose them, for he will be bound to render an accounting to the Lord
if he has proceeded without discernment in this and other matters.

As for the brothers who go, they can live spiritually among the Saracens
and other believers in two ways. One way is not to engage in arguments
or disputes but to be subject to every human being for God's sake and to
acknowledge that they are Christians. The other way is to announce the
Word of God, when they see it pleases the Lord, in order that [unbelievers]
may believe in almighty God, the Father, the Son and the Holy Spirit, the
Creator of all, the Son, the Redeemer and Savior, and be baptized and
become Christians because no one can enter the kingdom of God without
being reborn of water and the Holy Spirit.

They can say to them and the others these and other things which please
God because the Lord says in the Gospel: 'Whoever acknowledges me
before others I will acknowledge before my heavenly Father' [Matt. 10: 32].
'Whoever is ashamed of me and of my words, the Son of Man will be
ashamed of when he comes in his glory and in the glory of the Father' [Luke
9: 26].

Wherever they may be, let all my brothers remember that they have given
themselves and abandoned their bodies to the Lord Jesus Christ. For love of
Him, they must make themselves vulnerable to their enemies, both visible
and invisible, because the Lord says: 'Whoever loses his life because of me will
save it in eternal life' [Luke 9: 24]. 'Blessed are they who suffer persecution
for the sake of justice, for theirs is the kingdom of heaven' [Matt. 5: 10].
'If they have persecuted me, they will also persecute you' [John 15: 20]. 'If
they persecute you in one town, flee to another' [cf. Matt. 10: 23]. 'Blessed
are you when people hate you, speak evil of you, persecute, expel and abuse
you, denounce your name as evil and utter every kind of slander against you
because of me. Rejoice and be glad on that day because your reward is great
in heaven.'

I tell you, my friends, do not be afraid of them and do not fear those
who kill the body and afterwards have nothing more to do. See that you
are not alarmed. For by your patience, you will possess your souls: whoever
perseveres to the end will be saved.[14]

Francis sends his brothers to the Saracens as lambs among wolves, just as
Jesus had sent his Apostles among the nations. The friars who hear the call
to mission should ask permission from their superiors who, in turn, should
not refuse them unless they judge them unprepared. The rule specifies that
there are two ways to live among the Saracens: humbly, avoiding dispute

and simply professing that one is Christian; or, on the contrary, boldly preaching the Word in hopes to convert the Muslims. For the latter, the rule enjoins courage and forbearance: a string of Gospel citations reminds them not to fear martyrdom.

This chapter of the rule shows how Francis and his brothers perceived mission to infidels two years after the meeting with al-Kâmil and one year after the martyrs of Marrakech.[15] The chapter is interwoven with Gospel exhortations: the friars are asked to take the Apostles as models, to go into infidel lands to preach the Word of God to them. The Apostles, of course, were martyred, put to death by the pagan Roman state. Elsewhere in the rule, Francis exhorts his brothers to hate their bodies, to joyously accept the sufferings inflicted by illness and ascetic rigours, as well as those inflicted on them by others. Here he reminds the friars 'that they have given themselves and abandoned their bodies to the Lord Jesus Christ'. The lines that follow, a patchwork of Gospel citations, encourage the friars along the path of martyrdom, supreme act of denial of their bodies, and of imitation of the Apostles.

The *Regula non bullata* was approved at the order's General Chapter meeting of 1221. But it caused discord within the order and it was never approved by the pope. After two years of negotiations, a simplified and modified version of the rule was ratified by a bull from Pope Honorius III (Innocent III's successor): the *Regula bullata*, rule of the order of friars minor still in use today. It has often been said that the first rule embodied Francis's own vision of the order and that the rule of 1223 was a compromise more or less imposed on the order by the pope and by Ugolino, cardinal protector of the order, with the connivance of some friars. Yet Francis always speaks in the first person in the *Regula bullata*, and he affirms his authorship of the rule elsewhere, until the *Testament* which he wrote at the end of his life. The new rule (eight pages in the English translation) is much shorter than the first (thirty-six). The tone has changed: the *Regula non bullata* exhorts the friars, in lyrical passages peppered with Gospel citations, to the perfection of apostolic life; the *Regula bullata*, in its language and in its form, is a legal text. Most of the biblical passages have disappeared. While the *Regula bullata* is more succinct than the *Regula non bullata*, it is often more precise, anticipating practical problems where the first rule merely reiterated admonitions found in the Gospel.

Concerning preaching to the Saracens, the chapter which I cited above is reduced to the following lines:

> Let those brothers who with by divine inspiration to go among the Saracens or other non-believers ask permission to go from their provincial ministers. The ministers, however, may not grant permission except to those whom they see fit to be sent.[16]

The bare bones are preserved, but all the biblical citations have disappeared, and with them the exhortations to martyrdom. No doubt Ugolino and Honorius thought that the Franciscan missionaries could be more usefully employed in serving the Church than in engaging in pious suicide. Martyrdom remained a goal for some Franciscans: six friars were martyred in Ceuta in 1227, five in Marrakech in 1232; ten Franciscans were martyred in the Near East between 1265 and 1269; seven in Tripoli in 1289. These martyrs no doubt inspired ambivalence: the 1220 martyrs were not canonized until 1481, when they became useful for crusade propaganda against the Turks.

Yet not all Franciscans who went to Muslim lands were in search of the martyrs' palm. The *Regula non bullata*, as we have seen, distinguished between two authorized ways of living among infidels: either humbly, avoiding dispute and confessing to be Christians or boldly preaching the Word. In 1225, with the bull *Vinee Domini custodes*, Honorius III authorized the Franciscan and Dominican missions in the Almohad caliphate. The pope instructed the missionaries to convert the infidels, to bring errant Christians back to the Church, and to fortify the weak.[17] On 17 March 1226, Honorius III issued another bull, *Ex parte vestra*, which sheds light on those Franciscans who wished to live 'humbly, avoiding dispute'.[18] He asks the friars to think not only of the conversion of the infidels, but also of the needs of the Christians living in Morocco. In order better to satisfy the needs of these local Christians, the friars should be discreet, avoid provoking the Muslims; they could abandon their habits and let their beards and hair grow, the better to go about their business without being noticed, in order to minister to the Christians of Morocco. The friars could even accept monetary donations (something normally prohibited to the friars, according to the *Regula bullata*) if circumstances did not permit them to beg for food. A few years later, the Franciscan minister and Dominican prior in Tunis wrote to Ugolino, who was now Pope Gregory IX, to ask him a series of specific questions concerning penitential practice for the Christians of Tunis. In 1234, the pope had Raymond de Penyafort respond to them in a long, detailed missive. The pope himself had in 1233 sent letters to three Muslim princes, urging them to convert. According to chronicler Matthew Paris, missionary friars had sent letters to the pope explaining the 'false doctrine' of Muhammad to the Christian world. The Franciscans and Dominicans were a discreet presence in the cities of North Africa and the Near East; they catered to the spiritual needs of European Christian merchants, mercenaries, adventurers, and captives. The dramatic provocation made by a handful of friars in quest of martyrdom could only make their work more difficult.[19]

Francis's mission to Egypt is thus neither an aberration nor a simple footnote to the history of the fifth crusade. It is a key moment in his life, essential for those who wish to understand Francis and the attitude of his new mendicant order towards Islam. This is one of the reasons why it is interesting to examine closely the texts of the first authors who speak of his Egyptian mission, chroniclers of the crusade and Franciscan hagiographers. Yet these early texts, just like those of the nineteenth and twentieth centuries, are partisan. Some chroniclers, wishing to legitimate and glorify the crusades, present Francis's mission as an audacious and even admirable, but in the end futile enterprise; his failure to convert the sultan through preaching confirms the necessity of military crusades.

Franciscan hagiographers had a very distinct perspective. For them, Francis, founder of an order destined to a tremendous success, canonized just two years after his death, is a new model of sanctity. His intrepid voyage to the sultan's camp shows his 'great thirst for martyrdom', brilliant proof of his sanctity. Francis preached the apostolic life, and he went to Egypt to live this life to its logical end: like the Apostles, he wanted to preach Christ to the infidels and be killed by them. The order that Francis founded soon was riven by conflict and discord, and his heirs disputed his heritage, each party claiming that their vision of Franciscan life was the true vision espoused by their saintly founder. For some of these authors, Francis had succeeded in proving, by logical argumentation, the truth of Christianity to the 'Saracen' doctors of the sultan's court. For others, the saint walked through fire to offer miraculous proof of the truth of Christianity.

In the modern period, the encounter between Francis and al-Kâmil continues to interest a variety of authors and artists. In the sixteenth century, as Ottoman armies conquer large swathes of Europe, Francis figures as a quixotic Christian hero confronting the overwhelming power of a Muslim enemy. Protestant polemicists mock his Egyptian mission, which for them is simply further proof of the folly of the founder of the friars minor. Franciscans and Jesuits, on the contrary, see Francis as a model for mission to the infidels. In the nineteenth century, as we have seen, some authors and artists make the saint into a European civilizer of barbarous Arabs, precursor to the European colonizers of modern times. Subsequently, starting in the mid-twentieth century, Francis becomes a man of peace who sought a peaceful alternative to the crusades and who initiated an ecumenical dialogue with the sultan.

Over the centuries, then, this encounter between the foremost saint of medieval Europe and a Muslim prince known for his erudition and justice has fascinated many. Each interpreter reads into encounter his or her own preoccupations. Hence rather than try to establish the historical truth of what happened in the meeting between these two men in September 1219, I propose in this book to examine how the changing portrayals of this event show the evolving fears and hopes inspired by the encounter between Christian Europe and the Muslim East.

In Part I, I will examine the principal texts and images of this encounter during roughly the century that followed it: from 1220 to 1337. In each of the nine chapters of this part, I present first the text describing the encounter (or a reproduction of a painting) and then attempt to explain this particular vision of the encounter, placing it in its historical context. The first chapter is devoted to Jacques de Vitry, bishop of Acre, who participated in the Egyptian crusade and who twice described Francis's mission to the sultan: the first time (in a letter dated 1220), the bishop was rather sceptical about the utility of Francis's endeavour; the second time, in his *Historia occidentalis* (1225), on the contrary, he presented this intrepid mission as a model for the evangelical life destined to renew the Church. In the second chapter, I examine the narrative of an anonymous chronicler who was also present in the crusader camp and who uses the mission of 'two clerks' (whom he does not name) to the Egyptian camp to emphasize the sagacity and justice of the sultan al-Kâmil, worthy adversary of the crusaders.

The following chapters are devoted to the image of this encounter in Franciscan hagiography. Thomas of Celano (Chapter 3), author of the official *vita* of the saint commissioned by Pope Gregory IX at Francis's canonization in 1228, insists on the 'great thirst for martyrdom' that propelled the saint to 'Syria' to find the sultan. The sultan, impressed by the saint's courage and eloquence, received him courteously and listened with interest, but did not convert. Henry of Avranches (subject of Chapter 4), poet at Pope Gregory IX's court, presents in his *Versified Life of Saint Francis* (1232) an epic Francis, hero of a sacred adventure, who courageously confronts the enemy and who preaches brilliantly, like a professor of theology. His preaching was well received by the 'king of the Persians' and his courtiers, but he did not have enough manpower to pursue his mission and he had to return to Italy without having converted the 'Persians'.

Devotional paintings offer different versions of the encounter. In the fifth chapter I examine the 'Bardi altarpiece', painted probably about 1240, which shows the saint preaching, gospel in hand, to the sultan and to an attentive crowd of subjects. The altarpiece was probably painted for a Franciscan convent and its artist sought to present Francis as a model of the apostolic life that the friars should lead; preaching the Gospels to the infidels is an integral part of this life.

In the sixth chapter I examine the works of Bonaventure, general minister of the Franciscans (1257–74), in particular his *Legenda major* (*c.*1260) which became the new official version of the life of the founder of the order. Bonaventure places Francis's mission to Egypt under the rubric of his burning love for God, a love which compels him to seek martyrdom. Beaten by the Egyptian soldiers, then courteously welcomed by the sultan, Francis preached eloquently and impressed the sultan and his courtiers. In order to prove the truth of Christianity, Francis proposed to enter a fire along with the 'Saracen priests', who refused. The saint then proposed to confront the flames alone, which the sultan also refused. In this way, Bonaventure concludes, Francis showed that reason alone is not sufficient to prove the truth of Christianity, that miracles are sometimes necessary to incline the hearts of infidels to the True Religion.

Bonaventure's vision was translated into images by the painter of the series of twenty-eight frescos in the upper basilica of Assisi at the end of the thirteenth century (as we will see in Chapter 7). The eleventh fresco presents a confrontation between Francis and the Saracen 'priests'. Taking inspiration from the fire which (according to Bonaventure) Francis asked the sultan to light, the artists places the saint at the centre of the composition, before a fire which separates him from the Saracen 'priests', from which they flee in fear. Francis looks behind him, towards the sultan, enthroned and surrounded by his men. The sultan gestures towards the fire and looks in the direction of his fleeing priests. Francis's mission to Egypt has become a dramatic confrontation, a trial by fire of which we do not see the final outcome, but which succeeded in humiliating the priests of the rival religion, showing the superiority of Christianity and the courage of the saint.

The two final chapters of Part I are devoted to authors from the 'spiritual' branch of the Franciscans in the fourteenth century. The order, which had suffered from conflict and division even during Francis's life, was rent by a veritable schism in the first third of the fourteenth century, between the 'conventuals' on one hand, obedient to the order's hierarchy, and the 'spirituals', condemned as heretics. Chapter 8 examines the work of one of the most fervent partisans of the spirituals, Angelo Clareno, for whom Francis's voyage to the East permitted the Devil to infiltrate the Franciscan order. Indeed, the 'rapacious wolf' took advantage of the saint's absence to sow chaos in the order and to encourage the weaker friars to disguise their laziness as wisdom and moderation. This opened a rift between, on the one hand, the worldly friars, who would rather follow their own desires and ambitions than the life and rule that Francis gave them and, on the other hand, the small band of brothers who remained faithful to their founder's teachings, who lived in absolute poverty and humility. Francis could have converted the sultan, who received him hospitably and who was receptive to his evangelical message, but the saint's stay in Egypt was cut short by the crisis in the order.

About 1330 Franciscan Ugolino da Montegiorgio compiled his *Deeds of Blessed Francis and his Companions*, a text which became something of a best-seller, particularly in its Italian translation, *I Fioretti*. The rendering of the mission to 'pagan lands' is much more elaborate and dramatized than in the earlier texts. Francis travels with twelve companions; their fervour for martyrdom compels them to seek out the sultan. Ugolino describes the admiration that Francis inspires in the sultan, who grants the friars the right to preach anywhere in his kingdom. Not wishing to let his hero leave without converting the sultan, Ugolino relates that the sultan promised to convert and that Francis promised for his part to send friars to baptize him *in extremis*—which he subsequently did, miraculously, after his own death. There is no longer any shadow or any suggestion that the mission was anything other than a tremendous success: the friars preach to the infidels, convert many of them, and even succeed in converting the sultan.

The nine chapters in Part I examine in detail each of the major representations of the encounter between Francis and al-Kâmil. In the following centuries, numerous authors and artists describe the meeting between the two men, presenting it, often, as an emblematic encounter between the Muslim East and the Christian West, as we will see in Part II. Chapter 10 traces the iconography of the encounter from Giotto at the beginning of the fourteenth century to the first printed editions of Bonaventure's *Legenda maior* in the sixteenth: the trial by fire, following the model established by the fresco of Assisi, dominates this iconography. But where the artist of Assisi, whose frescos served as model, depicted Francis *before* he had placed his foot in the flames, some fifteenth-century artists place the saint firmly in the midst of the fire, emphasizing the brilliant miracle performed by the saint before the Muslim king.

Chapter 11 shows how different authors and artists, beginning in the fifteenth century, emphasize the violence and power of the sultan and his lackeys. Various artists depict the saint being beaten, his hands tied, or being dragged brutally into the presence of a sultan who seems little inclined to listen to him—a sultan who now appears more Turkish than Arab. In the context of the rise of Ottoman power, the saint appears audacious but his endeavour ultimately futile: if St Francis himself was unable to soften the hard hearts of the Muslims, they must be impermeable to the Christian message. This justifies the fight against infidels, Moors or Turks, but also Protestant 'heretics'.

The situation changes after the failure of the Ottoman siege of Vienna in 1683; now the declining power of the Turk no longer seems a threat to Europe. Chapter 12 examines portraits of Francis sketched in the eighteenth century. The *philosophes* criticized the religious orders, in particular the Jesuits and Franciscans, which they considered a dead weight on society, so many indolent layabouts who did not work and did not reproduce. In order to attack these orders, one attacked their founders, especially Francis. Thus Voltaire presents Francis as a fanatical madman and the sultan as a wise and tolerant ruler; Voltaire emphasized the demential desire for martyrdom which pushed Francis and his followers first to Egypt, then to Morocco. For Jean Henri Maubert de Gouvest, Francis's mission was an attempt by Elias of Cortona, true leader of the Franciscans, to get rid of the saint by sending him to his death. Against these critics, other writers and authors defended the traditional Catholic vision of the saint.

Chapter 13 shows how different authors used the story of the encounter to justify the Franciscan presence in the Holy Land, which in fact was the fruit of privileges granted to the order by Mamluk sultans in the fourteenth century. For some Franciscan authors, Francis's mission to the East becomes the founding and legitimating act for the Franciscan custody of the holy places. They affirm that the saint came and visited the Holy Sepulchre, the Cenacle, and the other holy places; he predicted that these places would be granted to his order. Some even claim that al-Kâmil himself gave the holy places to Francis. Starting in the sixteenth century, when the privileged role of the Franciscans is threatened by Greek and Western rivals, the friars defend their privileges by invoking this now-mythical past. Other European writers, beginning in the nineteenth century, celebrate the heroic renunciation of these friars and decry the persecutions that they suffered at the hands of the Ottomans, all in order to call for new crusades to take back the Holy Land. For some of them, such as Michaud and Doré, Francis's voyage east becomes a civilizing mission amongst barbarous Orientals, precursor to the colonial movements of the nineteenth and twentieth centuries.

In the final chapter of Part II, we will see how various authors of the twentieth and twenty-first centuries transformed Francis into an 'Apostle of Peace', strident opponent to the crusades, who went to Damietta in search of ecumenical dialogue. This vision, the polar opposite of those of the nineteenth and early twentieth centuries, is equally dependent on a voluntary deformation of the medieval sources, which, we are told, did not comprehend the radically new nature of Francis, enemy of the crusades, admirer of Islam, even (for some) a budding Sufi. This vision of a pacifist saint continues to provoke debate in the Catholic Church: we have seen that Cardinal Ratzinger in 2002 (three years before his election as Pope Benedict XVI) affirms that Francis was opposed to the crusades and that his voyage to the sultan's court shows us 'the path towards peace' that we must follow.

As with any 'lieu de mémoire', the encounter between Francis and al-Kâmil constantly changes in meaning. One tacks onto it the preoccupations of one's day, whether they involve the role of religious orders in eighteenth-century France, the colonization of Muslim lands in the nineteenth century, or the violence in the Near East in the twenty-first. But before examining this encounter through the prism of modernity, let us examine it through the sources of the thirteenth century, starting with two works by a man who knew Francis, Jacques de Vitry.

PART
I

Thirteenth to Fourteenth Centuries

I

Francis, Model for the Spiritual Renewal of the Church

Jacques de Vitry (1220 and 1223–1225)

Lord Rayner, Prior of St Michael, has entered the Order of Lesser Brothers. This Order is multiplying rapidly throughout the world, because it expressly imitates the pattern of the primitive church and the life of the apostles in everything. Nevertheless, this Order seems very dangerous to us, because it sends out two by two throughout the world, not only formed religious, but also immature young men who should first be tested and subjected to conventual discipline for a time. The head of these brothers, who also founded the Order, came into our camp. He was so inflamed with zeal for the faith that he did not fear to cross the lines to the army of our enemy. For several days he preached the Word of God to the Saracens and made little progress. The Sultan, king of Egypt, privately asked him to pray to the Lord for him, so that he might be inspired by God to adhere to that religion which most pleased God. Colin, the Englishman, our clerk, also has joined this Order, as well as two more of our company, namely Master Michael and Lord Matthew, to whom I had committed the care of the Church of the Holy Cross. I am having a difficult time holding on to the cantor and Henry and several others.   (Jacques de Vitry, *Letter* 6: February or March 1220)[1]

Not only Christ's faithful but even the Saracens and people in the darkness of unbelief admire their humility and virtue, and when the brothers fearlessly approach them to preach, they willingly receive them and, with a grateful spirit, provide them with what they need.

We have seen the founder and master of this Order, Brother Francis, a simple, uneducated man beloved by God and man, whom all the others obey as their highest superior. He was so moved by spiritual fervor and exhilaration that, after he reached the army of Christians before Damietta in Egypt, he boldly set out for the camp of the Sultan of Egypt, fortified only with the shield of faith. When the Saracens captured him on the road, he said: 'I am a Christian. Take me to your master.' They dragged him before the Sultan. When that cruel beast saw Francis, he recognized him as a man of God and changed his attitude into one of gentleness, and for some days he listened very attentively to Francis as he preached the faith of Christ to him and his followers. But ultimately, fearing that some of his soldiers would be converted to the Lord by the efficacy of his words and pass over to the Christian army, he ordered that Francis be returned to our camp with all reverence and security. At the end he said to Francis: 'Pray for me, that God may deign to reveal to me the law and the faith which is more pleasing to Him.'

In fact, the Saracens willingly listen to all these Lesser Brothers when they preach about faith in Christ and the Gospel teaching, but only as long as in their preaching they do not speak against Muhammad as a liar and an evil man. When they do speak in such a manner, the Saracens irreverently put them to the lash and savagely expel them from their cities; they would kill them, if God did not miraculously protect them.   (Jacques de Vitry, *Historia occidentalis* (1223–5?))[2]

J acques de Vitry, bishop of Acre, was in the crusader camp when Francis arrived in July or August, 1219. He recounts Francis's mission to al-Kâmil twice (in 1220 and then between 1223 and 1225); the differences between these two versions show Francis's increasing reputation of sanctity and the growing enthusiasm for the apostolic life he preached. Jacques's testimony is interesting for a number of reasons: a partisan of and participant in the crusade, admirer of the piety of the friars minor, he initially expresses some misgivings about the zeal of the young Franciscan recruits and some ambivalence about Francis's missionary project; yet he in the end becomes their fervent partisan. According to numerous sources, Jacques was one of the most brilliant and eloquent preachers of his century. He preached in particular about his two passions: the reform of Christian life and the pursuit of the crusades. The two were closely linked, for him, and Francis's mission to the sultan of Egypt represented, for Jacques, the perfection of apostolic life, combining as it did the ideals of reformed Christianity and militant mission.

Jacques was born in the 1160s into a noble family of the Perthois.[3] He was a student in Paris as the new university was taking shape. He studied with preaching masters Jean de Liro and Jean de Nivelles, who in turn had been taught by Peter the Chanter. The secular clerics and canons of this milieu, associated with reformist elements in the church, were dismayed by what they presented as the moral turpitude that reigned in Paris, a place of debauchery and vain curiosity. They saw preaching as a privileged tool of teaching and of moral and spiritual reform. They developed a panoply of practical tools for the use of preachers: *artes praedicandi* (preaching manuals), collections of model sermons and of *exempla*.[4] Jacques, in other words, found himself in the midst of a considerable intellectual ferment. Inspired by the will to pursue and encourage reform at every social level, he preached publicly to the Parisians. Jacques proved to be the most effective and prolific preacher trained in this milieu, producing 410 model sermons, a number of which contain *exempla,* short edifying stories meant to capture the listener's attention and illustrate the preacher's moral and spiritual message. But these model sermons are the products of the final years of his life (1226–40). Let us return to 1208: in this year, thanks to his master Jean de Nivelles, Jacques is established at the Augustinian priory of Saint-Nicolas d'Oignies, in the diocese of Liège, where he meets Marie, Jean de Nivelles's wife, who had retired to Oignies to live a life of extremes ascesis. Or perhaps it is Marie herself who is responsible for Jacques's arrival: she affirmed that she had prayed that God send her a preacher since, as a woman, she could not preach.[5] God heard her prayers and sent Jacques; Jean, Marie's husband and Jacques's teacher, was simply God's intermediary in this affair. Jacques became Marie's confessor and, after her death in 1213, wrote her biography, which he completed before 1216.

In his *Life of Marie d'Oignies*, Jacques draws a portrait of the beguine, describing how, in accord with the standard hagiographical *topoi,* as a young girl, she had no interest in children's games or in material things, devoting herself to prayer and contemplation. Her worried parents had her marry, at the age of 14 (in 1181), Jean de Nivelles, but her admiring husband respected his young wife's chastity and finally let her leave to lead a live of ascesis and contemplation in a hermit's cell near the Augustinian convent of Oignies. Jacques describes the beguine's privations and the simplicity of her life; she is filled with a great 'love of poverty'; she wishes to 'follow naked the naked Christ'.[6] Through her ascesis, according to Jacques, Marie receives numerous visions, in which she consorts with her Divine Husband and frequently witnesses bitter fights between demons and angels over the souls of the dying. Her Husband permits her to intervene in these struggles through prayer; in this way she helps the angels fight off the demons and saves the souls of the dying. Thanks to these ecstatic visions, she feels less and less the need for terrestrial sustenance; her body is racked by the privations that she inflicts on it. She even takes a knife to mutilate herself and then, in shame, buries the flesh that she had cut from herself. Was she marking her flesh with stigmata in imitation of Christ? Jacques does not explicitly say so, but he says all should be 'astonished at such fortitude in the frail sex of a woman who, wounded by charity and invigorated by the wounds of Christ, neglected the wounds of her own body'.[7] A few years later, camped before Damietta, Jacques perhaps spoke with Francis about this exemplary ascetic and the wounds that she had inflicted on herself for the love of Christ. In April 1213, Marie announced that she would soon die and that she would no longer eat. She died fifty-three days later, 23 June 1213; she was 46 years old.

Jacques presents the beguine as a model of piety and renunciation, a saint who could inspire spiritual renewal, a renewal all the more necessary in the face of the growing threat of Catharism. Jacques dedicated his *Life of Marie d'Oignies* to the bishop of Toulouse, Foulque de Marseille (1205–31), who, exiled from Toulouse by Cathar sympathizers, had come to the diocese of Liège. Jacques describes the prophetic visions Marie received concerning the crusade against the Cathar heretics: she saw a multitude of crosses descend upon Languedoc, prefiguring the victory of God's army over the heretics; God showed her a sneak preview of the massacre of the crusaders at Mongausy.[8] Another vision involved 'one of our close friends who lived at our house in Oignies and who had been signed with the cross [and] was dying'. As a flock of demons descend upon the crusader, Marie takes up his defence and, in spite of his many sins, prays to God for his soul. An enormous cross descends from heaven, protecting the dying man and chasing away the demons.[9] For Jacques, this *exemplum* proves two things: it shows the efficacy of a model ascetic's prayers, and it demonstrates the protection offered by the cross to those who take the crusader's vow.

This text perhaps shows us less about Marie's personality than about that of her confessor and hagiographer. Ardent supporter of reform, product of Parisian spiritual and intellectual movements, Jacques approved of the new spirituality of the beguines, these lay women who, without taking monastic vows, devoted themselves to a life of renunciation. For Jacques, praising beguines and preaching crusades go hand in hand: to crush heresy, military battle must be accompanied by moral and spiritual renewal. His vision is the same as that of Foulque, bishop of Toulouse, who approved the preaching of the Dominicans around 1215.[10] Pierre des Vaux de Cernay, in his chronicle of the Albigensian crusade, relates that Jacques de Vitry and Guillaume, archdeacon of Paris, had been invited by papal legate

Raymond d'Uzès to preach the crusade. The two preachers toured France and Germany (*Franciam et Allemanniam*) during the winter of 1211–12 and succeeded in recruiting 'an incredible multitude of the faithful'. Pierre notes the arrival of a considerable number of soldiers recruited by these two preachers in April 1212.[11] Jacques left Oignies for a preaching tour in spring 1213.[12] Pierre des Vaux de Cernay relates the presence of other crusaders recruited by Jacques in April 1214, in spite of the fact that in theory there had been no more recruiting of crusaders against the Cathars for over a year.[13]

In April 1213, Innocent III promulgated the bull *Quia maior* to launch the fifth crusade. The bull revoked the indulgences accorded to the fight against Cathar heretics and against the Muslims of Spain, affirming that the successes of these endeavours had rendered these privileges superfluous. But clearly the purpose was to prevent the Albigensian crusade and the Spanish *reconquista* from diverting knights from a new expedition against Jerusalem, now in the hands of the Ayyubids, a dynasty founded by Saladin who had captured the holy city in 1187.[14] It is at this time that Jacques de Vitry began to preach the crusade to the Holy Land; there too, his successes were famous. According to Dominican Humbert of Romans, Jacques, 'using *exempla* in his sermons, provoked the enthusiasm of all of France. I can think of no one, before him or after him, who so inflamed his listeners.'[15] Jacques himself related, in one of his model sermons for the preaching of the crusade, that one day when he had come to a town to preach the crusade, a woman had locked her husband in the attic of their house to prevent him from listening to Jacques and from taking the cross. But the man listened to the sermon from a window and, moved by the promises of spiritual rewards, leapt from the window and ran towards the preacher in order to be the first to take the cross, provoking an enthusiastic crowd to follow his example.[16] An anonymous crusade chronicler sang the praises of the 'good cleric' Jacques, who recruited many crusaders and who was subsequently elected bishop by the canons of Acre, who asked Pope Innocent III to confirm their choice and to send them their new bishop.[17]

Jacques was elected bishop of Acre in 1216; he set off for Italy, was consecrated in Rome by Pope Honorius III, embarked at Genoa, and sailed to Acre. There he impatiently awaited the arrival of the troops of the fifth crusade. Jacques gives a lively description of his travels and of the hopes that the crusade inspired in him; he then narrates the events of the crusade until April 1221, in six letters that he sent to the pope, to his former Parisian teachers, to Jean de Nivelles, to the beguines of Oignies, to the Cistercian nuns of Aywières and to their abbess, to Leopold VI, duke of Austria (after his departure from the crusade), and to various unnamed friends.[18]

Jacques wrote his first letter in the port of Genoa, aboard the ship that would take him east. He told of his trip to Italy: he had travelled with a donkey, which he had loaded with two trunks containing cloths, personal effects, a reliquary containing the finger of Marie d'Oignies and above all (like many who studied in Paris before and after him) books—perhaps too many books, for, as he was crossing a river, 'the devil dumped into the river my arms, which is to say my books, with which I had decided to combat him'. The violent currents carried away one of his trunks, but not the one containing the finger of the saintly beguine, thanks to which, Jacques affirms, he was able to reach the other side of the raging river. He found the other trunk a bit further downstream, caught between the roots of a tree: miraculously, his books were almost dry. The devil had not been able to disarm the future bishop, thanks no doubt to divine protection and to the intervention of Marie d'Oignies. This episode shows the importance, for Jacques, of books and study, which should serve neither vain curiosity nor personal ambition, but must be deployed in the battle against the forces of evil.

Jacques arrived in Perugia the day after the death of Pope Innocent III (16 July 1216). He tells how brigands came in the night to despoil the pontiff of his clothes; Jacques contemplates the papal cadaver, naked and malodorous, and reflects on the vanity of worldly glory. On 18 July the cardinals elected Honorius III to succeed Innocent. Jacques presents the new pope as 'a good and pious old man, of great simplicity and kindness'. On 31 July the pope consecrated Jacques bishop of Acre and agreed to support the women's convents of the diocese of Liège. It was no doubt on this occasion that Jacques offered the pope a copy of his *Vie de Marie d'Oignies*. Yet during his stay in Rome, Jacques 'encountered a great deal that was repugnant to me'; those in the pope's entourage were too concerned with the things of this world, the affairs of kings and kingdoms.

> I did find, however, one source of consolation in those parts. Many well-to-do secular people of both sexes, having left all things for Christ, had fled the

world. They were called 'Lesser Brothers' (*Fratres minores*) and 'Lesser Sisters' (*Sorores minores*). They are held in great reverence by the Lord Pope and the Cardinals. They are in no way occupied with temporal things, but with fervent desire and ardent zeal they labor each day to draw from the vanities of the world souls that are perishing, and draw them to their way of life. Thanks be to God, they have already reaped great fruit and have converted many. Those who have heard them, say 'come', so that one group brings another.

They live according to the form of the primitive Church, about whom it was written: 'The community of believers were of one heart and one mind' [Acts 4: 32]. During the day they go into the cities giving themselves over to the active life in order to gain others; at night, however, they return to their hermitage or solitary places to devote themselves to contemplation. The women dwell together near the cities in various hospices, accepting nothing, but living by the work of their hands. They are grieved, indeed troubled, by the fact that they are honored by both clergy and laity more than they would wish.

With great profit, the brothers of this Order assemble once a year in a designated place to rejoice in the Lord and eat together; with the advice of good men they draw up and promulgate holy laws and have them confirmed by the Lord Pope. After this they disperse again for the whole year throughout Lombardy and Tuscany, Apulia and Sicily. Not long ago, Brother Nicholas, a provincial administrator for the Lord Pope and a holy and religious man, left the Curia and took refuge with these men, but because he was so needed by the Lord Pope, he was recalled by him. I believe, however, that the Lord desires to save many souls before the end of the world through such simple and poor men in order to put shame to our prelates, who are like 'dumb dogs not able to bark'.[19]

Jacques provides key evidence about the organization of the Friars minor at this time (summer 1216). He does not mention Francis, but speaks of brothers and sisters who live in poverty and who inspire rich men and women to convert, leading them into lives of renunciation. He mentions the annual meeting of the order, which establishes its rules and submits its decisions to papal approval. He affirms that the friars minor are revered by the pope and the cardinals.[20] According to Franciscan tradition, Innocent III met Francis and approved the new order in 1209 or 1210, though there is no papal document to confirm this. Perhaps the Franciscans invented this tradition in order to affirm that the friars minor had been blessed with papal approbation *before* the council of Lateran IV (1215), which prohibited new religious orders.[21] The primitive Franciscan rule that Innocent supposedly confirmed orally—in 1209, 1210, or just before his death in 1216—is lost, though it has perhaps left some traces in the writings of Franciscans of the mid-thirteenth century.[22] In any case, Jacques's letter is the earliest text that shows the enthusiasm for the new order at the papal curia.

It should come as no surprise that Jacques admires the Franciscans. The 'lesser brothers' and 'lesser sisters'—just like the beguines of the Lowlands whom he so passionately championed—led a life of exemplary piety and ascesis. Their preaching bore fruit precisely where it was most needed: in the cities and towns, among the 'rich and worldly'. The Franciscans' success highlighted the inefficacity and mediocrity of many clerics, who proved themselves incapable of watching over their flocks or who showed little concern for them, like dogs who do not bark at the wolf. Franciscan life, far from being a novelty, is a return to the simplicity and purity of the primitive church. God himself is responsible for the emergence and success of the Franciscans, which is part of His plan for the fast-approaching end of the world. The friars permit Jacques to insert a note of optimism into his description of a papal court that was too preoccupied with the things of this world. There is a certain tension in this description between, on the one hand, his boundless admiration for those (beguines from Liège or lesser brothers and sisters) who spurn worldly affairs, and, on the other, the practical and material concerns of a priest and bishop responsible for his flock. He mentions the case of Brother Nicholas, called back by the pope to the responsibilities he had sought to abandon. Franciscan vocation provokes admiration, but it also can hinder the proper functioning of the church.

Jacques left Rome for Genoa, his port of departure. On his arrival, the Genoans seized his horses: they needed them for their war against Pisa. Jacques took vengeance by preaching the crusade to their wives: 'a great number of rich and noble women received the sign of the cross: their compatriots had taken my horses, and I marked their wives with the sign of the cross' (*Letters*, 1. 169–71). The men came back from the war and returned Jacques's horses; when they learned that their wives and children had taken the crusader's vow 'they in turn received the sign of the cross with great fervor and great desire'. Jacques proudly says that he recruited many thousands of Genoans for the crusades and anticipates the important role the maritime republic could play in the crusade.

Having spent September in Genoa, Jacques reserved a place on a brand-new Genoese ship in October. He rented a quarter of the upper level and set up a study; he also rented three cabins: one for himself, one for his servants, and a third to house his clothes and seven days' rations. In the hold, he installed his horses along with enough wine, biscuit, and other rations to last three months. The bishop of Acre admired the simple life of the beguines and Franciscans much as twenty-first century Europeans and Americans admire the simple life of the poor: without imitating it. No doubt Jacques, worried about his affairs, preoccupied about his new diocese, and anxious about the coming crusade, envied a bit those ascetics who indulged in the luxury of despising the world. He sent his letter to his Flemish friends before setting sail.[23]

Jacques sent his second letter from Acre in March 1217: one copy to his former teachers in Paris and another to the Cistercian nun and future saint Lutgarde of Aywières. He describes his five weeks as sea, tossed by the winds and by the waves which finally 'chased the storms from the hearts of most of the sinners'. The ship's merchants took the cross at Jacques's bidding; this appeased the elements and permitted a calm voyage. The wind in its sails, escorted by a bevy of dolphins, the ship arrived in Acre on Friday 4 November 1216 (*Letters*, 2. 119–21). Jacques's parishioners welcomed him with expressions of joy, but the new bishop was alarmed by what he found in his see. First of all, there was the diversity of rites and doctrines of the city's Christians: there were Jacobites, Melkites, Nestorians, Georgians, and Armenians. Some of them were circumcised; some girls walked about veiled; some priests were allowed to marry; some Christians used leavened bread for communion. To this cacophony of cults and rites were added the divisions between European Catholics: Genoans, Pisans, and Venetians had their own priests and refused to recognize the bishop's authority. Only the 'Poulains' (Franks established or born in the East) recognized him, but they were plunged in the sin of fornication. Acre was a 'monstrous city' whose inhabitants gleefully indulged in murder, prostitution, and debauchery. All of this caused Jacques to tremble in terror, to cry, and to pray. Yet Jacques was an effective preacher, by his own account: he preached to the men and women of his diocese and gradually 'where sin abounded, grace did much more abound' (2. 238–9; Rom. 5: 20): men and women ran to him, weeping and moaning, confessing their sins, and took the crusade vow. Jacques ordered the men among the new recruits to 'prepare arms and other useful things to succor the Holy Land'; he had the women give of their riches to support the army.

But Jacques's preaching did not touch only Christians, or so he claimed:

Some Saracens, learning of the beauty of the Lord's works, came running to be baptized; many of them said that they had in dreams seen either Lord Jesus Christ or the Holy Virgin, or a saint, who told them to abandon Muhammad's error and to turn to the grace of Christ. The Virgin said to them, they say, that if they did not become Christians, they would soon perish when the Christian army arrived and was victorious.   (*Letters*, 2. 247–54)

These 'Saracens' may be slaves who sought baptism in hopes of improving their living conditions or obtaining freedom. Little did it matter, for Jacques; the point was that the Saracens responded favourably to his sermons and that they predicted their own imminent military defeat. This could only reassure the anxious bishop who often, tears in his eyes, gazed westwards over the sea, eyeing the horizon in ardent desire to see the 'pilgrims' arrive. 'If we had four thousand armed men here' he writes, 'we would find no one, thanks be to God, able to resist us' *(Letters*, 2. 432–7). The Saracens are divided, politically and religiously: some drink wine and eat pork, in defiance of Muhammad's law. What's more, there are more Christians under Saracen rule than there are Saracens: 'they daily await, in tears, the aid and succor of the pilgrims' *(Letters*, 2. 273–6).

He did not wait in vain. In summer 1217, numerous crusader ships arrived in Acre, bearing among others King Andrew II of Hungary and Duke Leopold VI of Austria with their troops, ready to fight the Ayyubids. The sultan al-'Âdil, brother and principal heir of Saladin (who had died in 1193), was backed by a number of his relatives: his eldest son, Muhammad al-Kâmil, was the governer (*na'ib*) of Egypt; the sultan had given Syria and Palestine to his son al-Mu'azzam, upper Iraq to another son, al-Ashraf; other sons, nephews, and cousins, members of the Ayyubid clan, had obtained different principalities and al-'Âdil remained in theory the sultan of all these lands. The crusaders began, in the winter of 1217–18, by launching raids against the territories of al-Mu'azzam. In spring 1218, large contingents of Frisians, Germans, and Italians arrived. The plan was, it seemed, to wage war on two fronts: in the north the crusaders, in alliance with the Seljuk sultan of Rûm, would attack the territories of al-Mu'azzam and al-Ashraf, while another part of the crusader army would invade Egypt. But the Seljuk strike against Aleppo failed and the crusaders sent most of their army to Egypt. Why Egypt, when in theory the goal, promoted by two popes and so many eloquent preachers of the crusade, was to 'liberate' Jerusalem? It would be easy to reply cynically that, just as the fourth crusade resulted in 1204 in the sack of Constantinople, the richest city in Christendom, providing enormous booty to the 'pilgrims' who participated, the new crusaders longed more than anything for the considerable wealth of Egypt. Perhaps. But they had also understood that they could not conquer Jerusalem, much less keep control of it, if Egypt stayed in the hands of their enemies. The conquest of Egypt would crush the Ayyubids and would give the kings of Jerusalem the wealth and manpower necessary to dominate the region, including the Holy City. Al-'Âdil, having heard rumour of the imminent attack, ordered the rapid construction of a land wall along the Nile at Fustât (Old Cairo); the following year, al-Kâmil and his brother al-Mu'azzam built another wall, linking Fustât with the newer part of the city, al-Qâhira.[24]

In May 1218 the crusaders landed near Damietta; Jacques de Vitry was with them. The target was well chosen: Damietta is on the Nile delta, at the mouth of one of its principal branches, the easternmost one, the one closest to the Palestinian coast. The crusaders succeeded in establishing a camp just across the Nile from Damietta, and they subsequently were reinforced by more troops, including John of Brienne, titular king of Jerusalem. They laid siege to the city, whose inhabitants sent word to al-Kâmil; he arrived on 6 June and set up camp close to the city.[25] Thus began a year and a half of siege and battles which exhausted both armies. Tall, thick walls protected the city; its port was sealed off by a chain across the Nile, from the city's ramparts to a tower on the other side of the river, guarded by about 300 men. For three months, the crusaders concentrated their attacks on this tower. Finally Oliver of Paderborn had the idea of building a floating offensive tower, built atop two ships, and sending it against the chain tower; through this stratagem, the crusaders finally took the tower on 24 August 1218, to the great consternation of the Egyptians. When al-'Âdil heard the news, it is said, he had a heart attack. At any rate he died in December 1218, leaving al-Kâmil sole master of Egypt.[26]

From Egypt Jacques wrote four more letters: 21 September 1218 (fourth letter); September 1219 (fifth), February or March 1220 (sixth) and 18 April 1221 (seventh).[27] These letters describe the riches and the strategic import- ance of Egypt, recall the Holy Family's flight into Egypt (which in some way, for Jacques, sanctifies and justifies the Christian conquest), and relate the events of the military campaign. Jacques speaks of his own role in these battles, describing for instance how he equipped a boat in which his men fought on the Nile (*Letter*, 5. 70–4). He asserts that those who fall in battle 'receive the crown of martyrdom' (*martyrio coronati sunt*, 4. 275–6). He describes the crusaders' ordeals: death on the battlefield, epidemics, famines, floods, the departure of colleagues who have decided to return home. But he remains resolutely optimistic. During the siege of Damietta, he reports, some Saracens cross the Nile to be baptized; only the dangers of the crossing keep more of them from doing the same.

In the fifth letter, Jacques explains how he sees the crusade as an essential part of God's plan for Christian reconquest and spiritual renewal of the Orient. The oriental church shone in antiquity, explains Jacques, spreading its rays to the West, but 'from the time of the perfidious Muhammad until our own time' has been in decline, seduced and weakened by 'the fallacious suasions of the pseudo-prophet and the dissolute wanton charms of lust' (*Letter*, 5. 8–16). The remnant of the Oriental Church, surviving 'like a lily among thorns', cries out like the poor widow of Lamentations: 'behold, and see if there be any sorrow like unto my sorrow, which is done unto me, wherewith the Lord hath afflicted me in the day of his fierce anger' (Lamentations 1: 12). In response to this cry for help, Jacques continues, many sons of the church are rushing to the aid of their Mother, leaving behind wives, children, and lands in order to secure a place in heaven.[28] Jacques is confident that they can succeed. The Eastern Church is riven by sects and heresies: the West flies to its rescue, bringing its soldiers and its church reformers.

The crusaders finally captured Damietta on 5 November 1219.[29] The following February or March, Jacques wrote a letter describing this conquest: he sent one copy to the pope, one to Jean de Nivelles, and one to the Cistercian abbess of Aywières. He exults in the victory, seeing the realization of the prophecy of the Psalms: 'For he hath broken the gates of brass, and cut the bars of iron in sunder. He has subdued the people under us, and the nations under our feet.'[30] 'Where once the accursed name of the perfidious Muhammad was often invoked, an abominable name from the Devil's mouth, from now on the blessed name of Jesus Christ will be pronounced' (*Letter*, 6. 21–4). Jacques tells how the crusaders, after a long siege and many battles, took the city almost without striking a blow, 'miraculously': the inhabitants, racked with illness and famine, were no longer able to resist. The Christians cleaned and purified the city: this involved a number of practical sanitary measures (in particular, the burial of the numerous bodies lying in the streets) but also ritual purification: Jacques describes a solemn procession for the feast of Candlemas (2 February 1220): the Patriarch of Jerusalem took possession of the main mosque and, 'after the perfidious Muhammad was banished from there', consecrated it as a church (*Letter*, 6. 113–37). The crusaders had taken many Muslim captives: they ransomed the rich and sold the poor as slaves. Jacques himself bought 500 children and had them baptized.[31]

It is at the end of this sixth letter, and only in the version that he sent to Jean de Nivelles and the abbess of Aywières, Jacques narrates Francis's mission to al-Kâmil, in the passage cited at the beginning of this chapter. In the letter he sends to the pope, he does not mention it.[32] He describes it to his friends only at the end of his letter, well after his description of the capture of Damietta. This shows that, for Jacques, Francis's mission was not one of the fundamental episodes of the crusade: it did not merit inclusion in his narration of the events of autumn 1219 (in his fifth letter); nor was it worth relating to the pope; it is simply a curious footnote to the crusade, to be related to his Flemish friends. Jacques is ambivalent about Francis and his order. He praises their ambition to imitate 'the forms of the primitive Church and the life of the Apostles'. But he feels, nevertheless, that the order is 'very dangerous': young idealistic friars, burning with zeal, travel the world, two by two, at their great peril. The danger is physical but also spiritual, for Jacques. He feels that these young friars 'should first be tested and subjected to conventual discipline for a time'. Jacques is here echoing St Benedict, whose Rule criticized 'gyrovague' monks who wouldn't stay in their monasteries, and who ruled that those who wanted to live as hermits should first submit to the rule and discipline of a monastic community. It is perhaps not a coincidence that on 22 September of this same year of 1220, Pope Honorius III, in his bull *Cum secundum*, imposed a period of novitiate for new Franciscan friars.[33] Jacques is more ambivalent about the friars minor than he had been in his first letter, where, as we have seen, he presented them as a remedy to the worldliness of the Roman curia. For this reason, Franciscan scholars Martiniano Roncaglia and Girolamo Golubovich thought that this passage was a scribal interpolation that did not reflect Jacques's thought; but R. Huygens accepts it as authentic. The passage is extant in a number of thirteenth-century manuscripts and it indeed seems to correspond to Jacques's attitude: admiring but worried by the zeal of the young Franciscan acolytes.[34]

One of the reasons for this ambivalence, already expressed in his first letter, resurfaces here: the longing to live the apostolic life can inspire the church's ministers, leading them to abandon their flocks, to the detriment of the church. We saw how in the first letter he mentioned a certain brother Nicholas, who had left the curia to join the friars minor, only to be recalled to his duties by the pope. Here the defections affect Jacques directly, and he, unlike the pope, does not have the authority (or perhaps the will) to oblige them to return. Four clerics in Jacques's entourage became Franciscans, no doubt inspired by Francis's preaching. We can easily imagine the bishop's mixed feelings as he attempted to carry on with four fewer clerics. Even more revealing, perhaps, are the last words of this passage: 'I am having a difficult time holding on to the cantor and Henry [probably his seneschal[35]] and several others.' We can imagine the bishop using all his persuasion and influence to retain his underlings, in a sort of duel with Francis: two of the thirteenth-century's most charismatic preachers fighting over these men. Francis manages to take four of them from the bishop; Jacques manages to convince the others to say. His 'vix ritineo' testifies to the time and effort he must have spent to avoid the dispersal of his entourage. It should come as no surprise that his admiration for Francis and his order is tinged with reticence.

This same ambivalence colours his narration of Francis's mission to al-Kâmil, to which he devotes two sentences, without naming the 'founder of this Order'. Francis burns with a zeal that gives him the audacity necessary to cross over to the Egyptian army to find the sultan, to whom he preaches for 'a few days'. Jacques admires this courage but emphasizes that the result is nevertheless disappointing: *modicum proficuit*, he 'made little progress'. As he wrote this letter from Damietta in early 1220, the bishop envisaged the imminent conquest of Egypt and as a result he thought that Francis's missionary strategy was of little use. This explains why he gave it such a minor place in his letters: an inconsequential event, a curiosity more than anything else. In 1220, Jacques is not a partisan of Franciscan mission.

Yet the second sentence mitigates this impression. The sultan asked Francis to pray for him, to ask God to reveal to him which religion he preferred. It is tempting to imagine that al-Kâmil really said something along these lines, as a gracious and polite way to end the discussion with the Christian preacher and send him on his way. Francis, who had succeeded neither in converting the sultan nor in becoming a martyr, clung to the sultan's words, which offered him a glimmer of hope and could lead him to think that his voyage from Assisi to Damietta had perhaps not been in vain. Francis then recounted this to Jacques, who recorded it in his letter. A plausible chain of events, given what we know of the three men, but of course this is only speculation. What is clear from this brief description of the episode is that Jacques admires Francis's zeal and courage but considers them ineffective.

But the bishop's perspective will be quite different after the crusade. The new Christian masters of Damietta hoped to conquer Egypt, but they couldn't agree on how to go about it. They were waiting for reinforcements, in particular for the arrival of Emperor Frederick II Hohenstaufen, who, kept back by revolts in Sicily, did not come. Chronicler Oliver of Paderborn relates that, in the long waiting period that followed the capture of Damietta, a book in Arabic came to light. This book recounted the history of the world from the creation to the end of time.[36] It spoke, in particular, of the crusaders' capture of Damietta, which, it predicted, would be followed by the triumphal arrival in Jerusalem of two Christian kings—one coming from the East, the other from the West—in the year in which Easter fell on 3 April (which was the case in 1222). Oliver says that the pontifical legate Pelagius had the book translated and read aloud 'to the multitudes'. Through this public reading, Pelagius no doubt hoped to reassure the crusaders, to discourage them from leaving Damietta, and encourage them to wait. The fateful day, 3 April 1222, was close enough to keep the flames of hope burning, far enough in the future to justify further waiting. Who was this Eastern Christian king, this ally who would come and lay siege to Jerusalem along with the Western king? Jacques de Vitry and Oliver of Paderborn place their hopes in the Christians of Georgia and in the legendary King David, to whom were attributed exploits derived from the life of Genghis Khan. The end result would be nothing less than a final and definitive victory of Christianity over Islam; the book predicted that 'a certain king of the Christian Nubians was to destroy the city of Mecca and cast out the scattered bones of Muhammad, the false prophet, and certain other things which have not yet come to pass. If they are brought about, however, they will lead to the exaltation of Christianity and the suppression of the Agarenes.'[37] The capture of Mecca, and the scattering of Muhammad's bones (erroneously believed to lie in Mecca), will mark, it is hoped, the decisive victory of Christianity over Islam. Let the crusaders at Damietta wait patiently, then, if they wish to participate in this glorious enterprise.

The wait dragged on: from November 1219 to July 1221. According to Oliver of Paderborn, this was a time of debauchery and shamelessness: 'No one can describe the corruption of our army after Damietta was given us by God, and the fortress of Tanis was added. Lazy and effeminate, the people were contaminated with chamberings and drunkenness, fornications and adulteries, thefts and wicked gains.'[38] Oliver wrote after the failure of the crusade, of course, and sought to explain why God revoked all that he had bestowed upon his army. Just as Muslim chronicler Sibt Ibn al-Jawzî explained that the Muslims lost Damietta because of their sins,[39] Oliver and other chroniclers give the same explanation when the crusaders subsequently lose the city. At any rate, all the Western sources agree that it was a long period of waiting, incertitude, and false rumours concerning the imminent arrival of reinforcements. Some crusaders went home; the legate Pelagius attempted, using all the means at his disposal, to prevent them from going. Should the crusaders go out from Damietta, attack the Egyptian army, and then conquer Cairo? This is what some thought, including Pelagius. Others, led by John of Brienne, argued that they did not have enough men; they should keep waiting for new arrivals, in particular for the Emperor Frederick. John of Brienne himself left Damietta: his father-in-law, the king of Armenia, had died, and he sought to affirm the rights of his wife and their son to the throne. His departure deprived the crusaders of one of their principal chiefs. Finally, on 17 July 1221, the troops left Damietta and marched south along the Nile, towards Cairo; John of Brienne returned as they were leaving and quickly joined the expedition that he had tried to discourage. At Mansûra, where al-Kâmil had established his camp and where his brothers al-Ashraf and al-Mu'azzam had recently arrived with reinforcements, the crusaders fell into a trap. Stuck between two branches of the river, they could no longer advance. Al-Kâmil broke open the dikes on the Nile, flooding the crusader camp. Cut off from any possible retreat, knee-deep in water, harassed by the Egyptian archers, the crusaders had no choice but to surrender. Al-Kâmil imposed his conditions: in exchange for the freeing of the crusader army and the end of hostilities, he demanded the return of Damietta and the departure of the crusaders from Egypt. All prisoners on both sides would be freed and an eight-year truce would be proclaimed between the Francs and the Ayyubids. The crusaders had little choice and accepted; some of them, such as Oliver of Paderborn, praised the generosity of the terms offered by al-Kâmil who could have imposed much harsher conditions on the crusaders.[40] For Jacques and the other crusaders, it was of course a tremendous disappointment: the conquest of Egypt, which was supposed to have led to the ultimate defeat of the 'Saracens', had failed.

In Damietta, soon after the crusaders took the city, amidst the general optimism and enthusiasm that reigned, Jacques began writing his chronicle, *Historia hierosolimitana abbreuiata, The Abbreviated History of Jerusalem.* He probably planned to write three books, but only completed two. The first, the *Historia orientalis*, which he completed in 1220 or 1221, relates the story of the crusades and the Holy Land up to 1216 (it does not include a description of the latest crusade).[41] While Jacques does not himself write of his role in the final debacle of the crusade, we know that he was there: the anonymous *Chronique* attributed to Ernoul says that he accompanied John of Brienne to negotiate the crusaders' surrender. The bishop figures among the hostages who remained in captivity until Damietta was restored to the Egyptians.[42]

In the second book of *The Abbreviated History of Jerusalem*, the *Historia occidentalis,* written after he returned to Europe, between 1223 and 1225, Jacques tells once again of Francis's preaching to the sultan. The *Historia occidentalis* paints a portrait of the Western Church:[43] a rather dark portrait indeed, particularly at the beginning of the text. Jacques describes a society plunged in the mire of sin. 'All gave themselves over to lust, like the pig in his mud hole, and made this plague their delight.'[44] The powerful fleeced the poor, the avaricious practised usury, the princes let cabarets and whorehouses flourish, the peasants refused to pay their tithes and rents, the priests celebrated mass with filthy hands and hearts, war and terror everywhere reigned.

Jacques paints a vivid portrait of Paris, new Babylon, where the houses are brothel-studies: upstairs the students spar in intellectual *disputationes*; downstairs they enjoy the embraces of prostitutes. All nationalities live cheek and jowl, but often clash: the French are said to be proud, the English drunkards, Burgundians idiots, Lombards avaricious. Insults quickly lead to fist-fights. The Parisian student, when he is not in the arms of a prostitute, has only one obsession: 'to study or hear something new. Some learn in order to know, which is vain curiosity; others, in order to be known, which is vanity; others for personal profit, which is cupidity and simoniacal vice. A small number of them, nevertheless, learned in order to be edified.'[45]

Thanks to this last group, all hope is not lost. Jacques presents his Parisian friends and professors: Peter the Chanter, Foulque de Neuilly, Jean de

Nivelles. He insists on their humility, their sobriety, their skills as teachers and preachers. He then describes the reform movements in the Western Church: 'Day by day, nevertheless, the state of the Church of the West reformed itself, improved, and those who had long lived in darkness and in the shadow of death were illuminated by the candor and the word of the Lord.'[46] In this context of spiritual renewal, Jacques presents, in thirty chapters, the principal orders regular of the Western Church, explaining, for each, how its members dress, the life they lead, the rule they follow. For each he gives a sort of moral inventory of the order, explaining and praising the motivations of its founder, criticizing those of its members who no longer respect the rule of the order, and noting with satisfaction those who devote themselves humbly to the life of a monk or canon.

The Franciscans, last of the orders that Jacques presents, have a special place:

> As we have seen, there have been three religious orders: hermits, monks, and canons. But in order that the state of those living according to a rule might rest firmly on a solid foundation, the Lord in these days has added a fourth form of religious life, the embellishment of a new order, and the holiness of a new rule.
>
> But if we carefully consider the form and condition of the primitive Church, the Lord has not so much added a new way of living as renewed an old one; he lifted up one that was being cast aside, and revived one that was almost dead. Thus, in the twilight of this world that is tending to its end, at a time when the son of perdition is soon to arrive, he might prepare new athletes to confront the perilous times of the Antichrist, fortifying and propping up the church.[47]

Gone are Jacques's worries, expressed in his sixth letter, about the perils of Franciscan life for young recruits; here on the contrary, the friars minor are at once the most recent order and the one most worthy of praise, established by God to revive the apostolic life. Jacques describes the Franciscan rule, granted by the pope, which prohibits all material possessions so that the friars can follow naked the naked Christ. As in his first letter, he insists on how these friars succeed in converting the rich and powerful, who show good business sense in trading their material possessions for spiritual riches far more precious.

Jacques cannot say enough in praise of the Franciscans: 'salt of the earth', 'light of the world', 'valiant knights of Christ', such are the epithets he uses for the friars minor, who lead 'a religious way of life which should

be imitated'.[48] Their life is based on the precepts of the Gospels and on
the life of the Apostles. 'These poor men of Christ carry on their journey
neither purse nor pouch nor bread, nor money in their belts; they possess
neither gold nor silver, nor do they have shoes on their feet', he explains,
reiterating Jesus' words to the Apostles according to the Gospels.[49] This
return to apostolic purity is laden with eschatological significance: these
knights of Christ will combat Antichrist and his disciples. There is only
one cautionary note in this panegyric: the order is not for the weak and
imperfect, who venture into it at their own risk. For them, implicitly,
one of the other orders, honourable but less perfect, would be more
appropriate.

This is the context in which Jacques describes anew Francis's preaching
to al-Kâmil. This is the only time he mentions Francis in the *Historia
occidentalis*, the only episode from his life that he relates, no doubt in part
because he enjoyed telling a story which he witnessed, at least partially,
as he saw Francis in Egypt. But this also shows that Francis's mission to
Egypt plays an integral role in the *vita apostolica* which Jacques admires so
much. In his letters narrating the crusade, Jacques considered the encounter
a detail or afterthought: Francis's project, while it did not hinder the
crusade, proved fruitless. Jacques, bishop of Acre, was an important leader
in the crusader army, while Francis, inspired barefoot preacher, was not.
Jacques was convinced, until his final letter, that he had embarked upon
the conquest of Egypt, which in turn would result in the domination of the
Holy Land. As much as he admired the life that Francis led and preached,
the bishop's primary concerns were his entourage, his church functions,
and the success of the crusade. When he wrote his *Historia occidentalis*,
between 1223 and 1225, things had changed. The crusade had ended in a
debacle. The friars minor were a popular and swiftly growing order and
Francis, still alive, already benefited from a reputation for sanctity. Now
Jacques is proud that he met Francis in Egypt.

He gives a much more detailed description of the episode than he had
for his Flemish friends in his sixth letter. It is close to hagiography: Francis
is *tantum ebrietatis excessum et feruorum spiritus raptum*, 'moved by spiritual
fervour and exhilaration'. Driven to Damietta, he is captured (*captum*) by
Saracens who take him before the sultan, a 'cruel beast' who is calmed when
he sees Francis. The man of God who tames wild beasts is a hagiographical
topos of long date: one finds it, for example, in the texts relating the lives
of the Egyptian desert fathers who tamed lions and who crossed the Nile

on the backs of crocodiles. Here the *bestia crudelis* is the sultan, enemy of the crusaders, and Francis tames him. Subsequently, as in the letter, Jacques relates that Francis preached to the sultan for several days and adds that the sultan 'listened very attentively to Francis as he preached the faith of Christ to him and his followers'. According to his letter, Francis had accomplished little. In the *Historia*, on the contrary, he begins to convince his audience and the sultan, 'fearing that some of his soldiers would be converted to the Lord by the efficacy of his words and pass over to the Christian army', has Francis sent away. In other words, it is in order to avoid the conversion and defection of his own troops that the sultan sends Francis back to the crusader camp. As in the letter, the sultan asks Francis to pray that God reveal to him 'the law and the faith which is more pleasing to Him'. Francis's sermon sowed doubt in the sultan's heart, causing him to ask the saint for his prayers, which could ultimately lead to the sultan's conversion. Jacques adds that the Saracens listen gladly to the Franciscans' sermons as long as they simply preach the Gospel, but that they beat them when they insult Muhammad.

For the bishop, Francis's preaching could have succeeded in accomplishing what the crusade failed to do. This episode occupies a central role in the *Historia occidentalis*: it is the only event that he narrates from the life of Francis, founding father and model for the friars minor, the order destined to revive the Western Church and to wage spiritual war against the forces of Antichrist. Francis's preaching to the sultan is a model to be followed. Jacques, who had boasted in his letters of having baptized hundreds of Saracens, recognizes the limits and dangers of this preaching: any attack against the 'false prophet' Muhammad could provoke the animosity of the friars' listeners, endangering the preachers' lives and preventing the Saracens' conversion. Better simply to preach the Gospel in a spirit of friendship, like Francis.

Few medieval authors will give such an important place to Francis's mission to the sultan in their biographies of Francis or in their praises of the Franciscans. For Jacques, this mission brings together three elements necessary for the triumph of Christianity: first, moral and spiritual renewal, through a life of ascesis, simplicity, and humility (a way of life incarnated first by Marie d'Oignies, then by Francis and the friars minor). Second, preaching, propagating the Word which inspires one's listeners and leads them to conversion. This conversion leads them to reform their lives to live according to the Gospels, to take the crusader's vow or (for non-Christians), to accept baptism. Finally, the third element is the confrontation with the Saracens, to come to the help of the Oriental Church in tears and hoping for liberation.

Francis most probably did not preach the crusade like Jacques, though many Franciscans would subsequently do so. One can of course contrast the two men's strategies for confronting Muslims: Jacques preached to them when he could, but he was first and foremost an active promoter of the crusades; Francis preached humbly and peacefully to the sultan. Jacques, however, sees no contradiction between crusade and preaching; on the contrary, the two are complementary. For him, Francis's mission (had the sultan not brought it to a swift close) could have resulted not only in the conversion of Saracens to Christianity, but in their desertion of the Egyptian army and in their joining the crusaders. Far from being an alternative to the crusades, preaching to Muslims could prove to be a way to recruit them to the crusader army.

After the debacle at Damietta, Jacques continued to call for crusades, composing model sermons for those who preached crusading. But the *Historia occidentalis* presents Francis's preaching as exemplary: where the crusaders' arms were able to accomplish nothing, the preaching and the apostolic life of the friars minor offered fresh hope. This text revises and corrects the first impression that Francis and his mission made upon Jacques. One sees here how Francis's sanctification has already begun several years before the saint's death. No doubt the letter from Damietta more faithfully transmits the impression that Francis's mission left in the crusader camp. This impression is corroborated by another crusader chronicler in the 1220s.

2

Al-Kâmil, Worthy Adversary
of the Crusaders

Anonymous *Chronicle* of the Crusade
(1227–1229)

Now I am going to tell you about two clerics who were among the host at Damietta. They came before the Cardinal, saying that they wished to go preach to the Sultan, but that they did not want to do this without his leave. The Cardinal told them that as far has he was concerned, they would go there neither with his blessing nor under his orders, for he would never want to give them permission to go to a place where they would only be killed. For he well knew that if they went there, they would never come back. But they responded that, if they were to go there, he would have no blame, because he had not commanded them, but only allowed them to go.

And thus they begged the Cardinal incessantly. When he saw that they were firm in their resolve, he told them: 'Sirs, I do not know what is in your hearts or in your thoughts, whether these be good or evil, but if you do go, see that your hearts and thoughts are always turned to the Lord God.' They responded that they only wanted to go to accomplish a great good which they longed to carry to its conclusion. Then the Cardinal said it was indeed good for them to go if they wished, but that they were not to let anyone think that he had sent them.

And so the two clerics then left the Christian camp and headed towards that of the Saracens. When the Saracen sentinels saw them coming, they thought that they were messengers or perhaps had come to renounce their faith. When they met them, they seized them, and led them to the Sultan.

When they were brought into his presence, they greeted him. The Sultan returned their greeting and then asked if they wished to become Saracens or perhaps had come with some message. They responded that they would never want to become Saracens, but that they had come before him as messengers on behalf of the Lord God, that he might turn his soul to God.

'If you wish to believe us,' they said, 'we will hand over your soul to God, because we are telling you in all truth that if you die in the law which you now profess, you will be lost and God will not possess your soul. It is for this reason that we have come. But if you will give us a hearing and try to understand us, we will demonstrate to you with convincing reasons, in the presence of the most learned teachers of your realm, if you wish to assemble them, that your law is false.'

The Sultan responded that he had qâdîs and good clerics [archbishops, bishops, and good clergy] of his Law, and that he could not listen to what they had to say except in their presence. 'Very well,' responded the two clerics, 'order them here, and if we cannot demonstrate with solid arguments that what we tell you is true, that your law is false—that is, if you are willing to listen and understand—then you can have our heads cut off.' So the Sultan ordered them to join him in his tent. And so some of the highest nobles and wisest men of his land and the two clerics were gathered together.

When they had all assembled, the Sultan explained the reason why he had called them together and brought them into his presence, and what the two clerics had said, and the purpose they had in coming to his court. But they answered him: 'Lord, you are the sword of the law: you have the duty to maintain and defend it. We command you, in the name of God and of Muhammad, who has given us the law, to cut off their heads here and now, for we do not want to listen to anything they have to say. We also warn you not to listen to them, because the law forbids giving a hearing to preachers. And if there should be someone who wishes to preach or speak against our law, the law commands that his head be cut off. It is for this reason that we command you, in the name of God and the law, that you have their heads cut off immediately, as the law demands.'

Having said this, they then took their leave and departed, without wanting to hear another word. There remained only the Sultan and with the two clerics. Then the Sultan said to them: 'My lords, they have told me in the name of God and of the law that I should have your heads cut off, because it is so prescribed. But I am going to act against the law, because I am never going to condemn you to death. For that would be an evil reward for me to bestow on you, who conscientiously risked death, as you believe, in order to save my soul for God.' After saying this, the Sultan told them that if they wished to remain with him, he would give them vast lands and many possessions. But they replied that they did not want to stay, from the moment they saw that he did not want to listen to them or understand their message, and that they would return to the Christian army, if he would permit them.

The Sultan replied that he would gladly have them returned safe and sound to the Christian camp. Furthermore, he brought great quantities of gold, silver, and silk garments and invited them to take whatever they wanted. They said that they would take nothing, since they could not have his soul for God, for it was in their eyes more valuable to them than all that he possessed. They said it would be sufficient if he would give them something to eat, and then they would be on their way, since they couldn't accomplish anything else there. The Sultan gave them plenty of food to eat, whereupon they took their leave of him and he had them escorted safely back to the Christian army.[1]

Here is a narrative no doubt based, like that of Jacques de Vitry, on the testimony of someone who was at the crusader camp before Damietta and who had seen Francis and his companion. This version corresponds with Jacques's on a number of fundamental points: the two men audaciously cross enemy lines; the sultan shows them hospitality and respect and expresses admiration for their intentions; he provides them with an armed escort to return them safely to the crusader camp. This agreement in the two best-informed sources renders these details all the more likely. Yet there are important differences between the two accounts. The anonymous chronicler gives a description roughly four times as long as that by Jacques, in his *Historia occidentalis*. He does not give the name of either of the 'two clerics' who proposed to prove the truth of Christianity 'through convincing reasons' to the Saracen clerics. The latter refuse to listen to the Christians and condemn them to death. But this only highlights the sultan's magnanimity, as he rejects their sentence and offers lands and riches to the two Christian clerics. This seems to indicate that at least two versions of Francis's mission circulated in the crusader camp. Some of these differences are the result of the author's perspective: he is probably a layman in the entourage of the king of Jerusalem, John of Brienne.

This text is often called the *Chronique d'Ernoul et de Bernard le Trésorier*. A misleading title, since the narration of the two clerics' mission was written neither by Ernoul nor by Bernard, and since this 'Chronicle' has only survived in the form of continuations added to a French translation of William of Tyre's Chronicle of the crusades, the *Historia rerum in partibus transmarinis gestarum*. William had related the history of the Holy Land from Muhammad to 1184, concentrating on the first crusade and on the political and military history of the crusader kingdom of Jerusalem. William's chronicle was translated into French in the first quarter of the thirteenth century; this translation adds to William's text a number of other elements, which show that the translator and compiler probably belonged to the lay nobility of the kingdom. The French text is often called the *Eracle*, since this name (i.e. the emperor Heraclius) is mentioned in the first paragraph of the text. Other anonymous writers subsequently add other texts to the *Eracle*, continuing the narrative. Of the sixty-four manuscripts of the *Eracle*, fourteen contain only the French translation of William's chronicle, while the rest contain continuations, relating events up to 1229, 1249, 1261, 1265, or 1275. Numerous authors wrote these diverse continuations; one finds in them divergent versions of the same events.[2]

Though these texts are the works of diverse authors, one version has been traditionally associated with the names of Ernoul and of Bernard le Trésorier. Ernoul, a valet of Balian d'Ibélin, is mentioned in a passage of the text concerning the year 1186: he is presented as 'he who put this story into writing'.[3] According to historian Margaret Morgan, this Ernoul is the author of a chronicle relating events in the Holy Land and Cyprus during the years 1184–97—he would thus not be the author of the description of the crusade to Damietta and of the audacious mission of the 'two clerics'. Bernard le Trésorier's name is found in the colophons of two manuscripts of the *Eracle*.[4] This treasurer of the abbey of Corbie apparently recopied a manuscript of the *Eracle* with continuations, including Ernoul's text and the text concerning Damietta; Bernard may have interpolated other materials.[5]

It is hence impossible to identify the author of this passage, though we can extrapolate a number of things about him from the text. First of all, while he certainly is not the same Ernoul who, in 1187, thirty years before the beginning of the fifth crusade, served Balian d'Ibélin as squire, he is no doubt from the same milieu of lay nobles of the kingdom of Jerusalem. The author probably belongs to the entourage of King John of Brienne, whose deeds, words, and travels he describes in detail. The chronicle ends, in many manuscripts, with John's crowning as Latin Emperor of Constantinople (in 1231). According to Oliver of Paderborn, the Frisians and Germans were the great heroes of the crusade, especially those from his own diocese of Cologne; the anonymous chronicler does not mention them at all, preferring to emphasize the valorous deeds of the 'poulains', the knights of the crusader states. His point of view is resolutely lay and noble, as is clear when we compare his text with those of clerics Jacques de Vitry and Olivier of Paderborn. The latter two continually describe the role played in the conflict by God and also by his ministers, the clerics. In describing the capture of the chain tower, for example, Oliver stresses the prayers of the priests as much as the prowess of the soldiers, implying that the former's piety and fervour guaranteed the latter's success. Throughout his chronicle, the priests' prayers, processions, and tears play a central role. There is no trace of any of this in the lay chronicler, who rarely mentions clerics; when he does, it is usually to criticize them bitterly.

The author is hostile to Cardinal Pelagius, the pontifical legate, whom he presents as the prime culprit responsible for the crusade's failure. He relates that, after the capture of Damietta, 'there was great discord between King John and the Cardinal' (p. 426)—discord which culminated in the cardinal excommunicating the district of Damietta under royal control. John 'was greatly pained that the cardinal held lordship over him' (p. 427); when he learnt of the death of his father in law, the king of Armenia, he set off, happy to leave Damietta, to try to claim the throne of Armenia in the name of his wife (who died soon after, bringing an abrupt end to his plans). While the king was away, the army was more and more mistreated by the cardinal, who prohibited all, even the poor and those in debt, from sending anything to their families in Europe; he tried to prevent the crusaders from returning home or from leaving Damietta with their goods. He indiscriminately excommunicated those who opposed him. Having been alerted, twice, that the Egyptian navy threatened European ships, Pelagius refused to believe it; the Egyptians subsequently attacked two ships in Cyprus that were preparing to bring fresh supplies to Damietta. The consequences were disastrous for the crusaders and the cardinal bitterly regretted his error (p. 429). When al-Kâmil proposed exchanging Jerusalem for Damietta, it was Pelagius who refused, going against the advice of King John, of the Templars, and of the principal barons of the Holy Land (p. 442). And it was again the cardinal who provoked the final debacle; John of Brienne joined the army to try to prevent the disaster but was unable to do so, confronted with the legate's obstinacy. Our author's hostility is so blatant that, when he recounts the death of Cardinal Robert de Courçon in the crusader camp in 1218, he regrets that Pelagius is still alive: 'Cardinal Robert died. And Cardinal Pelagius lived on, which was a great shame, for he did much evil, as you will learn in due time, in this chronicle' (p. 417). At the end of the crusade, John of Brienne goes to Rome to complain to the pope about his legate's behaviour (p. 449). Throughout the text, the author imputes the responsibility for the failure of the crusade to Pelagius and exonerates John.

It is in this context that one must place the narration of the two clerics' mission, to which the author devotes a fairly long development, four pages, in Mas-Latrie's edition, out of forty devoted to the entire crusade. He places it not in chronological order, but after the description of the capture of Damietta and of the 'great discord' caused by Pelagius, before the telling of the crusaders' march south towards defeat. The author apparently sought to use this episode, among other things, to further discredit the cardinal. The first paragraph of the chapter, concerning the two clerics and the cardinal, is almost comical. The clerics explain that they want to preach to the sultan but that they do not want to do so without permission from the cardinal. Pelagius refuses to grant them leave, fearing that this would be sending them to their death. The clerics insist, and the legate finally lets them go but washes his hands of the responsibility for what may befall them.

The clerics cross over to the Egyptian army. The Egyptian soldiers assume that they must be either renegades or messengers; they seize them and take them to the sultan. When the sultan greets them and asks them whether they have come to become 'Saracens' or as messengers, they respond that they are messengers sent by God to save his soul, affirming, 'if you die in the law which you now profess, you will be lost and God will not possess your soul'. The two clerics assert that they can prove 'with convincing reasons' *(par droite raison)*, in other words through logical argumentation, the truth of Christianity and the falsity of Islam. They propose a debate 'in the presence of the most learned teachers of your realm'. The sultan responds that he has *caadiz et bon clers de lor loi*, 'qâdîs and good clerics of his Law'. One of the scribes of the continuation did not understand the word *caadiz* and replaced it with 'archbishops [and] bishops'. The chronicler knew enough about Islam to know that a qâdî was a Muslim judge and supposed that his reader knew as well. But the scribe did not understand and imagined that the sultan, like any respectable prince, surrounded himself with bishops and archbishops.

The Christians tell the sultan that he may have their heads chopped off if they fail to prove, through rational arguments, the superiority of their religion. The Saracen sages urge the sultan to decapitate the Christians without any debate, since the law prohibits them from hearing preaching and imposes death on anyone who dares preach against the law. They remind the sultan that he is 'Sword of the Law', translation of Saîf al-Dîn (in fact the honorific title *(laqab)* of his father, al-'Âdil) and that he is obliged to defend the law by killing the two Christians.

The Saracen 'clerics' are avatars of obstinacy and blindness. Refusing to listen to their adversaries, they react with violence. This stereotypical image of the violent Saracen is a common trope in Christian texts about

Islam in the thirteenth century.[6] The Saracens' supposedly wise men, who do not dare use their knowledge and reason to defend a religion that is a priori indefensible, impose the silence of death on those who invoke reason against the law. Jacques de Vitry, in his *Historia occidentalis*, affirms that the sultan and his men listened to Francis for days and that their Saracen faith began to weaken, such was the power of Francis's words. He adds that the Saracens listen gladly to Franciscan preachers as long as they limit themselves to explaining Christianity and avoid attacks against Muhammad and the Qur'ân. The idea, as we have seen, is that mission to Muslims, when it is properly conducted, can bear fruit. In the *Chronique d'Ernoul*, on the contrary, neither the sultan nor the men of his court let the two clerics speak, and Saracen law imposes death on any who dare preach against it. The reader cannot know whether the assertion by the two Christians that they could prove the truth of their religion is true or false, since they never had a chance to try. Their declaration, threatening the sultan with damnation if he does not convert, could be seen as showing exemplary courage and forthrightness, inspired by God. Yet one could also read this, on the contrary, as the sign of the same obstinacy and arrogance that the Saracen clerics show. The chronicler's point of view is not clear.

The ambiguous portrait of the Christian clerics and the negative image of the Saracen priests serve to highlight the sultan's qualities. He listens to both sides calmly, without being intimidated by the divine punishments threatened by both the Christian and the Saracen clerics. He makes his judgement without hesitation, calmly and with justice: he refuses to listen to the Christians' preaching, but he also refuses to put them to death, 'for that would be an evil reward for me to bestow on you, who conscientiously risked death, as you believe, in order to save my soul for God'. In other terms, he appeals to general principles of justice and equity which transcend and supersede the religious laws of the clerics. A good king has clerical advisers and listens to them politely and attentively. But he judges himself, according to universal principles of justice, rather than blindly following their dictates. He takes into account the motivation of the two Christians, which merits reward rather than punishment. The chronicler here presents the sultan as a model, as much for Christian princes as for Muslim ones, we may suppose. His only flaw, it seems, is that of not being Christian, a flaw caused by the fact that it is prohibited for him to hear the preaching of the Gospel.

The following passages in the chronicle confirm this interpretation. The sultan shows that he possesses a key attribute of the good ruler, generosity: he offers lands and riches to the two Christians, if they wish to stay with him. When they reply that they prefer to return to the crusader army, he offers them gold, silver, and silks; this they also refuse, accepting only a meal before leaving. This emphasizes the sultan's generosity and shows that the author knew the principles of the religious life of the Franciscans, who refuse all gifts of money or other material possessions but who humbly accept to eat whatever is presented to them.[7]

The chronicler admires the courage and abstinence of the two clerics, yet he shows that their endeavour was futile. Franciscan mission is neither a complement nor an alternative to crusade. The true hero of this episode is the sultan, symbol of wisdom and justice. Thanks to his qualities and his patience, he succeeds in vanquishing his enemies in the crusade. The clerics are kept in their place. The caliph of Baghdad 'who is the Apostle of the Saracens', who was thought to play the same role in Islam that the pope did for Latin Christians, had the holy war preached 'in pagandom just as it was in Christendom'[8]. Yet the 'Saracen Pope' does not meddle in military affairs, which are left to the sultan alone. This is not the case for the Christians: Pelagius, the papal legate, directs the Christian forces and leads them to their ruin.

This episode paints a portrait of a just and generous ruler, a portrait which is developed in the narration of the negotiations which followed the final debacle of the crusade. The cardinal, having refused the sultan's offer of Jerusalem in exchange for Damietta, orders the crusader army to march south. John of Brienne, hostile to this expedition, nevertheless joins the army to try to avert catastrophe. Harassed by the sultan's archers, the Christian army marches straight into a trap. Egyptian ships cut off communications between Damietta and the army, which is deprived of rations. The sultan floods the camp of the crusaders, who try to withdraw. At this point King John proposes a duel with the sultan, who refuses but invites the king to negotiate. The king goes to the sultan's tent, with Pelagius's agreement, and takes Jacques de Vitry with him.

The sultan serves a banquet to the king, then tells him, 'Sire, I have great pity for you and your people who die in great pain, for they will die of hunger or be drown. And if you wish to have pity on them, you will save them from death' (p. 445). The king asks what he must do and the sultan demands the restitution of Damietta as the price of freedom for the crusader

army. John sends Jacques back to the crusader camp to communicate the
sultan's proposal, which is quickly accepted. Each side promises to free
its prisoners and the sultan promises to return the relic of the true cross
to the Christians. Among the hostages who stay with the sultan until the
surrender of Damietta, the chronicler says, are King John and Jacques de
Vitry (p. 446).

At the end of the negotiations, King John, from the bluff on which the
sultan's tent was pitched, gazed across at his flooded camp and his men
who had no food, and began to weep. The sultan saw him and asked 'Sire,
why are you crying? A king should not cry.' The king responded 'Sire, it
is proper that I weep, for I see the people that God entrusted to me die
of hunger, standing in that water.' The sultan, gripped with compassion,
looked across at the enemy host and began to cry with the king. Then
he comforted him and said he would send food to the crusader camp. He
continued to supply the crusader army for fifteen days, while waiting for
the surrender of Damietta (pp. 446–7).

The chronicler expresses his respect for the empathy shown by king
and sultan. Far from being distant or arrogant, they are saddened by the
suffering of the Christian army. The sultan is both a model of inspiration
for Christian princes and a valiant adversary against whom defeat is not
shameful. This positive portrait of al-Kâmil resembles the one painted by
many European authors of his uncle, Saladin.[9] The chronicler attempts to
relieve John of any responsibility for this defeat. If the war was lost, it was
because of the skill of the sultan and the numerous errors of Pelagius, the
arrogant legate who did not stay in his place.

In the following chapter, the author relates John's travels after his
liberation: to Rome, where he is received by pope and emperor 'with
great honour' and where (as we have seen) he bitterly complains to the
pope 'about the shame of the loss of Damietta, which the Cardinal had
caused'. As if to emphasize that the shame was the cardinal's and not
John's, the chronicler relates the king's European tour, which reads like a
society column in a tabloid newspaper: he betroths his daughter Isabelle to
Emperor Frederick II, then goes to St Denis for the funeral of French King
Philippe II Auguste, then to Reims for the coronation of Louis VIII, then
to Spain to undertake the pilgrimage to Santiago de Compostella, where
he is welcomed by the 'King of Spain' (Alfonso IX of León); he then
marries Berengera, daughter of the queen of Castile, returns to Louis VIII's
court, and goes to Puglia for his daughter's wedding with the Emperor.

The author is clearly in John's entourage and seeks to show that his master is accepted as an equal by all the crowned kings of Europe, the failure of the crusade notwithstanding.

This royal and anti-Pelagian point of view contrasts with the ecclesiastical perpective of other crusade chroniclers, who describe the rapacity, the lust, and the impiety of the crusaders after the capture of Damietta: so many sins which ultimately provoked God's righteous anger and caused the crusaders' defeat. Olivier de Cologne, for example, denounces the corruption of an army that had become effeminate through inaction and which wallowed in the mud of drunkenness and lust. The fault was largely King John's, for he had broken his crusader vows by abandoning the army to pursue his vain personal ambitions in Acre and Armenia. If they had listed to good Pelagius, Olivier affirms, the crusaders would have left for Cairo much earlier and all Egypt would have been conquered.[10]

The idea that the crusaders' defeat was a punishment for their sins of debauchery is also found in another anonymous continuation of the *Eracle*. The chronicler evokes Francis, whom he names, the better to emphasize the turpitude in which the Christian army wallowed; he does not mention the mission to the sultan.

> That man, who began the Order of Lesser Brothers—a brother called Brother Francis—who was later made a saint and officially raised to that dignity, so that we call him Saint Francis, came to the army at Damietta. He accomplished many good things and remained until the city was captured. He saw the evil and the sin which began to grow amongst the people of the army, and it displeased him. For that reason, he left there and stayed for a while in Syria, and from there he returned to his country.[11]

This text, clearly written soon after Francis's canonization in 1228, portrays the saint's presence in the army as a symbol of the harmony that reigned among the crusaders and the divine favour that they enjoyed. Their fall into sin, which the saint who 'accomplished many good things' was unable to prevent, finally discouraged him and made him abandon the army, a harbinger (if only the crusaders had paid attention to it) of God's coming punishment through the crusaders' defeat. 'For very shortly afterward they lost, through their sins, all that they had won through God's help.'[12]

Francis's mission to al-Kâmil is perceived in different ways by the crusade chroniclers. Oliver of Paderborn does not mention it. The anonymous continuer of the *Eracle*, as we have just seen, uses Francis's disapproval and desertion of the army to dramatize the moral turpitude of the crusaders which leads to their defeat. Jacques de Vitry perceives Francis's mission first (in his sixth letter) as a minor event which shows the *poverello*'s courage and faith but which bore no real fruit; in his *Historia orientalis*, in contrast, this event becomes the paradigm of the apostolic life which could revitalize the church, one positive episode in a failed crusade.

The perspective of the *Chronique d'Ernoul* is quite different. It offers no moral or religious explanation for the military failure of the crusade: the fault is Pelagius's and, indirectly, the pope's, since he named the legate. The 'pope of the Saracens', the caliph of Baghdad, does not try to tie the sultan's hands. The Saracen equivalents of Pelagius are perhaps the clerics who order the sultan to decapitate the two Christians. But the sultan ignores their advice. This author is not anti-clerical: he praises good clerics such as Jacques de Vitry. The two Christians who risk their lives to see the sultan are more ambiguous: they are perhaps naïve to think they can obtain an audience, arrogant in affirming that the sultan is damned by his law, excessively zealous in proposing to be put to death if they are unable to convince the sultan and his 'wise men'. But the author expresses his admiration for the two men's courage. An ambiguous image, deliberately or not. But the story serves, as we have seen, to blacken a bit more the portrait of Pelagius and to glorify the sultan.

This version of the interview between the two Christian clerics and the sultan of Egypt had a certain literary success. It was known, first of all, in the twenty-odd manuscripts which contain this anonymous version of the continuation of the *Eracle*. It is recopied and abbreviated by an anonymous chronicler of the fourteenth century.[13] But the readers of this text do not necessarily associate the event with St Francis, as we see in the sole manuscript of the *Chronique* which contains an illumination of the preaching of the two clerics (Fig. 2). The manuscript was produced in Flanders at the end of the thirteenth or beginning of the fourteenth century, and it narrates events up to 1228.[14]

Nothing in the image indicates that the two preachers are Franciscans, much less that one of them is Francis himself. Nothing suggests the threat of violence that, according to the *Chronique*, the Saracen clerics made to the two men, nor their refusal to listen to the Christians' preaching. On the contrary, the two Christians seem to be preaching in the tent of the infidel king. One of the preachers, standing, dressed in blue, with red cape and socks, black shoes and simple white bonnet, gesticulates with both

Fig. 2. The two clerics preach to the Saracens, Brussels, Bibliothèque Royale, MS 1142, fo. 120.

hands. Behind him, a second cleric wears a brown habit which indeed could recall the Franciscan habit, but the grey socks, black shoes and white hat show that he cannot be a friar. The two men are standing, legs apart in a position that suggests energy and movement, as if they were walking, with conviction, towards the sultan. Across from the two preachers the

Saracens are seated. Among them, the sultan, presented in the semblance of a crowned European king, seems to respond to the Christians, as he also gestures with his hands. Behind him two seated men show no reaction but seem to listen to the preachers. This illumination suggests a slightly different interpretation of the Christian mission than that proposed by the text. The two clerics courageously encounter the sultan and his men, who receive them in their tent and listen to them attentively.

The anonymous Tuscan author of the *Conti di Antichi Cavalieri* (last quarter of the thirteenth century) takes up the *Chronique*'s narration of the mission and offers an abbreviated version with a clear moral:

> When the law of the Saracens was brought to the Saladin and read to him and he had to swear on it, as does every sultan, he began by swearing to obey the law which most pleased God. Two Christian friars one day came to him and said: 'We have come to save your soul. Summon your wise men, and we will prove that your law leads to damnation.' The Saracen wise men came, and after a long dispute, they finally said to the Saladin that he was obliged to kill the friars, for it was written in their law that anyone who argued against it must be killed. The Saladin responded: 'It is true that that is written in the law but I must obey the law which most pleases God. I know that these men have come to me to save my soul, and I know that it would not please God if in exchange for this I gave them death.' Then he honoured them greatly and let them leave.[15]

Here the sultan is not al-Kâmil but his uncle, *il Saladino*, Saladin. The two clerics of the French *Chronique* have become *doi fratri*, two brothers (or friars), which suggests that the author knew they were mendicant friars. We easily recognize, in this abbreviated version, the essential elements of the story: the Christians affirm that they can prove the falsity of Islam; the Muslim wise men say that the sultan must put them to death; the sultan refuses and 'honour[s] them greatly', without showing the slightest interest in the Christian doctrine which they wish to preach to him. But there is a new element which makes the story into a moralizing *exemplum*. The author affirms that every sultan, when he takes power, swears to obey the law, and that Saladin promised to obey 'the law that most pleases God'. It is in the name of this law, superior to that of his religious advisers, that he refuses to kill the two friars. The prince must obey justice over the written law and cannot accept that the clerics' good intentions be punished by death.

This brief story is part of the twenty-one *Tales of Ancient Knights*, devoted to the exploits of fourteen heroes, twelve of which are non-Christians, mostly from antiquity: from Hector and Agamemnon to Caesar and Brutus. Five tales relate the adventures (partly based on historical facts, partly legendary) of Saladin, presented as a model of a chivalrous prince. This collection celebrates a sort of confraternity of knights which goes well beyond the chronological, geographical, and doctrinal boundaries of Christendom: Saladin, like Hector or Caesar, proves that there is no need to be a Christian in order to be a valiant knight and a just prince. The *Conti*'s Saladin, like al-Kâmil in the anonymous *Chronique*, knows how to keep his clerical advisers in their place and follows universal principles of justice which his bigoted clerics ignore. He, more than his clerics, understands and respects the 'law which most pleases God', a law which is incomprehensible to the Saracen and Christian clerics who are too obsessed with their doctrinal differences.[16]

The author of the *Conti* has understood and reproduced the spirit of the anonymous *Chronique*. The moral of the story, implicit in the *Chronique*, explicit in the *Conti*, is that a prince must respect universal principals of justice rather than listening to clerics and their laws. In the *Chronique*, written in John of Brienne's entourage, the objective was to place the responsibility for defeat on the shoulders of the pontifical legate. If only the crusaders had reacted like their adversary, the sultan, if only they had given full power to the king and not to the clerics, things would perhaps have turned out quite differently.

3

Great Thirst for Martyrdom

Thomas of Celano, *Vita prima* (1228)

Now in the thirteenth year of his conversion, he journeyed to the region of Syria, while bitter and long battles were being waged daily between Christians and pagans. Taking a companion with him, he was not afraid to present himself to the sight of the sultan of the Saracens. Who is equal to the task of telling this story? What great firmness he showed standing in front of him! With great strength of soul he spoke to him, with eloquence and confidence he answered those who insulted the Christian law. Before he reached the sultan, he was captured by soldiers, insulted and beaten, but was not afraid. He did not flinch at threats of torture nor was he shaken by death threats. Although he was ill-treated by many with a hostile spirit and a harsh attitude he was received very graciously by the Sultan. The Sultan honored him as much as he could, offering him many gifts, trying to turn his mind towards worldly riches. But when he saw that he resolutely scorned all these things like dung, the Sultan was overflowing with admiration and recognized him as a man unlike any other. He was moved by his words and listened to him very willingly. In all this, however, the Lord did not fulfill his desire, reserving for him the prerogative of a unique grace.[1]

Thomas of Celano, the Franciscan Friar whom Pope Gregory IX enjoined to write Francis's life in the wake of his canonization, gives a very brief version (compared with those of the *Historia orientalis* of Jacques de Vitry or of the anonymous *Chronique*) of Francis's meeting with the 'Sultan of the Saracens'. He places the encounter vaguely in 'Syria' and emphasizes the beatings that Francis and his companion received from the Saracens, trials which the two friars confronted courageously, showing their merits. For Thomas, Francis's voyage east testifies first and foremost to his great thirst for martyrdom. Francis, who led the apostolic life, wanted to live it to its logical end, to die the glorious death of the Apostles, martyrdom at the hands of the infidels.

We have little reliable information about Thomas of Celano. He was probably from the town of Celano, in Abruzzi. In 1221, at the General Chapter of the Portiuncula, Thomas is one of the brothers chosen to preach in Germany; in 1222, he becomes guardian (*custos*) of Mainz, Worms, Cologne, and Spire.[2] He returns to Italy in 1223 or soon thereafter; he no doubt met Francis and spoke with him in the later years of his life, without ever being a close associate. He was probably present at Francis's canonization in 1228. It was then, perhaps, that the Pope asked Thomas to write the official *Vita* of Francis, an essential element for any canonized saint. Normally the writing of a *vita* precedes canonization; here it comes after, underlining the rapidity with which Francis was made a saint. Perhaps to recompense him for his work as hagiographer, Thomas subsequently receives several relics of the saint; he later gave some them to Giordano di Giano, to the delight of Giordano and his fellow friars in Germany.[3]

Gregory IX canonized Francis in Assisi on 16 July 1228 (canonization which he confirmed in the bull *Mira circa nos* three days later). Before becoming Pope Gregory IX, Ugolino, cardinal of Ostia, had been Francis's admirer, friend, and protector. Thomas mentions him often. He praises the warm welcome that the cardinal extended in Rome to the saint, who had come to preach before Pope Honorius III and the pontifical curia. Thomas presents Ugolino as the paternal protector of the new order at a time when Francis had only recruited a few friars (1C 74–5). Francis predicted the cardinal's promotion to the papacy (1C 99–101). Ugolino was over 70 years old when, on 27 March 1227, he was elected pope to succeed Honorius III. In the second year of his pontificate, he opened the canonization process of his old friend Francis and dispatched it with a singular rapidity.[4] In order to understand this canonization—and to understand Thomas of Celano's *vita*—both must be situated in the political and institution context of the papacy and the Franciscans in 1228.

When the pope pronounced Francis's canonization in July 1228, he was in exile: he had fled Rome after he had provoked a revolt by excommunicating Emperor Frederick II Hohenstaufen. This situation explains, at least in part, the apocalyptic tone of the bull of canonization: the eleventh hour is at hand, pronounces the pope.[5] Frederick had become emperor, after a contested succession, with the help of Pope Innocent III. He had promised to abdicate from the throne of Sicily to keep it separate from the empire and to embark on a crusade to come to the aid of the kingdom of Jerusalem. The emperor subsequently showed no intention of letting go of Sicily, though he did prepare several times to embark on a crusade; each time his departure was postponed by rebellions (in Sicily, in Germany, or in the cities of northern Italy, which had banded together to form a new Lombard League).[6] We have seen how, after the capture of Damietta, the crusaders waited in vain for Frederick to come. The emperor managed nonetheless to maintain cordial relations with Popes Innocent III and Honorius III, repeatedly assuring them of his respect for pontifical authority and his desire to undertake a crusade. This desire seemed all the more compelling on 9 November 1225, when he married Isabelle (also called Yolanda), queen of Jerusalem, daughter of Queen Mary and of John of Brienne. During the wedding, he took the title of king of Jerusalem and asked the nobles of the kingdom of Jerusalem who were present to pay homage to him, which irked John of Brienne, who affirmed that *he* was still the king of Jerusalem, thanks to his marriage with the late Mary.[7] When Gregory IX was elected, Frederick was once again preparing to set off on crusade. He set sail from Brindisi in September 1227, but he and other crusaders fell ill and returned to Italy. The pope, furious at this new setback, excommunicated Frederick on 18 November 1227. It is possible, as David Abulafia suggests, that the pope took advantage of this pretext to excommunicate an emperor with whom he had many disagreements.[8]

Gregory reiterated the sentence of excommunication at St Peter's on 23 March 1228; this provoked a riot in Rome, obliging the pope to flee the city on 27 March. Over the next two years, he mobilized money and political and military allies to undermine the emperor's power. The two camps lobbed polemical bombast at each other: Gregory accused the emperor of persecuting the Sicilian church, in addition to having violated his crusader's vow. Frederick wrote letters of warning to Kings Louis IX of France and Henry III of England: Gregory, he intoned, sought wealth and power to the detriment of Europe's kings, even though poverty, and not worldly wealth, should be the foundation of the church. With the pope, nonetheless, Frederick was more diplomatic: he sent an embassy in June 1228, but Gregory refused to receive it. On 28 June 1228, the emperor set sail from Brindisi, having decided to undertake the crusade even though he was excommunicated.

His was a singular crusade. For several years, bitter rivalries had divided the Ayyubid brothers. Al-Kâmil sought out an alliance with Frederick to counter the power of his brother al-Mu'azzam; the chronicler al-Makîn affirms that he promised Jerusalem to the emperor in exchange for this alliance.[9] The goal of the sultan's negotiations with Frederick was double: first, to avoid having Egypt become once again the target of a major crusade; second, to use the *Ifranj* (Franks), particularly Frederick, as a counterbalance to al-Mu'azzam. In 1226 or early 1227, al-Kâmil sent his close adviser Fakhr al-Dîn ibn al-Shaykh to Sicily to negotiate the alliance.[10] But al-Mu'azzam died in October 1227; when Frederick arrived in Acre in October 1228, al-Kâmil no longer had any need of him. The two princes negotiated nonetheless, and on 11 February 1229, signed the treaty of Jaffa. Al-Kâmil gave over Jerusalem to the emperor but prohibited him from rebuilding its defensive walls. The Haram al-Sharif, with the Dome of the Rock and the al-Aqsâ mosque, stayed in Muslim hands. Frederick had succeeded in obtaining the Holy City without striking a blow; to mark this victory, he solemnly wore the crown of Jerusalem in the Church of the Holy Sepulchre. But the situation in Italy was troubling; he returned to Brindisi in June 1229, succeeded in reaffirming his rule, and finally obliged the pope to lift his sentence of excommunication.

During Francis's canonization in July 1228, then, Gregory was in a bind: exiled from Rome, trying (without much success) to forge an anti-imperial alliance and to pull together an army under John of Brienne, who was now the enemy of the son-in-law who had usurped his title of king of Jerusalem. John, who had no doubt met Francis in the camp before Damietta, was probably present in Assisi, along with the pope, for his canonization.[11] On 29 April 1228, a year and a half after Francis's death, Gregory (in his bull *Recolentes qualiter*) authorized the building of a basilica in Assisi to receive the saint's body;[12] this was three months before his canonization, which had apparently already been decided. Why hasten this canonization? No doubt Gregory's admiration and friendship for the poor man of Assisi were an important motivation. Nevertheless, in the troubled situation in which he found himself, Gregory sought no doubt to reaffirm his belief in the principles of poverty and simplicity incarnated by Francis. It is also possible that he saw the Franciscans as the new shock troops of the papacy: directly dependent on the pope and not on the episcopal hierarchy, these friars minor (like the friars preacher or Dominicans) could play a key role in the promotion of the Holy See's spiritual, institutional, and political programmes. Some Franciscans helped disseminate the pope's anti-imperial propaganda.[13] The canonization of the founders of the two orders, Francis and Dominic (canonized by Gregory six years later, in 1234), underlines the key role played by these two orders. At the same time, the pope reinforced the Franciscans' implantation in the Italian cities: in Florence, for example, he accorded privileges to the Church of Santa Croce, taking it under the protection of St Peter and the pope, which meant that the Franciscans could use it without worry, as the pope was legal owner of the building and the land on which it was built. (This avoided, for the friars, any disobedience of the Franciscan rule, which prohibited ownership.[14])

By championing the Franciscans and the veneration of Francis, Gregory also hoped, no doubt, to influence the order, whose cardinal protector he had been, at a time when the friars were riven by conflicts that followed the death of their founder. In the election of the new Minister General of the order, Elias of Cortona, a close associate of the saint, had been passed over in favour of John Parenti. Elias had subsequently been charged with the construction of a sumptuous basilica destined to receive the body of the poor man of Assisi; this incongruity scandalized some of the friars.[15] Elias finally succeeded John Parenti as minister general in 1232, but was finally deposed in 1239 and excommunicated.

Gregory played an active role in the institutionalization and the promotion of the order of friars minor, beginning with his first meeting with Francis in 1217. Cardinal Ugolino was preaching the crusade in Florence when Francis passed through bound for France, where he had decided to preach. The cardinal convinced Francis that his brothers in Italy needed him, that he could not abandon the new fraternity of which he was the head and founder.[16] Francis was torn between his desire to lead a model life (to set off, like his brothers, to faraway lands to preach the Gospel) and his responsibilities as head of a burgeoning institution. This conflict troubled the saint until his death and subsequently haunted the order for centuries.

It is not easy to understand the situation of the friars minor between Francis's death and his canonization; we know the period chiefly through later partisan texts, in particular those written in the fourteenth century when the order was riven by bitter debates between 'spirituals' and 'conventuals', each side claiming to represent the true heritage of their founding saint. Some historians have been too quick to lend credence to certain spiritual Franciscans, who affirm that Elias, Gregory IX, and others violated Francis's wishes and hijacked the order, transforming it into a worldly institution serving the needs of the Roman Church, in the face of a stiff but ineffectual resistance from Francis's closest companions. From this perspective, Thomas's *Vita prima* is simply a work of propaganda designed to serve the interests of Gregory and Elias. Yet nothing indicates the existence of two harshly opposed camps at the time of Francis's canonization.

Division and discord indeed existed in the order at this time, as they had during Francis's life. The saint himself was divided between, on the one hand, the desire to promote his order, to assure that it obtained papal approval, to give it a rule, and, on the other hand, the longing to abandon this world of rules and institutions to follow the call of poverty and simplicity. It was clear, during Francis's lifetime, that an order with hundreds or thousands of friars spread all over Europe and the Mediterranean world could not survive without rules and a hierarchy, as had been possible for the dozen brothers of the order's initial years. Francis no doubt was proud of and pleased with the order's successes, yet probably also nostalgic for the heady early days when a few brothers shared a life of simplicity which was now forever lost.

Thomas of Celano, in the *Vita prima*, says not a word about divisions in the order, during Francis's lifetime or afterwards. He nevertheless seems to be a partisan of Elias, whom he presents as a regular companion of the saint (1C 69). When Francis was troubled by a multitude of illnesses at the end of his life, Elias intervened on many occasions to oblige him to see a doctor (1C 98, 105). Elias was the one person who had a special privilege: he saw Francis's stigmata, including the wound in his side, when the saint was still alive (1C 95). God revealed to him, in a dream, the date of Francis's death two full years in advance (1C 109).

Francis's deathbed scene clearly shows favour to Elias. Francis, blind, in the presence of many friars, places his hand on Elias's head and asks 'over whom am I holding my right hand?' When they answer 'over Brother Elias', Francis replies:

> And this is what I wish to do. I bless you my son, in all and through all, and just as the most High has increased my brothers and sons in your hands, so too, upon you and in you, I bless them all. May the king of all bless you in heaven and on earth. I bless you as I can, and more than I can, and what I cannot do may the One who can do all things do in you. May God remember your work and labors, and may a place be reserved for you among the rewards of the just. May you receive every blessing you desire and may your every worthy request be fulfilled.   (1C 108)

Elias was chosen by the saint's hand, through this special benediction, as his legitimate successor as head of the order, a responsibility which logically followed that of vicar (to which he had previously been named). By electing John Parenti, the friars thus went against the will of the saint, for Thomas.[17] Some spiritual Franciscans of the fourteenth century saw John Parenti as one of their own, who respected the simplicity and poverty of the poor man of Assisi; for them, Elias had abandoned the life of simplicity and poverty and usurped the memory of Francis, just as he had usurped his body to place it in a sumptuous and pretentious basilica. But once again, this is projecting onto the thirteenth century the divisions between spirituals and conventuals which in fact erupt in the fourteenth. John Parenti indeed led a life of humility and walked the paths of Italy barefoot to visit the order's convents. But John was a lawyer, and he also represented the first successes of the class of university professors who would take control of the order. Here Elias signalled a return to the tradition of the simplicity of the unschooled, and during his generalate he fought against the growing role of the learned in the order. It would thus be overly simplistic to reduce the conflicts among the friars minor to a bipolar struggle between 'spirituals', faithful to Francis, and 'conventuals', dominated by Elias and the pope, who sought to corrupt the primitive brotherhood.

Thomas's *Vita prima* is hence not a simple work of propaganda in the service of Elias and Gregory, as some critics (in particular Paul Sabatier) have claimed.[18] It is nonetheless clear that Thomas supported Elias at a time when he, passed over for the generalate, was beginning work on the enormous basilica which was destined to become a major pilgrimage site. Thomas, like Elias, sought to present Francis not only as a model for the friars, but also as an exceptional saint worthy of devotion for pilgrims from all over Europe. This will shock some friars for whom the cult of the saint, and the sumptuous basilica which is to become its centre, profane the ideal simplicity taught by the poor man of Assisi.

Thomas divided the *Vita prima* into three parts: the first relates the life of Francis up to 1225; the second narrates the end of his life, insisting on his illnesses and sufferings, then describes his death and the stigmata found on his body; the third relates his posthumous miracles. Thomas no doubt used the oral accounts of various friars; as Jacques Dalarun has shown, he also used three written texts: in the first part, Francis's *Testament*; in the second, the letter that Elias sent to the friars in 1226 to announce the saint's death—Elias describes in detail the stigmata, which he presents as an exceptional proof of Francis's sanctity; in the third, Gregory IX's bull of canonization.[19] Through the three parts of the *Vita* the image of the saint progresses. He is at first the saint of apostolic poverty, model of ascesis and simplicity for the brothers who accompany him. In the second part of the *Vita*, he has become the saint of the stigmata, now impossible to imitate, closer to Christ than to the Apostles. Finally, in part three, he is a healing saint who performs miracles for his devotees, as do countless other saints.

Throughout the *Vita prima*, one senses a certain tension. On the one hand, Thomas seeks to cast Francis in the standard mould of sanctity, to use hagiographical *topoi* and biblical citations to show that he corresponds to the standard model of the saint (a model which of course imitates that of Christ and the Apostles). On the other hand, he wants to give a living and vibrant image of a unique man. The two goals are not contradictory for Thomas: he was convinced of Francis's sanctity, a sanctity which of necessity conformed to canonical models, but he was also struck by Francis's exceptionality. Hence the impression that Thomas, even as he tries to confine himself to the typological exigencies of hagiography, is constantly trespassing them. Sometimes he seems aware of the constraints that hagiography imposes on him and consciously thwarts them, insisting on the uniqueness of his subject. After his narration of a miracle of exorcism that Francis accomplished during his life, Thomas remarks:

> But we have not chosen to describe miracles—they do not make holiness but show it—but rather to describe the excellence of his life and the honest form of his manner of living. Passing over the miracles, because they are so numerous, let us return to narrating the works of eternal salvation. (1C 70)

As a hagiographer, Thomas is obliged to recount miracles; but this is clearly not what interests him. When he arrives at Francis's *post-mortem* miracles, he narrates them conscientiously, but in a way which clearly shows his principal interests: they are relegated to the third part of the *Vita prima*, which accounts for just 16 per cent of the text (20 out of 128 pages, in the English translation).

Some modern readers, apparently not understanding that this is a work of hagiography, criticize Thomas for his use of *topoi*: N. Tammassia speaks of a 'Celano's plagiarism', a simple 'cold imitation of the standard *Lives of the Fathers*'.[20] Certain passages of the *Vita prima* indeed seem simply to reproduce well-established hagiographic themes: for example, the motif of the whiteness and beauty of Francis's cadaver.[21] One could easily multiply the examples of passages where Thomas, like any other hagiographer, takes inspiration from hagiographical models, either to introduce into the *Vita* typological 'events' which may never have taken place, or to colour his presentation and interpretation of other events. As Jacques Le Goff noted in his *Saint Louis*, the saints themselves read hagiography.[22] When their biographers use these *topoi* to describe their deeds, is this because they wish to attribute to them words and deeds considered obligatory in a work of hagiography? Or do the future saints themselves model their words and behaviour on the lives of their saintly predecessors? Some of the passages of the *Vita prima* often considered the most authentic, because they show Francis's uniqueness, are equally problematic. One example is the well-known scene (1C 15) where the young Francis strips naked in the square before the cathedral of Assisi and gives his clothes to his father, a rich clothes merchant. This dramatic confrontation marks the conversion of Francis, year one (from which Thomas dates all subsequent events in the *Vita*). The rejection of worldly clothing, that of a merchant to boot, symbolizes his renunciation of worldly values; his nudity represents the absolute poverty that he seeks. The bishop of Assisi takes Francis in his arms and covers him with his coat, marking the welcome that the church extends to Francis and his brotherhood. This scene strikes Thomas's readers and becomes a central element in the saint's iconography: it seems a key moment in the life of a unique saint. Yet we find echoes of hagiographical *topoi* here as well: as Ruth Wolff has shown, Thomas is here reworking a story told by Pope Gregory I the Great, concerning a rich young merchant who wished to renounce worldly goods. Surrounded by demons who attempted to prevent him, he ultimately took off his clothes, threw them behind him, and ran naked to a nearby monastery, where he was accepted as a novice.[23] Any attempt to disentangle the 'real' Francis from hagiographical convention is doomed to failure.

We confront the same problem in Thomas's description of Francis's voyage to the Holy Land, which he places in the first of the three parts of the *Vita prima*, devoted to 'the purity of his blessed way of life, to his virtuous conduct and his wholesome teaching' (1C 2). At the outset, Thomas narrates Francis's life in chronological order: his carefree youth, his conversion and the subsequent conflict with his father, the conversion of the first brothers, his trip to Rome where he received the approbation of Pope Innocent III, after which he proclaimed that he wanted his brotherhood to become the Order of Friars Minor. Henceforth, Thomas no longer narrates in chronological order, but describes the ascesis of the brothers, their love for and obedience to Francis, and the saint's exceptional qualities: his clairvoyance, his abstinence, his goodwill towards his brothers, his humility.

Immediately after these descriptions, Thomas evokes the 'desire for holy martyrdom' which thrice compelled Francis to seek death at the hands of the infidels.

> In the sixth year of his conversion, burning with the desire for holy martyrdom, he wished to take a ship to the region of Syria to preach the Christian faith and repentance to the Saracens and other unbelievers. But after he had boarded a ship to go there, contrary winds started blowing, and he found himself with his fellow travelers on the shores of Slavonia [Dalmatia]. (1C 55).

To return to Italy, he snuck onto a ship as a stow-away; when the winds died down and the crew had to row for many days, Francis's modest provisions miraculously multiplied and sufficed for all on board. He tried a second time to obtain the martyr's palm, this time in Morocco, 'to preach the gospel of Christ to the Miramolin [the Almohad caliph] and his retinue' (1C 56). But he fell ill in Spain and was forced to return to Italy.

Why did God prevent Francis from obtaining his goal of martyrdom? Because 'God, out of pure kindness, was pleased to be mindful of me and many others', says Thomas. When he returned to the Portiuncula, 'literate men and nobles gladly joined him. He received such men with honour and dignity, since he himself was very noble and distinguished in spirit, and respectfully gave to each his due. In fact, since he was endowed with out-standing discernment, he wisely considered in all matters the dignity of rank of each one' (1C 56). Among these new disciples was Thomas of Celano himself. This is one of the rare pieces of autobiographical information that Thomas gives in his writings. This took place, most probably, in 1215.

The arrival of these 'literate men and nobles' is indeed an important moment in the new order's expansion. Previously, Thomas had mentioned only twelve brothers, including Francis: the number of the Apostles, which corresponded to the apostolic life which the brothers led (even if in fact the years 1210–15 saw a significant growth of the order, who probably numbered much more than twelve[24]). The arrival of these new disciples (Thomas does not say how many they were) nevertheless probably represented a significant augmentation of the order. Yet one senses a tension or contradiction here. Francis's writings and Thomas's *Vita* exalt the notion of absolute poverty and total equality between brothers; Francis rejects social distinctions and disdains erudition. But Thomas asserts that Francis 'respectfully gave to each his due', that is, that he showed particular respect to these nobles and men of letters. Thomas relates with pride the warm and respectful welcome that the founding saint of the order extended to him. Here we see already, in 1215, or at least in 1228 when Thomas wrote this *Vita,* tensions in the order.

After this interlude, Thomas returns to Francis's desire for martyrdom; he relates the passage cited at the opening of this chapter. This is the third attempt to obtain the martyr's crown. Thomas situates this episode vaguely in the Orient, in 'Syria', where Christians and 'pagans' wage bitter battles. Thomas knows little about the crusades and cares little, compared to Jacques de Vitry or to the anonymous author of the *Chronicle of Ernoul.* Thomas asserts for example that Francis and his companion went to see 'sultan of the Saracens', as if there was one sole ruler of all the Muslims.

In his description of Francis's quest for martyrdom, Thomas naturally follows established hagiographical models, in particular the *passiones* which related the suffering and death of the martyrs of antiquity, put to death by the pagan Roman state. Thomas's use of the word 'pagans' to describe the Saracens thus corresponds to hagiographical tradition.[25] The ancient *passiones* delighted in the detailed descriptions of the tortures that the evil 'pagans' inflict on their Christian victims, who confront these tribulations courageously, showing that God favours them and gives them strength. Thomas tells us that Francis is captured by Saracen soldiers who beat him, who 'insulted the Christian law', and who threatened torture and death. In other words, the Saracen soldiers perfectly played the role of vicious torturer assigned to them by hagiographic tradition. And Francis played his role: he 'was not afraid. He did not flinch ... nor was he shaken.' On the contrary, 'With great strength of soul he spoke to him [the sultan], with eloquence and confidence he answered those who insulted the Christian law.' Was Francis in fact beaten? Or were these beatings imagined by his hagiographer, as necessary tribulations according to the *topoi* of the hagiographic genre? It is of course quite plausible that, in the midst of war, two barefoot friars found wandering between the enemy camps should be soundly beaten. But neither Jacques de Vitry nor the anonymous chronicler, both better informed than Thomas, say anything about Francis being beaten. On the contrary, the *Chronicle,* as we have seen, has the Saracen guards simply ask the friars if they are messengers or if they wish to 'become Saracens'; when they respond that they have a message for the sultan, they bring them to him. No doubt Thomas describes the saint's tribulations as he thought they must have happened, according to the traditions of hagiography. These tortures compensate, so to speak, the fact that Francis did not in the end obtain the crown of martyrdom which he so passionately desired.

Thomas describes Francis's meeting with the sultan very briefly, in just a few lines. He affirms, like the *Chronique d'Ernoul*, that the sultan offered 'many gifts' to Francis. For the *Chronique*, this was proof of the sultan's generosity and openness and of the respect which the two clerics inspired in him. For Thomas, on the contrary, the sultan is trying to lay a trap; he wishes 'to turn his mind towards worldly riches'. The sultan, just like his soldiers who beat the friars, plays the traditional hagiographical role of Satan's agent: he is the tempter who tries to lure the potential martyr with promises of earthly delights. And Francis rejects these gifts *velut stercora*, 'like dung', says Thomas, expressing the disgust that money and worldly riches inspire in the saint. It is only at this point that the sultan 'was overflowing with admiration and recognized him as a man unlike any other'. For the *Chronique d'Ernoul*, on the contrary, the sultan was not the least bit astonished. Subsequently, says Thomas, the sultan 'was moved by his words and listened to him very willingly'. According to the *Chronique d'Ernoul*, the sultan refused to allow the two clerics to preach to him; Jacques de Vitry, like Thomas, describes him listening with pleasure and attention. In both cases, we sense that Francis's preaching is effective and that it could result in the conversion of his audience. For Jacques, it is precisely because he fears that his army will convert (with disastrous military results for the Egyptian army) that the sultan cuts short Francis's mission and sends him back to the crusader camp. Thomas offers no explanation for Francis's failure, other than the assertion that it was not God's will: 'the Lord did not fulfill his desire'. The sultan makes a brief appearance in the *Vita prima*: he plays first the role of tempter, then that of the good infidel who listens attentively to the man of God. Thomas shows little interest in this man: Francis abandons him without having either converted him or obtained the martyr's crown from him. Why did God refuse to grant the saint's most ardent desire? Because he was 'reserving for him the prerogative of a unique grace'. This unique grace is the privilege of receiving the stigmata, a unique gift superior to that of martyrdom, a gift that shows Francis's singularity. Julian of Spire, who uses Thomas's text as a basis for his own *Vita Sancti Francesci* (written between 1232 and 1235), makes explicit what Thomas had merely suggested.[26] Martyrdom is a rather banal fate which God granted to a large throng of saints. God had something more original, something better, in store for this exceptional saint, Thomas seems to be saying.

Francis may have seen this episode as a double failure, since he had obtained neither the sultan's conversion nor the prize of martyrdom. But Thomas says nothing about this. He says nothing, either, about the divisions in the order which (as we shall see) obliged Francis to cut short his travels in the Holy Land and to come back quickly to Italy. As if to offer consolation for the fact that Francis succeeded neither in converting the sultan (as the hagiographer admits) nor in resolving the conflict among the friars (about which he says nothing), Thomas places immediately after the passage on Francis's preaching to the sultan a description of his preaching to the birds, showing the respect and attention that they show the saint. Birds listen to Francis and obey him better than do men. In the rest of the *Vita prima*, the brothers who had been, alongside Francis, the heroes of Thomas's narrative now retreat to a subordinate role, as simple witnesses to the saint's holiness: to his healing miracles, his ascesis, his stigmatization, his illness and death.

In Thomas's *Vita*, Francis's passage to the East marks a turning point in his life. Before, Thomas relates the saint's conversion, the foundation of a brotherhood living in poverty and in joyous devotion, recreating the simple life of the Apostles. Francis is above all a model, an inspiration, a companion in the pursuit of this ideal life. After his return from the East, he is a singular, inimitable man: one who speaks to animals and makes them obey him, who performs miracles, who receives the divine mark of the stigmata. Did his voyage to the Holy Land and his preaching to al-Kâmil produce this change in Francis or magnify his reputation for holiness? Or was it simply his absence which permitted, whether he wished or not, his order to develop in accordance with the desires of the friars and of the papacy? Francis resigned as head of the order in 1220, yet perhaps his real resignation was in 1219, when he embarked for Egypt in search of death, rather than in 1220, when he in fact continued to influence and control the order.

In any case, though Thomas passes over the subject in silence, Francis's sojourn in the East was the occasion for major conflicts and disagreements among the friars. During his absence, the Order of Friars Minor confronted a number of concrete problems stemming from its rapid growth—and from the opposition that its success created among members of the secular and monastic clergy. Ugolino, cardinal protector of the order (the future

Gregory IX), persuaded Pope Honorius III to promulgate a bull (11 June 1219) instructing the clergy to treat the friars with respect and to allow them to preach.[27] This measure sought to regulate or avoid conflicts between the friars and other clerics, while it confirmed the role of the Franciscans (and the Dominicans) as preachers. On 22 September, Honorius ruled that all those who wished to enter the order should first complete a year of novitiate.[28] Here the pope sought no doubt to avoid quick and impulsive adhesion of men who were little prepared for the life of Franciscan poverty. By the same logic, the monastic orders had long required a year of novitiates for new recruits, a measure included in the *Rule* of Saint Benedict.[29] The new rules show the extent to which Ugolino had taken the order under his wing and had sought to give it a coherent legal status—at the risk, for some, of destroying the spontaneity and humility of the primitive brotherhood. Francis had left in quest of apostolic death and according to chronicler Giordano di Giano rumour had it that he had in fact died, either at the hands of the Saracens or in a shipwreck.[30] The order continued to grow and change without its founder.

But of course Francis was not dead. Giordano relates that one friar, troubled by the turn of events in the order, travelled to Acre to find Francis and inform him.[31] Whatever the truth of this account, Francis indeed came back to Italy, probably sometime between June and September 1220.[32] He was probably unhappy with the institutionalization of an order which he no longer fully controlled. Some of the hagiographical texts speak, for example, of his ire when he discovered that the friars of Bologna had a house: he refused to set foot in it and ordered the friars to abandon it. He saw it as a violation of the principle of poverty: the order must not have any possessions. Ugolino intervened and swore that the house was his and that he simply allowed the friars to live there; the saint, pacified, allowed the brothers to return.[33] These stories appear for the first time in texts from the 1240s and are part, as we shall see, of polemics within the order. But it does indeed seem that Francis looked on with some consternation at developments in the order.

On 29 September 1220, Francis was probably in Assisi for the General Chapter meeting. He renounced the direction of the order and named Peter Catani as vicar. Peter Catani was head of the order until his death the following year (10 March 1221);[34] Francis then named Elias. Thomas presents this episode as a supplementary proof of his humility; yet it is also the sign of his frustration with recent changes in the order, with the institutionalization of the little brotherhood that he had founded and which had turned into a large institution that he was no longer able to control.[35] Yet Francis continued to hold the reins of the order, even if he was no longer in charge of its administration; Pope Honorius III and Jacques de Vitry consider him, and not his vicar, to be the real head of the order.[36] This is clear during the meeting of the General Chapter on Pentecost 1221, when (according to Giordano di Giano) Francis, ill, tugs on Elias's sleeve in order to whisper his wishes—which are quickly adopted by the chapter.[37] Francis tried to take control: he wrote with his associates a first version of the order's written rule, the *Regula non bullata*, in 1221; when the pope refused to approve this rule, he wrote another, the *Regula bullata*, which Honorius III approved in 1223.

These conflicts and negotiations no doubt inspired, in Francis and other brothers, nostalgia for the early years of the brotherhood. This nostalgia permeates Thomas's descriptions of these years: it seems more than a mere hagiographical *topos* and reflects neither the interests of Elias (who was building his sumptuous basilica) nor of Gregory IX, searching for legitimacy in his fight against Frederick II. One cannot reduce the *Vita prima* to a simple work of propaganda for the use of those who commissioned it. Thomas's treatment of the stigmata clearly shows his independence *vis-à-vis* Elias and Gregory, as Chiara Frugoni and Jacques Dalarun have shown.[38] Elias, in his *Encyclical* of 1226, describes the stigmata as *wounds,* identical to those that Jesus had on his hands, his feet and in his side. Gregory, in his canonization bull, does not mention the stigmata; he seems not to have accepted this miracle until 1237. Thomas, as we have seen, presents them as 'a unique grace', the culminating event in the life of a singular saint, marking the passage from the apostolic life to a life modelled on that of Christ himself. But for Thomas, the stigmata are not wounds: they are miraculous brown fleshy growths in the form of nails. Thomas clearly did not simply follow either Elias or the pope.

At any rate, the *Vita prima* became the official biography of the founding saint of the Friars Minor, basis for all the other narratives concerning Francis until the approbation of Bonaventure's *Legenda maior* in 1263. Thomas himself wrote an abbreviated life for liturgical use in 1230, the *Legenda ad usum chori*, in which he briefly evokes Francis's desire for martyrdom, his voyage towards Morocco cut short, the voyage to 'Syria', the beatings he received, and the fact that he preached Christ to the sultan.[39] Other Franciscan authors reproduce Thomas's version of the event: Julian of

Spire in his *Vita Sancti Franciscani* (composed between 1232 and 1235),[40] an anonymous friar who wrote a *Vita* about 1250–6,[41] Giordano di Giano in his 1262 *Chronicle*.[42] Julian and other first-generation Franciscans composed liturgical texts in honour of the saintly founder of their order, but these texts rarely mention Francis's preaching to the sultan. Only one of these texts, the *Laetabundus* attributed to Cardinal Thomas of Capua, alludes to it.[43]

Meanwhile, the Franciscan order continued to grow, and with it grew the tension and discord among its friars. We find evidence of these conflicts in 1230, concerning Francis's *Testament*. Francis, in this text composed towards the end of his life, declares (among other things):

> I strictly command all the brothers through obedience, wherever they may be, not to dare to ask any letter from the Roman Curia, either personally or through an intermediary, whether for a church or another place or under the pretext of preaching or the persecution of their bodies. But, wherever they have not been received, let them flee into another country to do penance with the blessing of God.   (*Testament*, 25–6)

Must the friars minor respect these last wishes of their founder, as they appear in this text? No, rules Gregory IX in his bull *Quo elongati* (4 October 1230): Francis was no longer Minister General of the order when he wrote the *Testament* and hence could not impose his will on the order without the agreement of the chapter. Though Thomas's *Vita prima* remained the official biography of the saint, other Franciscans wrote their versions of the sayings and deeds of Francis; many of these writings were also tinged with nostalgia for the early brotherhood. While these texts are difficult to date, some of them were first composed, it seems, in the 1240s: the *Anonymus perusinus* (*Anonymous of Perugia*), the *Legenda trium sociorum* (*Legend of the Three Companions*), and the *Compilatio Assisiensis* (*Assisi Compilation*).[44]

At the Chapter of Genoa in 1244, Minister General Crescent de Iesi asked the brothers to write down their memories of Francis and to send them to him. We have a letter written by friars Leo, Rufino, and Angelo on 11 August 1246, which they sent along with their text (probably what is now known as the *Legenda trium sociorum*, though this text may have subsequently been modified). Crescenti asked Thomas of Celano to bring together these different texts; the result was the *Vita secunda*, a sort of anthology of Francis's words and deeds, drawn from the *Anonymus perusinus*, the *Legenda trium sociorum*, the *Compilatio Assisiensis,* and probably, as well, from other texts now lost, from oral testimonies, and from Thomas's own memories.

This text is not, strictly spreaking, a *Vita*: it does not present a narration of the life and death of the saint, but a collection of brief anecdotes loosely organized by themes. Thomas does not relate Francis preaching to the sultan; he no doubt judged that he had given it sufficient treatment in the *Vita prima*. He does, however, write of Francis's sojourn in the crusader camp before Damietta; he relates an episode worth presenting, notably because it is extensively used by historians of the twentieth century. Thomas places this anecdote in the midst of a series of miracles concerning Francis's gift of prophecy. He says:

> How he foretold the massacre of Christians at Damietta.
>
> When the Christian army was besieging Damietta, the holy man of God was there with his companions, since they had crossed the sea in their fervor for martyrdom. When the holy man heard that our forces were preparing for war, on the day of battle he grieved deeply. He said to his companion: 'If the battle happens on this day the Lord has shown me that it will not go well for the Christians. But if I say this, they will take me for a fool, and if I keep silent my conscience won't leave me alone. What do you think I should do?' His companion replied: 'Father, don't give the least thought to how people judge you. This wouldn't be the first time people took you for a fool. Unburden your conscience, and fear God rather than men.'
>
> The saint leapt to his feet and rushed to the Christians crying our warnings to save them, forbidding war and threatening disaster. But they took the truth as a joke. They hardened their hearts and refused to turn back. They charged, they attacked, they fought, and then the enemy struck back.
>
> In that moment of battle, filled with suspense, the holy man made his companion get up to look. The first and the second time he got up, he saw nothing, so Francis told him to look a third time. What a sight! The whole Christian army was in retreat fleeing from the battle carrying not triumph but shame. The massacre was so great that between the dead and the captives the number of our forces was diminished by six thousand. Compassion for them drove the holy man, no less than regret, for what they had done overwhelmed them. He wept especially for the Spaniards: he could see their boldness in battle had left only a few of them alive.
>
> Let the princes of the world take note of this, and let them know: it is not easy to fight against God, that is, against the will of the Lord. Stubborn insolence usually ends in disaster. It relies on its own strength, thus forfeiting the help of heaven. If victory is to be expected from on high, then battles must be entrusted to the divine spirit.   (2C 30)

Thomas presents this episode as a wondrous example of Francis's gift of prophecy: God revealed to him that the day was not propitious for combat, and the crusaders who did not heed the saint's warnings were killed or captured. To put this story in its context, all the more important since the second part of the *Vita secunda* is organized thematically and not chronologically, Thomas says that Francis and his companions had come to Damietta *fervore martyrii*, because of their fervor for martyrdom. While in the *Vita prima* Thomas had placed the encounter with the 'sultan of the Saracens' in 'Syria', here he says that it was during the siege of Damietta.

The purpose of the story is simple and clear: Francis feels both the grace and the weight of responsibility of the God-given gift of prophecy. God revealed to him that the Christian army would lose that day; Francis knows that the soldiers and their leaders will not heed his warning. Hence his doubt: should he warn the army and risk being ridiculed by the soldiers? His companion gives the expected answer: it is better to fear the wrath of God than the derision of men. The subsequent rout proves Francis right; his reputation as a prophet is confirmed. For the reader, his humility and compassion are also corroborated. He hesitates to speak up, remains anxious during the battle, feels compassion and regret for those who were killed or captured. He felt particularly for the Spaniards whose exemplary heroism only brought them death.

The moral of the story, for Thomas, is one of humility: we must not fight against God's will, and we should humbly listen to his messengers. The saint's compassion and tears, according to his hagiographer, are reserved for the Christian victims of this battle. Nowhere does he suggest that Francis felt the slightest compassion for the Muslims who fell in battle. On the contrary, the most ferocious Christian warriors, the Spaniards, cause him to shed his hottest tears. Nothing in this passage suggests that Francis had said anything against war in general or against the current crusade, or against the siege of Damietta. He had merely foreseen the disastrous consequences of battle, *on one particular day*, consequences decreed by God for reasons which only he knows. Neither the saint nor his hagiographer criticizes the crusaders (contrary to Jacques de Vitry or to Francis himself according to the anonymous continuator of the *Éracle*); their only error seems to be not to have heeded the saint.

I am insisting on the fact that, for Thomas, Francis wished merely to dissuade the crusaders from waging battle on this particularly unpropitious day. Some twentieth-century authors have used this passage to present

Francis as a pacifist searching for a peaceful resolution to the conflicts between the two camps.[45] Nothing justifies this interpretation.

Thomas's version of Francis preaching to the sultan, in the *Vita prima*, remained the official Franciscan narrative of Francis's life, and the most widely read, for twenty-five years, and the principal source for all Franciscan authors until Bonaventure. While Jacques de Vitry and the *Chronique d'Ernoul* showed real knowledge of the political and military context in which Francis's mission took place, Thomas ignores this context completely and makes al-Kâmil the 'Sultan of the Saracens', residing in 'Syria'. The sultan is cast in the role of the good infidel king who politely listens to the saint and gives signs of his admiration; in the following centuries, he will more often than not remain confined to this role. Thomas simplifies the encounter in order the better to insert it into his life of the saint, to make it into yet another testimony to the qualities which make Francis exceptional: his eloquence, his courage, and his admirable thirst for martyrdom.

4

Epic Hero and Eminent Professor

Henry of Avranches (1229–1230)

All this, however, cools down not the passion for virtuous
Death that was born in his heart. Far from it;
For he boards ship, and the ship he commits to wind and wave,
And wind and wave unto God, who as steersman,
Carries him safe into Damietta's coveted harbor.

Christ's faithful and Gentile, the one in turn against the other,
Were locked in great conflict there: Damietta was the constantly
Shifting hub of the war, and the prize in a future of triumph.
    With neither savage close combat nor hand-to-hand fighting
Could they take it; but only with long-distance bow,

With sling and with engines of siege: blows fell like hail.
Nor could they attack it at a much closer range,
For between flows the seventh of its river's branches:
Its source must be none, or else torrid zone hides it
From every explorer, and eyes of ours may never reach it.

Midway between the armies the waters flowed,
And they grabbed the missiles raining down from either side.
But though the water moved, it never spread out in rings,
And there was no measuring by circles the strokes
That came, for their points of entry were everywhere.

What manly courage in a man to cross that great river
In a tiny skiff! Alone and unharmed he moves towards
The weaponed and hostile host, through darts, through
Unquenchable 'Greek fire,' through a thousand mortal perils!
A thousand dangers strewed his path, yet more the menace

At journey's end. Fears he neither till the greedy river
He crosses and, nothing daunted, reaches the enemy's midst.
But before he can advance further to reach the presence
Of the King of the Persians, to whose ears
The word of the Lord he intended first to convey,
He must take furious treatment in plenty, with cruel club
Be smitten. His flesh is livid, his blood pours out;
Violet is his body from violence, and rose-red his wounds
Within. Nor does the soul within him any sorrow feel
For those tortured limbs now all swathed in purple.

While the flesh is hostile to the soul, why should
Its wounds be pitied? Anyone who boosts his foe
Leaves himself in a weaker position. Hence the inner
Francis sought nothing of outer honors, through the losing
Of which he has his will set on salvation's gaining, on

Reaching heights through being brought low, on winning
Through losses, on living through dying, on delights
Through pain. For the flesh's woes cheer the soul, groans
Are comfort, wounding brings healing, agreeable are insults,
Hurts are helpful, distress spells relief.

　　When the fair name of the holy man who was indomitable
Under every affliction had spread through the Persian camp,
Such was a kingly king's admiration for his great spirit
That he gave him a great reception and offered him precious
Gifts. He content with what he has, declines the king's
Offer, and asks for that gift of gifts, to be given a hearing.
So as to hear him, the king himself bids the crowd to be silent
And orders every noise to cease, while to his attendants
He said: 'Fetch me my sages; let them be the judges
If this man's teaching be genuine, or if he's not minded
Rather to lead multitudes astray.' And so, as he speaks
To the wise ones gathered together, this wise man
Proves the source out of which he has drawn his philosophy.
All of his reasoning he hastens to carry onto celestial things;
He discourses on things unheard before, as though beyond
Mere human ken: here is one to whom nothing's unknown.
He reasons matters which few mortals have ever perceived,
Or on the origins of the universe manifest only to God.
Whence he introduces reflexions upon the first cause;
Then he condemns the perverse school of Mohammed, proves
That God is one, and that a host of Gods has no existence;

How it is that all things come from one source, how a moment
Of that first principle is simple substance, a simple
Moment in the present, a substance simpler than
A mathematical point; how its essence is wondrously present
Wholly, always and everywhere outside of place and time.
Where pride comes from, and how Lucifer, once 'morning star',
Is now laden with murky mud; at what price the world's
Redemption was wrought; and what reasons brought
The Incarnation; how it was the ancient serpent seduced
Eve, Eve the first man formed, the first-formed man
His posterity, how that posterity betrayed Christ, how Christ
Outwitted the serpent, death now driven back whence it sprang.
How not only is Christ's body glorified,
But while it glorifies other bodies,
His living flesh adorning the soul with gifts,
He is fully at one and the same time in divers churches,
And how Christ assembles all his holy people into his Church;
How Baptism is a spiritual cleansing power
That purifies souls of the stain of the first parent.

While he thus teaches the articles of faith with skillful
Tongue, he impresses sages and king, and nobody dares
to harm him. Indeed heralds are bidden to make this
Their cry: 'Often may he come and go among us.' Yet on his own
He is unable to convert so many Persians; and as ministers
Which his plan badly needed are missing, he is forced to give up
The venture, and is borne over the seas by a homeward wind.[1]

Henry of Avranches, poet in the court of Pope Gregory IX, presents an epic Francis, hero of a sacred adventure, who courageously confronts his enemy and preaches brilliantly, like a professor of theology. His preaching was well received by the 'King of the Persians' and his courtiers; in order to explain the failure to convert the 'Persians', Henry briefly and vaguely evokes a lack of *ministri*. Here is a Francis who does not resemble either that of the crusade chroniclers, or that of Thomas of Celano—even though Thomas is the only written source that Henry used.

Henry of Avranches inhabits a different world from Thomas of Celano and the first Franciscans. One might be tempted to say that he represents everything they abhorred: obsequious submission to the powers of the day, the use of complex, ornate rhetoric, pride and ambition. Henry of Avranches was a court poet; his talent and success made him famous. He

graced the courts of Emperors Otto IV and Frederick II, of Kings John
and Henry III of England, of King Louis IX of France, and of numerous
abbots and bishops, in England and on the continent. While most of his
compositions were poems ordered by his patrons, in others he flattered
princes whose patronage he hoped to obtain. It has been said that Henry
was the most successful poet of his generation and that his life of Francis
was his major work.[2]

Born in the Norman town of Avranches about 1190, Henry began his
study of letters about 1205, probably in Paris.[3] Around 1212 or 1213, he
frequented the court of King John. In one of his poems from this period,
Henry presents himself in the guise of a poet who needs royal generosity:

> You have, John, a name of divine origin, not undeservedly
>   The name fits its object.
> May you then either be supremely gratified or be of supreme grace:
>   For me, one or the other fits.
> If you are supremely gratified, you are the disciple of piety;
>   Hence you give alms to the poor.
> Hence to me, since I am poor. If you are of supreme grace,
>   You give of what you possess to all—therefore also to me.
> Therefore, if you are well-named according to grace,
>   Clearly I will have some of your riches gratis.[4]

Henry probably served as a messenger between King John and Emperor
Otto IV when they were negotiating the anti-French alliance which would
ultimately be crushed by the troops of Philip II Augustus at Bouvines on
27 July 1214. In 1215, he wrote a poem to the curia of Pope Innocent III
to defend Otto's imperial title against the claims of his rival, Frederick II
Hohenstaufen. In the following years, he travelled between England and
the empire:

> Exiled, I wander the world
> And inglorious, I err through barbarous lands.
> A barefoot, naked poet, with no prince taking pity on me.
> I do not walk wide roads, but stuck among the thankless English
> I write verses for which no one pays me.[5]

He was in England again from 1219: he wrote an epitaph for William
Marshall, count of Pembroke, who had been one of the principal vassals of
Henry II. He subsequently wrote for various ecclesiastical patrons, English
bishops and abbots, composing poems which mixed lives of saints and

panegyrics of his patrons.[6] Among his hagiographical works are two texts on Thomas Beckett written for Archbishop Stephen of Canterbury; a *Life of St Hugh* for Bishop Hugh of Lincoln; a *Life of St Edmund,* for the abbot of Bury St Edmunds; a *Life of St Birinus* for the bishop of Winchester.

In 1228 or 1229, Henry was in the papal curia, which he accompanied to Perugia, Spoleto, Rome, and Anagni. He wrote numerous works commissioned by members of the curia, then composed his *Legenda Sancti Francisci,* which he read aloud to the pope. Gregory IX, to thank him for his poem, granted him two prebends: Henry became clerk of Santa Maria di Trastevere in Rome and canon of Avranches.[7] Proud of his success, around 1232 he does not blush to write to Emperor Frederick II:

> Just as your excellence surpasses that of the other kings,
> I am the supreme professor of poetry in this world,
> One might say, excuse the ambiguity, that we are both monarchs.[8]

He probably stayed in the papal court until 1239, when he went to France; perhaps he accompanied Jacques de Vitry, now cardinal-bishop of Palestrina and papal legate charged with negotiating an anti-imperial alliance with King Louis IX. Henry was in Paris in 1241, when the relic of the crown of thorns arrived; he wrote a poem for the king in commemoration of the event. In 1242, he returned to England, where he entered into the service of Henry III: a number of documents in the royal archives (between 1243 and 1262), show that the king gave to his *versificator* money, clothing, and casks of wine.[9] A venerable poet and an agile courtier: this is the image of Henry that one gleans from the poems and the archival documents. John of Garland, around 1257–9, listed among the king's principal vassals *regius vates Henrycus*; John affirms that Henry's financial success is reflected in his name: since, in latin *v* and *u* are interchangeable, *Avrans* (of Avranches) is the same as *aurans* (golden).[10]

Henry participated in three poetic debates which give a similar impression of the poet. These debates consisted in veritable verbal jousting, as poets attacked and insulted each other in verse. In the first debate, which took place in Angers, probably between 1240 and 1243, Henry confronted two poets named Peter Siler and John Bordo. A second verbal duel, with William, deacon of Laval, is from the same period. Only Henry's poems have survived; those of his adversaries have disappeared.[11] A third debate pitted Henry against Michael of Cornwall; in this case, only the latter's poems have survived, and they were quite popular: Michael recited them in public four times in 1254–5.[12] In these poetic jousts, the professors displayed their oratorical and poetic skills to amuse their students and to lambast their colleagues and rivals. William FitzStephen, clerk in the entourage of Thomas Becket, affirmed that such events happened regularly, in the twelfth century, in the schools of London during Carnival.[13]

During his debate with Peter Siler and John Bordo, Henry insults his adversaries in well-crafted verse. The bishop of Angers, Michel de Villoiseau, presides over the event. All verbal blows are permitted: Henry accuses Pierre Siler of having contracted leprosy by sleeping with a leprous woman; he describes the consequences in detail. He affirms, for example:

> Should I not call leprosy the disease that has infected your entrails and that is now rotting them? It makes your lungs stink, it turns your vicious face green; it makes your throat swell and makes your voice croak. Your voice indeed is inaudible when it comes out of your oesophagus. Scabs make your skin itch and your breath is putrid.[14]

He makes puns with his opponents' names: 'Peter Siler, be silent like a stone … You are silent about the good things and you poorly sing lies' (vv. 1, 30). 'It is impossible to teach you anything, Peter (*Petrus*) hard as a rock (*petra*). On the other hand, *siler* (willow) is rather soft: you are too hard to receive impressions and too soft to retain them' (vv. 370–9). 'With willow we make brooms to clean out latrines: this is an appropriate vocation for you, that of your parents' (vv. 309–14).

For Bordo, Henry plays on the two meanings of his name: donkey (*burdus* or *bordus*) and bumble bee (from late Latin *burdo*). 'The people know that Brother Bordo is only a mule. He displays neither sense nor reason but brays both to himself' (vv. 84–6). Bordo's hee-hawing shows that he is a bastard, like his brother Siler, but we do not know if they are of the same species. Henry concludes that he was wrong to call Bordo a mule:

> What can I say? I was wrong, Bordo, to call you a quadruped. I take it back; I now believe that you emerged alone from decomposed excrement. … You are not a mare but a nuisance, and you were born not from a donkey, but from bovine shit.   (vv. 237–9, 251–2)

Siler and Bordo, for their part, call Henry an old, blind, drunken hunchback. Henry defends himself: if he is hunchback, it is from having borne the sky on his shoulders, as Atlas and Hercules had done before him (vv. 126–32). If he is blind, it is from having studied Ovid. No one mocks Tobias, the old blind prophet. If the years have made him blind, he can still see that the evil life of his adversaries is an insult to men and God. As for wine, it is worthy of praise: but it is normal that the mule Bordo does not appreciate it, since he only drinks from streams (vv. 140–59).

Henry appeals to the judge, Michel de Villoiseau, flattering him: 'Orator of the Truth, admirable and dignified clergyman', 'flower of prelates' (vv. 40–2). He asks him to punish his opponents severely:

> I ask you for your verdict: these idiots should be stoned
> With a hundred turds, since they have attempted
> To usurp such talent and have refused to cede the place of honor to Homer.

(vv. 54–6)

One imagines the laughter that shook the episcopal court when Henry proposed this punishment. These debates, sophisticated amusements for clerks (for no layman could compose such poems in Latin), permit the masters to display their poetic talents. The humour lies in the exaggeration (for example, in the frequent comparisons between the protagonists and the poets or heroes of antiquity), in the mock solemnity of a bogus trial, in the skilful wordplays and in the contrast between the refinement of the verses and the vulgarity of the insults.

Henry of Avranches is a brilliant and worldly poet. His poems earned him ecclesiastical prebends and a salary in the English royal court. Proud of his success, he enjoys showing off his linguistic prowess in verbal duels. It would be hard to imagine a man of the cloth less likely to sing the praises of Franciscan poverty and simplicity. Yet Henry, who specialized in hagiographic poetry, was in the papal court of Gregory IX in 1228, the year of Francis's canonization; indeed he may well have been present for the canonization. Henry composed poems in which he presented to the papal curia praises of his patrons: he pleaded that the archbishop of Bourges, Simon de Sully, and not the archbishop of Bordeaux, might become primate of Aquitaine; he defended Conrad, abbot of Lorsch, whom Gregory had deposed in 1226; lobbied for the nomination of John of Blund as archbishop of Canterbury. It was no doubt thanks to these poems that the pope noticed Henry's talents and asked him to versify the *Vita prima* of Thomas of Celano, which he did most probably in 1232 or 1234.[15]

The three manuscripts which we possess of the *Legenda Sancti Francisci versificata* give three different versions of the text: manuscript 338 of the library of Assisi, composed before 1279, contains the version closest

to the original, dedicated to Pope Gregory IX. A manuscript dated
c.1250, now in Cambridge University Library, has a version reworked
by Henry after the destitution of Elias (1239) and the death of Gregory
IX (1241); this manuscript belonged to Matthew Paris, who made some
marginal annotations.[16] A third manuscript, today in the municipal library
of Versailles, dated late thirteenth or early fourteenth century, has a text
that has been reworked to better correspond to Bonaventure's *Legenda
maior*, which became the sole biography of Francis recognized by the friars
minor.[17] I will refer almost exclusively to the Assisi version, which has the
oldest version of the poem. For the passage which interests us (on Francis's
mission to the 'Persians'), the text of the three manuscripts is identical.

The pope appears clearly as the patron of the poem. Henry praises him:

> You, Holy Father, good shepherd, Gregory Ninth,
> Making orison for gregarian sin, watching over congregational
> Pastures, you fill the measure of so great a name
> Prithee be gentle with me and deign to accept in your kindness
> This smallest of gifts, O greatest of mortals!
>
> (*ED* i. 429)

Gregory appears three times in the *Legenda,* just as in its source, Thomas
of Celano's *Vita prima*.[18] The initial verses of the fourteen books of the
Legenda form an acrostic: if one takes the first letter of each book, one
obtains Gregorius Nonus, Gregory IX.

Henry's Francis is an epic saint, a new hero inspired by God, described
in verses inspired by those of Virgil and Ovid. The poem opens with the
verses: *Gesta sacri cantabo ducis, qui monstra domandi | Primus adinvenit tribuitque
Minoribus artem*, which echo the beginning of the *Aeneid: Arma virumque
cano, Trojae qui primus ab oris | Italiam, fato profugus, Laviniaque venit*. Just as
Virgil sang the praises of the armed exploits of Aeneas, Rome's national
hero, Henry sings the epic of the 'saintly general'. The military metaphor
is central to Henry's poem. The first word, *gesta,* which is often translated
as 'acts' or 'deeds', refers in particular to military exploits in epic poetry,
in the *chansons de geste*. Our hero, Francis, has become a *dux*, a veritable
military leader.

Henry's poem is saturated with these echoes of classical epic poetry,
peppered with references to ancient history and mythology. In the opening
verses, Henry affirms that Francis is superior to the two great heroes of
antiquity, Julius Caesar and Alexander the Great:

For what, compared with Francis, did Julius Caesar,
Or the great Alexander, that we can recall?
Julius vanquished a foe, Alexander a world; Francis did both.
Nay, Francis not only overcame a world and a foe,
But also himself: victor and vanquished in the same war.

(ED i. 428)

Francis's exploits surpass those of the ancient heroes. This *Christi miles* (1. 12), soldier of Christ, bears the wounds which are the signs of victory over his own body and of his glory: the stigmata. Henry is not the first author to use the martial figure of the *Christi miles* to describe the heroic renunciation of the ascetics: it is a *topos* of hagiography from the fourth century on. Nor is he the first to play on the apparent contradiction between the image of the classical hero and that of the ascetic; Henry takes great pleasure in this game. Francis *pede nudo mundum calcavit* (1. 7–8: trampled the world barefoot). Henry does not tire of such comparisons: in his poems commissioned by English ecclesiastical patrons, he had already compared Saints Guthlac, Birin, and Oswald with Alexander the Great.[19]

He peppers his *Legenda* with classical allusions. When confronted with bad monks, Francis flees them just as Ulysses fled the Cyclops, the Sirens, or the lotus eaters (4. 112–13). When Francis, dying, arrived in the town of Rieti, everyone in the town crowded around to see the saint. This was normal, since Francis is greater than all the marvels of antiquity:

Great may it have been to set eyes on two-bodied
Chiron, or the bull of Minos that ravaged the Athenians
Or the lynxes of Bacchus with the all-piercing stare
Or rejuvenated Phoenix after momentary death,
Or the wild boar let loose in Calydon, or the Emperor's
Elephant, or the wild asses whose nostrils spouted
The swamp of Maeos on to hostile shores
Or all the secrets in the sea's far corners
That we in our clime are not wont to see:
How far more wondrous this man to behold
Here now—though not here, for he is totally in a realm above—
And on earth to have sight of a celestial citizen

(ED i. 512)

Henry deploys military metaphors throughout the *Legenda*. In the second book, he adds a long digression (not in Thomas of Celano's text) on the vices and virtues. The culminating point of this excursus is the description of Francis, *miles Christi,* armed with the virtues:

> Charity, head of the virtues, to her hero hands heaven-made weapons;
> Unerring Modesty tightens the reins on the steed of his flesh,
> Upon which two spurs, Love and Fear, their full vigor impose;
> Action and Contemplation form the double greave protecting his legs;
>
> On his breast is the cuirass of Justice; by his left flank
> Hangs the 'shield of Faith'; Patience makes sure his helmet
> Is securely strapped round his neck; and the crest of that helmet
> Is Hope, that shines with the brightness of a host of stars.
> The first movement of battle is made with his spear; the shaft
> Of that spear is right Judgment, and its point is fervent Devotion.
> When at last the spear falls broken from so many throws, in the thick
> Of the fight that still furiously rages, there flashes from his right
> Flank the sword of the Cross for cutting to pieces those savage hordes.
> Thus was he equipped; and from that time forward, nothing could he
>
> Accomplish that did not bring him military honors,
> And nothing stood in the way of his fierce valor.
>
> (*ED* i. 440–1)

In the *Aeneid,* Venus brings to her son Aeneas arms forged by Vulcan, so that he can fight his rival Turnus. Here it is Charity, *virtutum Princeps,* 'prince of the virtues', who provides Christ's soldier with spiritual arms for the combat against *catervas,* his diabolical enemies. Later, Henry presents Francis, accompanied by one lone soldier (*miles*), 'planting the foot of virtue upon the neck of vices' (*virtutum pedibus vitiorum colla prementes,* 6. 7). The friars, through their ascesis, 'wage war upon the malicious demons' (*bella malignis | Indicunt furiis,* 6. 26–7). Presiding over the General Chapter in Assisi, the saint is a *dux* surrounded by his troops:

> Compelled to return to Assisi, he fits out all he can
> Of recruits for Christ's army. With unerring command
> He shows the way to the trophy to all who will carry his banner.
>
> (*ED* i. 485)

Henry's penchant for bellicose language transforms (and at times deforms) his principal source, Thomas of Celano's *Vita prima.* Let us look, for example, at two descriptions of how, in the early history of the order, when it had only eight friars, Francis convoked them and sent them out two by two to preach the Gospel. In Thomas's text, Francis's words are modelled on those of Christ in the Gospels.

> At that same time, another good man entered their religion, and they increased their number to eight. Then the blessed Francis called them all to himself and told them many things about the kingdom of God, contempt of the world, denial of their own will, and subjections of the body. He separated them into four groups of two each.
>
> 'Go, my dear brothers,' he said to them, 'two by two through different parts of the world, announcing peace to the people and penance for the remission of sins. Be patient in trials, confident that the Lord will fulfill His plan and promise. Respond humbly to those who question you. Bless those who persecute you. Give thanks to those who harm you and bring false charges against you, for because of these things an eternal kingdom is prepared for us.' (1C 29)

Thomas in this brief passage includes seven Gospel citations.[20] Just as Jesus sent his disciples out into the world two by two (Luke 10: 1), Francis sent his. He speaks to them of deprivation and humility, renunciation of the world and of one's own will. He told them to announce peace and penance. When confronted with hostility, the Franciscan friar, new apostle, must respond with humility, patience, and blessing.

Here is how our poet Henry transforms this passage:

> Meanwhile another good man of acceptable life, so that he'd be
> A better Christian and his life be still more acceptable,
> Comes to take up arms and engage in brave battles under Francis,
> That wager of brave wars, and consecrate himself a soldier
> Under a holy commander

> Their number reached eight, Francis calls them together
> And sends them in twos throughout the world, to pass on
> What they learned of the art of combat. He commands them to show
> Courage in battle, be patient in affliction, whatever might happen,
> And be constant in purpose, not to seek easy ways nor fear opposition,

> To cast a wary eye on successes, and all the more readily accept
> Adversities. Without opposition no one is toughened; no one fights
> A war without being tough; but there is no triumph if there's no war,
> And the kingdom of heaven does not come, unless it is won.
> And, directing his words to them, he said:

> 'Note well the situation you are in, and know that life here
> Is but a military campaign, and sides now eager for battle

Have declared an unending war; each against the other.
Souls belong to the side of heaven, bodies to the side of earth.'

(ED i. 465)

Gone are the invocations to humility, penance, and peace. In their place, Henry uses the vocabulary of war. He employs seven times the word *bellum* (war) and its cognates; twice *fortia* (force or violence) and *triumphus* (triumph); he also uses *miles* (soldier or knight), *militia* (army), *princeps* (prince), *agon* (combat), *arma* (arms), *rebelles* (rebels). Thomas's Francis, in the image of Christ surrounded by his friars, the new apostles, is all gentleness and humility. In Henry's poem, he becomes a prince at the head of a valiant band of knights who wage perpetual war.

Thomas and Henry both insist on Francis's skill in preaching. But here again, they do so from very different perspectives. Thomas describes how Francis preached in Assisi, at the beginning of his calling:

> He then began to preach penance to all with a fervent spirit and joyful attitude. He inspired his listeners with words that were simple and a heart that was heroic. His word was like a blazing fire, reaching the deepest parts of the heart, and filling the souls of all with wonder. He seemed entirely different from what he had been, and looking up to heaven he refused to look down upon earth. It is truly amazing that he first began to preach where he had learned to read as little boy.   (1C 23)

Francis, inflamed by divine love, finds the words to touch and inspire the people of Assisi, who had mocked him before. Fire is here the dominant metaphor: the saint is animated by a great fervour (*magno fervore*); his words are like a blazing fire (*ignis ardens*). This ardour fills his audience with wonder. It comes from Francis's heart and pierces the hearts of his listeners: Thomas uses the word *cordis* (heart) three times in this passage. Francis speaks simply (*verbo simplici*) but efficaciously. The transformation of the young Francis, rich and mundane, lover of worldly pleasures, into an ascetic and a preacher who cannot take his eyes off the heavens, fills the Assisians with admiration.

Here is what Henry makes of this passage:

> Though he not know the Pagasean spring
> Or ever see Parnassus's twin-peaked heights, he is not slow
> To master sacred truth. The Holy Spirit's stronger flame ignites him,
> Whence the knowledge of all words proceeds. He who had no doctor

Teach him, teaches now a multitude. Those who know him stand
Astonished as he speaks on things transcending human ken;

A pupil they had never seen him, now they listen to a teacher.
'Nothing has he ever learnt, nothing will he ever teach':
So supposes the common saying, and it holds in the natural run of things;
But let the common rule be broken, as when miracles occur, that saying
Is no longer true. Presumptions human often cloak the true meaning.

Of things. Needs he a teacher from outside whom within the Spirit
Instructs? By his courtesy Francis receives the doctrines he imparts
With skill. The more graciously God instructs the heart, the more
Clear the message of the tongue. O secrets of God, hidden from all
Mortal beings! Here is one who earthly interests left for his sake,

And now the obdurate converts, when from being obdurate turned
But a while away himself. Behold a distinguished master now,
While townsfolk and companions gaze, and wonder how their simple friend,
Whom they had thought quite out of mind, true wisdom
Meanwhile has acquired!

(ED i. 460–1)

Francis burns with the 'fire of spirit' (*igne Pneumatis*), which inspires him and permits him to inflame his audience. But he does not speak *verbo simplice*: on the contrary, he seems gifted with exceptional knowledge: he has become an erudite professor *(magister egregius)*. He has learnt church doctrine directly from the Holy Spirit; he teaches it eloquently. For Thomas, the audience admires Francis's fervour and piety, his eloquence which comes from the heart. For Henry the Assisians are stupefied by the transformation of the simpleton into a *magister egregius*: while Thomas simply said that Francis had learnt to read in the same place where he now preached, Henry affirms that he was considered stupid by his fellow pupils, all the better to dramatize his transformation into one who masters true wisdom (*vera sophia*).

Thomas describes Francis's charisma by emphasizing his simplicity, sincerity, and warmth. Henry praises him by attributing to him the qualities he admires: eloquence, discernment, erudition. We find the same contrast in another episode from his life: his preaching before the papal curia and Pope Honorius III (1C 73). For Thomas, Francis's preaching shone in its simplicity, purity, and fervour, qualities which his friend Cardinal Ugolino admires. When the cardinal introduces the saint into the papal court,

Francis's feet move as if they are being burnt by the fire of divine love; he seems to dance as he speaks. Ugolino is nervous: he fears that Francis's simplicity and the unusual behaviour will provoke the ridicule of the curia. But on the contrary, the pope and the cardinals are moved by his faith and confidence; they weep in admiration. Here we are far from hagiographical *topoi:* Thomas is aware that the saint's simplicity, a quality which both Thomas and Ugolino admire, can provoke derision from the worldly. Yet Francis's grace and simplicity, and the force of divine love, vanquish all reticence.

Henry reproduces nothing of this when he describes Francis's preaching before the pope (10. 5–30; *ED* i. 498–9). Francis displays no simplicity, Ugolino not the slightest doubt. The movement of Francis's feet and body, for Henry, is not laughable; it is not even inspired by divine love, but by the mastery of gesture, as taught by the rhetoricians: 'making use of rhetorical gesture he involves not only his tongue but his total body in speaking'. Francis declaims a speech which he seasons with the sayings of the sages of old (*verba priorum*)—just as Henry himself does in citing the classical poets. No text is too complicated for this expert orator: neither the enigmas of the prophets, nor the riches of the Gospels; Francis is an unequalled exegete. All admire him, but the learned most of all, for his knowledge surpasses theirs. Francis is an erudite professor, expert exegete, eloquent orator, skilful courtier. This is the Francis, as we will see, who preaches eloquently to the sultan and his court. Even though Thomas's *Vita prima* is his sole written source, Henry's image of the saint is the polar opposite of Thomas's.

For the twenty-first-century reader, to go from Thomas's *Vita prima* to Henry's *Legenda* is to pass from three dimensions to two. Thomas portrays a complex and lively Francis, continually tossed by emotions and regrets; the saint's charm and vivacity overflow the constraints of hagiography. This is particularly true of the passages which precede his departure for the East: Thomas paints an idyllic picture of the simple life led by the little band of friars minor, for whom the rigours of asceticism are accompanied by joy and harmony. Henry has nothing of this: he describes an epic hero ready to wage war against the forces of evil. We have already seen that for Thomas Francis's Egyptian voyage marks a turning point in his portrayal of the saint: before, he is first among equals, the centre of a vibrant community of friars who share the same simple pious life. After his return from Egypt, he is more distant: he preaches to birds and animals, meditates in solitude, receives the stigmata: all this makes Francis unique and distances him from his friars. For Henry, this distance seems to be there from the beginning, or at least since his conversion. An epic hero is out of necessity somewhat two-dimensional. Thomas sought to present a warm and vivid image of a man he knew and admired, who had founded the order to which Thomas had devoted his life. Henry sought above all to display his poetic prowess to Pope Gregory IX and his curia by transforming a vagabond clothed in rags into an invincible knight of Christ armed with the celestial virtues. Henry has no visible affinity either for Francis or for the friars minor.

In the seventh and eighth books, Henry evokes Francis's desire for martyrdom and his three attempts to obtain it. Henry is not enthusiastic:

> With a martyr's death, therefore, longing to crown his labors
> He sets his mind on making for Parthian regions.
> But with the Church's house in flames within, what is its
> Watchman looking outside it for? Italians, more than Parthians,
> Need a good preacher to teach them the faith—the populace,
> I speak of, not of the nobles. Just one error made the Parthian
>
> Slip; not one but every error made Italy slip.
> The Parthian preserves a schism taken up from of old;
> The Italian rebuffs the precepts of faith he embraced.
> To one foundling heresy the Parthian is guardian;
> The Italian is founding father of thirty-two!
> And this gives the latter more license to sin.
> While freedom belongs to Italians, Syrians are slaves;
> It was not they that owed God the first fruits of the tithe
> Prescribed in the law; they sin, but without an avenger.
> For should the Holy Father excommunicate them
>
> Or an irate Emperor threaten war on them,
> They couldn't care less, as for neither have they any respect;
> They've already consigned them to the yoke and the tax!
> Out there there are countless millions of people
> And there a knight is the same as a boor:
>
> The knight for his muscle, the boor for his hatred of lords.
> But enough! Certain things may be true but can't always be told.

Yet the holy simplicity of Francis sustains to the last,
And has no eyes for sins or for faults.
Meet he the crafty, he will take them for wise citizens

Of Italy; nor will he believe they need a schoolmaster.
And so, he embarks, with his heart in converting the Syrians.

(*ED* i. 479–81)

The mission to the 'Parthians' is a poor idea, thinks Henry. Francis should have concentrated his efforts on the Italians, who had greater need of him. The saint embarks for the Orient while the Italian church was burning. Henry here issues a sharp rebuke to Francis; this is the only such criticism in the *Legenda* (except for the description of the young man's dissolute life before his conversion). Thomas of Celano has of course nothing like this. Why, in this work dedicated to Pope Gregory IX, does Henry dare to criticize severely the project of the saint, Gregory's friend? No doubt he would not do so if he thought it would provoke the pope's displeasure. Was this in fact the pope's opinion of Francis's mission, or at least a view widely held in the curia? We have seen that Cardinal Ugolino (the future Pope Gregory IX) had discouraged Francis from setting off for France in 1217,[21] precisely because the young order needed its founder and chief. We have also seen that Francis's departure for the East left the friars headless, prey to internal divisions which finally spurred Francis to return hurriedly; Ugolino himself had to intervene to find a solution. No doubt the cardinal thought that the Egyptian mission was an error, and perhaps his opinion was known in the curia at the time when Henry wrote his *Legenda*.

Of course Henry, like Thomas, is careful to avoid mentioning any division among the friars. He invokes, more generally and grandiloquently, heresies and schisms. His Francis is a 'doctor' who could have instructed the Italians and purged them of their errors. This leads the poet into a long invective against the mœurs and the indiscipline of the Italians: the *miles* who abuses his power, the peasant who hates his master. The Italians, unlike the 'Syrians', enjoy freedom—a freedom which they squander, since they follow the teachings of thirty-six heresiarchs. They fear neither the pope's excommunication nor the sword of the emperor. Francis should have taken care of the Italians instead of setting off to preach to the Parthians.

In order to exonerate Francis, Henry invokes his *pia simplicitas*. *Simplicitas* is ambiguous: it sometimes suggests a regrettable lack of culture or discernment (simpleness), sometimes an exemplary modesty and honesty (simplicity). Henry plays on the double meaning: he qualifies Francis's *simplicitas* as *pia*, pious. It nevertheless has unfortunate consequences: it prevents the saint from perceiving the vicious nature of the Italians and their need of instruction. If Henry often presents the *poverello* as a professor whose astonishing knowledge and remarkable eloquence are directly inspired by God, here we see dimly reflected the opposite image—that of a pious but naïve man who cannot understand the world and its machinations. A slight disdain for Francis and his followers seems to flow, almost involuntarily, from the poet's pen. The resulting portrait is somewhat schizophrenic: Francis is at once an eminent doctor (*doctor disertus*) whom the Italians need and a simpleton incapable of seeing their vices.

Francis's audience is not the 'Saracens' of Thomas's text; Henry prefers the classical terms of *Parthi*, *Syrii*, and *Persae*, which he uses indiscriminately: his is a fixed and stereotyped Orient. The image that he paints of these peoples is borrowed from the poets of antiquity. The people of the Orient are the slaves of one man, the *Rex Persarum*. They are all caught in the same religious error, which Henry qualifies as both heresy and schism. We will see that he subsequently accuses Muslims of polytheism. These Persians are not worthy of our poet's curiosity, and it is difficult to understand why Francis sets off to preach to them.

After this passage, Henry relates Francis's three attempts to obtain the martyr's palm. He narrates at length the first ship voyage towards Syria, cut short by contrary winds. This misadventure gave him the opportunity to describe, dramatically and verbosely, storms at sea and the fear that they inspired in the sailors and passengers; he peppers this passage with verses borrowed from Virgil and especially Ovid. He describes the miracle in which Francis's frugal rations were multiplied to nourish, for days, the passengers and crew of the ship. After a brief description of Francis's endeavour to set off for Morocco—cut short this time by illness in Spain—Henry describes the voyage to Egypt, in the passage cited at the beginning of the chapter. Where Thomas vaguely evoked 'Syria', Henry places the encounter in Damietta; his source of information was perhaps Jacques de Vitry, whom he knew, as we have seen.

The setting permits him to compose epic verses: a real war at last, where his military vocabulary can finally be used literally! The poet indulges this desire: javelins and arrows fly; Greek fire rains down. Francis, a new stoic Aeneas, does not flinch: he crosses the mighty river standing at the prow of the boat, fearless and impassive. He sets off by himself (*tot solus*), which makes his heroism the more remarkable: Henry eliminates the saint's companion, mentioned in the first three sources. In this passage he uses numerous verses borrowed from ancient writers.[22]

Where Thomas had briefly invoked the blows which the Saracen soldiers inflicted on the saint, Henry elaborates: blood flows, the saint's body is beaten and bruised. His wounds, under the poet's pen, become roses, his bruises violets, which permits Henry to say that the saint's members are dressed in royal purple. The saint's heroic resistance to this treatment inspires the Persians' admiration. Their king receives Francis grandly and offers him sumptuous gifts, but Francis wants only one thing: to be heard. The king convokes his philosophers, asking them to listen to Francis and to judge the truth of his sayings.

Henry is the first author to relate what Francis supposedly said at the court of the sultan—or rather, here, of the *Rex Persarum*. For the anonymous *Chronicle*, as we have seen, the king's priests refused to listen to the Christian clerics and prohibited the king from listening to them. Jacques de Vitry and Thomas of Celano both affirm that Francis preached to the sultan for several days and that his preaching was well received. But neither of them says what Francis said. Henry is thus free to imagine the scene as he likes.

Henry describes the triumph of a brilliant philosopher and a peerless orator. Francis is wise (*sapiens*); he produces new sermons which surpass human understanding. Nothing escapes his intellect. He begins at the beginning, with the origins of the universe, the creation by the first cause, God who is unique. This gives him the occasion to condemn the 'perverse school of Mohammed' and to prove to the Persians that there is one sole God, not a multitude of gods. This declaration is involuntarily ironic, for anyone with the slightest knowledge of Islam: not only were the Muslims convinced that there was only one God, creator of the universe, but they accused Christians of having betrayed monotheism by 'associating' to the sole God a multitude of minor divinities: Christ, the Holy Spirit, the saints. But Henry knows nothing of all this: the Persian king is a product of his readings of ancient poetry and has nothing to do with real Muslims.

The king and his courtiers listen in astonishment to this professor of theology who explains to them the history of the world: the fall of Lucifer, his seduction of Eve, who provokes Adam's fall and that of all humanity, then the redemption worked by Christ, who is unique and indivisible and present in the various churches. Finally, he presents baptism as the rite which permits the purification of the sin of Adam and Eve and permits access to the church. The king and the philosophers are dumbstruck in admiration. The king authorizes Francis to leave and return as he wishes: he who before was a prisoner tortured by the Persians is now the great professor before whom all doors are open.

What follows (Francis's departure) is even more incongruous in Henry's version than it had been in Thomas's. Thomas had simply invoked God's will, suggesting that he reserved for Francis a destiny even more glorious than martyrdom (by which, as we have seen, he meant the stigmata). Jacques de Vitry, in his *Historia occidentalis*, affirmed that the fear of having his army convert to Christianity *en masse* and abandon him made the sultan send Francis back to the Christian camp. For Henry, the saint concludes by exhorting the Persians to accept baptism. Given the enthusiasm which his sermon provoked this should have led to the conversion of the king and his entourage. But this did not happen. Why not? Henry declared simply that Francis, lacking sufficient *ministri* to convert so many Persians, left. This precipitous abandonment of his mission solicits no further comment from the poet, who quickly turns to the preaching to the birds.

The *Vita versificata* by Henry of Avranches unwittingly highlights the perils which success held for the Franciscans: it could corrupt and denature the saint and the order he founded. While Francis's unusual qualities earned him a singular reputation for sanctity, once he was established in the communion of saints, he was transformed the better to correspond with conventional hagiographical *topoi*. We have seen that the problem is inevitable, that Thomas of Celano is torn between, on the one hand, a desire to faithfully depict a man that he knew and admired and, on the other, the need to prove his sanctity by tacking onto his life story a certain number of hagiographical *topoi*. But Thomas was of course a Franciscan who wrote a very Franciscan version of the life of the order's founding saint. Henry of Avranches, the polar opposite of Francis in his mœurs, his lifestyle, and his erudition, remakes the *poverello* according to his tastes: an epic hero, a great professor, and orator. The preaching to the 'King of the Persians' furnishes one of the best examples of this transformation. This version of the events will have direct little influence on the later sources, but other authors from other periods will revive this idea of a stalwart saint who through brilliant preaching 'proved' the truth of Christianity to breathless barbarians.

5

Bearer of the Precepts of Life

The Bardi Dossal (1240s)

Fig. 3. Bardi dossal: Francis preaches to the Saracens.

T he artist of the Bardi dossal renders a striking image of Francis's preaching to the sultan and his subjects (Fig. 3). Against a golden background, a crowd of men and women, clearly Oriental, is assembled in what seems to be a public square (flanked by buildings on both sides). On the left, Francis preaches standing, haloed, barefoot, in Franciscan habit, a cord tied around his waist, with two friars behind him. He preaches to a very attentive audience, an open book in his left hand; he makes a gesture of blessing with the right. To the right of the composition, the sultan sits in a throne before a building, perhaps his palace. His long beard indicates that he too is Oriental, but apart from this detail the artist graces him with all the attributes of a European king: a crown (visible in spite of the damage to the dossal), throne, sceptre topped with *fleur de lys*. Behind this king, a beardless soldier bears a lance and a shield. The artist presents Francis leading the apostolic life, faithful to the Gospel which he holds in his hand. Christ had ordered the Apostles to go through the world bearing the good news of the Gospel through preaching to infidels. This is exactly what Francis and his companions are doing in this scene. And they have found a receptive audience: all eyes are fixed on the saint.

This image is one of twenty scenes of the life and miracles of Francis painted on what art historians call the 'Bardi' altarpiece or dossal because it is now housed in the Cappella de' Bardi in Santa Croce, principal Franciscan church of Florence. The artist has been dubbed the 'Maestro del San Francesco Bardi', and the date of composition has been variously estimated between 1230 and 1270. For Miklós Boskovits, the artist was the Florentine painter Coppo di Marcovaldo, who painted it in the 1240s.[1]

In the centre of this large altarpiece stands Francis, haloed, in Franciscan habit (brown with pointed hood, with a knotted rope in place of a belt) (Fig. 4). He is tonsured. The stigmata, black, are clearly visible on his hands and feet. One foot is in profile while the other, turned towards the front, slightly overlaps the lower border, creating a suggestion of movement. The saint's face, hieratic, displays a perfect symmetry in a formalistic style inspired by Byzantine icons. His almond-shaped eyes and small closed mouth suggest serenity. His right hand is raised in a Christ-like gesture of blessing, while his left hand holds a book with a golden cover, marked with a large cross. Is this book the Gospels, as some commentators have affirmed, or rather the Franciscan rule, as others have argued? Are the two not the same, for Francis and his followers? To live according to the rule is to live according to the Gospels; Francis himself had presented the *Regula non bullata* as the 'life of the Gospel of Jesus Christ'.[2] The artist seems to affirm the same here. This sentiment is confirmed by the scene above the saint's head: the hand of God emerges from the blue vault of the firmament and

Fig. 4. Bardi dossal.

unfurls a parchment, towards which two angels point. On the parchment, we read: *Hunc exaudite perhibentem dogmata vitae* ('Obey this man, bearer of the precepts of life'). God orders the viewer to obey Francis, who bears in his hand the 'precepts of life', that is, the rule of the Gospel.

How is one to follow this divine order, to live according to the precepts of the rule/Gospel? That is what the artist shows in the twenty scenes placed around the central standing figure of the saint, who is both a model to follow and a saint to venerate. The artist has painted, in the corners of the borders between the scenes, a series of busts of Franciscan friars, all turned towards the central figure of their founding father, their hands joined in prayer. There are seventeen friars, but clearly there were more originally (perhaps thirty-six or forty): the dossal has been damaged and trimmed; the outer borders have disappeared, but at the bottom there are bits of heads of other Franciscans. These friars are an example for the viewer, who should turn to Francis in veneration and follow the *dogmata vitae* that he personified his whole life and that he established in the rule.

The twenty scenes present a narration, more or less chronological, of the life, death, and several *post-mortem* miracles of Francis. Whether we date it with Miklós Boskovits to the 1240s, with Chiara Frugoni to 1254, or with Eamon Duffy after 1263 (an issue to which I will return), the dossal is one of the first (at least in Europe) to depict the life of a saint. Previously, only Christ was the object of narrative series of scenes, often placed around a central image of his crucifixion. This fact can only confirm the sentiment that here Francis is an *alter Christus*.[3]

The narrative begins on the top left. Francis, on the right of the scene, haloed (in this scene and in all the others), is freed by his mother; according to Thomas of Celano, he had been imprisoned by his father, who was furious that his son gave away his money in order to pay for repairing a church (1C 12–13). In an act of maternal love and charity, the mother liberates her son; on the left is the father, who has returned and who seems to oppose in vain his wife's act. Directly underneath, the second scene shows Francis breaking the ties with his parents. Before the cathedral and the episcopal palace of Assisi, Francis tosses his clothes at his father's feet; the bishop of Assisi, a tall man with a grey beard, holding a book in his hand, puts his arm and his cloak around Francis, in a gesture of welcome and protection. In the centre are the blue and white clothes that Francis has spurned, symbols of the worldly life that he now renounces. In the third scene, Francis traces, using a stick as the bishop looks on, the habit in the form of a cross that he will wear in the seventeen other scenes, and which the seventeen friars in the margins wear also. In the following scene, Francis listens to the mass at the church of Portiuncula: when he hears Christ's injunction to the Apostles: 'Provide neither gold, nor silver, nor brass in your purses, nor scrip for your journey, neither two coats, neither shoes, nor yet staves', he removes his shoes and henceforth goes barefoot.[4]

These initial scenes emphasize Francis's rupture with a world ruled by monetary and material values. Francis has chosen to renounce his parental heritage. The dress and appearance of Francis and his friars clearly show this rupture: the habit in the shape of the cross, the lack of shoes, the simple cord instead of a belt, the refusal to handle money. In the fifth scene, the pope gives his approval to Francis, who kneels at the centre of the composition; the pope hands Francis a book with his left hand and blesses him with his right hand. Behind the pope, several cardinals look on; behind Francis are a friar and a priest. It has often been said that the pope here is Innocent III, but nothing indicates whether the scene is meant to represent the first approbation of the order by Innocent in 1209/1210 or the approval of the *Regula bullata* by Honorius III in 1223, or a mix of the two. In any case, the message is clear: both Francis and his rule have received the blessing of the pope, hence of the church. The book, like that held by the saint at the centre of the dossal, is both rule and Gospel, since, according to Thomas of Celano, Francis, in composing the first rule 'used primarily words of the holy gospel, longing only for its perfection' (1C 32).

The following scenes do not follow Thomas's chronological order, but seem rather to portray Francis's progression towards holiness and his growing resemblance to Christ. The sixth episode shows Christmas at Greccio (dated by Thomas 'three years before his death', i.e. 1223); Francis, to the right of the altar, attends a mass celebrated by a priest; in front of the altar is the stable scene with, between the ass and the bull, baby Jesus who (according to Thomas) appeared miraculously to the eyes of a 'man of great virtue' (1C 84–7). Next are two scenes of preaching: first to the birds, then to the sultan and his subjects. The order of the two scenes is inversed compared to Celano who, as we have seen, placed the preaching to the birds (1C 58) directly after Francis's return from the East.

Before examining in detail these preaching scenes, let us quickly survey the rest of the ensemble. The four following scenes are at the bottom centre, underneath the feet of the central figure of Francis. Two of these episodes show how Francis bought and freed lambs, for which he had a particular affection, for they reminded him of the 'gentle lamb', Christ (1C 78–9). The following scene shows the penance that Francis imposed on himself for having eaten chicken once when he was ill: naked, attached to a column (an echo of the iconography of Christ's supplications), he offers himself up to penitential punishment before the inhabitants of Assisi. As Eamon Duffy has remarked, this scene is closer to Bonaventure's description than to Thomas's.[5] Next is the stigmatization: Francis, kneeling before a chapel in the mountains, arms open, contemplates a seraph, which bears on its wings an image of the crucified Christ; golden rays emanate from the seraph to the halo of the saint. The stigmata appear on Francis's hands and feet. Next, the artist depicts the miraculous apparition of the saint to friars at the chapter of Arles. Next is a representation of Francis caring for lepers, probably inspired by the saint's *Testament*,[6] according to which lepers played a key role in Francis's conversion: they provoked a profound aversion in him, as long as he was enamoured of this world; it was by learning to love them and take care of them that Francis was able to turn to a life of ascesis and of serving the poor (*Testament*, 1–3). Francis appears twice in this image: on the left, he holds a leper in his arms; on the right, he washes other lepers' feet. The next scene is the saint's death: he is lying in bed, surrounded by his friars, holding a candle in one hand and a book in the other; two angels carry his soul, dressed in white, towards heaven. At the foot of his bed, four cripples raise their hands towards the saint, begging to be cured.

The five final scenes illustrate Francis's *post-mortem* miracles and his canonization. The sixteenth scene combines two miracles already well established in Franciscan iconography: the curing of a crippled girl and the exorcism of a young woman possessed by demons. The following image shows Pope Gregory IX canonizing the saint. Then two scenes show a miracle the saint performed for the benefit of sailors: first he appears to them to save them from shipwreck; next the sailors, barefoot and bare-chested, thank the saint in a solemn procession. The final scene (also well established in the earlier iconography) shows the cure of the cripple Bartholomew of Narni, who walks off happily at the right of the image.

The richness and coherence of this ensemble are striking. To better understand its importance, we need to place the Bardi dossal in the context of similar thirteenth-century devotional images.[7] This altarpiece is not the first of its genre: earlier painted boards depict Francis surrounded by scenes from his life and miracles. Only one of these pieces is dated and signed:

the Pescia dossal, painted by Bonaventura Berlinghieri, dated 1235, only nine years after Francis's death and seven after his canonization. For the other pieces, I follow the dating proposed by Chiara Frugoni, based on the relations between the different images. For her, the earliest paintings were rectangular painted boards, showing the saint surrounded by a few miracle scenes. While these early compositions (painted before 1235) are no longer extant, two mid-thirteenth century copies survive: one of them is now in the basilica of Assisi, the other in the Vatican.[8]

The four scenes surrounding Francis in the Assisi panel are inspired by miracles related by Thomas of Celano in the *Vita prima*. Above left is the cure of a girl whose neck is twisted: the miracle takes place in front of the church of San Giorgio, just outside the walls of Assisi (where Francis had initially been buried; according to Thomas the miracle took place during his funeral).[9] Before the altar kneel the girl and her mother, their hands jointed in supplication; behind the altar, Franciscan friars, arms open in prayer, contemplate the child; behind the mother, in front of the city of Assisi, a crowd of witnesses jostles, churchmen and laymen. The artist of the Bardi dossal will combine this with another miracle, to which the Assisi artist devotes a separate image (above right): the exorcism of a possessed woman.[10] A grey, winged, diaphanous demon emerges from the mouth of the young women whose dishevelled hair and dress are telltale signs of possession. Below left we find another scene which the maestro de Bardi will take up: the cure of Bartholomew of Narni, a cripple to whom (according to Thomas) Francis appeared in a vision, instructing him to go bathe in a fountain; there he feels Francis's hands putting his leg back into place; to the right Bartholomew walks off carrying his crutches on his shoulder.[11] On the lower right is the cure of another cripple (not depicted on the Bardi dossal), probably Nicholas of Foligno (1C 129). The Vatican panel has the same four scenes disposed in the same way around the central figure of Francis. If Chiara Frugoni is right to think that these are both copies of originals dating before 1235, this suggests that, for the first artists who painted Francis, the saint is above all a thaumaturge: we have here four scenes of miraculous cures and none inspired by the saint's life. Francis is presented as an object of veneration rather than of emulation: the spectator is incited to go to his tomb and pray for his intervention, not to enter into the order that he founded.

Bonaventura Berlinghieri, for Chiara Frugoni, is the first to innovate, in Franciscan iconography, by presenting the saint as an *alter Christus*. First, by an innovation in form: while in the beginning Francis is represented on rectangular panels, starting in 1228 Berlinghieri employs vertical pentagonal forms, closer, for Frugoni and Boskovits, to the historicized painted crucifixes, on which the crucified Christ is surrounded by scenes from his life.[12] Berlinghieri paints Francis standing, in Franciscan habit, a book in his hand, flanked by two angels, accompanied by two scenes from his life (the stigmatization and the preaching to the birds) and by four posthumous miracles; Berlinghieri's first dossal, the San Miniato dossal (dated 1228), is lost; a copy survives, a sixteenth-century drawing.[13] Next is the Pescia dossal, which Berlinghieri signed and dated 1235.

When we compare the Pescia dossal with the Assisi and Vatican panels, the differences in form and dimensions are striking: the Pescia dossal measures 1.60 metres in height and 1.23 in width (compared with 1.155 × 1.545 for Assisi and 0.67 × 0.865 for the Vatican). 'Through this disposition, which is an innovation in icon painting, the Franciscans created the dossal, whose form was not borrowed from other genres, but determined by its function.'[14] This is the first dated example of a painted altarpiece or dossal, whose functions, forms, and origins have been studied by Helmut Hager and André Chastel. It consists of a large painted wooden panel (or sometimes an ensemble of panels) with, most often, a central devotional image (depicting Christ, the Virgin, or a saint) flanked with other images (sometimes devotional, sometimes, as here, narrative). The dossal is designed to be placed upon or behind an altar—in the case of the Pescia dossal, probably in a lateral chapel, the cappella Mainardi.[15] The gabled vertical shape echoes the architectural forms of a church or chapel: beginning in the fourteenth century, altarpieces are given gothic vaulting. Often they are inserted in sculpted frames, with columns and arches: the Pescia dossal has twelve perforations along its edges, where it was no doubt attached to a frame. Placed behind the altar, the central image of Francis would become the focal point of devotion during mass or personal prayer. The narrative scenes, too small to be perceived from afar, are the object of individual contemplation and invite the faithful to learn of the saint and his curing powers. Like icons in the Orthodox Church, the Franciscan panels encourage devotion to a saint far from his relics.

Vertical, gabled, the Pescia dossal devotes a much larger space than the Assisi panel to the central figure of the saint, here accompanied by two angels, a book in his left hand, the right hand open in a gesture of blessing, with black stigmata on his hands and feet. Berlinghieri disposes six scenes around the saint in two vertical columns. Four depict miracles, three of which we have seen in the Assisi panel: the cure of the girl with the twisted neck, that of Bartholomew of Narni, and that of the possessed woman (here shown with two other possessed women). The fourth miracle combines various cures of cripples, paralytics, and one leper: they kneel before the altar; they have placed their crutches on the ground; on the right they walk off. Just as Thomas regroups multiple thaumaturgical miracles in his *Vita prima* (1C 127–35), Berlinghieri places them in one painted scène.

Berlinghieri, unlike the artists of the Assisi and Vatican panels, presents two episodes from Francis's life: the stigmatization (top left) and (just below) the preaching to the birds. These scenes are emblematic of the saint and are destined to be the two episodes most often illustrated from his life by artists from the thirteenth century to the twenty-first. While any self-respecting saint performs cures, the stigmatization and the preaching to the birds show Francis's singularity. These scenes invite the viewer to contemplate Francis's life, not just his miracles.

These panels show the importance of Francis's cult from 1228, the year of his canonization. Indeed, most of these miracles had been related by Thomas of Celano in the *Vita prima*: the *post-mortem* miracles, we have seen, constituted the third part of the text. But this third part is the briefest; it is only 16 per cent of the *Vita prima*: the accent, for Thomas, is on Francis's singular life. The miracles are there to confirm his sanctity, but they interest Thomas less than his exemplary life. The panels, on the other hand, present Francis above all as a healing saint, though Berlinghieri does emphasize the saint's singularity through the two scenes from his life.

Let us return to the Bardi dossal which, contrary to Pescia, is neither signed nor dated. The identity of the artist and the date have provoked lively debates among specialists. All agree that this is a dossal and that it was probably set behind an altar in a Franciscan church: in its form, it is similar to Berlinghieri's two altarpieces, although it is much larger (2.34 metres high, 1.27 wide): Francis is painted almost life-size. We do not know for which church it was painted: it was transferred to the Cappella de' Bardi of the Church of Santa Croce, principal Franciscan church of Florence, in 1595.[16] Francis is clearly a saint to venerate, here as in the panels of Assisi, the Vatican, and Pescia; he produces miracles depicted in the final scenes of the dossal. But the artist restores the proportions of Thomas's *Vita prima*: fourteen of the twenty scenes narrate the saint's life, providing a unique

iconographic visual narrative. This Francis is a model to imitate, he bears
the *dogmata vitae* that the Franciscan friars must follow.

Let us take a brief look at the principal interpretations of this piece. In
1568, Giorgio Vasari attributed it to Cimabue. In the following centuries,
most critics followed Vasari; others attributed it to Giotto, to Margaritone
d'Arezzo, or to Bonaventura Berlinghieri.[17] In the first comparative study of
Franciscan panels of the thirteenth century, Benvenuto Bughetti compares
the scenes from the Bardi dossal with Bonaventure's *Legenda maior* and
concludes that the artist knew Bonaventure's text, which would indicate a
date after 1263.[18] In 1943, Giulia Sinibaldi and Giulia Brunetti questioned
this dependence on Bonaventure; in 1961, William Miller, followed by
Judith Stein in 1976 and Chiara Frugoni in 1988, affirmed that almost all the
scenes were based on Thomas of Celano's *Vita prima* and (for the story of
the shipwrecked sailors) on Thomas's *Tractatus de miraculis*.[19] The latter text
is dated 1254, which for Stein provides the *terminus post quem* for the dossal.
Since the artist relies on Thomas and not on Bonaventure, the *terminus
ante quem* would be 1263, date of the approbation of the *Legenda maior* by
the General Chapter of Pisa, or 1266, when the General Chapter of Paris
orders the destruction of all lives of Francis written before Bonaventure's,
or even 1257, when Bonaventure becomes minister general of the order.[20]
Stein prefers 1257, which for her marks the rupture between the 'spiritual'
Franciscans under the leadership of John of Parma (who resigns as minister
general in 1257) and the conventuals, led by Bonaventure. Rona Goffen
(1988) follows and elaborates Stein's perspective: the Bardi dossal presents
'Celano's Francis', not the saint of Bonaventure and the conventuals whom
we will find in Giotto's frescos at the beginning of the fourteenth century,
on the walls of the same Cappella de' Bardi.[21]

Eamon Duffy questions the consensus which, starting with Judith Stein,
has seen 'Celano's Francis' in the Bardi dossal.[22] While most of the episodes
depicted are indeed in Thomas's *Vita prima*, some of them are closer to the
versions given by Bonaventure in his *Legenda maior*; for Duffy, this indicates
that the artist used both texts.[23] He is right to stress this connection and to
cast doubt on the often simplistic contrasts between a 'spiritualist' portrait of
Francis (in Celano and Bardi) and the 'conventual' version of Bonaventure
and Giotto. The reality is much more complex, since (as we shall see), the
split between the two movements dates from the fourteenth century, not
the mid-thirteenth.[24] Duffy, however, exaggerates the similarities between
the dossal and Bonaventure's text: the third scene, where Francis designs

his habit, sketching with a stick, indeed has no equivalent in the *Vita prima*; but nor does it correspond (as Duffy claims) to Bonaventure's description: Bonaventure merely says that Francis drew a cross on his habit with a piece of gypsum.[25] The eleventh scene, which illustrates Francis's penance before the people of Assisi, indeed shows similarities with Bonaventure's text. But must we necessarily conclude, with Duffy, that the artist had read the *Legenda maior*?[26] Would it not be equally plausible that Bonaventure had seen the altarpiece and had been influenced by this scene?[27] After all, this painting must have been well known among Franciscans in Italy, whether it was originally in Florence or elsewhere. Both hypotheses are plausible. We may conclude, as Klaus Krüger did in 1992 (in a book which Duffy does not cite) that the arguments about sources do not provide convincing evidence for dating the dossal; after all, painters and writers often worked from the same oral material, and it is impossible to say who used whom, the Bardi painter or Bonaventure. Krüger concludes that it is better to try to date the piece using other elements.[28]

Alongside these debates on the artist's textual sources, another, more fruitful discussion has involved the formal and stylistic aspects of the work. Klaus Krüger, Chiara Frugoni, and Miklós Boskovits have shown that the painter of an altarpiece in Pistoia, from *c*.1250, took inspiration from the Bardi dossal, which consequently was finished before 1250.[29] Boskovits compares the work of artists active in Florence in the mid-thirteenth century and concludes that the altarpiece was probably an early work of the Florentine artist Coppo di Marcovaldo, dating from the 1240s.[30]

Concerning the use of these panels, Klaus Krüger has compared the narrative scenes of Francis's life with Franciscan liturgical texts such as Thomas of Celano's *Legenda ad usum chori* (1230). These texts show that in 1230 the Franciscans already have a complete liturgy for the week of the feast of St Francis (4–10 October). For Krüger, the dossals could have had a function in this liturgy; he suggests that the Bardi dossal was used behind the principal altar of a church during these feast days.[31] Dieter Blume had already posited a liturgical use of the altarpiece, highlighting the role played by the seventeen busts of friars in the margins of the scenes: they testify to the devotion that the Franciscans should show towards their founding father and function as intermediaries between the saint and the friars who participate in the liturgy.[32]

Let us return to the two images of preaching: to the birds and to the Saracens. In both cases, a group of friars is on the left: at least three behind

Fig. 5. Bardi dossal: Francis preaches to the birds.

Francis above, two below (even though all the texts give Francis only one companion). In the preaching to the birds (Fig. 5), Francis holds a closed book in his left hand; his right hand is pointed towards his audience, his index finger raised. Before the Muslims, the book is open; the pages are blank; his right hand is raised towards heaven. In both cases, he preaches to an attentive and well-ordered audience. The birds are aligned in five rows, on the ground and on four perfectly horizontal branches of a tree; they are all shown in profile. They face Francis and seem to listen to him. They all have the same size and colouring; some hold their wings open. Other artists will take pleasure in depicting a great variety of birds before the saint, with a multiplicity of species, sizes, and colours—no doubt for aesthetic reasons, but also to symbolize the great diversity of the men and women to whom Francis and his friars are called to preach. Here, on the contrary, the accent is on the fundamental uniformity of God's creatures, all of whom should sing praises of their Creator. Below, the Saracens are also neatly aligned in five rows. Here, however, the artist has depicted them in all their diversity: cloths of different colours (red, pink, blue, white); women and men (though it is not always possible to distinguish a woman from a young beardless man). Some of the men have black or white beards, most of which (including the sultan's) are long and pointed, which marks them as oriental: the other men depicted in the dossal have closely trimmed beards. The headdress also distinguishes these Saracens: most of the men have their heads covered, whereas most Christian men depicted on the altarpiece go bare-headed (with the exception of the hoods of the friars and the mitres of the bishops, cardinals, and popes—and in one case, a shepherd's hat. Most of the Saracen women, however, are bare-headed, whereas all the Christian women in the altarpiece have their heads covered—with the sole exception of the possessed woman (in the sixteenth scene). Only an infidel woman or a possessed woman goes around with her head uncovered. The seated position of the men in the first row is also visibly oriental: on the ground, legs crossed, or in one case with his arms around his knees; these are positions that we find nowhere else on the panel. As Chiara Frugoni has remarked, the Saracens have disproportionately large heads, compared to the Franciscans; for her this suggests that the artist wished to emphasize the intense attention with which they listed to the saint.[33] As for the sultan, we have already noted that, apart from his long beard, nothing distinguishes him from a Christian king: he holds all the essential symbols of royal power. Among these is his *spatharius* or arms-bearer, behind him, who holds his spear and shield. Finally, we note that six persons make the same gesture (some with the left hand, others with the right): arm bent, they hold out a hand, palm open, towards Francis: this gesture is made by the sultan, by a friar behind the saint, and by four other people in the audience. This shows that these people, at least, are receptive to the saint's message; we find the same hand gesture elsewhere in the dossal: the friars who listen to the sermon of St Anthony of Padua, the bishop of Assisi (as Francis designs his habit), and another friar who stands behind Francis as he receives the rule from the pope.

How can we compare this image of Francis's preaching with the hagiographical texts, in particular with that of Thomas of Celano? Chiara Frugoni has shown how complex are the relations between images and their supposed textual 'sources'; the images are 'a distinct voice'.[34] When they take inspiration from a text, they nevertheless diverge from it by necessity. There are always some elements in the texts that the painter or sculptor cannot directly translate into an image. Conversely, the artist is obliged to make choices concerning things that his source did not mention:

for example, the physical appearance of people, their position relative to each other, their gestures, the landscape around them, etc. When an artist 'translates' a text into an image, he necessarily transforms it. Chiara Frugoni has in particular studied this transformation in the texts and images of Francis's stigmatization. Some artists, in order to dramatize the scene, painted golden or red rays between the seraph and Francis. Bonaventura Berlinghieri paints one single large golden ray which emanates from the seraph to Francis's golden halo. In the Bardi dossal, three rays connect the seraph and the halo. Later, as we will see, the frescos in the upper basilica of Assisi have thin rays directly connecting Christ's wounds with those of Francis: this will become the canonical image of the stigmatization. Neither Celano nor Bonaventure say anything about these rays; yet they are nevertheless a strong visual image familiar to all who contemplated any of the hundreds of representations of the stigmatization painted on panels, frescos, and in manuscripts. Frugoni shows how the fourteenth-century Dominican Catherine of Siena (according to her hagiographer) contemplated a crucifix and saw rays come from Christ's wounds and touch her hands, feet, and sides, causing her intense pain and marking her with the stigmata. This text suggests that Catherine (or at least her hagiographer) was familiar with the iconography of Francis's stigmatization; for Frugoni, this anecdote shows the importance of the contemplation of images in medieval devotion and mysticism.[35] An artist, though he may wish to be 'faithful' to the canonical text of Celano (or, later, Bonaventure), introduces new elements which influence devotion and which leave their mark on subsequent texts.

In the scene of Francis's preaching to the sultan in the Bardi dossal, the artist has first of all had to make a choice: he devotes only one image to Francis's mission to the East. He could have chosen, taking inspiration from Thomas's text, to paint the context of the crusade, placing the encounter in the midst of the tents of the sultan's army; on the contrary, he chooses an urban setting which—alongside the bucolic venue of the preaching to the birds—underlines the universal character of the Franciscans' preaching mission. He could have shown the saint being 'insulted and beaten' (as Thomas affirms) by the sultan's soldiers. Yet here nothing suggests the slightest threat of violence: the only weapon, the spear held by the *spatharius*, presents no danger; it is pointed upwards. As we have seen, it is a standard iconographic expression of a king's power. The artist could have shown the rich gifts that the sultan offered Francis, 'trying to turn his mind towards worldly riches'. Yet he chose to portray Francis preaching to the sultan who 'was moved by his words and listened to him very willingly' (1C 57).

This scene indeed corresponds more to 'Celano's Francis' than to that of Bonaventure, as many scholars have affirmed; it is perhaps even closer to the Francis who was author of the *Regula non bullata*, the primitive rule of the order written in 1221. In the *Regula*, as we have seen, Francis enjoins his brothers to preach 'among the Saracens and other nonbelievers', urging them on with the very words that Jesus addressed to the Apostles in the Gospels. Rule and Gospel are one, and Francis and his companions, new apostles, bring the book of life to the infidels. By the book he carried in his hand and by his exemplary apostolic life, Francis invites the Saracens to embrace the Gospel. The saint shows the way to his followers, who should go out and preach everywhere, in the countryside and in the cities, in the lands of Christians and of Muslims. This connection with the spirit of the *Regula non bullata*, which gave a central role to the preaching to the Saracens, reinforces the hypothesis that the panel expresses a 'spiritual' or 'protospiritual' point of view; the primitive rule will remain the text of reference for the spirituals, while the conventuals will insist on the superior authority of the *Regula bullata* (which, as we have seen, gives a less important place to the preaching to infidels).

What is the result of this preaching? The image does not show it. This underlines the limits of iconographic expression, but also its advantages, compared to texts. Thomas of Celano, like Jacques de Vitry before him and Bonaventure after him, could not merely say that Francis had preached to the sultan: he had to admit that he had succeeded neither in converting him nor in obtaining the palm or martyrdom; he had to explain the reasons for this apparent failure. The artist has no such constraint: he depicts the moment he has chosen, when the saint is fulfilling his apostolic duty of preaching to the infidel, without portraying the results of that preaching.

If we compare this image of Francis's preaching to the sultan with that proposed by Henry of Avranches, we distinguish two quite distinct portraits of Francis and of the Franciscan life. Both Henry and the Bardi panel depict an efficacious preacher before an attentive audience and a well-disposed monarch. Yet in Henry's version, the saint's sojourn in the court of the 'King of the Persians' was the occasion to present his hero as an erudite orator amongst astonished barbarians. Francis's mission was useless: he should have stayed in Italy to convert the heretics. There is no suggestion that it would be a good idea to follow Francis's example and go preach to the 'Persians'. In the Bardi dossal, on the contrary, the preaching to the sultan is an integral part of the apostolic life, a life that Francis incarnates and which is inscribed in the Rule/Gospel that every friar minor must follow. Like the *Regula non bullata*, the dossal incites the friars to follow their founder's example and to set off to preach to the infidels.

The variety of interpretations of this episode shows how divisive Francis's life and preaching could be: within two decades after his death, we find competing visions of his life and message within the church, and even within the order he founded. In the mid-thirteenth century there is not yet a 'schism' between spiritual and conventual Franciscans. Yet there is a struggle for the future of the order, and in this struggle, as often, part of the combat takes place on the field of memory, as all contestants reclaim the heritage of the founding saint.

6

Burning with a Perfect Love

Bonaventure, *Legenda maior* (1263)

But with the ardor of his charity urging his spirit on toward martyrdom, he tried yet a third time to set out to the non-believers, hoping to shed his blood for the spread of the faith in the Trinity.

In the thirteenth year of his conversion he journeyed to the regions of Syria, constantly exposing himself to many dangers in order to reach the presence of the Sultan of Babylon. For at that time there was a fierce war between the Christians and the Saracens, with their camps situated in close quarters opposite each other in the field, so that there was no way of passing from one to the other without danger of death. A cruel edict had been issued by the Sultan that whoever would bring him the head of a Christian should receive as a reward a gold piece. But Francis, the intrepid knight of Christ, hoping to be able to achieve his purpose, decided to make the journey, not terrified by the fear of death, but rather drawn by desire for it. After praying, strengthened by the Lord, he confidently chanted that prophetic verse: 'Even if I should walk in the midst of the shadow of death, I shall not fear evil because you are with me' [Ps. 23: 4].

Taking a companion with him, a brother named Illuminatus, a virtuous and enlightened man, after he had begun his journey, he came upon two lambs. Overjoyed to see them, the holy man said to his companion: 'Trust in the Lord, brother, for the Gospel text is being fulfilled in us: "Behold, I am sending you forth like sheep in the midst of wolves"' [Matt. 10: 16]. When they proceeded farther, the Saracen sentries fell upon them like wolves swiftly overtaking the sheep, savagely seizing the servants of God, and cruelly and contemptuously dragging them away, treating them with insults, beating them with whips, and putting them in chains.

Finally, after they had been maltreated in many ways and were exhausted, by divine providence they were led to the Sultan, just as the man of God wished. When that ruler inquired by whom, why, and how they had been sent and how they got there, Christ's servant, Francis, answered with an intrepid heart that he had been sent not by man but by the Most High God in order to point out to him and his people the way of salvation and to announce the Gospel of truth.

He preached to the Sultan the Triune God and the one Savior of all, Jesus Christ, with such great firmness, such strength of soul, and such fervor of spirit, that the words of the Gospel appeared to be truly fulfilled in him: 'I will give you utterance and wisdom which all your adversaries will not be able to resist or answer back' [Luke 21: 15].

For the Sultan, perceiving in the man of God a fervor of spirit and a courage that had to be admired, willingly listened to him and invited him to stay longer with him. Inspired from heaven, Christ's servant said: 'If you wish to be converted to Christ along with your people, I will most gladly stay with you for love of him. But if you hesitate to abandon the law of Muhammed for the faith of Christ, then command that an enormous fire be lit and I will walk into the fire along with your priests so that you will recognize which faith deserves to be held as holier and more certain.' 'I do not believe,' the Sultan replied, 'that any of my priests would be willing to expose himself to the fire to defend his faith or to undergo any kind of torment.' For he had seen immediately one of his priests, a man full of authority and years, slipping away from view when he heard Francis's words.

'If you wish to promise me that if I come out of the fire unharmed,' the saint said to the Sultan, 'you and your people will come over to the worship of Christ, then I will enter the fire alone. And if I shall be burned, you must attribute it to my sins. But if God's power protects me, you will acknowledge Christ the power and wisdom of God as the true God and the Savior of all.' The Sultan replied that he did not dare to accept this choice because he feared a revolt among his people. Nevertheless he offered him many precious gifts, which the man of God, greedy not for worldly possessions but the salvation of souls, spurned as if they were dirt. Seeing that the holy man so completely despised worldly possessions, the Sultan was overflowing with admiration, and developed an even greater respect for him. Although he refused, or perhaps did not dare, to come over to the Christian faith, he nevertheless devoutly asked Christ's servant to accept the gifts and give them to the Christian poor or to churches for his salvation. But, because he was accustomed to flee the burden of money and did not see a root of true piety in the Sultan's soul, Francis would in no way accept them.

When he saw that he was making no progress in converting these people and that he could not achieve his purpose, namely martyrdom, he went back to the lands of the faithful, as he was advised by a divine revelation. Thus by the kindness of God and the merits of the virtue of the holy man, it came about, mercifully and remarkably, that the friend of Christ sought with all his strength to die for him and yet could not achieve it. Thus he was not deprived of the merit of his desired martyrdom and was spared to be honored in the future with a unique privilege. Thus is came about that the divine fire burned still more perfectly in his heart, so that later it was distilled clearly in his flesh.

O truly blessed man, whose flesh, although not cut down by a tyrant's steel, was yet not deprived of bearing a likeness of the Lamb that was slain! O, truly and fully blessed man, I say, whose life 'the persecutor's sword did not take away, and who yet did not lose the palm of martyrdom!' (Bonaventure, *Legenda maior*, 1260–3)[1]

Saint Francis was chosen by God because of his indomitable zeal for the Christian faith. Of Saint Paul it is written: 'He is a chosen instrument of mine to carry my name before the Gentiles and kings and the sons of Israel' [Acts 9: 15]. The Apostle Paul was endowed with this zeal because he was consumed with desire to spread the faith among the Jews, then the Greeks, and afterwards among the Romans. Saint Francis wanted to be poor for Christ's sake, and because of his zeal for the faith he became God's chosen instrument. He journeyed into many countries to spread the Christian faith. On three occasions, he attempted to go overseas but was prevented by shipwreck. He traveled to Miramamolin in Spain and then to Morocco, where later our friars were martyred. On a third occasion, he went to the Sultan of Egypt and proclaimed the Christian faith to him, longing to be torn to pieces for the faith. The Sultan said to him: 'Let us bring in our wise men so that we can debate our faith and yours.' Saint Francis replied: 'Our faith is beyond human reason and reason anyway is of no use except to a believer. Besides, I cannot argue from Holy Scripture because your wise men do not believe the Scriptures. Instead, make a fire of wood, and I will go into it together with your wise men. Whichever of us is burnt, his faith is false.' On hearing this the Sultan's wise men withdrew. The Sultan began to smile and said: 'I don't think I will find anybody to go into the fire with you.' 'Then,' answered Saint Francis, 'I will go into the fire alone, and if I am burnt, account it to my sins; if I am not, then embrace the Christian faith.' The Sultan replied: 'I could not dare do that, for fear my people would stone me. But I believe that your faith is good and true.' And from that moment the Christian faith was imprinted on his heart.   (*Sermo de Sancto Francisco*, 4 October 1267)[2]

Note concerning Blessed Francis, who preached to the sultan. The sultan said that he should have a disputation with his priests. Francis told him that he could not dispute concerning the faith according to reason, because faith is beyond reason; nor could he dispute using the Scriptures, for they did not accept them. Bur Francis asked him to light a fire so that he could enter it with them. For we should not mix the wine of the Holy Scriptures with the water of philosophy. For that would be turning wine into water, which is a very bad miracle; we read that Christ turned water into wine, not the contrary. This shows that the faith cannot be proved through reason, but by

Scripture and miracles. Hence in the early church, books of philosophy were burned. One must not turn bread into stones.   (*Collationes in Hexaemeron*, 1273)[3]

For Bonaventure, 'Seraphic Doctor', minister general of the Franciscan order from 1257 until his death in 1274, the ardent thirst for martyrdom played a key role in Franciscan spirituality. It was the highest form of love: at once a longing for union with God and a desire to bring the souls of infidels to Him. Bonaventure's *Legenda maior*, which became the order's official biography of its founding saint, insists on the burning desire for martyrdom which drove Francis East. Bonaventure takes up and expands upon Thomas of Celano's version of Francis's series of failed attempts to obtain the crown of martyrdom from the Saracens. He embellishes the interview with al-Kâmil, having Francis propose an ordeal: he and the sultan's 'priests' would enter into a fire; he who came out unscathed would have proven that he followed God's true law. When the Saracen priests refused, Francis urged the sultan to light a fire anyway so that he could enter the flames alone. The sultan refused, fearing lest he provoke a revolt among his people. Francis then spurned the gifts that the sultan offered him; the sultan 'was overflowing with admiration, and developed an even greater respect for him'. Since the sultan did not wish or did not dare to convert, Bonaventure concludes, Francis left him. In two later texts, in a sermon in honour of St Francis and in his *Collationes in Hexaemeron,* Bonaventure returns to the incident and slightly changes his story: now the sultan proposes a debate between his 'philosophers' and Francis. The saint rejects this proposition, affirming that the faith is beyond human reason.

In order to understand how and why Bonaventure reworks and transforms Thomas's narration, let us take a look at the situation of the friars minor in 1260 and the conflicts that threaten them from outside and from within. The General Chapter of Narbonne, in 1260, asked Bonaventure to compose a new life of Francis; Bonaventure completed the text before May 1263, when the General Chapter meeting at Pisa approved the *Legenda maior*. In 1266, the General Chapter of Paris ordered that any other biography of Francis be destroyed: Bonaventure's *Legenda* is henceforth the only authoritative text on the founding saint of the order of friars minor.[4] Why did the order take these exceptional measures to commission a new biography of Francis, to give it the solemn approbation of the order, and finally to eradicate any variant version of the life of their founder? These measures are part and parcel of the order's response to two major problems: the controversy over the role of the mendicant orders (Dominicans and Franciscans) at the university of Paris, and the conflict within the Franciscan order between those who championed strict poverty and a refusal of any positions of authority in the church and those who believed on the contrary that the order should play an important role in church affairs. Bonaventure found himself at the heart of both conflicts when he became a Franciscan in 1243.

Born John of Fidanza, son of a doctor in the town of Bagnoregio, near Orvieto, *c*.1217, he went to Paris in 1235 to study in the faculty of arts.[5] The following year, 1236, Alexander of Hales, one of the most reputed masters of the university, became a Franciscan. In 1237 Gregory IX issued his bull *Quoniam abundavit iniquitas*, which obliged bishops to permit Franciscans to preach and hear confessions in their dioceses. In this bull Gregory follows, almost word for word, a bull that Honorius III had issued for the Dominicans in 1221.[6] The Franciscans, like the Dominicans before them, were becoming an order of preachers, priests, and confessors, an order of clerics, and less and less a fraternity that simply sought to lead an apostolic life.

These two developments, the Franciscans' entry into the university and their clericalization, represent a change in strategy that provokes the displeasure of some of the friars. They also provoked a hostile and defensive reaction from secular clergy: Parisian masters who looked askance at the Franciscan and Dominican intrusion into the university and bishops, canons, and priests who had no desire to see these friars usurp their prerogatives for preaching and hearing confessions. Bonaventure actively participated in both of these debates.

Did the example of Alexander of Hales inspire John of Fidanza to enter into the Franciscan order? It is possible. In any case, Bonaventure was a student before he became a Franciscan. A sole biographical detail suggests an early predilection for the friars minor; Bonaventure himself relates, in his *Legenda minor*: 'When I was just a child and very seriously ill, my mother made a vow on my behalf to the blessed father Francis. I was snatched from the very jaws of death and restored to the vigor of a healthy life.'[7] This story of the young John of Fidanza saved from death by Francis corresponds perfectly to hagiographical *topoi*: the saint protects the child who is destined to enter into his order and to become his hagiographer. But this is Bonaventure's version of the story when he is Minister General of the order in the 1260s; nothing indicates that the young Parisian student John of Fidanza was conscious of his Franciscan destiny in his first years as a student, 1235–43.

John of Fidanza entered the order in 1243, the same year he began his studies of theology, which he completed in 1248. He then stayed on in Paris to teach the Bible, and the *Sentences* of Peter Lombard. He obtained his *licentia docendi* in 1254 and became master *ad scholas fratrum* (in the school of the Franciscan friars). He was still in Paris on 2 February 1257, when the General Chapter of the order, meeting in Rome in the presence of Pope Alexander IV, elected him minister general.

Well before his election as minister general, Bonaventure took an active role in the defence of the Franciscans at the university. The Parisian secular masters asked how these regular clerics, who owed obedience to their hierarchical superiors, could freely swear allegiance to the faculty, as any master was supposed to do. Nor did they accept that these Franciscan and Dominican masters were named by their superiors in their respective orders. More to the point, they criticized the friars for their lack of solidarity with the other masters; their practice of teaching *gratis* was particularly irksome. In a conflict between the town of Paris and the university, the masters ceased all teaching from 1229 to 1231; but the friars continued to teach—the Dominicans even took advantage of the situation to establish a second chair in theology. In 1252, the secular masters limited the Dominicans to one chair; the Dominicans appealed to the pope and William of Meliton, regent of the Franciscans in Paris, signed this appeal. John of Parma, master general of the order, came to Paris, spoke before the faculty, and in an apparent gesture of pacification revoked the appeal to the pope. William of Meliton left for Oxford and John named Bonaventure in his place. When, in 1253, the masters called a new strike in response to the killing of a student by Parisian civic guards, the mendicants again refused to participate. In retaliation, the masters expelled the friars from the university and excommunicated them.[8] The friars appealed to Pope Innocent IV, who ordered that they be reinstated to the university while he studied the case in detail. In February 1254, the university published an *Apology* which presented its point of view.[9] Between May and July 1254, Innocent IV issued a series of measures obliging the mendicant masters to submit to the demands of the *universitas* of masters, in particular to respect the strikes declared by the masters. In November of the same year, in his bull *Etsi animarum*, the pope limited the mendicants' rights to preach and perform sacraments without the approval of the parochial clergy. This bull effectively revoked or limited a number of privileges that the two orders had received from Honorius III and Gregory IX and represented a serious blow to their development. But the pope died on 7 December. Some claimed that the Virgin Mary paralysed the pope the very day that he issued his *Etsi animarum*, in order to punish him for his anti-mendicant policies, and that she subsequently made him die in acute suffering. Thomas of Eccleston claimed that the pope, as soon as he had proclaimed the bull

> lost the power of speech directly he had uttered the words 'thou hast chastened man for sin.' ... Earlier, when he had been bishop of Ostia, Pope Alexander IV had predicted that the Lord would soon remove the pope from among men, because of the way in which he had supported the enemies of the Order. ... No beggar—though I could hardly say no man—ever died more wretched and neglected than this pope.[10]

Chronicler Thomas of Cantimpré claims that a holy man had a vision in which he saw the deceased pope appear before Christ for judgement, as Saints Francis and Dominic looked on.[11]

Rinaldo de Segni, nephew of Gregory IX, was elected pope on 12 December 1254; he took the name of Alexander IV. He proved far more favourable to the mendicants than his predecessor; he had been cardinal protector of the Franciscans. Ten days after his election, on 22 December, he issued his *Nec insolitum* which rescinded the restrictions imposed by Innocent IV in his *Etsi animarum*. On 14 April 1255, in *Quasi lignum vitae*, Alexander IV ordered the university to re-establish the mendicant masters and prohibited any restriction on their number. The secular masters responded with a tract, the *Radix amaritunidis*, *Root of Bitterness*. They sought to avoid contradicting the pope at the same time as they set out arguments against the friars. They were inadvertently helped by a Franciscan Gerald of Borgo San Donnino, who in 1254 had written an *Introductio in evangelium aeternum*, *Introduction to the Eternal Gospel*. Gerald, inspired by the quasi-apocalyptical ideas of Joachim of Fiore, affirmed that a new age of the spirit would begin in 1260 and that the mendicant orders would take the place of the corrupted secular clergy. This text accentuated the hostility and apprehension of the secular clerics, who exploited this text to their advantage. In 1254, they wrote up a list of the thirty-one heretical doctrines they had found in the text and sent the list to Pope Innocent IV.[12] Innocent ordered that a commission study the issue; as a result of this commission, the new Pope Alexander IV condemned the text and asked the bishop of Paris to have Gerald's book burnt and to excommunicate anyone who possessed it.

In this context, William of Saint-Amour, the leader of the Parisian anti-mendicant movement, broadened the polemic, attacking not only the presence of the friars in the university but even the very legitimacy and orthodoxy of their way of life. Bonaventure, in September or October 1255, when he was 'internal' master of the Franciscan convent in Paris (i.e. he taught in the convent, but his right to teach was not recognized by the university), determined the question *De paupertate quoad abrenuntiationem, On Poverty and Renunciation*.[13] He attempted to show that the renunciation of all material possessions, both individual and collective, was the height of Christian perfection; he provided a theological defence of the Franciscan way of life. William of Saint-Amour responded with his question *De quantitate eleemosyne, On the Quantity of Alms*; he affirmed that begging for one's bread is only allowed to those who have no choice because they cannot work. The life of a mendicant, he affirmed, is spiritually dangerous, because his material need can lead him into sin: flattery, lying, stealing, murder. True spiritual poverty is that practised by monks, not the dangerous novelty promoted by the Dominicans and Franciscans. These mendicants claim to lead the apostolic life, but even the Apostles carried a purse (*loculos*) according to the Gospels (John 12: 6). Those who beg out of choice and not necessity should be excommunicated.[14]

William carries this criticism further in his *De periculis novissimorum temporum, On the Dangers of the Most Recent Times*, which he wrote in 1255–6 to the bishops of France. He sketches an apocalyptic scenario of a world falling to pieces, seeing everywhere the signs announcing the end of time. The most fearful enemies are the false preachers, precursors of Antichrist, whom the reader easily identifies as the Dominicans and Franciscans. These false preachers undermine the authority of the bishops, for they have obtained permission to preach everywhere (*ubique*). The bishop can no longer watch over the orthodoxy of the preaching in his diocese and the false preachers take advantage of this to spread a new heretical gospel, the *Introductio in evangelium aeternum*. In October 1256, Alexander IV condemned *De periculis novissimorum temporum* and asked King Louis IX to expel William from his kingdom. At the same time, the pope confirmed the nomination of Bonaventure and Thomas Aquinas as *doctores theologiae* of the Franciscan and Dominican orders at the University of Paris.[15]

By October 1256 the affair seemed settled, but it was at about this time that the minister general, John of Parma, gave his adversaries fresh ammunition by espousing joachite ideas close to those of Gerald of Borgo San Donnino. The sources only let us glimpse imperfectly at what happened, giving the impression of an embarrassing affair for the order, concerning which the friars preferred to keep a discreet silence. Chronicler Salimbene of Adam says that John was well-loved by his friars, that he was a reformer who could have had a good influence on the Roman curia that needed reform, but that unfortunately he 'followed the prophecies of insane men', to the great disappointment of his friends.[16] At any rate, John resigned as minister general in February 1257, during a meeting of the General Chapter called by Pope Alexander IV. Some have suggested that the pope pushed John to quit. Salimbene relates that the friars asked John to nominate a successor; John proposed Bonaventure, who (as we have seen) had already succeeded him in Paris. John, 'after his absolution' (which suggests that he had retracted his joachite doctrines and had received formal absolution from the pope), retired to Greccio, where he led the life of a simple Franciscan friar.[17]

When Bonaventure became minister general in February 1257, the order counted about 30,000 or 35,000 friars residing in thirty-two provinces, from the Syrian littoral to Scandinavia and from Morocco to the Mongol lands. This is a far cry from the tiny fraternity of forty years earlier. Bonaventure was conscious of the difficulty of the task before him. He took inventory of the all-too-frequent failings of the order: failure to strictly obey the vow of poverty (through taking positions incompatible with poverty, through living a life of luxury, through construction of new and sumptuous convents), vagabondage, aggressive begging (some friars act like brigands, fumes the new minister), familiarity with women, arrogance towards the secular clergy, etc.[18] In the face of criticisms of the order coming from lay clerics, of rivalry with the Dominicans, and of problems created by the order's expansion, Bonaventure undertakes a major overhaul of the order which earned him the nickname of 'second founder' of the friars minor.

In October 1259, Bonaventure retired to Mount Alverno, where Francis had seen the seraph and received the stigmata, to walk in the saint's footsteps, as he explains in the prologue of his *Itinerarium mentis in Deum*, *The Journey of the Mind into God*, the founding text of Franciscan mysticism.

Here Bonaventure makes Francis a model to follow, both in action and in contemplation. Bonaventure opens the *Itinerarium* by invoking peace, the peace of Christ, the *pax* that Francis always had on his lips when he preached.[19] As its title indicates, the *Itinerarium* is a sort of road map to find God. But before beginning its journey, the soul must practise humility and prayer. In a passage meant perhaps to show the superiority of the Franciscan approach over that of the secular masters, but meant also to warn Franciscan masters of the dangers of pride, Bonaventure affirms:

> Therefore to the groan of praying through Christ crucified, through whose Blood we are purged from the filth of vices, I indeed first invite the reader, lest perhaps he believes that reading without unction, speculation without devotion, investigation without admiration, circumspection without exultation, industry without piety, knowledge (*scientia*) without charity, understanding without humility, study apart from divine grace, gaze (*speculum*) apart from divinely inspired wisdom is sufficient for him.[20]

Bonaventure maintains that the mind must begin by the contemplation of created beings and then raise itself, in six stages (symbolized by the six wings of the Seraph), to the contemplation of the uncreated Creator. Bonaventure's spirituality is both more intellectual and more mystical than Francis's. Yet he keeps the accent on simplicity of life, on the fervour of love, and on the positive role played by creation in the contemplation of God: all this indeed shows the mark of the Franciscan spirit. We also see the preoccupations of the master general in this brief pedagogical work that seeks to encourage his friars in the practice of a moderate ascesis, to urge them to study in a spirit of humility and piety, and to nourish their spiritual contemplation.

At the same time Bonaventure seeks to give his order a clear legal basis, in the spirit of the programme of reform outlined in the circular that he had sent to the provincials (his *Licet insufficientiam meam*) at his election in 1257. The result is the *Constitutions of Narbonne,* approved by the General Chapter of Narbonne in 1260. While the *Regula bullata* of 1223 remained the rule of reference, the new *Constitutions* refounded the juridical basis of an order far different from the *fraternitas* of 1223: an order, first of all, in which priests were now more prevalent than non-ordained friars and in which university masters played a key role. Hence, for Raoul Manselli, Bonaventure is the principal author of the clericalization of the order.[21] For Jacques Dalarun, the *Constitutions* 'placed this caste of university priests in a real position of power'.[22] This is not new in 1260; Dalarun shows how the *Constitutions* represent the culmination of twenty years of reflection and legislation within the order. Bonaventure's task was to compile, summarize, and complete this work, and then to have the chapter approve this new synthesis. As a final precaution, the General Chapter ordered the destruction of all previous legislation (with the exception of Francis's two rules of 1221 and 1223). Thus the intermediate legislation, a potential source of appeals or recriminations, was eradicated, the better to affirm the authority of the new *Constitutions*.

This same chapter of Narbonne in 1260, as we have seen, asked Bonaventure to write a new life of the order's founding saints. For similar reasons to those that motivated the *Constitutions*: first, to present Francis as an irreproachable saint, modelled on Christ and the Apostles, so that no new William of Saint-Amour could raise doubts about his saintliness which legitimized the order. For similar reasons, the chapter of Narbonne modified two lines of the liturgical text by Julian of Spire, the *Officium Rythmicum*, which described thus the young Francis before his conversion:

> Hic vir in vanitatibus
> Nutritus indecenter,
> Plus suis nutrioribus
> Se gessit insolenter.

> This man in vanities
> Was indecently nurtured,
> And he behaved in a manner even more insolent
> Than that of his parents.[23]

This image of a young party-loving Francis is in accord with Thomas of Celano's; it serves to dramatize the miraculous nature of his subsequent conversion. But this was not to the taste of the chapter of Narbonne, which establish the following purified version:

> Hic vir in vanitatibus
> Nutritus indecenter,
> Divinis charismatibus
> Praeventus est clementer.

> This man in vanities
> Was indecently nurtured,
> But by divine grace
> He was protected with clemency.[24]

In this way Francis is irreproachable from his youth and, though he is less colourful and interesting than Thomas's Francis, he is more presentable. Bonaventure uses the same logic as the driving principal behind his *Legenda maior*. He tries to present his friars with a powerful tutelary saint, guarantor of the holiness of life incarnated in his Rule and in his order. It has often been remarked that, compared with Thomas's Francis, Bonaventure's is more distant: a saint to whom one offers devotion rather than an example to follow. Part of the reason, no doubt, is the forty years that have elapsed between the saint's death and the chapter of Narbonne; Bonaventure, unlike Thomas, never knew Francis. But if Francis is now more distant, that is fine for the Franciscan hierarchy: it is by venerating their founding saint and humbly obeying the order he founded (an order now graced with a clear hierarchy and new *Constitutions*) that the friar can pursue the apostolic life, not in trying to imitate Francis's life. As Chiara Frugoni has observed, Bonaventure makes the stigmata into the central miracle of Francis's life; he is now in the image of Christ, a saint to venerate, and no longer a brother whose life can serve as a model.[25]

In 1260, then, Bonaventure takes up Francis's hagiography with the same rigour and spirit of synthesis that he had recently employed in the *Constitutions of Narbonne*. He bases his *Legenda maior* primarily on three texts of Thomas of Celano: the *Vita prima*, the *Vita secunda*, and the *Tractatus de miraculis*; he also says that he spoke with those of Francis's companions who were still alive. He reshapes Francis in the apostolic and Christic mould, multiplying the parallels between Francis and the characters of sacred history, citing copiously from the Bible. He smoothes over the rough edges in Francis's life, deleting whatever does not correspond to the image he wishes to give. Thomas himself, as we have seen, wrote his life at the request of Pope Gregory IX and presented a saint in accordance with hagiographical *topoi*. But the reader has the impression that Francis's strong personality, with his uncertainties, his fits of righteous anger, his enthusiasm, his charm, continually overflows the hagiographical frame. Bonaventure allows the saint no doubts, no spontaneity: he confronts all with serenity, sure that he is following the holy life clearly laid out in the Bible. Hence the disappointment of many of Bonaventure's modern readers, from Paul Sabatier in the nineteenth century to Jacques Dalarun, for whom the excision of the primitive hagiography and the consecration of only Bonaventure's text constitutes a 'Misadventure (*malaventure*) of Francis of Assisi'.[26]

In his prologue, Bonaventure (in keeping with the humility *topos* known as *captatio benevolentiae*) apologizes for his rustic prose and declares that he would not have dared to undertake the narration of the life of such a venerable man if he had not been pressed to do so by his brothers; it is here that he affirms that, as a child, he had been cured by the saint.[27] Not to write would be an act of ingratitude; his *Legenda maior* is a sort of *ex voto* offered to the saint in thanks. Bonaventure announces that he will not try to be exhaustive. In other words, he is free not to relate any episode that does not seem in conformity with the image of the saint that he wishes to present. 'To avoid confusion I did not always weave the story together in chronological order,' he explains. 'Rather, I strove to maintain a more thematic order, relating to the same theme events that happened at different times' (*LM* P:4). In this way he is free to organize Francis's life according to a clear spiritual itinerary: from the mud of worldly sin, through ascesis, up to the divine recognition symbolized by the stigmata, then to his death and canonization. This thematic organization echoes that of his *Itinerarium*: beginning with the meditation on the things of this world and slowly raising oneself to the contemplation of divine truth. Worldly layman in chapter 1, Francis converts and undertakes a life of preaching, contemplation, and reconstruction of churches (both in a literal and symbolic sense) (chapter 2). The order is organized under his direction, with the approval of two popes (chapters 3–4). Next are a series of chapters devoted to his qualities (5–12), beginning with those that all friars should try to follow (austerity, humility, ...) and reaching those which mark him as a man apart (his ability to communicate with animals, his desire for martyrdom, ...), then the singular miracle which he benefited from, the stigmata (miracle confirmed by his exemplary death and his canonization). This schema corresponds to Bonaventure's mysticism (strongly influenced by Dionysius the Areopagite) according to which one follows first the purgative way (austerity, obedience, poverty—here chapters 5–7), then the illuminative way (devotion, charity, prayer—chapters 8–10), and finally the unitive way (comprehension of scripture, preaching, stigmata—chapters 11–13).[28]

This structure also allows him to deftly avoid several embarrassing questions. We have seen that, according to Thomas, Cardinal Ugolino dissuaded Francis from going to preach in France, convincing him that he had to stay in Italy to rule and organize his young order.[29] In the same vein, Francis had been criticized for having thrice abandoned his friars in his individual quest for the palm of martyrdom; while Thomas says nothing of such criticism, Henry of Avranches mentions it.[30] Moreover, Thomas is unable to hide the problems and divisions that came to light in the order during Francis's voyage East, and the crisis in the order that followed. Bonaventure neatly sidesteps these issues: first, he says nothing about Ugolino's meeting Francis in Florence and sending him back to Assisi. Since Bonaventure's text is organized thematically rather than chronologically, the issues concerning the order and its organization are covered in chapters 3 and 4, while the voyage to the East is discussed in chapter 9. Francis's desire for martyrdom, testimony to his great love of God, comes logically after the concerns for the administration of the order, even though these concerns had not been settled when Francis left for Damietta.

This hagiographical overhaul is clear from the first chapter of the *Legenda maior*, devoted to 'his life in the world'. We have seen how Thomas of Celano paints young Francis before his conversion: a fun-loving carouser, a man 'still boiling in the sins of youthful heat' (lC 3). Generous and charming, Francis became the head of a band of youths that wandered through the streets of Assisi indulging in 'wit, curiosity, practical jokes and foolish talk, songs, and soft and flowing garments' (1C 2). Alas, sighs Thomas, Francis led many youths into debauchery. Bonaventure will have none of this: 'even among wanton youths, he did not give himself over to the drives of the flesh'.[31] Bonaventure no doubt remembers the attacks on the order made by the likes of William of Saint-Amour and seeks by all means to avoid giving fodder to the enemies of the order. Even Francis's pre-conversion debauchery is eliminated in order to present young Francis as already touched by God; here we see the same logic already used in the rewriting of the *Officium Rhythmicum* in 1260. The result is a less convincing portrait: the charm and fervour of the young Francis, tellingly evoked by Thomas, help us understand the success of the order he subsequently founded; these qualities enabled him to attract men and women to his movement and to convince two popes to approve it. *Malaventure*, indeed, this monochrome Francis. But let us not forget that Thomas himself was inspired by hagiographical models: stories of sinners converted from a life of debauchery to one of purity and piety were medieval best-sellers. Among many examples, we could cite the legend of St Mary the Egyptian, a beautiful prostitute who after years of indulging in lust converted and purified herself through seventy years of fasting and prayer in the desert. Thomas's reader might think of Augustine, whose

Confessions describe his dissolute youth. The band of young revellers in Assisi indeed corresponds to what we know of the bourgeoisie of northern Italian cities in the thirteenth century. Yet this image also fits the model of the sinner turned saint. Bonaventure chooses the contrary hagiographical *topos*, that of the youth already marked by destiny and free from sin. He does this no doubt because Francis is now the founding saint of a powerful order that has its enemies, and he thinks it safer to present Francis as untainted by sin.

Another important passage in Bonaventure's text, as shown by Jacques Dalarun, concerns the two Franciscan rules, the *Regula non bullata* of 1221 and the *Regula bullata*, approved by Pope Honorius III in 1223.[32] Thomas of Celano, in the *Vita secunda*, relates that, at the time when the friars were concerned with the approval of their rule by the pope, Francis had a vision in which God ordered him to collect tiny crumbs of bread from the ground and to make a eucharistic host from them; Francis obeyed and gave it to his friars. But some of those to whom he gave the eucharist treated it with disdain and were immediately struck with leprosy. The next day, a voice revealed to Francis the meaning of the vision: the crumbs are the citations from the Gospel, which together form the host of the Franciscan rule; the leprosy represents the sin committed by those who do not respect the rule (2C 209). For Thomas, the Rule, composed of Gospel precepts, already exists at the time of Francis's vision (even if it has not yet received the pope's official approbation); the vision lambasts lukewarm Franciscans who, even during Francis's lifetime, do not want to submit to the Rule. Bonaventure transforms this story: he relates this vision of the crumbs and the eucharist, but does not mention the leprosy: there are no bad Franciscans in the *Legenda maior*. The heavenly voice gives a different interpretation of the vision, which becomes an order to Francis, to draw up a rule for his friars. Subsequently, says Bonaventure, Francis withdrew to a mountaintop with two companions; he dictated to them an initial version of the rule which he gave to his vicar, who then lost it 'through negligence'. Francis returned to the mountain and rewrote the rule himself, in the form that the pope then approved. Bonaventure once again deftly manipulates his sources: the rule is the fruit of a divine revelation that Francis, like Moses, received on a mountaintop. Moreover, Bonaventure found a clever solution to the troublesome problem of the two rules: the first rule dictated to his companions, then lost by his vicar (Elias, whom he avoids naming) is the *Regula non bullata*; the second, true rule, that Francis wrote himself and that was approved by the pope is the *Regula bullata*. To those who invoke the authority of the primitive Rule, Bonaventure opposes the superior authority of the Rule of 1223.

In the same way, Bonaventure says nothing of Francis's *Testament*, a text which posed problems for the order. Nor does he mention various other sayings and acts attributed to Francis by his earlier hagiographers: his fulminations against books and learning, the most striking descriptions of his extreme ascesis, all the allusions to conflicts within the order. The specifically Umbrian or Italian references disappear: the *Legenda* is to be read in Franciscan convents from Portugal to Poland. Thomas had portrayed a Francis of an almost rustic simplicity. For example, he related another vision that Francis had, of a black hen protecting a multitude of chicks under her wings. The black hen is Francis himself, who watches after his numerous friars.[33] Bonaventure did not like this image: no doubt, he felt that a little black hen did not inspire the reverence and devotion that he wished to instill in his readers. As Jacques Dalarun has said, Bonaventure's task consisted in transforming the feathers of the black hen into those of the sublime seraph.[34]

The description of Francis's mission to the sultan again shows how Bonaventure uses and transforms his sources. Let us note first of all the length of his treatment of the topic: the passage given at the beginning of this chapter is four times longer than the corresponding passage of Thomas's *Vita prima,* his principal source. Bonaventure gives a much more developed and detailed narration. Bonaventure peppers his text with biblical citations meant to show how Francis corresponds to the models of Christ and his Apostles.

The principal motivating force of this adventure (for Bonaventure as for Celano) is a fervent love for God which compels Francis to seek martyrdom. Before describing Francis's mission to the sultan, Bonaventure presents his two earlier attempts to obtain martyrdom, using language imbued with fiery metaphors:

> In the *fervent fire* of his charity he strove to emulate the glorious triumph of the holy martyrs in whom the *flame* of love could not be extinguished, nor courage weakened. Set on *fire,* therefore, by that perfect charity which drives out fear, he desired to offer to the Lord his own life as a living sacrifice in the *flames* of martyrdom so that he might repay Christ, who died for us, and inspire others to divine love. In the sixth year of his conversion, *burning* with the desire for martyrdom, he decided to take a ship to the region of Syria

in order to preach the Christian faith and penance to the Saracens and other non-believers. (*LM* 9. 5; italics added)

This burning love compels Francis to seek martyrdom a third time. Following Thomas of Celano, Bonaventure says that Francis went to 'Syria' and sought out the sultan (the 'Sultan of the Saracens', for Thomas; here the 'Sultan of Babylon'). Francis is indifferent to the myriad dangers of his project, dangers which Bonaventure exaggerates when he affirms, 'A cruel edict had been issued by the Sultan that whoever would bring him the head of a Christian should receive as a reward a gold piece.' This is highly improbable, not only because no other source concerning the crusade mentions this, but also because, as we have seen, Francis's mission probably took place during a period of truce and negotiations. But this 'cruel edict' highlights both Francis's courage and the miraculous transformation that he will operate on the cruel sultan. Bonaventure deploys biblical citations to describe the saint's intrepidness: as he walks through the desert, Francis piously sings an appropriate psalm. He sets off with Friar Illuminatus: while the earlier sources said Francis had a companion, Bonaventure is the first to name him. 'Illuminatus of Arce' is mentioned as one of the companions of Francis in a letter appended to *Legend of Three Companions*, where he is presented as a source of anecdotes concerning the saint's life. It is possible, as some have suggested, that Bonaventure consulted him before writing his *Legenda major*. On the other hand, the oldest manuscript of the *Legend of Three Companions* is dated 1311: could it be that the scribe inserts the name of Illuminatus that he knew from Bonaventure's *Legenda*? Could it be that Bonaventure invented the name, eminently appropriate to the witness of Francis's proposition of a trial by fire?[35]

Along the way, the two brothers meet two little lambs (*oviculas*); the saint, recognizing a sign sent by God, reminds Illuminatus of the appropriate verse of the Gospel of Matthew: 'Behold, I am sending you forth like sheep in the midst of wolves.' The lamb often represents Christ: we have seen that the Bardi dossal had two scenes in which Francis saved lambs from the butcher; he had a great affection for them because they reminded him of Christ.[36] Here the two lambs symbolize not Christ, but the Apostles, sent by Christ to preach the Gospel to the infidels. Francis used this same Gospel passage, as we have seen, in the *Regula non bullata*, where it is used to encourage friars to set out and preach the good news to 'Saracens and other infidels'; the friars, like their founding saint, should have confidence in God and be prepared to submit to martyrdom, if necessary. Of course the *Regula bullata*, the only legitimate rule for Bonaventure, downplays this injunction. Bonaventure's Francis, as he resolutely marches towards enemy lines, displays not only unequalled courage (as he had in the previous texts we have examined); he also has complete confidence that his acts conform to the Gospel model. Everything, even the animals he meets along the way, confirm this certitude.

As soon as the two friars see the lambs, ferocious Saracens, as if on cue, swoop down on them 'like wolves swiftly overtaking the sheep'. Bonaventure, following Thomas, has the Saracen soldiers cruelly torture the friars before taking them before the sultan, in accordance with divine will. Francis declares that God himself had sent him to preach the Gospel. As in Jacques de Vitry's *Historia occidentalis* and the *Vita prima*, Francis preaches brilliantly and the sultan listens attentively and in admiration. Unlike Henry of Avranches, Bonaventure does not make him into an erudite professor of theology lecturing to awestruck students, but he insists on three essential qualities of Francis's preaching: *mentis constantia* (which could be translated as 'force of intelligence'), *virtus animi* (strength of soul), and *fervor spiritus* (fervour of the spirit). All this shows, once again, the perfect fit between Francis and the apostolic model found in the Gospel: 'the words of the Gospel appeared to be truly fulfilled in him: "I will give you utterance and wisdom which all your adversaries will not be able to resist or answer back."' (Luke 21: 15).

Next Bonaventure introduces a completely new element: Francis, seeing that, even though the sultan listens attentively to his preaching, he does not wish to convert, proposes a challenge, a trial by fire. He asks the sultan to light a fire so that he can enter with the sultan's 'priests'. The sultan responds that he does not think that any of his priests is ready to throw himself into the fire to defend his religion; on cue, a venerable priest flees the scene, frightened away by the challenge. Francis then proposes to enter the fire alone: if he burns, it will be on account of his sins, but if he comes through unharmed, it will prove the superiority of Christianity. Yet the sultan again refuses to light a fire, fearing to provoke a popular uprising.

Why did Bonaventure add this strange episode? Some Franciscan historians claim that he heard of this from Illuminatus.[37] Probably Bonaventure inserted this proposition by the saint (seconded by the well-named Illuminatus) the better to illustrate the fervour of his love, which is the subject of this chapter of the *Legenda*. This challenge allows Bonaventure to deny that Francis's mission was a failure, since he managed in a way to show the superiority of Christianity by daring to propose an ordeal which frightened off the Saracen 'priests'. The proposed confrontation allows Bonaventure to highlight the sultan's growing admiration for the saint. This esteem grows even more when Francis rejects the gifts he offers; the sultan recognizes and admires Francis's disdain for worldly wealth. But he does not share this disdain, for it is precisely his love of power in this world and the fear of his subjects which prevents him from granting Francis's request for a trial by fire. The saint concludes that the roots of faith are not present in the sultan's heart; he leaves for Italy.

The addition of this episode is even more peculiar when one notes that the judicial ordeal had recently been banned, in 1215, by the fourth Lateran council. Ordeals, which had been fairly frequent in Frankish territory but also in Celtic lands in the early Middle Ages, called upon divine intervention to signal the guilt or innocence of an accused person. There were several types of ordeals, including judicial duals, trial by water, and trial by fire. In all three cases, the participants and the objects involved were blessed in specific liturgical rites invoking divine intervention to make the truth appear. It is true that the ordeal Francis proposed is not the classic trial by fire, in which, most often, an iron object was heated in a fire; the accused or his representative held it in his hand and had to carry it a certain distance. The burn was then dressed and after three days it was examined to see if it was healing well (a proof of innocence) or poorly (guilt); needless to say, this left a wide margin for interpretation, manipulation, and negotiation.[38]

The liturgy for trial by fire often invoked Shadrach, Meshach, and Abednego, the three Jewish children thrown into an oven at the order of King Nebuchadnezzar for having refused to worship an idol. The guards who threw them into the flames died, but the three children, thanks to the strength of their faith, were not harmed by the fire; on the contrary, they sang prayer and praises of the Lord in the midst of the flames (Deut. 3). In the liturgical formulae for this type of ordeal, the priest asks God to intervene to protect the innocent. What could then be more logical than to ask God to show, in a spectacular manner, the superiority of the true faith? Bonaventure is not the first to have this idea—far from it. In the sixth century, Gregory of Tours describes an ordeal between a Catholic and an Arian: a ring was thrown in a cauldron of boiling water and each one had to plunge his hand in to grasp the ring.[39] The chronicler Widukind affirms (*c.*970) that, in order to convince the Danes to abandon their traditional gods, a priest named Poppo carried a burning iron.[40] Guibert of Nogent tells how a Christian who was unable to convince an obstinate Jew of the Christian truth finally gave a clear proof: he grabbed a burning log in his bare hand. But the Jew was not convinced, which for Guibert proves the perfidy of the Jewish people.[41]

Even more interesting for our point is a passage in Peter Damian's *Life of St Romuald*. It is the story of Bruno of Querfurt (here called Boniface), a disciple of St Romuald around the year 1000. This Boniface had heard the story of the martyrdom of the more famous (eighth-century) St Boniface and asked: 'why shouldn't I seek out martyrdom also?' He thus set out for 'Sclavonia' and converted numerous people. He finally arrived in the court of the pagan king of Russia, who declared:

> 'If indeed you want what you say to be believed, let us erect two tall towers made of wood, separated by a small space, and let us set them aflame. Once they are burning brightly, and so hotly that they seem like a single fire, you will pass between them. If any part of your body is singed, we will put you immediately into the fire so that you are burned completely. If on the other hand you come through hale and whole (which is impossible to imagine), we will all believe, without the slightest hesitation, in your God.' This proposition greatly pleased not only Boniface, but all the gentiles present. Boniface, dressed as if to celebrate the solemnities of the mass, blessed the fire with holy water and incense, entered into the blazing fire, then came through unharmed: not a single hair on his head had been singed. Then the king and all the others who had witnessed this spectacle fell together at the feet of the blessed man, tearfully begging for indulgence, and demanded to be baptized immediately.[42]

Here the infidel king, and not the Christian, proposes the trial by fire. The saint braves the flames alone and his success provokes the conversion of the Russians. Clearly this mission was more successful than Francis's, all the more so since Bruno finally obtained the martyr's crown that he (like Francis) so ardently desired: while the king was away, his pagan brother had Bruno decapitated.

If, unlike Bruno of Querfurt, Francis did not get to die at the hands of an infidel king, this is because God had even greater things in store for him, as Bonaventure states more clearly than Thomas: namely, the stigmata. Indeed, Bonaventure presents the stigmata as a sort of martyrdom: Francis's 'interior fire' burns so strongly in his heart that it ends up marking his body. Francis succeeds in obtaining a new form of martyrdom. The proposed trial by fire makes metaphorical sense, since Bonaventure's whole chapter sparkles with words pertaining to fire: his Francis was not about to propose a trial by cold water! The fire of spiritual love which burns the saint is much stronger than the mere wood fire that he dares to enter to prove the ardour of his faith to worldly men.

This dramatic confirmation allows Bonaventure to attenuate the impression of failure that a reader of Thomas comes away with. Bonaventure, who no doubt had read the life in verse by Henry of Avranches (which, we have seen, expresses doubts about whether the mission was a good idea), tries to prove that this mission was neither senseless nor useless: it represents a necessary stage, a salutary trial, along the spiritual path that leads Francis towards God. Francis demonstrated his burning desire for martyrdom, won the sultan's admiration, humiliated the Saracen priests. Then, notified by God that it was useless to stay with the sultan any longer, he returned to Italy to pursue his glorious march towards the martyrdom of the stigmata. Bonaventure says not a word, of course, about the divisions that troubled the order and which, according to some, explained Francis's premature departure. Francis does all calmly and with dignity, as is appropriate for a great saint. Nothing here would encourage a friar to follow in the footsteps of their founding father, to embark for Muslim lands to preach the Gospel. Bonaventure's Francis is, here once again, a saint to venerate, whose sanctity illuminates the order he founded, but not a model to follow.

Bonaventure's *Legenda maior* is henceforth the only official Franciscan version of Francis's life. Almost all the authors and artists whom we will see in the following chapters will have read this text and taken inspiration from it. But Bonaventure himself did not hesitate to modify his canonical vision of the encounter between Francis and al-Kâmil. He reworks it twice: first in a sermon preached for the feast of St Francis, 4 October 1267 (the second passage given at the beginning of this chapter), then, in 1273, in his *Collationes in Hexaemeron* (third passage).

Let us first look at the sermon. It is the second of five sermons that he devoted to 'our holy father Francis' in his *Sermones de sanctis*. Bonaventure takes the theme of the sermon from Isaiah 42: 1: 'Behold my servant whom I uphold, my chosen in whom my soul delights; I have put my spirit upon him, he will bring forth justice to the nations.' Who is this servant? The one we find in the Gospel of Matthew (24: 45, the text that serves as the protheme for this sermon, i.e. a Gospel passage which provides the subject of the sermon): 'Who, do you think, is a faithful and wise servant, whom his master has set over his household, to give them their food at the proper time?' This servant is Christ, Bonaventure declares, following the traditional exegesis of these passages. He is sent by his master, God the Father, to spread the true religion and to nourish a hungry world with spiritual victuals. But this passage can also apply to Francis, Bonaventure affirms, presenting the saint as an *alter Christus*. God chose Francis and ordered him to spread the true religion throughout the world; he placed him over his brothers to guide them and to provide them with spiritual nourishment. To show how Francis corresponds to this 'faithful servant', Bonaventure insists on three essential qualities of the saint, in the three parts of his sermon: his profound humility, his confirmed virtue, and his perfect love. Bonaventure divides his second part, on his confirmed virtue, into three sections: (1) Francis's complete obedience to the law and the Gospel; (2) his unsurpassable zeal for the Christian faith; and (3) his perfect love for the crucified Christ.

It is in the second section that Bonaventure returns to Francis's mission to the sultan, to show his 'unsurpassable zeal'. While Francis is now an *alter Christus*, he is also still a model of the *vita apostolica*. Bonaventure insists on the similarities between Paul and Francis: just as Paul, in his zeal, brought the Christian faith to the Jews, the Greeks, and the Romans, Francis sought to spread it to the infidels in Spain and Morocco before going to preach to the sultan. Sultan of what (Syria, Egypt, Babylon) Bonaventure does not say. He simply declares that Francis preached to the sultan and that he was 'longing to be torn to pieces for the faith': his zeal drives him to seek out martyrdom. In this brief narration, a mere dozen lines (probably the summary of an *exemplum* which he embellished orally) present a completely different version of the encounter than that of the *Legenda maior*. Here the sultan proposes a debate between his 'priests' and Francis, but the saint refuses because 'Our faith is beyond human reason'. He cannot preach from the scriptures because the sultan and his priests do not recognize their authority. The only remaining option is proof by miracle: Francis proposes to enter into the fire with the Saracen wise men, who demonstrate their wisdom by quickly fleeing, provoking the sultan to smile. Francis proposes to enter the fire alone; the sultan refuses. In the *Legenda maior*, the sultan did not dare light the fire for fear of a popular uprising; here he fears he may be stoned. The *Legenda maior* insists on the admiration that the sultan feels for the saint; he wanted to shower him with gifts. But nothing suggested that the sultan had the slightest intention of converting. But in this sermon, things have changed: the sultan says to the saint, 'I believe that your faith is good and true.' And Bonaventure concludes, 'from that moment the Christian faith was imprinted on his heart'. Bonaventure now wishes to affirm the success of Francis's mission; while he did not succeed in bringing the sultan to the baptismal fount (for the sultan, unlike Francis, fears death), at least he profoundly marked his heart with the Christian faith.

Let us return to the proposed debate, another important change in Bonaventure's new version of the events. We have seen that in the so-called *Chronique d'Ernoul*, the two Christian clerics offered logically to prove the superiority of Christians and the Saracen clerics refused, demanding the death sentence for the Christians who had dared to propose such a debate. In the version by Henry of Avranches, there was no debate, but Francis's sermon, which resembled the teaching of university masters of theology, deeply impressed the sultan and his 'philosophers'. Here, on the contrary, it is the infidels who propose a debate and Francis who refuses, claiming that faith is beyond human reason. Why this addition? We should no doubt place this in the context of Parisian university theology. Logical argumentation, of course, was the basis of teaching and of speculation in scholastic theology from the twelfth century. Bonaventure occupies an important place in this tradition. But he nevertheless distances himself from certain aspects of this tradition; he affirms (as does his contemporary, the Dominican master Thomas Aquinas) that reason alone cannot prove the truth of the Christian faith. The truths of philosophy, inferior to those of the faith, are useless for missions to infidels. As Bonaventure affirmed in his *Journey of the Mind into God*, human knowledge is worthless without divine wisdom. In this sermon destined for the ears of Franciscan friars (as he shows when he calls the martyrs of Morocco, 'our brothers', *fratres nostri*), this lesson is a warning for friars overconfident in their intellectual capacities, ready to affirm that logical argumentation can be the basis of Christian truth.

Who are these intellectual friars who think they can prove Christian truth through reason alone? The best-known among them is no doubt Roger Bacon, an English friar who, in his *Opus maius*, tries to found a science of religion on the solid foundations of philosophy and astrology.[43] Bacon does not hide his disdain for the lack of erudition of the Franciscan hierarchy, including Bonaventure, whom he attacks several times in barely veiled polemics. Bonaventure, for his part, was wary of the enthusiasm of Roger and other friars for the arts of astrology and alchemy.[44] Roger, who wrote his *Opus maius* (1266–8) at the request of Pope Clement IV, did so unbeknownst to his superiors. Bonaventure feared that Roger or other free spirits could become new Geralds of Borgo S. Donnino, that their clumsy speculations would prove embarrassing to the order.

Bonaventure has these same problems in mind when, in spring 1273, in Paris once again, he preaches a series of twenty-three sermons concerning controversies raging at the University of Paris, in particular concerning what has come to be known as 'Latin Averroism'. These sermons have come down to us (as often for this period) through *collationes*, reports written by listeners (often students), and which are generally corrected and approved by the authors of the sermons.[45] Since the *theme* (the biblical text that served as a point of departure for these sermons) was the Hexaemeron (the story of the creation of the world in six days, in Genesis), this text is called the *Collationes in Hexaemeron*, even though Bonaventure ranges widely beyond the biblical text. He organizes his sermons around four *visiones*: intelligence introduced by nature (*intelligentiae per naturam inditae, Collationes* 4–7), intelligence raised by the faith (*intelligentiae per fidem sublevatae, Collationes* 8–12), intelligence instructed by the scriptures (*intelligentiae per scripturam eruditae, Collationes* 13–19), and intelligence suspended by contemplation (*intelligentiae per contemplationem suspensae, Collationes* 20–3). Through these four themes Bonaventure sketches a spiritual and intellectual itinerary which echoes that of his *Journey of the Mind into God*: the study of nature, of the things of this world, has its place in this itinerary, but it is only the beginning, the basis of intelligence. This point of view permits Bonaventure to affirm the importance of scientific and philosophical inquiry but to relegate it to the beginner's phase of his intellectual road map and to subordinate it to the following phases, where intelligence develops through faith, scripture, and contemplation. Bonaventure had planned on giving more sermons, but he was named cardinal on 23 May 1273 and had to leave Paris.[46]

In the first *Collatio*, Bonaventure explains his method: 'Our goal is to show that in Christ "are hid all the treasures of wisdom and knowledge" [Col. 2: 3] and that He is the means (*medium*) of all the sciences'.[47] There is no wisdom or science without God, as even the philosophers of antiquity understood, for Bonaventure: 'all true philosophers adore one sole God'. Socrates understood this truth and prohibited sacrifices to Apollo—and for this reason was put to death. The greatest philosopher of antiquity was thus a martyr for monotheism.[48] While Socrates and his disciple Plato understood that all wisdom emanated from the sole God, this was less clear to some of their followers, according to Bonaventure. He notes various errors of Aristotle, in particular the notion of the eternity of the world; an honest, forgivable error, but one which shows the fallibility of human reasoning (*Collatio* 7). He criticizes certain doctrines of his Dominican friend Thomas Aquinas (particularly his idea of *creatio ab aeterno*) and attacks the Averroists whom he calls 'blind' (*Collatio* 6).

It is in the nineteenth *Collatio* that Bonaventure speaks of Francis's mission to the sultan. This was the seventh and final *Collatio* on the theme of intelligence instructed by the scriptures; the purpose is to show how 'through knowledge and through holiness we arrive at wisdom'.[49] The theme for this sermon is: 'And the Earth brought forth grass, and herb yielding seed, and the fruit tree yielding fruit after its kind' (Gen. 1: 12). The principal fruits of Bonaventure's sermon are love (*caritas*) and wisdom (*sapientia*). Wisdom must not be confused with knowledge (*scientia*), a dangerous thing inspired by curiosity (*curiositas*). One cannot pass from knowledge to wisdom without the help of sanctity. True wisdom is found in the scriptures, not in the writings of the philosophers, for 'the philosophers have no knowledge which provides remission of sins' (*Collatio* 19. 7, p. 421). It is nevertheless difficult to avoid the philosophers completely. To understand scripture, one must sometimes consult the commentaries of the fathers of the church (such as Augustine or Jerome), which involves a certain danger, caused by the beauty of their discourse (*pulchre sermo*). Then, to understand these fathers, one must at times read the *summae magistrorum*, the writings of the university masters of theology; here the danger is greater still. Finally, to understand these masters, one must examine the sayings of the philosophers. Here *maximum periculum*, maximum danger, for we risk being sidetracked from the true sources of wisdom: did not St Jerome himself admit that after reading Cicero he no longer wished to return to the study of the prophets?[50]

In order to present these ideas, Bonaventure returns to Francis's mission to the sultan, in a passage of the *Collationes* cited at the beginning of this chapter, as an *exemplum*. In the *Collatio*, we have once again a brief summary of Bonaventure's sermon; only the essential is transcribed. The narration is essentially the same as in the *Sermon on St Francis*: the sultan proposes a *disputatio* and Francis refuses, claiming that the faith is beyond human reason. Francis for his part proposes to enter into the fire. Then Bonaventure gives the lessons that he draws from this *exemplum*. Philosophy cannot bring infidels to the faith. To mix philosophy and scripture is to dilute the wine of wisdom with the water of knowledge or, worse, to turn wine into water or bread into stones. Poor miracles indeed: one would do better to burn the books of philosophy, as was done in the primitive church. The faith can be proven through scripture or through miracles, but not by reason.

We have seen that Bonaventure does not feel the least bit constrained to faithfully follow his own 'canonical' version of Francis's life, that of the *Legenda maior*; he modifies it according to the didactic needs of the moment. Here he invokes Francis as a model for a specific purpose: to show that it is impossible to convert the Saracens through rational or scriptural arguments. It is the sultan, in the *Collationes* and in the *Sermon*, who proposes a rational debate and Francis who refuses. But while in the *Sermon* the sultan seemed touched by the saint's words, now, apparently, Francis has decided that it is useless to preach, since he knows in advance that the sultan will listen neither to his rational arguments nor to the words of the Gospel. The proposed trial by fire, in the *Legenda*, came after his well-received preaching; here it seems to replace it.

But while Bonaventure casts doubts on his own version of the encounter, as related in his *Legenda maior*, his successors will not dare to do so: for them this narration of Francis's mission to the sultan remains the official Franciscan version, the point of departure for all Franciscan authors and artists, from the thirteenth century to the twenty-first.

7
Trial by Fire
The Assisi Fresco (Late Thirteenth Century)

Fig. 6. The trial by fire, Assisi, upper basilica.

In the upper basilica of Assisi, a series of twenty-eight frescos relates Francis's life and miracles. The eleventh scene presents a confrontation between Francis and the Saracen 'priests'. Drawing inspiration from the trial by fire which (according to Bonaventure) Francis proposed to the sultan, the artist places the saint in the middle of the composition, before a fire that separates him from the Saracen 'priests' and causes them to flee. Francis glances back at the sultan who, seated on his throne, surrounded by armed men, with a sweep of his arm exhorts Francis to enter the fire. Francis's mission to Egypt has become a dramatic confrontation, an ordeal whose final outcome is uncertain, but which has succeeded in chasing away the clerics of the rival religion, showing the superiority of Christianity and displaying Francis's courage.

This fresco, with the twenty-seven others that accompany it, has long been attributed to Giotto Bondone (c.1267–1337). This attribution, quite plausible considering the style of the paintings and what we know about the artist's itineraries, has nevertheless provoked disagreements among specialists.[1] Just as Bonaventure's text became the standard text on the saint's life, the fresco of the trial by fire became the emblematic image of Francis's mission to Egypt; dozens of medieval artists took inspiration from it, both because of the artistic qualities of the fresco and because of its place at the heart of the Franciscan universe.

The Basilica of St Francis at Assisi: 1228–1300

Upon his death, Francis was buried in the small church of San Giorgio, outside the city walls of Assisi. But plans soon began for a more sumptuous resting place for the poor man of Assisi.[2] On 29 March 1228, brother Elias obtained a piece of land just outside the city walls, in a place called the 'Hill of Hell'; according to legend, it had been the site of public executions.[3] The irony would no doubt have pleased Francis: the brothers converted this place of violence and vengeance into a haven of peace and reconciliation, with it henceforth being called the Hill of Paradise. The donor, Simone di Pucciarello, granted full property to Pope Gregory IX and designated Elias as the beneficiary of this donation to the pope.[4] This permitted the Franciscans to avoid owning the land and thus to obey the letter of their rule of institutional poverty: the pope, and not the friars, possessed the Hill of Paradise and the sumptuous church that would be built upon it. The pope thus played a key role in the construction of the basilica and in the orientation of the young order at a crucial moment in its history. One month later, 29 April 1228, a year and a half after the saint's death and three months before his canonization, Gregory (in his bull *Recolentes qualiter*) authorized the construction of a basilica in Assisi destined to receive the body of Francis (whom the pope describes as *beatus*); he accorded an indulgence of forty days to those who gave alms for the construction of the church.[5] On 17 July, the day following the canonization, the pope laid the cornerstone of the building. On 22 October, Gregory announced that the church would owe obedience only to the pope, guaranteeing the Franciscans' independence from the bishops of Assisi and again asserting his control over the principal church of the order; these declarations were no doubt contested, since the pope was obliged to reiterate them two years later. On 21 February 1229, he exhorted churchmen to promote the cult of the new saint.[6] He then declared that the new church was the *caput et mater* (head and mother) of the order.[7] Elias used all his powers of persuasion to raise funds for the church; according to the censorious *Speculum vitae*, he 'began to extort money by diverse means'; Giordano di Giano echoes these critiques, as do chroniclers of the fourteenth century.[8] Many Franciscans noted the paradox of a sumptuous basilica destined to receive the remains of the *poverello*: in the fourteenth century, some spiritual friars sharply criticized the sumptuousness of the church; the order's hierarchy defended itself, affirming that it helped encourage the devotion of the faithful.[9] The paradox continued to strike twentieth-century authors such as Henry James, who noted: 'The apostle of beggary, the saint whose only tenement in life was the ragged robe which barely covered him, is the hero of this massive structure.'[10] For Jacques Le Goff, the basilica is an 'insult to the spirituality of the saint'.[11]

The lower basilica, carved into the side of the hill, looks like an immense Romanesque crypt, dark because of the small size of its windows, the low ceiling, the thick walls (designed to sustain the weight of the upper basilica) and because the eastern end is buried in the hill. This lower basilica, built to receive Francis's body (and to accommodate crowds of pilgrims), was completed in 1230. A great festival was planned for the translation of the saint's body on 25 May 1230: more than 2,000 friars were there, with innumerable prelates, bishops, and laymen. All hoped to see the saint, perhaps even to touch him. Perhaps his body would be miraculously preserved, like those of many saints (at least according to their hagiographers). Perhaps one would be able to see the stigmata, as Thomas of Celano described them. But when the day came, there was no body! The texts concerning the event are confused and contradictory, but it seems that Elias, unbeknownst to minister general John Parenti and to the majority of the friars, but in accord with the civil authorities of Assisi, had Francis's body transferred secretly in the night, a few days before 25 May, and buried it beneath the altar in a place so inaccessible that it remained secret for six centuries—until 12 December 1818, when the saint's sarcophagus was found after fifty-two days of excavation.[12] Elias and the civil authorities perhaps feared that someone might steal the precious cadaver—or take away a piece of it. If Elias showed so little trust in his fellow Franciscans, it was no doubt because he knew that some of them looked askance at the new church and thought that the little church of the Portiuncula, which Francis frequented while alive and where he died, would be a much more appropriate burial site.[13] Or perhaps, as Richard Trexler has suggested, Elias did not want to show a body which did not correspond to people's expectations, either because it was in an advanced state of decomposition or because it bore no trace of the stigmata.[14] In any case, the incident provoked the ire of the friars and laymen present but succeeded, far better than a bevy of papal bulls, in consecrating the church as *caput et mater* of the order of friars minor.

The construction of the upper basilica began in 1230 and lasted about six years. In the form of a T, it contains a long gothic nave adapted to the preaching to crowds of pilgrims. At the end of the apse of the choir, a marble throne indicates that it is a pontifical church. While the lower basilica is low and dark, the upper basilica is high and luminous, lit by the rose window of the western wall and by large side windows. These windows are five metres above the floor, which leaves a large area for mural decoration, as we shall see.

Gregory IX's successor, Innocent IV, consecrated the basilica on 27 April 1253 and (on 10 July of the same year) authorized the raising of funds for its decoration.[15] At this point there were already narrative stained-glass windows in the upper basilica, but the friars had yet to establish an iconographical cycle for the walls of the two basilicas, a cycle which would celebrate Francis's life and the glory of his order. I will not describe the frescos of the lower church but will instead concentrate on those of the upper basilica, most of which were painted between 1265 and 1305. During the pontificate of Clement IV (1265–8) an artist known as the 'Master from beyond the mountains' painted the frescos of the north transept. Then the Florentine master Cimabue (Giotto's teacher) completed (between 1278 and 1280) the frescos of the transept and the choir, devoted to the Virgin, the Apostles, and the Apocalypse, in a cycle which celebrates the triumph of the church and which seems devoid of direct Franciscan themes. Yet various art historians, including Charles Mitchell, have shown the thematic coherence of the ensemble, which exalts the power of the church and the importance of Francis and his friars in the *diebus novissimis*, the final days before the Last Judgment: this is emphasized by the apocalyptic scenes in the south transept. While these paintings may seem to reflect certain joachite tendencies in the order, the message remains conventional (not to say conventual) and conservative, as Hans Belting has shown: the order is now an integral part of the church, with the Roman pope as its incontestable leader.[16]

The great cycle of frescos in the nave probably began under the pontificate of Nicholas IV (1288–92), the first Franciscan pope, who had been minister general of the order after Bonaventure (Jerome of Ascoli, 1274–9). The nave is divided into four bays. In each bay, two biblical scenes are placed on each side of the window: from the Old Testament on the north wall and from the Gospel on the south wall. Then, under each window, the space is divided into three frames, more or less square, reserved for scenes from Francis's life. Above the entry, around the rose window, are the Last Supper and the Ascension and, underneath, four scenes from Francis's life (one on each side of the door and one on each lateral wall of the entrance). The artist of the Franciscan cycle hence has twenty-eight large rectangles at his disposition (the one that contains the trial by fire measures 3.635 × 3.31 metres),[17] constituting a series which begins on the north wall near the altar and goes around the nave in a continuous band. These frescos, whose lower edges are two metres from the floor, are also the lowest, and hence most visible, of the upper basilica.

The Franciscan Cycle in the Nave of the Upper Basilica of Assisi

The artists to whom the Franciscans entrusted the cycle, whether or not Giotto was among them, painted an unprecedented narrative series which subsequently had a profound influence on sacred painting in Italy and all of Europe, especially (but not exclusively) in Franciscan art. No saint had hitherto been the object of such a monumental cycle.[18] We have seen that the Bardi dossal, in the 1240s, was already exceptional in proposing twenty scenes from the life and miracles of the saint, presenting a unique narrative cycle. The upper basilica of Assisi contains eight additional scenes, presented in a monumental setting: each of the twenty-eight paintings is larger than the whole Bardi altarpiece (which is 2.34 metres in height, 1.27 in width). Various factors permit us to date the cycle to the years 1291–1305, probably between 1295 and 1299.[19]

The twenty-eight scenes take their inspiration (with few exceptions) from the *Legenda maior*, official biography of the saint. Numerous commentators have noted that the artist closely respects Bonaventure's text. Underneath each scene is a caption in Latin, in upper-case letters, identifying the scene; most of these captions are citations from or paraphrases of the *Legenda maior*.[20] But as we saw for the Bardi dossal, a painter cannot simply 'translate' a text into images. Even with twenty-eight frescos, he must choose some episodes and exclude others. Each image must crystallize the essence of an episode that may occupy several pages in the text: here, too, the artist must make choices. The resulting image of Francis is to be seen by millions of pilgrims, most of whom have never read Bonaventure, and is reproduced, as we have said, by dozens of other medieval artists.

The series begins on the north of the nave, near the chorus. The first bay has three scenes from Francis's youth: in the first, a man to whom God had revealed Francis's future holiness spreads out his coat for the youth to walk across (Bonaventure relates this incident, *LM* 1. 1); the scene takes place on the communal square of Assisi (before the 'temple of Minerva', an ancient pagan temple transformed into city hall). In the second scene, the young Francis gives his coat to a poor man (following *LM* 1. 2). In the third, Christ appears to him to show him a house full of arms, which represent the future glory of his order, but Francis, still enamoured of this world, interprets this as the harbinger of a brilliant military career (*LM* 1. 3). The three panels of the second bay show his conversion. On the left (scene 4; *LM* 2. 1), he kneels before a crucifix in San Damiano, a badly damaged church that he vows to repair. None of these first four scenes has an equivalent in the Bardi dossal (whose first scene, Francis freed by his mother, is not shown in the basilica). The fifth scene at Assisi corresponds to the second in the Bardi dossal: Francis returns his clothing to his father and stands naked on the cathedral square; the bishop covers him with his mantle. The father holds the clothing on his left arm and looks at his son in anger and incomprehension; a man behind him holds his right arm, as if to prevent him from violence. People of Assisi, witnesses of this confrontation, are massed behind the father. The bishop wraps Francis in his blue mantle and turns his head towards the clerics behind him, who all have their eyes fixed on the saint. Francis looks at no one, but raises his eyes towards the sky, where the hand of God emerges from the clouds to bless him. Francis has broken the bonds that connected him to his father by the flesh; protected by his new adoptive father, the bishop (representative of the church), he has eyes only for his true father who is in heaven.[21] Next (scene 6) is Pope Innocent III's dream. The pope, asleep, sees the Lateran church leaning dangerously and an energetic Francis, dressed in the habit of his order, holding it up with his shoulder. This prepares the following scene (7, first in the third bay), where Francis, kneeling in the centre, receives from the pope a parchment containing the rule of his order. Behind the saint are eleven brothers: they were twelve at that time, like the Apostles, according to both Celano and Bonaventure. Behind the pope, six men (four of them wearing bishops' mitres) look on. After the saint's conversion, here is the official recognition of the fraternity by the church.

The following scenes, from the eighth to the nineteenth, present for the most part miracles that Francis performed during his life and visions which reveal his singular destiny. At night, Francis appears riding a fiery chariot across the sky, before a group of astounded friars (scene 8; following *LM* 4. 4). An angel shows a friar the celestial thrones, one of which is reserved for the saint (scene 9; *LM* 6. 6). At Francis's bidding, brother Sylvester orders the demons to leave the town of Arezzo: we see them flying away and looking back in fright, as Francis kneels and prays at the gates of the city (scene 10; *LM* 6. 9). It is in the midst of this series of miracles and visions that the artist places the trial of fire before the sultan (scene 11); we will come back to this scene. The following panels continue in the same vein, each showing a singular proof of his sanctity, often portraying astonished witnesses. The twelfth fresco shows Francis, arms wide open in prayer, in dialogue with Christ, who leans from the clouds to make a gesture of blessing; Francis floats above the ground, before four dumbfounded friars (cf. *LM* 10. 4). Next comes the Nativity scene at Greccio, where the baby Jesus miraculously appears in the saint's arms (scene 13; *LM* 10. 7). Francis's prayers cause a fountain to gush out of a rock to quench a peasant's thirst (scene 14; *LM* 7. 12). The saint preaches to the birds (scene 15). He predicts the death of a knight of Celano (scene 16; *LM* 11. 4). He preaches before Pope Honorius III and his court (17; 1C 73). He appears, floating in the air, to the chapter of Arles, during a sermon by St Anthony of Padua (18; *LM* 4. 10). And in the ultimate miracle *in vita*, he receives the stigmata (19; *LM* 13).

The following frescos relate his death (20), the visions which two people had at the moment of his death (21), the verification of the stigmata (22), the Poor Clares mourning his death (23), his canonization (24). In scene 25, Francis appears in a dream to Pope Gregory IX to display the stigmata, eliminating any doubts the pope had about them. The three final frescos (26–8) show posthumous miracles: Francis heals a wounded man (26); he resuscitates a dead woman just long enough for her to confess and avoid damnation (27); he liberates a prisoner unjustly accused of heresy (28).

This Francis is above all a worker of miracles and a beneficiary of visions. It has often been said that the artist follows faithfully, even slavishly, the *Legenda maior*. Indeed, each of the twenty-eight scenes is based on Bonaventure's text. But the artist has chosen to place the accent on the miracles and visions, presented as proofs of Francis's exceptional sanctity. The pilgrim who comes to contemplate these frescos learns little about the ascetic life of the saint or the community that he founded. This contrast, already stark between the frescos and Bonaventure's text, is all the more striking when we compare these twenty-eight images with the twenty of the Bardi dossal which, as we have seen, stress Francis's ascesis, his rejection of the world, the choice of his habit, his decision to go barefoot, his penance, etc. The Florentine friars of Santa Croce who observed the Bardi dossal could see their founder as a model to follow. In most of the scenes there, Francis is accompanied by friars who wear the same habit, who go barefoot like him; visually, only his halo distinguishes him from them. Moreover, in the margins of the scenes, as we have seen, are busts of Franciscans turned towards the saint with devotion, their hands joined in prayer. These friars serve, it seems, as intermediaries between those who contemplated the altarpiece and Francis, presented both as a founding patron saint and as a role model whose austere life each friar should follow. In the Assisi frescos Francis is also, in many cases, accompanied by friars, though they are usually wearing sandals, while Francis is always barefoot. During Pope Innocent III's approbation of the order (scene 7) they participate fully in the action, receiving the rule and the papal blessing with Francis, but elsewhere they are astonished witnesses to the miraculous manifestations of Francis's sanctity: they benefit from visions concerning the saint (scenes 8, 9); they watch, amazed, as he performs a miracle (scenes 12, 14, 16, 18; the exception here is scene 10, where brother Sylvester participates in the expulsion of the demons of Arezzo). The artist clearly stresses the distance between Francis and his companions; the gulf that separates the saint from the friars and pilgrims who look at the Assisi frescos can only be wider.

This inaccessible saint perhaps displeased some friars, though we have no direct testimony of this; it certainly has irked modern observers. Henry James, in his *Italian Hours* (1909) describes both the admiration for Francis that the frescos inspire in him and the 'impassable gulf' which they place between their subject and the spectator.[22] For Charles Mitchell, Bonaventure's Francis, faithfully and skilfully portrayed by the Assisi painter, captures the true character of the saint.[23] For others, it is a deformation of the *poverello*. Hans Belting sees it as a skilful 'integration' of the saint into the papal Church of Rome, but it is not a 'triumph of the historical Francis', but rather a 'triumph *over* this Francis'.[24] Nonetheless, just as Bonaventure's Francis pushes aside Thomas of Celano's, the Assisi basilica's Francis will replace the saint of the Bardi altarpiece. The iconography of these frescos quickly becomes the standard model for the representation of Francis's life.[25] Henry Thode affirms that the Assisi frescos mark the onset of the Renaissance: the artist (Giotto, for Thode) faithfully translates the wonderment and love that Francis and his brothers held for the natural world: birds, animals, landscape. Hence a new naturalism that was a real rupture with medieval art.[26]

Let us return to the trial by fire. The episode takes place outside, before two buildings, on the left, a structure with Doric columns, surmounted with small pillars on which one sees statues of winged figures; could the artist have in mind a pagan temple, with winged idols, which would correspond to widespread contemporary ideas about 'Saracen' religion?[27] Yet this is perhaps hasty: after all, similar statuettes decorate Pope Innocent III's palace in the sixth scene. The second building here is in the style know as 'cosmatesque', in multicoloured sculpted stone; it resembles the monument of Pope Hadrian V in the Church of San Francesco in Viterbo;[28] in front of this building is the sultan's elaborate throne, with (on its base), a sculpted golden frieze with lions. Behind the throne, a sumptuous red cloth edged in blue carries a kufesque inscription (i.e. it is meant to look like Arabic but it is not Arabic). The sultan and his entourage are clearly oriental: they are distinguished from the Europeans not by the colour of their skin but by their beards (long for the Saracen priests, short for the sultan and his men in arms, whereas in the other scenes laymen and most churchmen are beardless). The clerics are clearly distinguished (wearing white turbans and long coloured robes over white tunics). The clothing of the king and his entourage are quite exotic compared to that of the other laymen in the frescos, though they seem more Byzantine than Arab (the artist perhaps has used Byzantine models). For Henry Thode, this scene is a 'chef-d'œuvre of varied and lively expression... We see the anxious suspense of the magi, the disdain of the friar, Francis's humble and burning aspiration to produce proofs of his faith, and finally the astonished severity of the sultan towards his cowardly counselors!'[29]

Various critics have noticed a diversity of portraiture styles and of the use of colour in this fresco; some have concluded that several artists must have worked on it.[30] For Francesca Flores d'Arcais, Francis's and Illuminatus's faces are Giotto's work, whereas those of the soldiers, more archaic in style, were painted by other artists.[31] Underneath the image runs the caption: 'How Blessed Francis wished to enter into a great fire with the priests of the Sultan of Babylon, but none of them wanted to enter it with him, but they fled immediately from his sight.'[32]

In order to satisfy his taste for the miraculous and the dramatic, the artist (or artists) took liberties with Bonaventure's text. In the *Legenda maior*, we have seen, Bonaventure places Francis's mission to the sultan in a chapter on his burning love for God, which compels him to seek out martyrdom. He describes the saint crossing the enemy lines, his torture at the hands of rough Saracen soldiers, and then says that Francis preached to the sultan with attention; it is only after this preaching that Francis proposes the trial by fire. Among these different elements, the artist could have chosen to portray Francis being beaten by infidel soldiers (placing the accent on his sufferings and his courage) or shown him preaching to the sultan and his men (as the Bardi artist did). But the painter preferred the moment of dramatic confrontation when (according to Bonaventure) Francis proposed a trial by fire and this proposition caused the Saracen 'priests' to flee. Bonaventure has the sultan refuse the proposition; no fire is lit. Here, on the contrary, the fire burns at the centre of the composition and the sultan himself, it seems, urges Francis to enter with a sweep of his arm. Why this fundamental change, coming from an artist often said to slavishly follow the text of the *Legenda maior*? No doubt the artist came up against the limits of the 'translation' of a text into images: how indeed could he paint a man who proposed a trial by fire to another who refused? Simpler, better, to paint a fire burning in the middle of the scene. This changes everything, of course.[33]

The trial by fire, for Bonaventure, is only a proposal, but one that attenuates the impression of failure that Francis's mission to the sultan could give, as we have seen. By challenging the Saracen priests to an ordeal, Francis humiliates them, inspires the admiration of the sultan and his men, and demonstrates his courage and his burning love for God. By transforming the ordeal from a simple proposal into a historical event, the artist goes further. Through his fiery challenge, Francis has succeeded in driving away four Saracen priests; two of them look back in fear as they hurry away.

The other persons are witnesses to this victory. Brother Illuminatus, in the centre behind Francis, looks at the fleeing priests; the sultan and his men contemplate the whole scene: Francis, the fire, and the humiliated priests. The trial by fire has become one element in the series of miracles accomplished by Francis during his life. Indeed, tension remains in the scene: the saint stands before the fire and turns back to look at the sultan; he has not yet placed his foot in the fire. What will be the result of this ordeal? Other artists (as we will see), will place the saint in the midst of the flames, to show Francis victorious in the ordeal.

This image is very different from the preaching scene in the Bardi altarpiece. The Bardi artist had simply shown the saint preaching to an attentive audience. By going to the Orient to preach to the sultan and his subjects, Francis walked simply and solidly in the footsteps of the Apostles. In this image, as in others in the dossal, Francis is the model *par excellence* for the Florentine Franciscans who contemplate the altarpiece and who use it in their liturgy. In Assisi, on the contrary, Francis is a great saint who performs miracles his whole life long and who appears to the friars and pilgrims as the founding saint of a powerful order favoured by God. The trial by fire is one proof among many.

The Assisi fresco is the first of our documents to present Francis's mission as a glorious victory in a confrontation between Francis and Saracen clerics. The *Chronicle* attributed to Ernoul had, it is true, depicted the Saracen clerics quite negatively, affirming that they wished to put the Christian missionaries to death for having dared to wish to preach the Gospel; but if the Christians escape this fate, it is less through their own merits than thanks to the sagacity and justice of the sultan. Jacques de Vitry and Henry of Avranches affirm that Francis's preaching impressed the sultan and his men but had to admit that the saint did not succeed in converting them. In Assisi, the artist transformed this failure into a singular victory, worthy of figuring amongst the saint's miracles *in vita*.

8

Father of the Spirituals

Angelo Clareno (1326)

After Francis, in so far as he could by divine words and examples, established, fully instructed, solidified and confirmed the brothers toward revering and purely and faithfully serving the life of the promised perfection, Francis, moved by the active fervor of that seraphic love by which he, set aflame, had been borne to Christ, choosing to offer himself as a living sacrifice to God by the fire of martyrdom, tried three times to make a journey to the lands of the infidels; but divine providence prohibited him twice in order to test the flame of his fervor more fully.

On the third attempt, after Francis had suffered many reproaches, fetters, floggings, and labors, he was led to the Sultan of Babylon by the providence of Christ. Standing in front of the Sultan, completely on fire with the Holy Spirit, he preached to him Christ Jesus and the faithfulness of his gospel with such power, life, and effectiveness, that the Sultan and all of those who were present were astounded. Because of the power of the words that Christ had spoken through Francis, the Sultan, converted to mildness, against the decree of his impious law, freely heard Francis's words, and on the spot invited Francis to stay in his land longer. Finally, the sultan ordered that Francis and his brothers should be able to visit the sepulchre of Christ in Jerusalem without paying any tribute.

While the shepherd Francis was away in Egypt, a greedy wolf attempted to plunder and disperse his flock, and the gate was opened to him by those ministers who ought to have opposed his scoffing and who more than others were supposed to guard against his snares. These ministers who presided over others and seemed to be more prudent as well as more knowledgeable, relied on their own complacency. Hiding the wolf's lukewarm infidelity under the guise of discretion, they preached, cleverly by words and works, a different mode of living than the one that had been handed over to them from heaven by the shepherd, justifying it with scriptural quotations and the examples of other religious. They did not understand that by relying on human prudence, which the apostle called death [Rom. 8: 6], they dug for themselves a lake in which to fall and manufactured an idolatrous calf, having drawn back from the acme of the perfection they had vowed.

For the ministers judged that it would be impossible, dangerous, and foolish to imitate and simply and obediently follow Christ who had spoken to them in Francis and had opened to them the ways of life. The sons of Israel after the exodus from Egypt and the crossing of the Red Sea had become incredulous and complacent about their own self-sufficiency, dismissing as nothing all that they had experienced, seen, and heard, when God was speaking to them through Moses. Similarly, these ministers, who had exited from the world, renounced their own wills, and assumed the cross of the evangelical life, thought that it was less useful for themselves and others humbly and obediently to follow Christ who was preaching and working in the man sent from heaven, Francis. Therefore, the ministers thought it expedient, meritorious and just to draw after themselves the friars who were walking simply and faithfully.

The ministers' presumptuous audacity grew so much that, while Francis was on a pilgrimage to the lands beyond the seas to visit the holy places, so that he might preach the faith of Christ to the infidels and merit a martyr's crown, as I have said, in many provinces they treated harshly and cruelly those friars who resisted their efforts and assertions and who continued to follow wholeheartedly the footsteps and teachings of their father. The ministers not only imposed unjust penances but also expelled the friars from their fellowship and communion as if they were heretics.

For this reason, the ministers refused to receive many friars, especially those who were fervent in spirit, deeming them disobedient. A number of other friars, taking note of the furor, wandered hither and thither like sheep who have become separated from the flock. Lamenting the absence of their holy shepherd and director, they pled tearfully to the Lord with unbroken prayers for his return.

God on high, hearing their entreaties and vows and being sympathetic to their afflictions, appeared to Saint Francis—after the sermon that he had preached to the Sultan and his court—saying: 'Francis, return, because the flock of poor brothers whom you have brought together in my name is taking the wrong road and needs your guidance to unite, strengthen and enlarge it. Already your brothers have begun to leave the road to perfection that you handed down to them, and they are losing the desire for love, humility and poverty as well as the kind of straightforward behavior and innocence in which you rooted and planted them.'

After this vision and after a visit to the sepulchre of the Lord in Jerusalem, Francis returned immediately to the Christian lands. Finding his flock, that he had left united, scattered as the word of the Lord had described, he called his brothers together by means of much laborious searching and tears.[1]

For Angelo Clareno, Francis's voyage to the East permitted the devil to infiltrate the Franciscan order. The 'greedy wolf' took advantage of the saint's absence to sow dissention in the order and to encourage the weaker brothers to pass off their feebleness as wisdom and moderation. This created a fault line in the order between, on one side, the worldly brothers who were more interested in following their whims and desires than the life and rule that Francis gave them and, on the other, the small band of brothers who remained faithful to their founder's teachings, living in absolute poverty and humility. It is the beginning of a division into two opposing camps, those who will later be known as 'conventuals' and those called 'spirituals' or *fraticelli*.

This is at least how Angelo Clareno sees it when, about 1326, he writes, in his refuge at the Benedictine monastery of Subiaco, his *Chronica seu Historia septem Tribulationum Ordinis Minorum (Chronicle or History of the Seven Tribulations of the Order of Brothers Minor)*. The elderly friar (he was probably more than 70 years old), embittered by decades of conflict with the Franciscan hierarchy, wrote his chronicle to encourage his brothers to remain faithful to what was for him Francis's true spirit of poverty, as found in the *Regula non bullata* and the *Testament*, a spirit betrayed by the heads of the Franciscan order. The order had obtained from Pope John XXII the condemnation of the spirituals: the Inquisition had several of them burnt at the stake. Others had been imprisoned—including Angelo himself in 1317. Freed later the same year, he made his way to Subiaco, where the abbot protected him. Throughout his *Chronicle*, Angelo tries to show that the divisions in the order—and the persecution of the 'good' friars by the 'bad' ones—dates from the beginning of the order. He wants to recruit Francis and his earliest companions to the cause of the *fraticelli*; the spirituals are the real heirs of their founding saint, while the hierarchy of the order follows in the footsteps of those false Franciscans who, inspired by the devil, opposed Francis's will while he was alive, taking advantage of his absence in the East.

To understand this portrait of Francis, let us briefly sketch Angelo's life, devoted to the search for exemplary poverty. I will not try to relate all the complicated history of the 'spirituals' and the *fraticelli*, but simply explain the essentials of Angelo's and his companions' project and the hostility of the Franciscan hierarchy and Pope John XXII. I rely principally on the work of Gian Luca Potestà and David Burr.[2]

We know little about Angelo's youth. For some historians, he was born around 1255; for others, perhaps ten years before.[3] At any rate, in the 1270s the young friar was implicated in a conflict in the order. Before the Council of Lyon (1274) rumours circulated affirming that the council would oblige the Franciscans to accept full legal property of their convents. Some friars, particularly in the March of Ancona, declared that they would not respect this decision; others insisted on the obedience owed to pope and council. In fact, the council made no such ruling; but the lines of conflict within the order had been drawn, and several friars, including Angelo, were apparently imprisoned around 1279. They were not freed until 1290, at the accession of a new minister general, Raymond Geoffroi, who (according to Angelo), having learnt that these friars were imprisoned for excessive zeal for the Franciscan rule, declared: 'if only the entire Order were guilty of such a crime!'[4] He freed them but nevertheless sent them to Armenia, where they stayed until 1294, when (after conflicts with other friars there) they returned to Italy.[5]

In autumn 1294, these brothers appeared before the new pope, Celestine V, to ask his permission to form a separate order that would allow them fully to follow the rule and testament of Francis. The pope gave his approval, creating the order of the *pauperes eremite domini Celestini*, 'the poor hermits of Lord Celestine', according to one of Angelo's letters.[6] But in December 1294, the pope resigned. His successor Boniface VIII promulgated, on 8 April 1295 the bull *Olim Celestinus*, in which he declared that all the concessions and privileges granted by his predecessor were null and void, except those confirmed by the new pope. The bull does not mention the 'poor hermits', but nothing indicates that the pope approved the order, or even that they attempted to have their privileges confirmed by him. On the contrary, it seems that a number of them, including Angelo, had already left for Greece, where they could lead their life of poverty without interference.[7] The Poor Hermits continued to exist, but with a precarious legal status—in particular, they were never recognized by the Franciscan hierarchy, for whom these brothers were friars minor who should obey them. In 1307, Angelo became head of the Poor Hermits.[8] In 1309, Pope Clement V who, it seems, wished to find a compromise to end the conflict within the order, convoked the heads of the order along with prominent spirituals at Grozeau, near Avignon. The spiritual Ubertino da Casale proposed the creation of a new order, along the lines of that approved by Celestine V in 1294. The head of the friars minor, hostile to this proposal, reminded the brothers of their vow of obedience. The problem was submitted to the Council of Vienne (1311–12). The result was the bull *Exivi de Paradiso*, which rejected the division of the order but which took account of a number of criticisms made by the spirituals.

In his letters from this period, Angelo seems optimistic that a solution can be found to permit the spirituals to follow Francis's dictates and at the same time to be obedient to the pope. He exhorts his brothers to take Francis as a model, to follow his example just as the saint himself followed Christ's example. One must be ready to be crucified with Christ and for Christ, Angelo affirms in his letters, repeatedly echoing Christ's words to the Apostles in the Gospel: 'If anyone would come after me, he must deny himself and take up his cross and follow me. For whoever wants to save his life will lose it, but whoever loses his life for me will find it' (Matt. 16: 24–5). 'If anyone comes to me and does not hate his father and mother, his wife and children, his brothers and sisters—yes, even his own life—he cannot be my disciple' (Luke 14: 26). These are the same citations that Francis himself employed in his *Regula non bullata* to exhort his brothers to follow him.[9] Francis, with his *Rule* and *Testament*, is the reflection of Christ with his Gospels. The Rule is nothing more or less than the Gospel, and Francis is the model for the friars, the 'renovator of Christ's life' (*renovator vite Christi*). Francis reached the summit of mystical ecstasy, *concrucifixio*—crucifixion along with Christ. The friars must be ready to follow their founder and to be crucified with Christ.[10] The persecution and disdain which the friars suffer daily are neither to be feared not to be shunned. On the contrary, friars should seek out the hatred of the world, strive for the humiliation which Jesus endured. Life is martyrdom.[11]

Yet in spite of this exaltation of martyrdom, Angelo, contrary to other spirituals, still sought a compromise solution which would permit the *fraticelli* to live a life of absolute poverty while remaining under papal authority. In the years 1312–13, just after the bull *Exivi de Paradiso* (which rejected the division of the order), a number of spirituals in central Italy took control of their convents in an open revolt against the Franciscan hierarchy. The local bishops had to intervene to return these convents to obedience. In his letters, Angelo distances himself from the rebels, underlining the importance of submission to the church hierarchy. In a letter dated 9 September 1313, he condemns the rebels as schismatics.[12]

Other prominent figures of the spiritual movement, such as Peter John Olivi and Ubertino da Casale, embraced a vision of Franciscan history inspired by the writings of Joachim of Fiore, according to which the Franciscans would bring on the Age of the Spirit, purifying the church and the world. For Angelo, in his commentary on Augustine's *De vera religione*, the church, just like the Franciscan order, will always be a *civitas permixta*, a mixed city, containing some men pure in spirit and others only concerned with this world.[13]

Everything seems to indicate that, until the pontificate of John XXII (1316–34), Angelo sought to work with the ecclesiastical authorities. In 1317, the new pope, at the instigation of the minister general of the Franciscans Michael Cesena, intervened against the spirituals; he imprisoned Angelo. In his cell in Avignon, Angelo wrote a *Epistola accusatoria* to the pope, to justify himself and especially to defend the Poor Hermits, affirming that they did nothing more than follow the example of St Francis and respect his rule.[14] He recalls that the hermits had received the approval of Pope Celestine V, who permitted them to follow Francis's rule even though they were no longer friars minor.[15] As a result perhaps of this letter, but especially through the intervention of cardinals favourable to him, Angelo was freed on 23 June 1317. In his letters from this period, Angelo presents a much more apocalyptic vision of history; he repeatedly affirms that the age of 'future tribulations' has begun.[16] Francis himself had predicted that a majority of his friars would repudiate him, Angelo affirms in a letter written in the summer of 1317. This is why the saint preferred to speak of the 'life of the minors' (*vita minorum*) rather than the 'order of the minors' (*ordo minorum*): he foresaw the difficult situation of Angelo and his brothers and allowed them to reject the name of *ordo minorum* in order better to follow the rule.[17] On 1 October 1317, Ubertino da Casale took the Benedictine habit and entered the abbey of Gembloux; at about the same time, Angelo became a Celestine monk. By leaving the friars minor to enter into the Benedictine order, the two leaders of the spirituals removed themselves from the power of their erstwhile Franciscan superiors. This did not stop them from writing polemics against them, or from defending their spiritual brothers.[18] On 30 December 1317, John XXII issued his bull *Sancta romana*, condemning those who claimed to follow the rule of Francis without respecting the authority of the minister general of the friars minor. Angelo continues, in his letters from this period, to express the hope of finding a solution to the conflict and to remain obedient to the church hierarchy, yet these expressions of optimism ring increasingly hollow.

At the end of 1318, Angelo left Avignon for Subiaco, the monastery in central Italy founded by St Benedict of Nursia. There he was welcomed by the Benedictine abbot and from there, from 1318 to 1334, he sent missives giving advice to his brothers and defending them from their accusers. From 1321 to 1323, Angelo wrote his *Expositio regulae*, a commentary of the Franciscan rule, inspired in part by Peter John Olivi's *Expositio super regulam*.[19] In this tract, Angelo tries to find the spirit of Francis and the early friars by sidestepping the texts officially sanctioned by the friars minor (the *Regula bullata*, the *Legenda major*) and by concentrating on the primitive texts: the first Franciscan rule (*Regula non bullata*) and the hagiographical texts predating Bonaventure. Angelo attributes to Francis three prophecies concerning the future tribulations of the order: first, there will be a heretical pope who would split the order in two (whom Angelo does not explicitly identify with John XXII); next, most of the friars will cease to respect the rule; finally, the few friars remaining faithful to Francis's life will be persecuted.[20]

Meanwhile, John XXII was increasingly at loggerheads with the Franciscan hierarchy. In theory, Franciscans could not possess anything, either individually or collectively; the pope was the legal owner of their lands and convents. On 8 December 1322, in *Ad conditorem canonum*, the pope terminated this arrangement and gave all the convents to the order, which was henceforth to possess them *de iure* and not simply *de facto*. On 12 November 1323, the pope declared (in his bull *Cum inter nonnullos*) that it was heretical to believe that Christ and the Apostles possessed nothing in this world. The pope was attacking not just the spirituals, but the whole Franciscan order.

It was in this context that Angelo composed, around 1326, his *Chronicle* or *History of the Seven Tribulations of the Order of Brothers Minor*. It is the work of an aged friar, informal spiritual leader of the *fraticelli*, who sought to offer a vision of Franciscan history that could explain the persecution that the brothers faced and could encourage them to remain faithful to what was for him true Franciscan life, founded on poverty and on the absolute respect for Francis's Rule and *Testament*. By asserting that the conflict between spirituals and conventuals began during Francis's lifetime, he reassures his readers: we are neither the first nor the only friars to be persecuted by those who, at the devil's instigation, oppose the life of evangelical poverty. This perspective permits Angelo to recruit to his cause not only Francis himself, but also his first companions and the principal saints of the order, making the spirituals into the true sons of Francis.

It should hence come as no surprise that Angelo prefers to use the earliest Franciscan texts rather than to accept Bonaventure's *Legenda maior*, the official Franciscan version of the life of the founding saint. We see this at the outset of his *Chronicle*:

> For notable persons have written lives of the poor and humble man of God, Francis, founder of three orders. These brothers, noted both for their knowledge and their holiness, were John and Thomas of Celano, brother Bonaventure, a general minister after blessed Francis, and Brother Leo, a man of admirable simplicity and holiness and a companion of blessed Francis.[21]

Far from recognizing Bonaventure's text as the sole authorized version of Francis's life, Angelo mentions it alongside three others: Bonaventure, presented here simply as a minister general of the order, seems indeed to have less authority than brother Leo, who is both a man of admirable holiness and a companion (*socius*) of Francis—these facts imbue him with authority. For Francis's mission to the sultan, Angelo prefers Celano's version to Bonaventure's, as we will see.

Angelo offers a simplified, almost Manichean version of Franciscan history. In the passage cited at the beginning of this chapter, Angelo presents Francis as a new Moses who received his Rule and *Testament* through divine revelation, just as Moses received the Law. Francis, like Moses, was not obeyed by all of his followers. Francis and the other 'good' friars are, in Angelo's *Chronicle*, frequent beneficiaries of premonitory visions. Brother Bartolo had a vision in which he saw a meeting of demons in hell. Lucifer was complaining of the perfection of Francis's life, which seduced more and more followers. How can we oppose this Francis, asks a frustrated demon; it seems that he is not a man, but Jesus Christ himself! But the demons are clever: we just have to send some of our adepts to infiltrate the order and take the Franciscan habit, they decide.[22] This vision proves that the devil himself is the cause of division amongst the friars.

The demon compares Francis and Jesus: this idea, as we have seen, is well established in Franciscan hagiography: the saint is an *alter Christus*. Angelo insists on the links between Christ and the *poverello*: Jesus speaks to the saint, shows him how to lead a life of poverty and humility, explains to him (*pace* John XXII) that he and his Apostles lived 'without money, shoes, purse or wallet'.[23] The Rule comes from Christ himself who appeared to the saint, crucified and in the form of a seraph, and revealed the contents of the Rule and *Testament*.[24] This is an important difference from Bonaventure's version. For Bonaventure, as we have seen, this encounter produced the stigmata (which Angelo does not mention here), the mark of the Lord which designates Francis as an inimitable saint. For Angelo the crucified Christ reveals the Rule, infused with evangelical perfection: this Rule must henceforth guide the friars. Angelo insists repeatedly on the fact that Christ himself revealed the Rule and *Testament* to Francis: these texts, and not the stigmata, are the real miracles that God produced through the *poverello*. For Angelo, Francis predicted time and again that some brothers would try, with vain erudition, to empty the Rule of its spirit; they would pay a high price in the fires of Gehenna, he threatened.[25] The tribulations of the order, provoked by these demonically inspired men, would last until the 'end of the days' (*fine dierum*).[26] The faithful friars, a minority, will be recognized by their strict obedience to the letter and the spirit of the Rule: Francis even asked his brothers to die clutching a copy of the Rule. Reworking a passage of Celano's *Vita secunda*, Angelo tells of a friar who had gone to Saracen lands and was martyred. At the moment of his death, he took out his copy of the Rule (which he always carried with him) and asked Christ to pardon any sin he may have inadvertently made against it.[27]

If Francis is a new Moses, the majority of the friars are like the Israelites who, during their leader's absence, made and worshipped the golden calf. The golden calf represents the worldly values of the friars. The order is thus divided between the 'sons of Francis', who only wish to follow in the footsteps of their founder, and the 'sons of Elias', who seek to weaken the rule.[28] For Elias, according to Angelo, is Lucifer's principal helpmate, sent to sow dissention in the order. When Francis goes off with two friars (including Leo) to write (like Moses, Angelo again says) the Rule revealed by God, Elias and his companions plot to see how they can weaken Franciscan discipline. When Leo brings the new rule to the friars, Elias steals it and hides it, helped by other corrupted friars (whom Angelo again compares to those who worshipped the golden calf). Francis, *alter Moyses*, must rewrite the Rule.[29] Bonaventure, as we saw, had Elias lose the Rule 'through negligence', and Francis then rewrote it; this story was meant to show the superiority of the *Regula bullata* of 1223 over the *Regula non bullata* of 1221.[30] Angelo on the contrary relates the story in order to privilege the Rule of 1221. He adapts to his needs the version he found in the *Compilatio assiensis*, a collection of anecdotes about Francis and his companions (including Leo), probably composed between 1245 and 1260, which survives in a manuscript copied *c.*1311. Angelo, following the *Compilatio*, affirms that Elias and his co-conspirators hoped to pervert the order and weaken the Rule: they came to see Francis and pleaded with him to temper the Rule's ascetic rigour. In response, Francis began to pray, and Christ himself appeared to the dumbstruck friars and declared: 'This is my servant Francis, whom I have chosen and in whom I have placed my spirit; and I have ordered him to do what he has done, and to write the Rule which he wrote; and the life and the Rule that he wrote is mine. It is from me and not from him. Whoever hears him, hears me; and he who spurns him spurns me.'[31] And Christ adds for good measure that the friars must follow the Rule to the letter, without glosses: those who do not wish to do so should leave the order.

Angelo tries to give his brothers a clear and limpid vision of a Franciscan order split, from the very beginning, between the good friars (the 'sons of Francis') and the bad ones ('sons of Elias'). In this Manichean vision of history, rare are the friars who receive a more nuanced treatment. I will not relate in detail Angelo's narration of the first century of the order's history, which David Burr has compared to a roller-coaster tour, alternating 'good' and 'bad' ministers general.[32] Let us simply look at how he presents Bonaventure and his rule.

Bonaventure's predecessor, John of Parma, is firmly in the camp of the 'sons of Francis' for Angelo: he frees good brothers from prison; he tries to reform the lax mores of the Franciscans, for which those of Francis's first companions who are still alive praise him. John sees that some friars, lax in their obedience to the Rule, devote themselves to study out of pure curiosity and love of learning.[33] He denounces their sophisms. But John arrives too late: he preaches against corruption, affirms that one must obey the Rule, but finally, having understood the futility of his mission, retires from the head of the order; he tells the friars to choose a man 'who will be in agreement with your feelings and ways'; they unanimously choose Bonaventure.[34] But before giving way to him, John lambasts the friars for their lack of respect for the Rule, which he details in reviewing the Rule chapter by chapter.[35]

Bonaventure poses a problem for Angelo: he does not dare criticize him too harshly, but presents him as manipulated by the bad friars. He is hence one of the rare ministers general who is neither clearly a 'son of Francis' nor a 'son of Elias'. Stung by John of Parma's accusations, the friars push their new minister to attack him, provoking the son against his father. Bonaventure puts John on trial; he is condemned as a heretic for his joachite ideas, but these ideas are in fact just a pretext for the friars who viciously attack him for daring to defend the Rule. Bonaventure is not the main culprit, but plays the role of manipulated coward: he told John that he supported him and then said the opposite to John's accusers.[36] To lend credence to his version of the conflict, Angelo relates the visions that two friars (both 'sons of Francis', of course) had at this time. The first saw Francis, in heaven, curing a leper covered with sores: the saint explained that the leper was the Franciscan order, plagued by dissentions.[37]

Another brother, James of Massa, lay three days between life and death. During this time, he had a vision of a beautiful, huge tree with golden roots, silver trunk and branches, and gilded silver leaves. Its fruits were men—friars minor. Each branch represented a province of the order and at the summit of the tree perched John of Parma. Francis arrived, accompanied by angels, bearing a luminous cup filled with 'the spirit of life'. He offered the cup to John, who drank it all and became luminous like the sun. He then passed the chalice to the other brothers: a few of them followed John's example: they drank the whole contents of the chalice and became brilliant as well. Others poured out the spirit: they 'became dark, deformed and hideous, horrible to behold, like demons'.[38] Others drank part of the cup and emptied out the rest: they became more or less luminous or shadowy, depending on how much they had drunk.

From high atop his tree, John sees a storm coming; he takes refuge in a hollow in the trunk. Bonaventure, who had drunk a part of his cup and emptied out the rest, climbs atop the tree to take John's place. He has long iron fingernails, sharpened like razor blades, and begins to attack John, who calls out for help to Christ, who sends Francis to cut Bonaventure's nails. Then the tree is struck and felled by a whirlwind: the friars fall from the tree—and the first to fall are those who spilt their cups. These evil friars are 'transported by ministers of darkness to places of darkness and misery', while those who drank the cup of spirit are led to 'a region of life, light and splendor'. Once the storm has passed, a new tree begins to grow from the golden root: its branches, leaves, and fruit are all pure gold: 'Concerning its spread, depth, height, odor, beauty and virtue, it is better to remain silent than to speak.'[39]

This vision highlights the apocalyptic fears and hopes that conflicts within the order inspired among some brothers—presumably including Angelo himself. The storm will hit the order and will destroy it. But from its ruins will spring a new order, a golden one, which will be in harmony with evangelical poverty. In it there will be only good friars, those who have drunk the cup of spirit, following the examples of Francis and of

John of Parma. Those who refused the spirit offered by the founding saint, those dark and deformed false friars, will have no place in the golden tree: they will be relegated to a place of shadows. Angelo says nothing, though, about the destiny of those who drank a part of the cup and spilt the rest, including Bonaventure. Angelo's Manichean division between luminous and tenebrous friars does not seem to offer any place for intermediate beings. He does not apparently dare to place Bonaventure among the hell-bound sons of Elias, and he recognizes that some friars are neither *fraticelli* nor their persecutors. But clearly he does not know what to do with them.

After this interlude, Angelo relates that John of Parma was subsequently freed through the intervention of Cardinal Ottoboni Fieschi, the future Pope Hadrian V; the help that he received from the future pope is no doubt supposed to underline, for Angelo, John's orthodoxy and the injustice of his condemnation. For thirty years, John led a life of poverty and humility at Greccio; at his death, he performed miracles, a certain sign that he was a true 'son of Francis'.[40] As for Bonaventure, Angelo has little to say about him once John of Parma is sent off. As David Burr has noted, this probably indicates that there was not, in Bonaventure's time (contrary to what Angelo affirms), a well-defined group of spirituals at odds with their minister general; otherwise, Angelo would no doubt have related their conflicts.[41] Instead he passes directly from John's trial to Bonaventure's nomination as cardinal, against his will, 'because of his reputation for learning, eloquence and sanctity'.[42]

We will not follow Angelo's recital of the ups and downs of the order, the alternating periods of persecution under bad ministers and of peace under good ones. Let us simply note how, for Angelo, the true enemy is now within—not only within Christian society, but at the summit of the Franciscan order, even in the papacy. In consequence the infidel, Jew or Muslim, is less an object of diabolization; indeed, Angelo shows little interest in non-Christians. What need is there for an infidel persecutor, when one can be martyred at home in Europe, at the hands of evil Franciscan inquisitors?

The Saracen and the Jew, for Angelo, become scales by which to measure the perfidy of the Franciscans who persecute good friars: in these rhetorical comparisons, the infidel always plays the role of lesser evil. For example, during the conflicts of the 1270s which resulted in the imprisonment of numerous friars, another friar who criticized this punishment was himself thrown in prison, according to (says Angelo) a law 'similar to the law of Muhammad'. The Franciscans who imprisoned these friars showed themselves to be 'crueler than the Saracens'; they acted with 'cruelty and ferocity surpassing that of the Saracens and the Tartars'. Their actions are equivalent to the crime of placing 'the likeness of Antichrist in God's temple'.[43]

In the same vein, a Neapolitan inquisitor who violently attacked good friar Tommaso and his companions 'exceeded the Jews and pagans in malignant evil'. This inquisitor, not believing the friars' declarations of their innocence, tortured them to obtain confessions of heresy—confessions that they later retracted. The pagans martyred Christians who proclaimed their faith in Jesus Christ and refused to worship idols; this inquisitor tortures Christians to make them profess heretical doctrines! He is indeed worse than Jews and pagans, Angelo affirms: the Jews would not have killed Christ if they had recognized him, as the Apostle himself says (1 Cor. 2: 8). As for the pagan kings, they worshipped demons in the form of idols, thinking that they were true gods. They thought that their combat against Christians was just; for them Christians were arrogant adepts of the magical arts. This passage, imbued with a striking relativism, only highlights the iniquity of the inquisitor, who is a 'genuine preacher of Antichrist'.[44]

In Angelo's extended narrative, Francis's mission to the sultan is one of the causes of the first of seven tribulations suffered by the saint's true sons. But here Francis is conscious of the danger (mentioned neither by Thomas nor by Bonaventure) that his absence poses for the friars minor: he makes all the brothers promise to respect 'the life of the promised perfection' after his departure. His premonitions were justified: indeed it is the absence of the founding saint, as we have seen, that allows the devil to infiltrate the order.

As for the motivations that compel Francis to leave, Angelo insists on the force of the 'seraphic' love which burns in him. Like Bonaventure, he declaims the vocabulary of fire, using words like *succensus* (enflamed), *flamma* (flame), *ignis* (fire), *ardens* (burning). But there is no real fire: he does not take up the proposal for a trial by fire that we saw in Bonaventure; he is closer to Thomas of Celano's text. It is at any rate a burning love which pushes him to seek martyrdom *ad partem infidelium*.

Angelo says nothing about his voyage; he mentions neither the crusade, nor the presence of the saint in the Christian army, nor his crossing the enemy lines. He mentions only 'many reproaches, fetters, floggings, and labors' which preceded his audience with the 'Sultan of Babylon'. Angelo emphasizes the vivacity and effectiveness of Francis's preaching before the sultan and the positive effect it had on the sultan and his men. Indeed, it was Christ himself who spoke through Francis. Listening to him, the sultan is 'converted to mildness' and listens without protest to the attacks against his 'impious law'. He urges him to stay, but Angelo does not mention (contrary to Thomas and to Bonaventure) any gifts which the sultan offered the saint. Next Angelo introduces a new detail: the sultan authorizes Francis and his companions freely to go to the Holy Sepulchre, without paying any tribute. Other fourteenth-century authors will reiterate this affirmation, at a time when the Franciscan presence in the East is being established.[45]

We have seen how various authors (Jacques de Vitry, Thomas, Bonaventure) try to explain Francis's failure. His preaching, apparently brilliant and well-received, does not succeed in converting the sultan, and Francis returns to Italy without having accomplished much. Here the reason is clear, even if Angelo does not explicitly say it: the fault lies with the bad friars, the 'sons of Elias'. Francis is on excellent terms with the sultan, and the reader might think that he would convert him. But troubles within the order compel the saint to return to Italy and cut off any hopes of converting the 'sultan of Babylon'.

Indeed, to hope that Francis could convert the sultan is to forget the 'greedy wolf' (the devil) who 'while the shepherd Francis was away in Egypt, ... attempted to plunder and disperse his flock'. The devil himself sows dissention in the order, but the worst part of the story, for Angelo, is that 'the gate was opened to him by those ministers who ought to have opposed his scoffing and who more than others were supposed to guard against his snares', that is by the leaders of the order who, through laziness and arrogance, weakened Franciscan ascesis, permitting a softer life and the pursuit of vain erudition. The faithful friars who criticized this negligence were persecuted, expelled from their convents. They prayed to God that he send them back their pastor. God then appeared to Francis and told him: 'Francis, return, because the flock of poor brothers whom you have brought together in my name is taking the wrong road and needs your guidance to unite, strengthen and enlarge it.' Francis hurried home (without having time to convert the sultan, implies Angelo) and put things back in order.

Bonaventure had indeed already affirmed that Francis returned from the East because he had been 'advised by a divine revelation'.[46] But with

Bonaventure, we have the impression that the divine revelation simply concerns the futility of staying in Egypt: there is no point further trying to convert he who was convinced neither by preaching nor by the proposed trial by fire. Bonaventure does not hint that troubles within the order were the cause of this divine intervention; on the contrary Bonaventure (like Thomas before him) mentions no division within the order at this time. Giordano di Giano, in his *Chronicle* of 1262, affirms that a certain friar Peter, troubled by the changes in the rule made during Francis's absence, went to the East and found the founder of the order in Acre; Francis, troubled, came back quickly, accompanied by other friars—including Elias, then provincial minister of Outremer.[47] Angelo combines this anecdote with the allusion to divine revelation from Bonaventure. He amplifies this history by relating the words that Christ said to Francis. He of course does not say that Elias was in the Holy Land with Francis, preferring to suggest that he was among the evil friars who took advantage of the saint's absence to pervert the order.

Just in case his readers might think that it was only human differences of opinion and not diabolical design that caused this conflict, Angelo relates the premonitory vision of the council of demons, as revealed to the good friar Bartolo. The devil is indeed the author of the schism within the order. Over and against those who would wish to present a more nuanced, less Manichean vision of Franciscan history, Angelo simplifies and clarifies his subject: Christ intervenes directly on the side of Francis and his sons, the devil on that of Elias and his henchmen. Ordered by Christ himself to return to Italy, Francis can only obey (after a quick pilgrimage to the Holy Sepulchre).

The struggle between spirituals and conventuals is played out (at least in part) on the field of memory. Both sides claim to be the true heirs of Francis and condemn their rivals who do not respect the way that the saint had shown to his brothers. Angelo, better than anyone, constructed a coherent and polemical vision of the life of Francis and his first companions, the better to defend the life of the spirituals and their opposition to the Franciscan hierarchy. What interests Angelo in the encounter with al-Kâmil is less the fact that Francis went to meet the 'sultan of Babylon', however praiseworthy that may be, than the opportunity that his absence offered to the devil and his henchmen, the 'sons of Elias'.

9

The Sultan Converted

The *Deeds of Blessed Francis and his Companions* (1327–1337)

Our most holy father Francis, urged on by his zeal for the faith and by a fervent desire for martyrdom, crossed overseas with twelve of his most holy brothers, intending to direct their course straight to the Sultan.

After he arrived in the territory of the pagans where those who guarded the roads were so cruel that no Christian passing there could escape death, they did indeed avoid death by God's plan. However, they were captured, mistreated in many ways, very harshly bound, and led to the Sultan. In the Sultan's presence, instructed by the Holy Spirit, Saint Francis preached with such divine power about the holy Catholic faith that he offered himself for proof by fire. Observing this, the Sultan conceived a great devotion for him both because of the constancy of his faith, his contempt of the world—even though very poor, he did not want to accept anything from him—and also because of his fervent desire for martyrdom. From that moment the Sultan gladly listened to him, and asked that he come to him frequently. Moreover, the Sultan liberally allowed Saint Francis and his companions to preach freely anywhere they wished. He then gave them a particular sign: seeing it, no one would harm them.

With this generous permission, Saint Francis sent his chosen companions, two by two, here and there into various regions of the pagans, among which he with his companion chose one. When he arrived at an inn where it was necessary for him to stay in order to rest, he found there a woman with a beautiful face but a very filthy mind who solicited Saint Francis for a vile act. Saint Francis said: 'Come with me and I'll show you the most beautiful bed.' He led her to the huge fire which had then been lit in that house. In fervor of spirit he stripped and placed himself naked on that red-hot hearth as if on a bed. And calling her he said: 'Undress! Hurry! Enjoy this splendid, flowery, wonderful bed. You have to be here, if you wish to obey me.' That fire did no harm to Saint Francis. He lay smiling on that hot, burning hearth as if on flowers. The woman, dumbstruck on seeing something so amazing, was converted to our Lord Jesus Christ not only from the manure of sin but also from the darkness of unbelief, and she became a person of such admirable holiness and grace that, helped by the merits of the holy Father, she won many souls for the Lord in that region.

Saint Francis, however, seeing that he was unable to produce fruit there, by God's revelation decided to regather his companions and return to the lands of the faithful. Returning to the Sultan he explained his decision to return. The Sultan said: 'Brother Francis, I would willingly be converted to the faith of Christ, but I am afraid to do it now, because these men, if they heard of it, would immediately kill me and you with your companions. Since you can yet accomplish much and I have to put some great affairs in order for the salvation of my soul, I would not willingly bring about an unexpected death for you and me. But tell me how I may be saved. I am prepared to obey you in all things.' Saint Francis said to him: 'Lord, I am indeed leaving you now; but after I return to my country, at God's call I shall pass on to heaven. But after my death, by God's design I will send two of my brothers, from whom you will receive baptism and you will be saved, just as the Lord Jesus Christ has revealed to me. In the meantime, free yourself from all your present affairs so that, when the grace of God comes, it will find you prepared in faith and devotion.' The Sultan joyfully agreed and faithfully obeyed. Then Saint Francis bid him farewell and returned to the lands of the faithful with that venerable assembly of holy companions.

Some years later this Sultan fell ill. Awaiting the promise of the saint, who had already passed to blessed life, he posted lookouts at port entrances so that, when two brothers in the habit of Saint Francis appeared, the guards would quickly bring them to him. At that very time, blessed Francis appeared to two of his brothers and ordered them to go without delay to the Sultan and carefully see to this command. Crossing the sea, they were led to the Sultan by those lookouts. When he saw them, the Sultan was filled with great joy, and said: 'Now I truly know that the Lord sent his servants. Just as Saint Francis promised, by the Lord's revelation, he has kindly sent these brothers to me for my salvation.' From these brothers the Sultan received instruction in the faith and holy baptism. Reborn in this illness, his soul was saved through the merits of the holy father and he passed to eternal happiness in the Lord.[1]

A few years after Angelo Clareno penned his *Chronicle,* Ugolino da Montegiorgio, a Franciscan friar who appears to be close to the spirituals of the Marche d'Ancona, compiled the *Actus Beati Francisci et sociorum eius* (*Deeds of Blessed Francis and his Companions*), a text destined to a wide diffusion and great popularity, especially when it was adapted into Italian as the *Fioretti* (*Little Flowers*) at the end of the fourteenth century. It then became (and has remained until today) one of the most widely read and appreciated texts concerning the *poverello*.

The description of the mission to 'the territory of the pagans' is more developed and dramatized here than in any of the earlier texts. Francis travels with twelve companions; their fervour for martyrdom pushes them to seek out the sultan (the chapter title indicates that he is the sultan of Babylon). They go to 'certain lands of pagans' (*quasdam paganorum partes*); indeed, Latin authors of the Middle Ages often qualify Muslims as 'pagans', which can only further highlight the conformity of the life of Francis and his brothers with that of Christ and his twelve Apostles. The *Actus* say nothing about the crusades, but attribute to the pagans an implacable hostility towards Christians: any Christian who went to these lands was put to death. We are far from the Egypt of al-Kâmil, among whose subjects were many Coptic and Melkite Christians; Ugolino da Montegiorgio instead depicts a stereotypical pagan kingdom, ideal theatre for the audacious mission of Francis and his companions. The friars escape death thanks to divine intervention. Ugolino describes the admiration that Francis inspires in the sultan, who subsequently grants the friars the right to preach anywhere in his kingdom. During these preaching tours, Francis produced a miracle: to calm the burning desires of a beautiful pagan woman, Francis lies naked on a fire (reproducing a second trial by fire): this causes the woman to repent of her sins and convert to Christianity. Next follows the narration of the sultan's conversion. Not wishing to let his hero leave the pagan lands without having converted the sultan, Ugolino relates that the sultan promised to obey Francis and Francis in turn promised to send him friars to baptize him *in extremis*—which the saint indeed does, miraculously, after his own death. No shadow troubles this new version of Francis's mission: the saint and his friars preach to pagans, produce conversions, and succeed even in converting the sultan. Gone is any doubt or hesitation as to the success of Francis's endeavour.

Little is known about the author of the *Actus*, Ugolino da Montegiorgio.[2] Probably born in Monte Santa Maria (now Montegiorgio, in the Marche) in the mid-thirteenth century, he entered the friars minor before 1274. A few archival documents mention the friar, as a witness, between 1319 and 1342. The text of the *Actus* mentions Ugolino three times: twice in the first person (as author of the text) and once in the third person, as oral transmitter of a story transcribed by an anonymous 'I'.[3] This suggests that

Ugolino was the principal compiler of the sixty-eight chapters of the text, which was composed sometime between 1327 and 1337.[4]

The *Actus*, like Angelo's *Chronicle*, presents Francis as the model and inspiration for a community of friars which he accompanies in a life of exemplary piety and renunciation; these friars, like their leader, produce miracles that testify to their holiness. Much of the text is centred on Francis and his first companions, some of whom (Bernard Quintavalle, Leo, Massa) are accorded several chapters relating their exemplary life and their miracles. Other chapters of the text are devoted to more recent friars, in particular from the Marche of Ancona, which Ugolino praises: 'The province of the Marches of Ancona was like a beautiful starry sky, with outstanding stars, that is, with holy Lesser Brothers who high and low before God and neighbor shone with radiant virtues, and whose memory is truly held in divine blessing.'[5] The author frequently intervenes in the first person to speak of the holy men that he had seen and known in the province of the Marche.[6]

Ugolino of course knew Bonaventure's *Legenda maior*, which he cites. He also knew Angelo Clareno's *Chronicle*, from which he reproduces the James of Massa's vision of the Franciscan tree destroyed by a storm.[7] But while he uses Angelo, he does not cite him; this is no surprise as Angelo was *persona non grata* for the order's hierarchy. Ugolino shares with Angelo a quasi-apocalyptic image of a Franciscan order in decline, an image to which the storm-struck tree gives dramatic expression. But this vision, as we have seen, promises a new order, a new golden tree which will grow from the roots of the fallen tree. Ugolino takes from Angelo another, less optimistic vision, attributed to Francis himself. The saint saw the same statue which King Nebuchadnezzar had seen in the Bible: 'The head of the statue was made of pure gold, its chest and arms of silver, its belly and thighs of bronze, its legs of iron, its feet partly of iron and partly of baked clay' (Deut. 2: 32−3). Here the vision concerns the history of the Franciscan order, as the statue itself explains to Francis. The golden head represents the early order, brilliant in evangelical poverty and charity. The friars of the second generation are inferior to those of the first as silver is inferior to gold; they will nevertheless shine in their virtues and wisdom, and some of them will be prominent in the church. At the third generation, the belly of bronze, the friars will devote themselves to pleasures of the belly, abandoning ascesis; they will remain eloquent, however, and will show to others the good path that they themselves refuse to take. At the fourth generation, the legs of iron, the friars will be hard as iron, lacking the qualities of the friars of the first three generations, but like strong legs they will succeed in holding up the order. In the fifth period, the feet will crumble, the clay friars will oppose the iron friars, and the order will collapse. Contrary to the vision of James of Massa, no note of optimism lightens this prediction of the order's inexorable decline, other than the promise of individual salvation for those few brothers 'who will have persevered to the end'.[8]

A third vision is attributed to Brother Leo, one of Francis's companions. He saw a number of friars minor crossing a swollen river. Some, who carried large or small burdens, were swept away by the current and perished. Others, who crossed empty-handed, arrived safely on the far shore. Leo relates his vision to Francis, who explains it to him: the friars bearing burdens are those who have not embraced evangelical poverty; they are swept away by the river, which represents this world. The other friars, who wish to possess nothing in this world, cross it without difficulty and obtain celestial rewards.[9]

These visions set the tone and permit us to understand the subtext of the collected legends: Ugolino expresses nostalgia for the golden age of the early brotherhood, when Francis and his companions led an exemplary life and benefited from frequent visions and miracles. The *Actus* are nevertheless not a work of propaganda for the spirituals, like Angelo's *Chronicle*. Rather than directly attacking the bad friars, Ugolino prefers to describe the merits and miracles of the stars of the Franciscan constellation, to paint a forever-lost golden age, a mythic era of origins. It is true that he does not hesitate to lambast Elias, *bête noire* of the spirituals.[10] But Elias is a more nuanced, more ambiguous figure in the *Actus* than in Angelo's *Chronicle*: Francis has a vision in which Christ reveals to him that Elias will leave the order and will be excommunicated and damned; Francis subsequently avoids him until finally Elias confronts him and asks why he is avoiding him. Francis reveals his vision and Elias, in tears, asks the saint to beseech Christ to lighten his sentence; touched, Francis prays for him. Elias indeed leaves the order and is excommunicated, but thanks to Francis's posthumous intervention he is pardoned by the pope and saved.[11] Other than Elias, Ugolino chooses in general to blame the friars indirectly: he affirms, for instance, that Francis always refused to be called 'master', saying that Christ alone merited this title; this is of course an implicit criticism of the Franciscan university professors who prided themselves on this title.[12] Ugolino places another criticism of Franciscan professors in the conclusion to his story of simple friars who convert a group of brigands: 'The holy simplicity of those brothers bore fruit not by preaching about literary authorities or Aristotle, but about the pains of hell and the glory of paradise in brief words, as it says in the Holy Rule.'[13]

Francis is of course the hero of a number of stories in the *Actus*: he tames the wolf of Gubbio; God reveals to him the friars' secret thoughts; he fasts for forty days, eating only a single piece of bread; he converses frequently with God. But other friars also accomplish miracles and receive visions. In the first five chapters of the *Actus*, the protagonist is Bernard Quintavalle, presented as the equal of Francis in his ascesis and in his gift for contemplation; he speaks with God and is visited by an angel. Bernard was 'so holy that Saint Francis held him in great reverence'.[14] Sometimes the community of friars warns Francis against excessive rigour: the friars protest against his refusal to see Claire and against the way he humiliates a brother to whom he wishes to teach humility. On each occasion, Francis humbly listens to his brothers and follows their advice.[15] To know whether he should lead a life of contemplation or of preaching, he asks Claire and brother Sylvester and follows their advice.[16]

Francis is the protagonist of less than half the stories in the *Actus*. We read of the visions and miracles of many Franciscan saints: Claire who miraculously imprints crosses on loaves of bread by making the sign of the cross over them; Anthony of Padua who preaches to fish; other friars who are visited by Christ, the Virgin Mary, and a host of saints. Many of the visions concern the salvation of the friars' souls: a dead friar returns to tell his brothers that, thanks to his Franciscan habit and to the holiness of the order's life, he now tastes the pleasures of heaven.[17] Indeed, some of these are stories that Ugolino has found in earlier Franciscan texts. Francis, whose life mirrors that of Christ,[18] is the brightest star in the Franciscan constellation, but he is not the only one. Ugolino's Francis is hence quite different from the saint of Bonaventure or of the Assisi frescos. In the *Actus*, Francis does not overshadow his brothers, who share his exemplary life and reap the same benefits—visions and miracles. The other friars play a quite secondary role in Bonaventure's *Legenda maior*; in the Assisi frescos, as we have seen, they figure primarily as astonished witnesses to the great saint's miracles. Ugolino describes a community of brothers and celebrates their common life, as Thomas of Celano had done a century earlier. But Ugolino's Francis is a far cry from Thomas's; in the *Vita prima*, one manages to glimpse, behind the hagiographical façade, Francis's hesitations, uncertainty, and contradictions, as he tries simultaneously to lead a contemplative life, to live an exemplary ascesis, to preach in Umbrian towns, and to organize a stable and durable order. None of this is found in the *Actus*: on the contrary, Ugolino's Francis is guided by God, who constantly reveals his will. While this Francis can humbly accept correction coming from his brothers, one cannot imagine that non-Franciscans could possibly find fault with him. We have seen how Cardinal Ugolino (the future Pope Gregory IX) dissuaded Francis from going off to preach in France, since his order needed him in Italy.[19] The *Actus* indeed relate that Francis decided to go off to France with brother Massa. But he then has a vision in which Peter and Paul announce to him that Christ granted the friars minor the 'treasure of most holy poverty'. Francis and his companion were so moved by this vision that they 'forgot about going to France'.[20] Nor is this Francis that of Angelo Clareno, who always had to be on the lookout against the intrigues of the bad friars led by Elias. Here, on the contrary, Elias seems to be a solitary figure: he is the only one of Francis's companions who is criticized. The order's divisions, revealed to Francis in the vision of Nebuchadnezzar's statue, are future problems; they do not tarnish the golden age of the primitive confraternity.

This transformation of the poor man of Assisi into a flawless hero is clear in Ugolino's version of the mission to the sultan. There is not the slightest hint of failure or ambivalence. The saint did not obtain the martyrs' palm that he and his brothers longed for—because flames could not hurt him. Ugolino credits Francis and his companions with the conversion of 'pagans': thanks to the permission to preach obtained from the sultan, and thanks also to the miracle Francis performs before the astonished pagan woman. Ugolino claims that Francis did indeed convert the sultan, though secretly; his baptism was accomplished through a posthumous miracle of the saint.

Ugolino opens the chapter by saying that Francis brought with him 'twelve of his most holy brothers'—the apostolic number implicitly equates the Franciscan golden age with the age of the Apostles. Ugolino knows Bonaventure's text, but makes selective use of it. He does not place the encounter in Syria, as Thomas and Bonaventure had done, but simply 'in the territory of the pagans' (*paganorum partes*). This land is a far cry from Ayyubid Egypt; it comes rather from the apocryphal gospels and the passions of the early martyrs. The pagans are violently hostile to Christians, which can only heighten the reader's admiration for the courage of the saint and his brothers. Ugolino briefly relates Bonaventure's version of the beatings which Francis received and of his preaching to the sultan. He then evokes the trial by fire in a manner that is anything but clear. For Bonaventure, as we have seen, Francis proposed the trial by fire when he saw that his preaching, though it had been well-received, had not managed to convert the sultan and his men; the sultan refused to light a fire. Ugolino, for his part, claims that Francis 'preached with such divine power about the holy Catholic faith that he offered himself for proof by fire' (*tam divine de sancta fide catholica predicavit, quod per ignem hanc se obtulit probare*). For Bonaventure the proposal came after Francis's preaching failed to have the desired effect; here it seems to be the logical conclusion of his preaching. Ugolino says nothing of the sultan's reaction to this proposition; did he accept it? Did Francis confront the flames? The reader does not know. Ugolino simply affirms that the sultan was so admiring that he granted Francis and his brothers the right to preach throughout his lands.

The *Actus* are the first text to claim that the sultan granted Francis the right to preach in his territory. Other fourteenth-century texts will make the same claim, in part to affirm the legitimacy of the friars' role in the Holy Land, in particular their custody of the holy places.[21] In the *Actus*, Francis, like Christ, sends his brothers two by two to preach the Gospel to the infidels; the reader does not learn what the fruits of this preaching are, except for the beautiful pagan woman that Francis converts by lying naked on a blazing hearth. This incident replaces, in a way, the trial by fire before the sultan: the reader does not know if that trial took place, but the fire in the inn allows Ugolino to claim that Francis indeed confronted the flames as he wished. The woman burns with carnal desire, prefiguration of the flames of hell, but Francis, aflame with divine love, cannot be harmed by a mere wood fire. After she converts, the woman becomes a model of saintliness and succeeds in converting many other pagans. But Ugolino mentions no other conversions of pagans; on the contrary, he says that Francis saw (through divine revelation) that 'that he was unable to produce fruit there'—this is the sole failure acknowledged in this chapter.

The principal novelty here, of course, is the sultan's conversion. Ugolino could not imagine letting Francis leave the 'pagan' lands without having saved the soul he came for. In his *Sermon on St Francis*, Bonaventure claimed that the sultan told Francis, 'I could not dare do that [convert], for fear my people would stone me. But I believe that your faith is good and true.' Ugolino goes further; the fear of being killed (and of causing the death of Francis and his companions) prevents the sultan from converting immediately, but will not prevent him from becoming Christian in due course.

The sultan is humble and subservient towards Francis: 'tell me how I may be saved. I am prepared to obey you in all things', he says to the saint. Here again, Francis shows no hesitation: a revelation from Jesus Christ shows him what is to be done. He tells the sultan to unburden himself from the troubles of this world and to prepare himself for death; he, Francis, will send friars to baptize him when the time comes. The sultan 'joyfully agreed and faithfully obeyed'. Francis returns to Italy. A few years later, after Francis's death, the dying sultan remembers the saint's promise and posts watchmen in the ports to intercept the friars whom Francis promised to send. Francis miraculously appears to two of his brothers and sends them to find the sultan. They arrive, offer a quick catechism to the sultan, and baptize him; he can then die and obtain 'eternal happiness in the Lord'.

Ugolino transforms an ambiguous story into a total victory. For Bonaventure, Francis succeeded neither in obtaining martyrdom, nor in affronting the flames, nor in converting anyone. In the *Actus*, he lies in a blazing fire that does not burn him; how could he suffer martyrdom? He converts the pagan woman, who becomes his faithful disciple and wins over the souls of numerous pagans. And above all, he succeeds in converting the sultan himself.

PART II

Fourteenth to Twenty-First Centuries

Introduction to Part II

In the first part of this book, I have examined in detail nine representations of Francis's mission to al-Kâmil. These texts and paintings are sources for many other authors and artists who, from the fourteenth century to the twenty-first, portray the encounter between the two men. There is no point in trying exhaustively to catalogue these representations or to give detailed analyses of texts and images which often simply reproduce their models.

In this second part we will see how some of these authors and artists manipulate Francis's voyage to Egypt for diverse purposes. Chapter 10 traces the iconography of the encounter, from Giotto in the early fourteenth century to the first printed editions of Bonaventure's *Legenda major* in the sixteenth; the trial by fire, in the tradition of the Assisi fresco, dominates this iconography. Chapter 11 shows how different authors and artists, beginning in the fifteenth century, place the accent on the violence and power of the sultan and his henchmen; they emphasize the struggle against the infidel, Moor or Turk, but also against the Protestant 'heretic'. Chapter 12 examines portraits of Francis sketched in the eighteenth and nineteenth centuries: Voltaire, followed by others, presents the *poverello* as a wild-eyed fanatic confronting a wise and tolerant sultan; other authors and artists defended a traditional Catholic vision of the encounter. Chapter 13 shows how various authors used the story of Francis's voyage to the East to explain and justify the Franciscan presence in the Holy Land. In Chapter 14, we will see how various authors of the twentieth and twenty-first centuries transformed Francis into an 'Apostle of Peace', a stalwart opponent of the crusade who went to Damietta in hopes of initiating ecumenical dialogue.

The Trial by Fire in Painting and Sculpture

Bonaventure's *Legenda major* remained the principal source for medieval authors who wrote about Francis's meeting with al-Kâmil, even though the *Chronicle of the Twenty-Four Generals* (1374), the principal history of the order, mentions nothing of the proposed trial by fire, preferring to cite Jacques de Vitry *in extenso*.[1] The Assisi frescos founded a tradition which dominated the pictorial representation of Francis's life until the sixteenth century (and persisted until the seventeenth). Illuminators of the manuscripts of the *Legenda maior* had the possibility to devote multiple illuminations to Francis's trip East, while sculptors and painters in general could only depict one scene: they almost always chose the trial by fire.

Giotto and the Capella Bardi of Florence

During the first quarter of the fourteenth century, Giotto painted a series of seven frescos of Francis's life and miracles in the Cappella Bardi of Santa Croce church in Florence. Among them is a representation of the trial by fire before the sultan, inspired by the Assisi fresco. This cycle was probably a commissioned work for the patrons of the chapel, the Bardi, a family of bankers who were among the richest and most influential in Europe. The sumptuous basilica of Assisi, as we have seen, was perceived by some Franciscans (and by some writers of the twentieth century) as a betrayal of the apostolic life of the *poverello* of Assisi. These same friars looked askance at the alliance forming, in Florence as in other Italian cities, between the friars minor and rich families of bankers and merchants.

Fig. 7. Giotto, trial by fire, Cappella Bardi, Florence.

The rise of the mendicant orders of the thirteenth century coincided with a major demographic and economic expansion which affected all Europe and in particular the cities of the north of Italy. Indeed, this movement began in the eleventh century and resulted in the twelfth (in many towns) in the taking of power by the commune, acting in the name of the people, though in fact they often represented the interests of a small social and economic elite. The power of the traditional landed aristocracy, in Italy as elsewhere in Europe, was based on the control of agricultural lands and the revenues that they produced. The symbol of the lord's power was his castle, from which he dominated the surrounding territory and where he could take refuge in case of attack. These aristocrats had tight-knit relations with Benedictine and Cistercian monasteries: they sent their younger sons there, they gave land and other goods to the monasteries, and when they died they were often buried alongside the monks.

The mendicant orders of the thirteenth century, in particular the Franciscans and the Dominicans, led a life quite different to that of the Benedictine and Cistercian monks: one of the essential elements of their apostolic life was urban preaching. Francis himself preached in cities, and the Franciscan convents (like those of the Dominicans) were for the most part urban, unlike traditional monasteries. For these two orders, this orientation was an integral part of their active life: to seek out those most in need and to serve them. Just as Christ wanted to convert the prostitute and the money-changer, the friars should seek to save the inhabitants of the cities. In order to do this, of course, both orders sought out the assistance of the urban authorities: the communal governments and the rich families of merchants and bankers.

For the Italian communes, the mendicant orders offered considerable advantages. First, a Franciscan or Dominican convent could serve as a counterweight to the cathedral, which was controlled by the bishop and his canons. Second, it could rival the rural monasteries which often escaped the commune's control and which remained allied to the rural aristocracy. The Italian bourgeoisie and the mendicant convents developed the same kind of relations that the rural aristocracy had woven with the traditional monasteries: they gave lands to the brothers for the construction of convents and churches; they made donations for construction and decoration of those buildings, they asked to be buried in the convents. In some cities, the mendicants adeptly took advantage of divisions between bourgeois clans: the Friars Minor allied themselves with some, the Preachers with their rivals, and each tried to erect a more sumptuous church than the other.

The Franciscans were present in Florence during Francis's life; the saint sent two friars, Bernard and Giles, in 1208 or 1209. Francis himself passed through Florence perhaps in 1211; he was at any rate there in 1217: there, as we have seen, he met Cardinal Ugolino. At the time the friars minor already had a small convent in the city, near the Porta San Gallo; a few years later, they transferred it to a more central site, on an island in the Arno, where they built a church dedicated to the Holy Cross (Santa Croce).[2] The primitive church and convent were no doubt quite modest: in the beginning, the church essentially served the needs of the friars. They slept in the convent, but their mission was in the city, with the Florentines. On 14 September 1228, the feast of the Holy Cross, Gregory IX promulgated a bull in support of the Florentine convent. At the friars' request, 'we take the Florentine church of Santa Croce under Saint Peter's protection and our own'. In other words, Gregory affirmed the independence of the friars, and their church, from the bishop of Florence. He also proposed a solution to a thorny judicial problem: the rule prohibited the friars minor from possessing anything: how could they then have convents and churches and accept donations from laymen? We have seen how in the same year 1228 Simone di Pucciarello gave lands to the pope for the construction of the basilica of Assisi; the pope reaffirms his authority over the unfinished basilica in October of the same year. For Gregory, this was a way both to affirm his influence over the young order and to solve the problem of property: the pope was the owner of the basilica; the Franciscans merely had use of it.[3] This same logic was behind the bull of 14 September: to the bishop, the pope asserts his power over the friars minor and their Florentine church; at the same time, the friars would not be disobeying the Rule which prohibited them from owning property. This became the doctrine of *usus pauper*, confirmed by Gregory in the bull *Quo elongati* on 4 October 1230.

The early convent of Santa Croce was soon too small for the Florentine brothers, all the more so since more and more bourgeois wished to be buried there—a practice which Pope Innocent IV formally authorized in 1245. The same pope accorded, in 1252, indulgences to anyone who would make donations for the construction of a new Franciscan church at Santa Croce. Florence is not unique: new Franciscan churches were springing up all over Italy, for similar reasons, notably in Padua and Venice.[4] Before the end of the thirteenth century, the Florentine friars began plans for a third church, even bigger and more sumptuous, to replace the second. This project provoked the ire of certain friars, notably Ubertino da Casale, one of the heads of the spirituals who, as we have seen, wished to form a separate order.[5] According to a contemporary legend, the construction project was the brainchild of Giovanni degli Agli, a friar from a bourgeois family: he wanted a church more luxurious than Santa Maria Novella, Florence's Dominican church. After his death, Giovanni appeared to a spiritual friar and announced that he was condemned to the eternal flames for having transgressed Francis's Rule.[6] But the spirituals could not stop the project: in 1295, the Florence commune granted 1,200 pounds for the new church and the construction began; in 1297, the Franciscan pontifical legate Mattheo d'Aquasparta obtained an indulgence promising the remission of sins for those laymen who contributed alms for the construction. The new church was consecrated in 1320.

With a nave 115 metres long and 38.23 metres wide (and a transept 73.73 metres wide), Santa Croce is much larger than Santa Maria Novella. As Rona Goffen has remarked, the wooden roof is in accord with the rules proclaimed at the chapter of Narbonne in 1260 concerning the construction of churches, which were supposed to be simple. But nothing else in this church respected the spirit of these rules—neither the dimensions, nor the elaborate programme of decoration: sculptures, frescos, and stained glass.

The frescos draw parallels between the life of Francis and his followers and that of the Apostles.[7]

The patron of the Bardi chapel is Ridolfo Bardi, who by 1303 was one of the directors of the Bardi company, who had been given the title of *mercatores camerae*, merchants of the pontifical curia, by Pope Boniface VIII. The pope remunerated these services by, among other things, offering a prebend to Ridolfo's son. Ridolfo became the head of the clan of bankers who lent to the pope and to the kings of England, France, and Sicily; he was still at its head when the bank went bankrupt because its royal debtors defaulted. King Robert of Naples and his wife, Queen Sancia, came to Florence in 1310; they no doubt visited Santa Croce (still under construction) and almost certainly met Ridolfo. Robert named him *camerlengo* and *consigliere segreto* in 1324. Robert and Sancia were fervent partisans of the Franciscans; the king's brother, Louis of Toulouse, had renounced his claims to the crown in favour of Robert so he could become Franciscan; he was canonized in 1317.[8] This context helps explain the Bardis' patronage of Santa Croce, despite the fact that one of Ridolfo's brothers had financed a chapel in the Dominican church of Santa Maria Novella. The Bardis financed four chapels in Santa Croce: one dedicated to St Lawrence, another to St Sylvester, a third to Louis of Toulouse, and the chapel we know as the Bardi chapel, dedicated to Francis.[9]

This Bardi chapel, adjoining the choir, was no doubt one of the first chapels built in the church. We do not know at what date Giotto painted the cycle of frescos on Francis, but it was probably between 1310 and 1317.[10] He also painted portraits of Franciscan saints: Claire of Assisi, Elizabeth of Hungary, and St Louis of Toulouse. In his series of seven frescos on Francis's life, Giotto of course cannot offer a narrative series comparable to that of Assisi, which had four times as many scenes, nor for that matter to that of the Bardi altarpiece (which had twenty). As Jane Long has remarked, Giotto here does not attempt a biographical narration of the saint's life, but instead presents him as a model of Franciscan life, a model showing an equilibrium between the contemplative life shown in the three episodes on the north wall (the rejection of his layman's clothes, his apparition to the chapter of Arles, and his death) and the active life represented on the south wall (the approbation of the rule by the pope, the trial by fire, and two miraculous *post-mortem* apparitions).[11] The stigmatization is painted above the entry to the chapel: it is proof of Francis's unique place among the saints and makes him an image of Christ.

The choice of scenes is surprising both for what it includes and what is excluded. Compared to the Bardi altarpiece also in Santa Croce, a number of scenes celebrating the poverty of Francis and his brothers are missing: Francis choosing his habit, removing his shoes upon hearing the Gospel admonition (Matt. 10: 9–10); his extreme penance, his caring for lepers, his preaching to the birds. While the artist of the dossal presented a Francis enamoured of Lady Poverty, Giotto places the accent on the approval Francis received from church authorities (the bishop in his rejection of his clothes, the pope in the approbation of the rule), and on the events which show his close association with Christ and which affirm his sanctity (the stigmatization); his death (angels carry his soul up towards the clouds); his apparitions, both while alive and *post mortem*. For a contemporary Florentine, Dante, who no doubt had seen the Bardi altarpiece, Francis is above all the spouse of Lady Poverty. The poet reprimands the saint's fourteenth-century disciples, 'greedy for new dishes'; he was thinking no doubt of Florence's friars minor, who were building their new sumptuous church.[12] In the chapel constructed at the order of one of the richest bankers of Europe, there is little place for Lady Poverty. She was no doubt not a favourite of Ridolfo Bardi, and one indeed notices a softening of Francis's radical poverty in the frescos, perhaps to satisfy the banker patron. But we can also maintain, with Jane Long, that it was the conventual Franciscans of Florence, not the Bardis, who decided on the iconographical orientation of the chapel. We can see a rejection of the pretensions of the spirituals in the rejection of extreme poverty and the avoidance of apocalyptic themes. Giotto depicts a conventual Francis who receives the approval of his bishop and of the pope, and who lives a life well-balanced between contemplation and mission to the world.[13]

The frescos of Assisi presented a miracle-working Francis, a saint worthy of the devotion from the throngs of pilgrims who came to venerate him in his basilica. In the Bardi chapel, a funerary chapel of a powerful bourgeois family, the accent is placed on the saint as image of Christ and intermediary between the faithful and Christ. The last two paintings show death scenes (Francis's own death, then that of brother Augustine who has a vision of the saint); this is in keeping with the chapel's function and places the accent on Francis's role as intermediary for the dead.

What role does the fresco of the trial by fire (Fig. 7) play in this ensemble? The image is similar to that of Assisi: Francis prepares to step into the fire, which his companion contemplates with unease; the sultan, seated on an ornate throne, points toward the fire; the Saracen priests show their fear. But the composition of the Florence fresco is different. In Assisi, Francis occupied the centre of the scene, between the sultan and his lay councillors on the right and the Saracen priests on the left: the fire separated the priests, fleeing the scene, from the others. In Florence, however, Giotto places the sultan in the centre of the composition. The fire separates the two Franciscans, on the right, from the Saracens. In both frescos, the Saracen priests are white men with long beards, turbans, and long robes. The Assisi fresco shows, behind the sultan's throne, three men in arms, white and bearded, in exotic costume (and one that had little in common with the dress of thirteenth-century Egyptians). Giotto places two beardless black men, also wearing turbans, next to the throne. In Assisi, the sultan's gaze takes in the whole scene: the fire, Francis, the fleeing Saracen priests. In Florence, the sultan's arm indeed indicates the fire (to the right), but he turns his head towards his priests on the left. For Jane Long, the sultan's placement in the centre of the scene, and the movement of his arm in Francis's direction, suggest a judgement given in favour of the latter and of the Christian religion.[14] The attitude of the Saracen priests is also somewhat different: in Assisi, they flee, looking back in fear towards Francis and the fire. In the Bardi chapel, the priests refuse to look as the saint confronts the fire: the priest on the left turns away and covers his ears with his robe as if he did not want to hear. The other priest seems to turn, almost involuntarily, towards the saint, but he hides his eyes with his robe so as not to see. The two beardless Saracens look at the priests; one of them points to Francis, as if to urge the priests to look at him. If the Saracen priests of Assisi were cowards in flight, these ones are stubborn: voluntarily deaf and blind to the miracle which is about to happen in their presence. This corresponds to the increasingly common portrayal, in the fourteenth century, of Muslims (and for that matter Jews) as blind and irrational in their refusal to recognize Christian truth; we find this idea in the writings of a contemporary Florentine Dominican, the missionary Riccoldo da Montecroce.[15] The essence of the message is the same in both frescos: Francis shows his courage by affronting the flames; it is a victory over the Saracen priests who dare not enter the fire, who flee (Assisi), or who refuse even to look (Florence). But the Bardi chapel is more pessimistic: only the two Franciscans are on the right side of the fire, and none of the Saracens looks at them.

Giotto Becomes a Model

This vision of the trial by fire dominates the iconography of the encounter for more than two centuries. We see this first in one of Giotto's best-known disciples, Taddeo Gaddi, born in Florence in 1300 (he died there in 1366). We do not know if the young Taddeo was already working at his master's side for the frescos of the Bardi chapel. His work is marked by Giotto's style, in particular at the beginning of his career. It was probably between 1330 and 1335 that Taddeo painted a series of twenty-eight panels, illustrating scenes from the lives of Christ and Francis, for a cabinet in the sacristy of Santa Croce in Florence. This cabinet was taken apart in the nineteenth century and its panels sold off individually; different theoretical reconstructions have been proposed, but none of them has received the unanimous approval of the experts.[16]

In the choice and execution of his programme, Taddeo follows his master: he reproduces six of the seven scenes from Giotto's frescos in the Bardi chapel; eleven of the thirteen scenes chosen by Taddeo have an equivalent in the Assisi cycle. What is new is the systematic presentation of Francis as an *alter Christus*: the thirteen scenes of Francis's life are placed in parallel with thirteen episodes from the life of Christ. While the exact disposition of the panels is not certain, the correspondence between the scenes seems clear. First, two panels only are in the form of half-circles: the Annunciation and the Ascension. The twenty-six other panels all have the same size and are shaped like a four-leafed clover: each of the thirteen scenes from Christ's life corresponds to one from Francis's, as we see in the table.

Taddeo's painting of the trial by fire (Fig. 8) is inspired by Giotto's fresco in the Cappella Bardi: the sultan and his throne in the centre dominate the scene; on the right, Francis, with a sweeping movement of his arm, prepares to confront the flames; behind him, Illuminatus prays. On the left are the Saracens, one of whom lifts the corner of his robe to cover his face so as not to see, as in Giotto. But Taddeo puts one of the Saracen priests in the centre, in front of the sultan's throne, as the sultan points towards Francis. The priest is turned towards the sultan and lifts his arm in a gesture of helplessness. We have the impression that the sultan has asked him to enter the fire and that the priest is refusing. The parallel scene from Christ's life is his baptism. This gives a special meaning to the event: Francis is reborn in the flames, just as Christ was in the waters of the Jordan. Taddeo places

Table 1

	Life of Christ	Life of Francis
1	Visitation	Francis rejects his worldly clothing
2	Adoration of the shepherds	Nativity scene at Greccio
3	Adoration of the Magi	Dream of Innocent III
4	Presentation in the temple	Approbation of the rule
5	Jesus teaches the rabbis in the temple	Francis preaches before Honorius III and his curia
6	Baptism	Trial by fire
7	Transfiguration	Francis appears to his friars in a chariot of fire
8	Last supper	Death of the knight of Celano
9	Crucifixion	Stigmatization
10	Resurrection	Francis resuscitates a dead child
11	Apparition of Christ to the three Marys	Apparition of Francis to the chapter of Arles
12	Thomas places his hand in the side of the resurrected Christ	Brother Girolamo places his hand in the side of Francis (at his death)
13	Pentecost	Francis appears to the Franciscan martyrs of Ceuta

the accent on Francis's evangelical mission: the final, thirteenth episode is unprecedented in the cycles we have hitherto examined: Francis appears, after his death, to Friars Minor who are being put to death outside a fortified city, martyred by a huge bearded executioner accompanied by two Saracen soldiers whose coat of arms (on the shields they carry) is a Moor's head (Fig. 9). It is tempting to identify them with the seven Franciscans martyred in Ceuta (in 1227): there indeed seem to be seven friars. In this case, this final episode would be a *post-mortem* apparition of the saint. But on the left we see two standing Franciscans, who seem to be spectators, one of whom has a halo: no doubt St Anthony of Padua, who took the Franciscan habit upon hearing of the Marrakech martyrs of 1220. Taddeo perhaps has confused the two incidents, or means here to present a synthesis of the martyrs of Franciscans in 1220, 1227, and since. In parallel, the last episode in the life of Christ is Pentecost: just as God sent the Holy Spirit to bestow the gift of tongues on the Apostles to permit them to evangelize the world, Francis floats in the air (like the Holy Spirit) and reaches his arms out towards his dying friars. On both panels, the hand of God emerges from

Fig. 8. Taddeo Gaddi, trial by fire, panel of a cabinet in the sacristy of Santa Croce, Florence, now in the Alte Pinakothek, Munich.

the clouds to bless his followers. Francis was baptized in fire, and the holy martyrs confirm the apostolic mission of the friars minor.

Giotto's frescos in the Cappella Bardi and especially the frescos of Assisi become models reproduced, more or less faithfully, in new Franciscan churches. For Dieter Blume, this was an iconographical programme diffused from Assisi and controlled by the order; Louise Bourdua, however, has shown that, at least in the Franciscan churches of the Veneto in the fourteenth centuries, lay patrons also played an important role in the choice

Fig. 9. Taddeo Gaddi, martyrdom of Franciscan friars, panel of a cabinet in the sacristy of Santa Croce, Florence, now in the Galleria della Accademia, Florence.

of iconographical programmes.[17] In San Francesco di Pistoia, whose frescos, by an anonymous artist, have been damaged, those which survived are for the most part copies of the Assisi frescos, as we see in the fresco of the trial by fire, even though a quarter or a third of its surface has been damaged.[18]

On the right the sultan is enthroned, surrounded by his men; in the centre is Francis before the fire; on the left, we can perceive on the damaged surface the robes of the Saracen priests. While in many details the artist innovates (the form of the throne and of the sultan's palace, the clothes of the sultan and his men), it is essentially the same confrontation that we find in Assisi.

Observants and Illuminations of Three Manuscripts of Bonaventure's *Legenda maior*

In 1266, as we have seen, the *Legenda maior* became the sole authorized version of Francis's life. Each Franciscan convent was required, in theory, to possess at least one copy. Hundreds of copies were produced: most of them are quite modest, but beginning in the fourteenth century we also find richly illuminated manuscripts. We will see how three illuminators of the fourteenth and fifteenth centuries depicted Francis's mission to the sultan.

Let us first look at a manuscript probably produced in Bologna in the last quarter of the fourteenth century, which contains a series of seventeen illuminations, placed in general at the beginning of chapters of Bonaventure's text. This manuscript may have been commissioned from a lay woman close to the friars minor: there are a number of depictions of a kneeling woman: with three Franciscans, flanked by the Virgin and John the Baptist, before Christ in *pietà*; under an image of Francis surrounded by birds and lambs; or again before Francis receiving the stigmata. One of the friars who accompanies her in the first image is wearing a red cardinal's hat; Silvia Mazzini identifies him with Tomasso Frignani of Bologna, minister general of the order from 1367 to 1372, then cardinal from 1378 to 1381, fervent partisan of the Observant movement.[19]

The Observants emerge in the fourteenth century in a sort of epilogue to the conflict between conventual and spiritual Franciscans. The abolition of the spirituals during the pontificate of John XXII did not put an end to conflicts within the friars minor. While the order hunted down spirituals and brought them before the Inquisition, friar John of Valle, disciple of Angelo Clareno, founded a hermitage at Brugliano, near Foligno, in 1334 and withdrew there with a group of brothers who wished to live simply, in accordance with the Rule. In 1350 John's successor, Gentile di

Spoleto, obtained from Pope Clement VI exemption from obedience to his Franciscan superiors, giving *de facto* jurisdictional independence to the Observants of Brugliano. But in 1354 the Franciscan Chapter General at Assisi condemned Gentile and his friars as *fraticelli* and dispersed them; the same chapter for the first time authorized friars to accept money donations, which for the Observants only confirmed that the order no longer followed Francis's Rule.

In 1368, friar Paul of Trinci obtained the permission of the minister general to refound the hermitage of Brugliano: there, the friars lived in extreme poverty. Other hermitages were established by the friars of Brugliano: in 1380, the order granted to Paul the control of twelve convents of the Observance; at his death in 1390, he ran twenty-two. In the first quarter of the fifteenth century, the most charismatic and dynamic Franciscans are Observants: Bernardino da Siena, John of Capistrano, Albert of Sarteano, James of the Marche. The Council of Constance in 1415 permitted the Observants to elect their own hierarchy. Towards 1500, the number of Observants surpassed the number of conventuals; in 1517, Pope Leo X formalized the definitive split of the friars minor and recognized the Observants as the principal branch of the order.[20]

Let us return to the manuscript, probably produced in an Observant convent at the time when the branch was rapidly growing. In this context, it is not surprising that the manuscript's seventeen images show an independence from the canonical conventuals' model of the Assisi frescos. As Mazzini has shown, the accent is on ascesis and poverty: next to classic scenes on this theme (for example, Francis's renunciation of his secular clothes), we find new expressions. There is the miracle of a bag full of money that a friar finds along a road; the friar is tempted to take it, but before Francis the bag is transformed into a snake. This scene may be read as a criticism of the amendment of the Rule in 1354 which permitted the friars to accept money. We also find Francis kneeling before the three virtues, one of whom is Lady Poverty.

As for Francis's mission to the sultan, we can perceive both echoes of the Assisi model and important differences. The scene is painted at the beginning of the ninth book of the *Legenda* within the initial 'C' of 'Caritatem ferventem, qua Sponsi amicus Franciscus ardebat, quis enarrare sufficiat?' (Who could relate the fervent love with which Francis, friend of the Bridegroom, burned?) (Fig. 10). The fire, at the right of the scene, symbolizes the burning love which is the subject of the book. The sultan, sitting on his throne on the left, looks like a Western king: dressed in purple and red, crowned, holding in his hand a sceptre topped with a *fleur de lys*. Between the sultan and Francis are three soldiers wearing pointed helmets, lances in hand. At the centre of the composition we see two priests in long robes with their back turned, leaving the scene. The treatment is less adept than in the Assisi frescos, where we saw the astonished, fearful faces of the fleeing priests; here we see only their backs, and their movement betrays neither fear nor haste. Francis stands between the priests and the fire, which his habit and his left hand almost touch. His arms open, he looks straight at the sultan, who looks back at Francis and extends his right hand in the same gesture we saw in Assisi, which seems to invite Francis to enter the fire.

Fig. 10. The trial by fire in a manuscript of Bonaventure's *Legenda maior*, Rome, Biblioteca Nazionale, MS 411.

We find the same Observant perspectives and preoccupations in two manuscripts of the *Legenda maior* which contain a major iconographic programme: manuscript 1989 of the Archivo Ibero-Americano de Madrid, from the first quarter of the fourteenth century, has 163 illuminations of Bonaventure's text; manuscript 1266 of the Museo dei Cappucini in Rome, probably a copy of the Madrid manuscript, has 183. This is the most complete Franciscan iconographic programme of the Middle Ages, far surpassing the twenty-eight frescos of Assisi.[21] Unlike the Biblioteca Nazionale manuscript, neither of these two contains images of patrons or other indices which permit us to identify them with the Observants. However, the themes chosen by the Madrid illuminator and their execution by the two artists show a clearly Obervant orientation.

Some of the miniatures take the Assisi frescos as models, as Jürgen Einhorn has remarked. But in general, the illuminators place the accent on Francis's poverty and ascesis, and much less on his miracles. This is no doubt in part because of a difference in audience: the Assisi frescos were meant to be seen by thousands of pilgrims, in whom they sought to instill or reinforce veneration for the saint whose sanctuary they were visiting. The manuscripts of the *Legenda*, in contrast, were composed for Observant friars minor for whom Francis was a model to follow. Let us look at just a few examples that show the Observant point of view of these manuscripts. Numerous miniatures show Francis with the poor: we see for example Francis as a youth, before his conversion, giving his coat to a poor man whose brown, ripped robe seems to prefigure the Franciscan habit; other poor people wear the same ripped habit, suggesting a parallel between the Franciscan voluntary poor and the involuntary poor.[22] The painters illustrate the physical suffering of Francis who is beaten by his father in two images; in another, the people of Assisi throw stones at him; in another, brigands pummel him.[23] In one image, his mother frees him from captivity: but whereas the hagiographers and the Bardi altarpiece had shown him locked in a room, the illuminators have him tied to a column, just like Christ when he was tortured by Roman soldiers. We also see the suffering that Francis imposed upon himself: shirtless, he whips himself on the back (62). He cares for poor and lepers, whose feet he washes (as in the Bardi dossal) (19). The choice of poverty and the rejection of worldly belongings is seen in an image where Francis puts on his habit and abandons, at his feet, a series of objects: lay clothing, a hat, shoes, belt, walking stick, and money bag. This is a reminder of the absolute poverty of the Franciscan life and a rejection of the conventuals who in 1354, as we have seen, authorized the acceptance of money donations. Francis and his companions are always shown barefoot. In one scene, a black man offers a bag full of gold coins to two Franciscans who refuse it (48). This message is reiterated in another painting which illustrates the story of the money bag transformed into a snake (87).

In this presentation of Francis as a model of poverty and ascesis, the artists devote nine paintings to his voyage to the East. The first scene shows Francis sitting in the middle of a ship setting off from the coast of Italy: one companion speaks to him and another holds the rudder. A second image shows an angel bringing bread to the ship immobilized because of lack of wind. Next we see various scenes of the two friars before the sultan. All of these paintings present the sultan in the image of a European king: a white man with a black beard in some images, grey beard on others, seated on a throne, sceptre in hand. He wears a turban (the only sign that he is oriental) topped with a crown. Francis is at the left in these images, with Illuminatus behind him and the sultan on the right or in the centre. First (Fig. 11), the sultan seems to speak to Francis who listens to him with his arms folded; behind the king, two black men gesture in apparent surprise.

Fig. 11. Rome, Museo dei Cappuccini, MS 1266, illustration 114, fo. 54ʳ.

On the next page (Fig. 12, top), Francis gestures while speaking to the sultan who listens: in the centre, between the two, two lambs look at Francis.

Fig. 12. Rome, Museo dei Cappuccini, MS 1266, illustrations 115 and 116, fo. 55ʳ.

This is a reference to Bonaventure's text, according to which, as we have seen, the two friars encountered two lambs on their way to see the sultan; Francis interpreted this as a good sign and reminded Illuminatus of the verse from the Gospel of Matthew: 'Behold, I am sending you forth like sheep in the midst of wolves' (Matt. 10: 16). On the same page (Fig. 12, bottom), two black men beat the two Franciscans. Here too, the artist follows Bonaventure's text; he also echoes it in other illuminations in the manuscript where, as we have seen, Francis is beaten by his father or by brigands. In all these images, the saint accepts these beatings without resisting: his prostrate position is one of submission and prayer.

The following image shows Francis once again before the sultan. Now in the centre of the composition, Francis preaches to the sultan, who holds a book open on his lap. A Qur'ân? A Bible brought by Francis? Behind the two Franciscans, the two black men observe the scene.

Next is the trial by fire, where we of course perceive the echo of the Assisi frescos and perhaps those of Giotto in the Bardi chapel, although this image is not a simple copy of either. In Assisi, Francis was at the centre of the composition: the sultan and his men were on the right, the fleeing priests on the left. In Florence, the sultan was in the centre, high on his throne, dominating the scene; Francis prepared to affront the flames on the right before the frightened Saracens (the priests covering their faces and two black men who seem to be the inspiration for those found in the two manuscripts). In the Madrid and Rome manuscripts, the fire occupies the centre along with Francis who continues to speak with the sultan. The sultan looks at Francis and gestures towards the saint and the fire with his right arm, with two fingers extended. Behind him, in the Madrid manuscript (Fig. 13) are the two black men. Curiously, the artist of the Roman manuscript replaces them with two white women (118; fo. 55ᵛ). Behind the Franciscans, two Saracen priests with white beards, wearing turbans, far from fleeing (as in Assisi) or covering their faces (as with Giotto), seem to speak to each other, completely unconscious of what is going on behind them. No one shows a hint of astonishment or fear. The dramatic tension of Assisi and Florence is missing; whether or not this was the artist's intention, one has the impression of a benevolent or (for the two Saracen priests) indifferent welcome for Francis and Illuminatus. In a final scene (119), the sultan offers to the friars a bowl or basket of money; Francis pushes it away.

These illuminations faithfully follow Bonaventure's text, even if the order of the scenes is somewhat confused: why show the friars conversing with the sultan *before* being beaten by his soldiers, in flagrant contradiction of the *Legenda maior*? The trial by fire, the subject of one of the nine illuminations of Francis's voyage East, becomes merely one episode among others. A few folios later is an illustration of Francis predicting the defeat

Fig. 13. Rome, Museo dei Cappuccini, MS 1266, illustration 118, fo. 55ᵛ.

of the crusaders before Damietta on an unpropitious day (illustration 132). Francis speaks to Illuminatus on the left, and on the right the crusaders (who have not heeded the saint's warnings) are routed. Nothing in the clothing or equipment of the soldiers distinguishes crusaders from Saracens, except their banners: the Christian standard, white with a red cross, lies on the ground, while the Saracens' bears a golden image of an animal (calf? lion?) just like many Saracen coats of arms in the *chansons de geste*.

The artist at times presents the Saracens as Europeans: the sultan, his soldiers, and many of the men and women are white and dress like Europeans. Only two (the bearded turbaned priests of the trial by fire) are in clearly oriental dress. And then there are the two black men who appear in several scenes; it is they who beat the two Franciscans.

The Trial by Fire in Fifteenth-Century Painting

While the miniature cycles in the manuscripts of Bonaventure's *Legenda* developed the narrative possibilities offered by a series of scenes, the painters of Franciscan monumental cycles (frescos or panels) continued to privilege the trial by fire. Some fifteenth-century artists made this confrontation more dramatic: Francis, with increasing audacity, propels himself into the flames.

Let us look at a panel (Fig. 14) by the Sienese painter Taddeo di Bartolo (1362/3–1422), today in the Niedersächsiches Landesmuseum in Hanover along with five other panels representing scenes from the life of the saint: the approbation of the Rule, the Nativity scene at Greccio, a miracle in which Francis makes a spring spout out of a rock, his preaching to the birds, his apparition in a chariot of fire. A seventh panel, showing the apparition in Arles, was probably originally part of this cycle. These panels, now separated, were probably once part of the praedella of an altarpiece

Fig. 14. Taddeo di Bartolo, *Trial by Fire*, Niedersächsiches Landesmuseum, Hanover.

devoted to the Virgin Mary and Francis. On the front of the altarpiece (now in the Galleria Nazionale dell'Umbria), the Virgin and child are in the centre, flanked by Saints John the Baptist, John the Evangelist, Mary Magdalene, and Catherine. An inscription reads: 'Taddeo di Bartolo of Siena painted this work in 1403'. On the back, which probably faced the presbytery, we see Francis flanked by Saints Anthony of Padua, Louis of Toulouse, Constantius, and Herculanus. Francis is stepping on three small characters who represent the vices of lust, pride, and avarice.[24] It is possible that the seven panels in Hanover are only a part of the original praedella: if we imagine a praedella on both sides of the altarpiece, we would need six or seven panels on each side to occupy the available space beneath the standing saints. The surprising absence of some of the essential episodes of Francis's life (in particular the stigmatization) may be explained by the loss of some of the panels.

Taddeo gives a simplified and dramatized version of the trial by fire. Only five people occupy the scene. The sultan, identified as *soldanus babilonis*, 'sultan of Babylon', is seated on a throne covered with a golden cloth, at the centre of the composition. He is clearly oriental, wearing a pointed hat whose lower part nevertheless has the form of a crown; he is dressed in a red and purple robe fringed in gold, he holds a sceptre in his left hand. He is looking at the fire and pointing at it with his right hand. On the left are two Saracen priests, also clearly oriental: one, dressed in blue and wearing a turban, holding a book in his hand, flees the scene. He glances back towards Francis and the fire, his faced deformed by a frown which clearly shows his defeat. Behind him, the second Saracen, apparently more receptive to Francis's message, moves in the opposite direction, towards Francis in the fire, hands open. Francis, who is identified by name, raises his arm above his head (as he does in Giotto's fresco in the Bardi chapel). But in Giotto's fresco he was immobile, standing before the fire, while here he is in motion: with an energetic stride, he places his foot before the fire; it is clear that his movement is carrying him into the fire. Behind him, Illuminatus, whose face is hidden behind the saint's halo, contemplates the scene. It is this impression of movement which distinguishes Taddeo di Bartolo's rendition from that of his models, the Assisi and Florence frescos. And there is another new element: the book that the Saracen priest holds in his hand. Is it the Qur'ân? This suggests that the artist (or rather his Franciscan patrons) drew inspiration not only from Bonaventure's *Legenda maior* but also from his *Sermones de S. Francisco* or his *Collationes in*

Hexaemeron, where the Saracens propose to dispute (*disputare*) with the saint in order to establish which of the two religions is better; Francis refused, affirming that the faith was beyond human reason, and proposed the trial by fire instead of a *disputatio*.[25] It is curious to see this element appear in the iconography for the first time in the fifteenth century, a century after Bonaventure. The Saracen priest flees, book in hand; all his knowledge cannot help him confront the militant faith of the *poverello*. The movement of the other Saracen priest, towards Francis and the fire, hands open, suggest that it is possible to convert some infidels to the Christian faith.

Taddeo di Bartolo's work probably inspired another altarpiece devoted to the Virgin and Francis. Stefano di Giovanni (d. 1450), better known as Sassetta, one of the masters of the Italian Gothic style in the early fifteenth century, painted a large altarpiece for the Franciscan conventual Church of Borgo San Sepolcro, in south-west Tuscany. The piece was commissioned in 1437 and completed in 1444.[26] It was later disassembled and its panels dispersed between museums across Europe. In a number of contractual documents between the artist and two friars of the convent, the Franciscans specify the disposition of the panels and the episodes to be depicted. One document mentions drawings that Sassetta drew for the friars. Like the altarpiece by Taddeo di Bartolo, that of Borgo San Sepolcro has, on the front, a large Virgin and child flanked with saints. On the back, a large Francis is in the centre; as in Taddeo's painting, he steps on personifications of the vices. Around this central image are eight scenes from Francis's life; a letter from the two friars to Sassetta in 1439 enumerates what they are to be:

> Eight stories concerning Saint Francis, namely: 1. when [in a dream] the palace was shown to Francis. 2. When he rejected the inheritance of his father [and placed himself] in the hand of the bishop. 3. When the pardon of Assisi was confirmed by the pope. 4. When he received the stigmata. 5. When he appeased the people of Gubbio with the wolf. 6. When he married the three virtues. 7. When he went before the sultan and entered into the fire. 8. When he died.[27]

The choice of scenes is original: this is the first time, for example, that we find the wolf of Gubbio. As James Banker has suggested, the two friars preferred episodes showing the saint's miracles and his acceptance by the church hierarchy; this is indeed a conventual Francis. We do nevertheless see him marrying the three virtues (including Lady Poverty), a favourite scene of the Observants.

The trial by fire (Fig. 15) takes place in a palace, before the throne of a young, beardless sultan (at the right) who leans towards the saint and looks at him fixedly. Behind the sultan on his right are two turbaned Saracens who also look on and, in front of them, Illuminatus, hands joined in prayer. In the centre, Francis enters the fire. Sassetta goes further than Taddeo di

Fig. 15. Sassetta, *Trial by Fire*, London, National Gallery.

Bartolo who, as we have seen, shows Francis advancing towards the fire in great strides, at the moment when he is about to place his left foot in the flames. With Sassetta, the left foot is in the middle of the fire, and the saint shows no sign of discomfort. The scene corresponds to the instructions that the artist received from the friars, who specified that he should paint the saint as he 'entered into the fire'. Francis is driven with the same energy that we see in Bartolo's painting, but while Bartolo depicted the Saracen priests in movement (one fleeing Francis, one moving towards him), for Sassetta, Francis alone is in movement (if we except the sultan's leaning forward on his throne). The Saracens do not move: none of them flees, none hides his face, none holds a book which he could use to argue against the saint. On the contrary, all eyes are on the miracle which is happening before them: two of them raise their hands in astonishment.

We could add to this catalogue of representations of the trial by fire that of Fra Angelico, now in the Lindenau-Museum Altenburg: Francis walks towards a small fire set in the middle of a flowering meadow as the sultan and his men look on.[28] We find the trial by fire depicted by Sienese painter Giovanni di Paolo (d. 1483), in an illumination of an antiphonary painted c.1450, today in the Széchényi National Library of Budapest (Fig. 16).[29] The scene, placed inside an initial C, is set in a gothic throne room. Francis preaches to the sultan, counting on his fingers. Behind the saint, Illuminatus holds a bell, which underlines the idea of a preaching mission—with this bell the friars would have called their audience together. The sultan sports a red beard, a crown, and European-style sceptre; he also has a turban and exotic pointed shoes. This exoticism is seen also in the clothing of the men standing behind him, in particular in their varied hats. The threat of violence is more clearly present here than in other representations of the trial by fire. The men on each side of the sultan hold large swords: one of them, bared, is held over the flames, pointed towards Francis. The sultan raises his right hand as if to prevent Francis from being harmed by the sword.

In 1452, Benozzo Gozzoli completed a series of frescos for San Francesco church in Montefalco, a town perched on a hill about 30 kilometres south of Assisi. The iconographical programme reveals an Observant orientation: a series of vignettes contains portraits of numerous Franciscans, among whom we find John of Brienne (identified simply as 'emperor of Constantinople'), King Robert d'Anjou, and his brother St Louis of Toulouse.[30] The portraits of numerous princes, doctors, and saints associated with the Franciscans celebrate the glory of the order and also legitimate the Observants, presented

Fig. 16. Giovanni di Paolo, trial by fire, antiphonary (*c.*1450). Széchényi National Library, Budapest.

as the sole true heirs of this Franciscan tradition. This becomes even clearer when we notice the presence of Peter John Olivi, spiritual hero subsequently adopted by the Observants, a *bête noire* of the conventuals.[31]

Gozzoli indeed paints an Observant Francis. In the arch at the entrance to the chorus, we find Francis (at the summit) surrounded by twelve friars, like Christ and his twelve Apostles. In the adjacent vault, Gozzoli presents Francis as an *alter Christus*, in glory, surrounded by seraphim in the midst of a luminous circle, holding in one hand a book proclaiming 'I bear the stigmata of Lord Jesus', a citation from the Letter to the Galatians which Bonaventure had used to affirm the *rapprochement* between Francis and Christ.[32] Gozzoli introduces scenes found neither in the Assisi frescos nor in Bonaventure's *Legenda maior*.[33] Thirteen frescos from the choir have survived (a fourteenth was destroyed when a window was enlarged), containing nineteen episodes, most of which are inspired by those of Assisi, from the homage given by the simple man of Assisi to the saint's death. But other scenes are new, for example, Francis's meeting with Dominic, inspired by the *Golden Legend*, or that of the saint blessing the town of Montefalco. Particularly remarkable, as Diane Ahl has noted, is the scene of Francis's birth: Christ, disguised as a pilgrim, announces to the saint's pregnant mother that Francis will be born in a stable; on the left we see the new-born Francis, haloed, receiving his first bath in the stable between a bull and a donkey.

Gozzoli also innovates in his depiction of Francis's preaching to the sultan (Fig. 17). The scene is a courtyard, with the sultan sitting on a raised throne in a columned arcade; in the background is a walled garden with trees, including palms. Behind Francis, two friars look on. Around the sultan are his men, who contemplate the scene: among them is a bearded turbaned priest and a soldier in armour. Francis holds a golden crucifix in his left hand, raising the right in a sign of blessing. Where Sassetta had the saint placing his left foot in the fire, Gozzoli goes further: Francis has both feet in the fire and he continues calmly to walk towards the sultan. The sultan stares at him and raises both hands in astonishment. Gozzoli, like Sassetta, removed any ambiguity from the trial by fire: it is clearly a miracle; Francis walks through fire.

Gozzoli adds another element to the story. A young blonde woman stands at the back of the scene: she also raises her hands in amazement. Who is she? The inscription below the fresco tells us: 'When the sultan sent a girl to tempt blessed Francis and he entered into the fire and all were amazed.'[34] The young woman is the one who tried to seduce Francis, according to the *Actus beati Francisci*; Francis lay in a fire and invited her to join him on his 'bed'.[35] But in the *Actus*, the episode takes place in an inn, far from the court of the sultan, who has nothing to do with the incident. Gozzoli brings her to the sultan's court and fuses into one the two separate fires in the *Actus*: the one that Francis proposed to enter before the sultan and the one in the inn. In Gozzoli's version, the sultan tried to burn Francis with the fire of lust by sending the beautiful young girl to lead him astray. But the saint, who burns with a higher love, walks through the flames to show the strength of his faith.

We could continue our catalogue of representations of the trial by fire across Europe through the sixteenth, seventeenth, and eighteenth centuries.

Fig. 17. Benozzo Gozzoli, fresco in the choir of San Francesco church, Montefalco.

Between 1479 and 1485, for example, Domenico Ghirlandaio paints a series of frescos in the Cappella Sassetti of Santa Trinità in Florence, the first major iconographical cycle devoted to the saint in a non-Franciscan church; he includes a painting of the trial by fire very much influenced by those of Giotto and Taddeo Gaddi in the nearby Church of Santa Croce.[36] In the first quarter of the sixteenth century, Benedetto da Rovezzano depicts the trial by fire in a bas-relief for the pulpit of the Chiesa di Ognisanti in Florence: the sultan vigorously gestures to his men, ordering them to enter the fire, while Francis, immobile, hands joined in prayer, lowers his eyes. In the cloister of San Francesco church in Padua is a series of twenty-five frescos of Francis's life; one of them is dated 1647. In front of a sultan in Turkish garb surrounded by numerous soldiers, Francis places his left foot in the fire.[37]

The birth of printing permitted a much greater diffusion of devotional images of saints—notably of Francis. The trial by fire is not the most popular episode from the life of Francis, far from it: in the many devotional images printed in Flanders in the sixteenth and seventeenth centuries, we find many representations of the stigmatization and the preaching to the birds, but not a single one of the mission to the sultan.[38] We do find it in many of the numerous printed editions of the *Legenda maior*, in particular in its German translations.[39] It appears, for example, in three translations printed at the end of the fifteenth and in the first quarter of the sixteenth century: before the throne of a European-looking king, a fire burns. On the left, Francis approaches; on the right, a Saracen argues, his finger pointed towards the saint, a book in hand. In two of the three images, we also see a priest who turns his back and leaves. In the other, Francis proclaims: 'I do not hold my life too dear. I go immediately with you in the fire' (Mein leben act ich nit zu teur. Ich ge bald mit euch in das feur) (Fig. 18).[40] Thanks to these images, the iconography of the trial by fire is diffused in northern Europe.

These prints do not depict the triumphant miracle that we find in Benozzo Gozzoli or Sassetta, but a much more ambiguous confrontation. We do still see, on some of these images, a priest who turns his back and flees the trial by fire. But sharing the centre with Francis is a Saracen, book in hand, who seems to show neither amazement nor fear, and who argues with Francis, presumably using material from his book. At a time when the Ottomans dominated a large part of Europe, triumphalism is no longer the order of the day.

Towards the Fear of the Turk: Benedetto de Maiano's Pulpit for Santa Croce

Let us return to the Florentine Church of Santa Croce, at the beginning of the 1480s, where we find a testimony of fear of the Turk. Sculptor

Mein leben acht ich nit zu reiz
Ich ge bald mit euch in das feur

Fig. 18. Trial by fire, woodcut, *c.*1470–80.

Benedetto da Maiano carved a series of five bas-relief panels for a new pulpit.[41] This is the fourth narrative cycle of the saint's life in Santa Croce, after those of the Bardi altarpiece, Giotto's frescos in the Cappella Bardi, then Taddeo Gaddi's panels for the sacristy cabinet. Benedetto draws inspiration from Giotto and Taddeo, but gives an original version in which the confrontation with the Saracens plays an important role, receiving two of the five scenes. The five episodes are the approval of the Rule, the trial by fire, the stigmatization, the saint's death, and his apparition to the martyrs of Morocco. This last scene was depicted for the first time by Taddeo, as the last of his thirteen episodes.

The depiction of the meeting with the sultan is different from the three previous versions in Santa Croce. In the Bardi altarpiece Francis preaches, open book in hand, to the attentive Saracens and their sultan. In Giotto's fresco, the sultan presides over a judgement by fire and his priests covered their eyes so as not to see the saint confront the flames. For the sacristy cabinet, Taddeo Gaddi added to the scene inspired by his master Giotto, a Saracen priest, seen from the back, who stood before the throne and raised his arms towards the sultan, expressing his refusal to enter the fire. Benedetto da Maiano (Fig. 19) makes this person more confident and defiant; he turns towards the fire and looks at Francis: it is Francis, and not the Saracen, who looks down. None of the Saracens show the slightest astonishment or fear when confronted by the trial by fire: in the Assisi frescos, the priests fled; Giotto and Taddeo Gaddi had them hide their faces; Benedetto has them stand firm. Moreover, one of the Saracen priests, on the left, holds two books in his hands, as if the Egyptian priests wanted to answer Francis with arguments gleaned from their books. It is impossible to say whether the artist meant to depict the Qur'ân, the books of Arabic philosophers, or perhaps both (which could explain the presence of *two* books). We have seen that Taddeo di Bartolo placed a book in the hand of a Saracen priest in flight, as if to say that the burning faith of Francis had vanquished the knowledge of the Saracens. Benedetto's Saracens, far from fleeing the encounter with Francis or covering their faces in fear of shame, confront him bravely and counter him with arguments from their books.

This image of a militant Islam which resists the evangelizing message of the friars minor is reinforced by the last of the five sculpted panels (Fig. 20), representing the martyrdom of Franciscans. Benedetto's model is once again Taddeo Gaddi: as with Taddeo, the dominant figure here is the executioner who raises his huge sword—for Taddeo, he was on the left; Benedetto places him in the centre of the composition: the corpses and severed heads of the martyred friars litter the ground; other friars, kneeling in prayer, await their turn. Above them, Francis floats in the air. There are also two standing friars in the background, who correspond to Anthony of

Fig. 19. Benedetto da Maiano, trial by fire, bas-relief for the pulpit of Santa Croce, Florence.

Padua and his companion in Taddeo's painting. Benedetto depicts Anthony in the background on the left, in front of a church upon a hill: surrounded by other friars, he enters into the order, inspired by the example of the martyrs.

Fig. 20. Benedetto da Maiano, martyrdom of Franciscans, bas-relief for the pulpit of Santa Croce, Florence.

There are nevertheless important differences in the two versions of the martyrdom scene. Taddeo places it outside a fortified city; the only Saracens present are two soldiers and the executioner. Benedetto brings the drama into the city, before the throne of the sultan: the severed heads roll at the foot of his dais. The sultan and the men around him resemble those of the trial by fire. Indeed, the sultan seems to be the same man, other than the slightly different form of his hat; he turns to speak to a young man identical to the one who confronted Francis in the first scene; a bearded man is also in both scenes. All of this suggests that the two episodes are closely linked: the Saracens and their sultan refuse to be convinced by Francis and his trial by fire; these same Saracens kill Francis's companions who come bearing the Gospel message. The sultan here shows no signs of hatred or violence, but rather of indifference: he doesn't even look at the executioner, but turns to speak with his young courtier; he does not react to the heads that roll at his feet. The violent death of the friars minor does not seem to provoke the slightest emotion in the sultan.

It is indeed not surprising to find a hostile vision of Islam in Italy in the 1480s. Ottoman sultan Mehmet II had taken Constantinople in 1453, provoking an exodus—many took refuge in Italy, where they painted a bleak picture of the Turkish conquerors.[42] Meanwhile, Mehmet continued his conquests in Europe: his troops conquered large swathes of Bosnia and Croatia: in March 1480, their camp fires could be seen from Venice. In July of the same year, Mehmet captured Otranto, in the south-east of Italy (on the heel of the boot), sending a shockwave through the peninsula. On 18 November, Pope Sixtus IV proclaimed the canonization of the five friars martyred in Marrakech in 1220: no doubt the Ottoman menace inspired, at least in part, the timing of this canonization.[43] It is in this context that Benedetto presents the meeting between Francis and the sultan as a heroic but futile confrontation with an implacable enemy.

This fear of the Turk, mixed, beginning in the sixteenth century, with the fear of the 'heretic' Luther and his followers, colours the depiction of the encounter between Francis and al-Kâmil by authors and artists of the sixteenth and seventeenth centuries, as we will see in the next chapter.

11

The Saint of Assisi Confronts Barbarous Infidelity

Sixteenth and Seventeenth Centuries

While Bonaventure's *Legenda* and the Assisi frescos dominate the representation of the encounter between Francis and al-Kâmil in the fourteenth and fifteenth centuries, other models exist. Some authors and artists preferred to place the accent on the hostility that the Saracens showed towards Francis, on the beatings that they inflicted on the friars, beatings described by Bonaventure but absent from the painted images we examined in the previous chapter. By presenting a Saracen Orient hostile to Francis's message and violent towards him, these authors affirmed that the 'Saracens' (or 'Moors' or 'Turks') were irremediable enemies who must be fought. We have seen how Benedetto da Maiano portrays the encounter between Franciscans and Muslims in a way that reflects the fear of the Ottoman menace, a real enough menace in fifteenth-century Europe. Mehmet II took Constantinople in 1453 and Otranto in 1480; his successors dominated the Balkans and twice laid siege to Vienna, in 1529 and in 1683. In the portrayals of the encounter between Francis and al-Kâmil, the sultan now often is a Turkish sultan surrounded by intimidating soldiers.

Even more troubling, for many Franciscan authors, was a second threat coming from the heart of Europe: the Protestant 'heresy'. In 1517, Martin Luther nailed his ninety-five theses on the door of the church of Wittenberg Castle. Luther and other Protestant leaders attacked the monastic orders that for them embodied the corruption of the Catholic Church: isolation, riches, celibacy, blind devotion to the papacy, the superstitious cult of the saints. Some Protestant polemicists attacked the Franciscans, whom they accused of turning their founder, Francis, into an idol that they adored instead of Christ. Various Franciscan authors responded to these accusations. Thus we need to place the sixteenth- and seventeenth-century portrayals of the encounter between Francis and al-Kâmil in the context of the Protestant attacks on Catholicism, of Ottoman expansion, and of the Catholic reactions to these two threats.

Francis's Tormenters in the Texts and Images of the Fourteenth and Fifteenth Centuries

Pedro Pascual, bishop of Jaén at the end of the thirteenth century, in his description of the encounter between Francis and al-Kâmil, paints the sultan in a wholly negative light: if he let the saint leave at the end of their interview, it was not because of any generosity or sympathy, but out of a calculated animosity, in order to deprive the Christians of a new martyr. The sultan said to Francis: 'On your way! I do not want to make you a martyr so that the Christians can then celebrate your feast day.' Pedro concludes: let's celebrate it anyway, to spite the sultan.[1] Dominican missionary Riccoldo da Montecroce complains of his lack of success in converting the Saracens of Baghdad and invokes Francis:

> O blessed Francis, for whom I have had a particular devotion from my childhood to this day, O true lover of poverty, to you I cry ceaselessly, in tears and moaning; you who, inflamed with the zeal of faith and devotion, went to find the sultan of Babylon, whom you asked to put you in the fire with the Saracens or even alone, to destroy the perfidy of Muhammad. That is what you wanted, but you could not achieve it.[2]

How had Riccoldo dared think he could convert the sultan and 'destroy the perfidy of Muhammad', when Francis himself had been unable to do so? Francis's example shows the impossibility of mission to the Saracens, their impermeability to the Christian truth.

A promoter of crusade, Venetian Marino Sanudo, incorporates the story of Francis's mission to Egypt into his *Book of the Secrets of the Devotees of the Cross for the Recuperation and the Conservation of the Holy Land*, which he presented to Pope John XXII in Avignon on 24 September 1321. Sanudo had been in Acre at the age of 14, in 1286, only five years before the Mamluks captured the city, the last crusader outpost in the Holy Land. He subsequently was one of the many authors who called for new crusades to recapture Jerusalem and the Holy Land. The first of the three books of his treatise is devoted to the first phase of his proposed new crusade, consisting of a commercial boycott of Mamluk Egypt. The second book sets out his plan for a crusade against Egypt: he has thought of everything, from the financing of the ships and their equipment to the strategic targets to attack. He opines (just like the crusaders of 1219–21 and 1248) that, once Egypt is conquered, it should be easy to conquer and to hold the Holy Land.[3]

The third part of the *Book of Secrets* contains a history of the Holy Land from Noah to the year 1302. Sanudo devotes numerous pages to the crusades. In this context he narrates the history of the fifth crusade. His principal source seems to be the anonymous continuation of the *Eracle*, from which he learnt, among other things, that after the conquest of Damietta, Francis, disgusted by the lust and avarice of the victorious crusaders, abandoned them to their fate.[4] Sanudo also uses Bonaventure's *Legenda maior*: he relates that Francis predicted the crusaders' defeat of 29 August 1219, then describes the saint's mission to the sultan, recounting the proposed trial by fire in Bonaventure's words. For Sanudo, this episode illustrates the glorious history of the crusades, a history which is destined to continue. Sanudo travelled from court to court in Europe, in particular between Avignon, Paris, and Naples, to try to persuade popes and princes to take up the crusading banner. He was received politely, sometimes even enthusiastically, but his project of a grand crusade against Mamluk Egypt never came to pass.

While Sanudo uses the encounter between Francis and the sultan to underline the need for a new crusade, others take it up for quite different purposes. An anonymous Franciscan friar composed, in 1437, in Constantinople, a *Treatise on the Martyrdom of the Saints* (*Tractatus de martyrio sanctorum*). The author was a recent convert to the Friars Minor; he converted so that he could accompany three friars in their mission to the Turks, from whom he hoped to obtain the palm of martyrdom. Before leaving Constantinople, the new friar wrote his treaty to explain and to justify the active pursuit of martyrdom. Against the military might of the infidel, he affirms, arms are not the answer. He is indignant against those who affirm that Christians should humbly submit to Turkish power and discreetly practise their religion. This would lead to the gradual disappearance of the Christian community and their conversion to Islam, he asserts. On the contrary, Christians should actively preach against the infidel faith in order to galvanize the Christians and to inspire conversion in the Muslims. He affirms that this was the solution favoured by Francis himself, who had recognized the futility of the crusades. In his Rule, Francis encouraged the friars to preach to Muslims, exhorting them to serenely accept death. Just as the martyrs of the early church finally conquered and converted the pagan Roman Empire, the martyrdom of Franciscan friars would succeed where the force of European arms had proved impotent.[5]

The Saracen torturer of Franciscans is also illustrated in the large (5.57 × 5.58 m) Bañeza altarpiece by Leonese artist Nicolás Francés, who from the 1430s until his death in 1468 was the most illustrious painter in León, where he introduced French Gothic style.[6] Among his numerous pieces, the best-known is the grand altarpiece of the Cathedral of León (1434). However, we do not know for which church Nicolás painted the Bañeza altarpiece. Along the base, in the praedella, are seventeen prophets and apostles. The central panel has a Virgin and child surrounded by angels playing musical instruments. Above is the Assumption of the Virgin and, on top, the Crucifixion. The lateral panels, each divided into three parts, relate scenes from the lives of the Virgin (on the right) and Francis (on the left). The three scenes from the Virgin's life are (from top to bottom) the Annunciation, the Nativity, and the Presentation of the baby Jesus in the temple; for Francis, the passage before the sultan, the approval of the Rule, and the stigmatization. The choice is surprising: the stigmatization, central event of the saint's life for Bonaventure, is indeed the episode most often portrayed by painters. The approval of the Rule, much less common, is nevertheless frequent in Franciscan cycles, because it places the accent on the legitimacy of the friars minor in the church. The mission to the sultan is relatively rare; in general we find it only in the extended cycles, i.e. those which contain a large number of scenes from Francis's life. Yet Nicolás Francés decides to give it an important place in his altarpiece.

The treatment of the subject is even more exceptional: it corresponds to no previous model. While the Bardi altarpiece showed Francis preaching to the Saracens and the Assisi master (followed by numerous artists) depicted the trial by fire, Nicolás Francés (Fig. 21) shows Francis and Illuminatus roughly treated by ferocious and barbaric men. The saint, in the centre of the composition, is in Franciscan habit, haloed, wearing sandals. The cord around his waist is held by a small black devil dressed in red, who leads him towards the sultan. The sultan, seated on his throne, sports a thick black beard, a golden headdress (which seems to be a cross between a crown and a turban), and a blue robe trimmed in red. He points an accusing finger towards Francis. Around his throne stand his armed men: one of them holds a shield bearing a grotesque golden mask—it echoes the shields and standards carried by the Saracen troops in the manuscripts of the *chansons*

Fig. 21. Nicolás Francés, Bañeza altarpiece, detail: Francis before the sultan.

de geste and of certain crusade chronicles.[7] Four other armed men, accompanied by two dogs, surround the friars: one holds Illuminatus roughly by his wrist and places his other hand on Francis's shoulder. Another grabs Francis's habit; another raises his fist to beat an old person; a fourth looks on malevolently from the back of the scene. The sultan's soldiers are animated by a hostility that clearly shows on their ugly scowling faces. Their expressions, especially that of the man who holds Francis by his habit and presses his face against the saint's, echo those of Christ's persecutors in Passion scenes.[8]

Francis is here an *alter Christus* dragged before a new Pontius Pilate. The sultan is neither the attentive listener of the Bardi altarpiece nor the witness/judge of the trial by fire. The Saracens and their sultan are the implacable enemies of Christ and his servants. We do not know for whom Nicolás Francés painted this altarpiece, nor why he paints this image of hostility between Francis and the sultan. Fear of the Turks could indeed have played a role in this portrayal. But the fight against Muslims closer to home is probably more central in the artist's mind. In the Iberian Peninsula, there are fresh projects for crusade: the Portuguese had already captured the port of Ceuta on the Moroccan coast in 1415; the Aragonese raided the Tunisian coasts; and in the 1430s King Juan II of Castile tried to convince King Duarte of Portugal to participate in a new crusade against the emirate of Granada. In this context, Nicolás's message seems clear: the Moors are our enemies.[9]

The violence towards Francis and Illuminatus is even more starkly portrayed in the frescos of the Franciscan church of Santa Maria delle Grazie, in Bergamo (built between 1422 and 1427), painted by Jacopino de' Scipioni probably in summer or autumn 1506.[10] The church was demolished in 1856 and its frescos dispersed. Twenty-one of them are extant; there were no doubt others, since certain key scenes from Francis's life (in particular his death and canonization) are missing. Some of the frescos echo the Assisi cycle, in the choice of episodes and in style, but others are quite different. Some of the frescos seem to be inspired by the illuminated manuscripts of Bonaventure's *Legenda*, such as those of Rome and Madrid: Francis's penance before the people of Assisi, the stoning that the young Francis receives from the people after his conversion, or the money bag that changes into a dragon.[11] On these frescos, Francis and his friars sport beards and sandals; they wear the pointed hood of the Capuchins.

In this series, Francis's voyage East plays an important role: it is the subject of three of the twenty-one frescos. A first fresco depicts the miracle produced during the aborted trip towards Syria: in the background on the left, we see an angel present food to an astonished sailor who glances back at Francis, standing in the centre of the ship; on the right, the saint distributes the food to the passengers. The exotic nature of the travellers is striking; the few previous portrayals of this scene tend to show Francis with one fellow friar and perhaps a sailor. Here there are at least five men wearing turbans, including a sailor climbing up the mast. The man to whom the saint hands a piece of bread extends his hand to receive it and gazes, amazed, at the saint. This is Francis's first miracle performed for the benefit of the 'Turks', an important part of his mission to the infidels.

On the following fresco (Fig. 22), Francis and Illuminatus walk between the two camps at Damietta. In the background on the left, we see the crusaders' tents, with banners and red shields marked with white crosses. On the lower left, Francis and Illuminatus meet two lambs: the saint turns to his companion, no doubt (as Bonaventure relates), to cite the appropriate Gospel passage, which we find in the legend below the fresco: the two friars are sent like lambs unto wolves.[12] On the right, three men—two

Fig. 22. Francis and Illuminatus go to meet the sultan, fresco in the Church of Santa Maria della Grazie, Bergamo.

black men carrying sticks, a turbaned white man holding a spear—beat the two friars. At the top right, the three same men lead Francis and Illuminatus towards the sultan, who is seated at the entrance to his tent, surrounded by soldiers. This fresco faithfully follows Bonaventure, placing the accent on the beating that the friars received from the Saracen soldiers. Here again, we see the influence of the illuminators of the *Legenda*; Jacopino de' Scipioni condenses into one fresco three scenes which we found in the Madrid and Rome manuscripts, placing for the first time on the walls of a church these episodes which had previously been reserved for the Franciscan readers of Bonaventure's Latin text. These episodes stress the brutality of the Saracens: the cruelty of the soldier at the centre of the composition would recall for the Italian observer the more recent violence inflicted on Europeans by 'the Turk'.

The following fresco presents the trial by fire. Francis 'having preached God triune and one', as the legend reads, 'wanted to enter into the fire'.[13] He stands before the fire, feet together, hands joined in prayer and pointed towards the flames, as he looks off into the distance. Across from him, a puppy contemplates the fire. The sultan, turbaned, seated on his throne under an arch, turns towards two of his men who look at him. In his right hand, the sultan holds a book which he is giving to one of his counsellors. On the left, another man wearing a turban glances towards the fire as he leaves the scene. At the right, behind a colonnade, the sultan offers the saint a bowl full of gold coins; Francis's backward movement shows that he rejects the gift (as the legend confirms).

This all suggests that the episode was particularly important for the artist or for the Franciscans of Bergamo. On the whole, Jacopino follows Bonaventure closely and seems to draw inspiration from the illuminated manuscripts of the *Legenda maior*. In the second of the three frescos, he emphasizes the violence that the friars suffered at the hands of the Muslim troops. In the first and third frescos, Jacopino accentuates the miracles Francis produced for the benefit of Muslim witnesses, all dressed in Turkish garb: the passengers on the ship, the sultan and his men. This Bergamo Francis bravely confronts the Turks and their sultan and his miracles give a glimmer of hope to a Christian Europe under increasing threat from the Ottomans.

Francis Attacked by Lutheran 'Heretics'

The harshest attack against the Franciscans in the sixteenth century came not from the Turk, but from another kind of 'infidel', the Lutheran Erasmus Alber, who published his *Der Barfusser Münche Eulenspiegel und Alcoran* in 1542; the Latin version, *Alcoranum Franciscanorum* came out the following year. An English translation was published in London in 1550, *The alcaron of the barefote friers*; there were also French and Dutch translations.[14] Alber explains that in 1542, the margrave Joachim-Hector von Brandenburg proclaimed that all his subjects, including Catholic clerics, should listen to the missionary sermons of Lutheran preachers. Alber went to a Franciscan convent to communicate this order to the friars, but he found them to be blinder than Jews or Turks, he says. They praise Francis so much that they place him on Lucifer's throne. Just as the Jews vainly wait for their Messiah, the Franciscans place all their vain hopes in the pope. The title of the book reveals its highly polemical tone: it is an attack on Bartholomew of Pisa's *De conformitate*, which, according to Alber, has become the Franciscans' new 'Qur'ân' and has replaced the Gospel just as Francis has replaced Christ in their devotions.

Bartholomew of Pisa had written his voluminous *De conformitate vitae Beati Francesci ad vitam Domini Iesu* in 1385; the text was approved by the General Chapter of the order in 1390.[15] As the title indicates, Bartholomew's goal is to show the conformity between Francis's life and that of Jesus. This idea, that Francis was an *alter Christus*, had had an important place in Franciscan tradition since Celano. The Florentine artist Taddeo Gaddi gave, in the 1330s, a striking iconographic expression of this idea by presenting, in parallel, thirteen scenes from Jesus' life and thirteen from Francis's.[16] What is new with Bartholomew is the amplitude of the project: more than 1,100 pages (in the edition in the *Analecta franciscana*), consisting in three books containing forty 'fruits' or 'conformities'. Each 'fruit' is divided into two parts, the first devoted to Christ and the second to Francis. The tenth fruit of part one is called 'Iesus Doctor Mirabilis—Franciscus Praedicator'. First, Bartholomew shows, using biblical citations, that Jesus is a *Doctor mirabilis*. Then he offers the reader, through a sort of anthology of Franciscan sources, everything that concerns Francis's preaching. It is in this context that he narrates Francis's mission to the sultan. He recopies Bonaventure's text, than adds that of the *Actus* relating the conversion of the woman in the inn and the promise that Francis made to send the sultan friars to baptize him—a miracle which is subsequently narrated in the thirty-eighth fruit, where Francis sends out his friars just as Jesus sent out his Apostles.[17] Bartholomew's text was widely read in Franciscan circles in the early sixteenth century, as we see in particular through the numerous printed editions of the text (the first, in Milan, in 1510, followed by a second in 1513).

The alcaron of the barefote friers takes the form of a summary of the *De conformitate*; occasionally Alber adds a caustic commentary, but mostly he simply summarizes Bartholomew's text, so that his Christian (i.e. Protestant) reader can laugh at the ridiculous beliefs of the papists. The very narration of these legends, which could inspire admiration in Catholic readers, shocks Protestant readers. The frontispiece of a seventeenth-century English translation presents the stigmatization. It is identical to devotional images that we find everywhere in Catholic Europe, but it is here meant to provoke ridicule and disgust; for the stigmata, Alber explains, are either the work of Satan or an invention of the Franciscans themselves.[18] The author wants his Christian readers to be shocked by these legends and to mock them.

Among the Franciscan legends that Alber offers up for derision is that of the miraculous conversion of the sultan, which Bartholomew had found in the *Actus*: the saint appeared *post mortem* to two Franciscans and asked them to go baptize the sultan. The sultan, on his deathbed, declared 'now I know of a Truth, that the Lord hath sent his Servants, as St. Francis promised; so he was baptized and saved, by the Merits of St. Francis, the Lord Jesus co-operating with them'; he accepted baptism from them before dying.[19] Alber also ridicules the idea that 'The Mahometans are to be converted by St. Francis' (11). At the end of his diatribe, Alber concludes: 'There are many other Signs and Wonders that St. Francis did, which are not written in this Book; but there is so much written, as you may believe Friar Francis to be a mad, deceiving, lying, thievish, truce-breaking, phanatical, funestous, filthy, fierce Servant of the Son of Perdition, and that they believe in him may be damned in his name' (137).

Martin Luther wrote a preface to the *Alcoran of the Franciscans*. He relates that he himself had once been a monk (in fact, an Augustinian canon) and was obliged to participate in their superstitious cult.[20] Luther affirms, with Alber, that the Franciscans have replaced the Gospels with Bartholomew's *Conformities*, just as they adore Francis in place of Christ. Here, as in other writings, Luther abhors the very idea of a monastic order based on vows of poverty, obedience, and chastity. Among the legends which Alber mocks is the snow woman: Francis, troubled by sexual desire, made a woman out of snow and chilled his fervour in her arms. Luther compares this story to one from the life of St Benedict, who threw himself naked into a briar patch to fight his sexual desires. Luther concludes that both men would have done better to marry.[21]

Luther discusses Francis in other works, often offering similar criticisms. He does indeed retain a certain admiration for the *poverello*, 'driven under Power of Holy Spirit'.[22] But Francis's error was to take the Gospel, meant for everyone, and to reduce it to a rule that benefited only the friars minor, and what is worse a rule in which the obsession with purity led Francis to prohibit what the Bible permits to all: marriage and the use of money. Francis, inspired with admirable piety, shows great naïveté in trying to found an order on the basis of poverty; yet his modern followers 'look out for themselves and their kitchens rather well'.[23] The Franciscans raised up their founder to adore him instead of Christ. 'They crawl into monasteries to have peace and happy days, leave other people in trouble and toil, and still claim to be holier in doing that than all others.' In fact, they have replaced the Gospel with Francis's rule; they imagine that they can be saved if they follow it.[24] In his commentary to Psalm 45: 11, Luther compares the Franciscans to the Muslims: Muhammad 'conceived himself to be God's right-hand man and thought God spoke with him as with a son. Thus a Franciscan venerates his rule and his Saint Francis and an idol.'[25]

Luther distinguishes between Francis (pious but naïve) and his disciples who idolize their founder; other Protestant authors are harsher towards the *poverello*. Johann Gerhard (1582–1637) calls Francis a 'holy man' (*heiligen Mann*) but thinks that he is superstitious; this places him among the adepts of Antichrist.[26] For Matthias Flaccius (1520–75), Francis and Dominic are precursors of Antichrist, while Peter Waldo, who preached evangelical poverty and was condemned as a heretic, tried courageously to dispel the darkness of error and to spread the light of truth.[27] The very fact of acceptance by the Roman Church, it seems, places Francis firmly in Satan's camp; those who are rejected by the popes are on Christ's side, they are honorary Protestants *avant la lettre*.

French Protestants offer up the same kind of anti-Franciscan invectives. Nicolas de Vignier, a Protestant from Blois, published in Leiden in 1608 his *Légende dorée ou sommaire de l'histoire des frères mendiants de l'ordre de S. Dominique et de S. François*.[28] For Vignier, the mendicants had over-turned the Gospel and initiated 'Anti-Christianity'. He makes little use of previous Protestant polemics against the friars minor, preferring to use anti-mendicant texts from the University of Paris in the thirteenth century. Pierre du Moulin, Protestant theologian of Sedan, published in 1641 a diatribe against the Franciscans called *Le Capucin*.[29] The titles of his chapters give the tone: 'XX. Under the guise of humility, Saint Francis showed un-equalled pride. ... XXII. That the Holy Scriptures are falsified and deformed in St. Francis's rule. ... XXIV. On the vow of poverty, leisurely begging, and superogatory works'. For these sixteenth- and seventeenth-century Protestant authors, Franciscan life and the cult of the order's founding saint are the epitome of all they despise about Roman 'Papism'.

The Jesuits' Francis: The Chiesa del Gesù

In the very heart of sixteenth-century Counter-Reformation Rome, in the Chiesa del Gesù, head church of the Order of Jesus, we find a defence of Francis and his order.[30] In a painting in this church, we see Francis and his friars dragged before the sultan, sitting on his throne in the midst of a vast military camp where, amongst the palm trees, there is a veritable forest of spears. This painting, along with seven others presenting episodes from the saint's life, was painted for the St Francis chapel of the Gesù. Why devote a chapel to Francis in the mother church of the Jesuits? The chapel, founded at the instigation of Francisco Borgia, minister general of the order, shows the admiration in which the Jesuits had held the *poverello* ever since their foundation by Ignatius of Loyola.

In 1540, Pope Paul III approved the new Order of Jesus. Thirteen years before, Pope Clement VII had recognized the independence of the new order of Friars Minor Capuchin, who preached the return to the primitive ascesis incarnated in Francis's Rule. The two orders, Jesuits and Capuchins, are from the time of the Council of Trent (1545–63) indispensable to the papacy for the affirmation of Catholicism in the face of Protestantism, for the enactment of the reforms proclaimed at Trent, and for missions to Africa, Asia, and America. While the Observants succeeded in obtaining (in 1517) their official separation from the Conventuals, some friars charged the Observants of having forsaken the true poverty required by the Rule. These friars came together in hermitages where they practised extreme ascesis and sought to follow the Rule to the letter. They wore beards and long pointed hoods (*cappucci*), sewed to their habits, which, they claimed, were identical to those worn by Francis and his companions: hence the name *cappuccini*, Capuchins. They were officially recognized by the pope in 1527; the Franciscan order was then divided into three branches: Conventuals, Observants, and Capuchins.[31]

Pope Paul III's grandson, Cardinal Alexander Farnese, financed the construction of the Gesù, one of the largest and most sumptuous churches of sixteenth-century Rome. The dominant theme of the programme of decoration is mission and martyrdom in imitation of Christ. The central apse is devoted to Jesus' circumcision, the first occasion, for the Jesuits, on which Christ had to give his blood for humanity. Elsewhere in the church (as in many other Jesuit churches of the sixteenth century) the theme of martyrdom dominates, as a reminder to the new missionary order of its duty to preach the Gospel to infidels and to Protestant heretics. In this the Jesuits echo the thirteenth-century Franciscans, and thus it is not surprising that they devote a chapel in their mother church to the *poverello*, all the more so since their founder Ignatius will not be canonized until 1622.[32]

When the Jesuits decided to devote a chapel in the Gesù to Francis, they naturally turned to the Capuchins who, more than the other two branches of the friars minor, are their allies and collaborators. It is thus a Capuchin Francis that we see portrayed in the eight paintings in the chapel: barefoot, bearded, wearing the pointed hood. Most of the eight scenes chosen are by now classics of Franciscan iconography; two only are unusual: the pacification of the wolf of Gubbio and the apparition of the saint to a friar. In their portrayal of the other scenes, the artist (or artists) does not follow any of the medieval iconographic models, but gives new versions of the episodes.[33] In the face of Protestant criticisms of the use of images in churches, the Council of Trent had affirmed that they could be a spur to devotion, but had also warned Catholics against the use of immoral or lascivious images. In Rome, Michelangelo was harshly criticized for his penchant for painted nudes. Pope Pius IV (1559–65) had hired painter Daniele da Volterra to 'clothe' Michelangelo's nudes in the Sistine Chapel. Francis hence does not appear naked in the Gesù. In the medieval images, his nudity represented his absolute poverty: it was found in particular in two scenes, his rejection of worldly possessions (he takes off his clothes to give them to his father) and his death (he dies naked, lying on the naked earth). But in the Gesù, he stands before his father in a nightshirt and he wears a loincloth as he dies.

Unlike Jacopini de' Scipioni, the Gesù artist paints one sole image of the encounter (Fig. 23). The sultan, richly dressed, wears a fez and a turban sporting a gleaming ruby; around his neck he wears a golden necklace bearing a crescent. Seated on his high throne, he looks down upon Francis and his companions (there are twelve Franciscans in all) who have their hands tied with ropes, by which grimacing soldiers lead them roughly. The scene takes place, as already noted, in the midst of a military camp: we see lances and tents (many of which are topped with crescents). The sultan is the embodiment of worldly power, surrounded by the symbols of his military might, his riches, and his lust. The golden armrests of his throne are in the form of naked women: the sultan places his hands on their heads. These are the only naked bodies in the paintings, and no doubt in the whole church of Gesù: in Counter-Reformation Rome, this is a potent symbol of Turkish lust. Behind the sultan, in the semi-obscurity of his tent, we see two large chests, which represent the sultan's considerable riches. The interior of the tent is dark, like the lair of a dangerous beast; two counsellors stand at the entrance; a hand emerges from the shadows, pointed towards

Fig. 23. Francis before the sultan, Chiesa del Gesù, Rome.

Francis. The symbols of the sultan's violence and his power over men are omnipresent: the arms (the lances and a gilded scimitar held by a man on the right), the soldiers, the turbaned counsellors behind the throne. In the foreground on the right is a dog held back by a black soldier. The dog and the man look at Francis; their bodies, tensed like springs, suggest all the energy and violence that could be unleashed against the friars, energy held at bay by the saint's preaching.

This vision of the encounter is similar to that of Nicolás Francés: cruel soldiers brutally drag the Franciscans before a powerful and pompous sultan. This artist does not use the same symbolic language as Nicolás Francés, who (as we saw) populated his scene with a devil, ugly soldiers with grotesque grimaces, and shields bearing pagan emblems which come from the medieval literary imagination. In the Gesù, on the contrary, realism reigns: we seem to be in an authentic Turkish military camp. The Gesù artist, like Nicolás Francés, tries to instill in his viewer an admiration for the courage of Francis and his brothers, but also the sentiment that his mission is doomed to failure. Even St Francis could not succeed in this world so foreign to his values of humility and poverty. High above the *poverello* on his golden throne with its lascivious armrests, the sultan cannot understand the saint's message. While the Turks in the Gesù painting are not the diabolical, deformed Moors of Nicolás Francés, they represent the love of this world that Francis and his friars have surpassed.

We find another vision of the encounter in a contemporary Roman painting by Niccolò Circignani, better known as 'il Pomerancio', between 1583 and 1585. Circignani no doubt knew the artists who had worked at the Gesù where he himself painted frescos in 1584. He was active in other Roman churches as well; he became something of a specialist in martyrdom scenes rich with gory details. While most of the martyrs he portrayed were those of the primitive church, others were the recent victims of the English Protestants, which could only confirm that the fight against the devil waged by the sixteenth-century church (in particular by the Franciscans and Jesuits) was a continuation of the struggles of the early church.[34] In his fresco showing Francis before the sultan for the Church of San Giovanni dei Fiorentini, Circignani revisits the trial by fire. Francis, bathed in light at the centre of the canvas, walks slowly but surely towards the fire without even looking at it. In his left hand he holds a crucifix; he raises his right arm and points his finger towards heaven as he gazes skywards. The scene takes place not in a military camp, but in the heart of a city, before the sultan's palace. The monarch's throne is in darkness; the sultan hence plays a secondary role in the composition. Indeed, the sultan seems almost lost amidst the crowd of bearded turbaned men, some of whom look at the saint in astonishment or apprehension. In the foreground, four soldiers prepare the fire: one of them points his finger towards heaven, just like Francis. In the sixteenth-century world where Franciscan and Jesuit missionaries braved dangerous encounters with infidels from China to America to Protestant Europe, Circignani presents Francis as a model to follow: he braves the flames in full view of the astonished infidels, his gaze imperturbably heavenwards.

The Encounter in Franciscan Hagiography, Sixteenth–Seventeenth Centuries

In this same context of Franciscan missions to the infidels and in response to the Protestants, but perhaps even more so in the context of the divisions in the Franciscan family, we must place the huge chronicle of Observant friar Mark of Lisbon in 1557. The *Crónicas da Ordem dos Frades Menores* (*Chronicles of the Order of Friars Minor*) enjoyed a considerable readership: translated from Portuguese to Spanish and Italian, then from Italian into French and French into English, the chronicles were published in eighty-four printed editions between 1557 and 1889, forty-three of which were in Italian.[35] In this text, widely diffused in Franciscan circles throughout Europe, Friar Mark relates the history of the order of friars minor, with the accent on its most famous members, from the birth of the order until the sixteenth century. While Mark was an Observant, the Italian translation modified his version of the birth of the Capuchins to present them in a more favourable light. The French translator, Jean Blancone, saw in the *Chronicles* a tool useful for affirming the legitimacy of the Observants against the Récollets, who had separated from the Observance.[36] In this context, the polemics between branches of the Franciscan family often took the form of partisan chronicles of the order: among the many examples, we can cite the chronicles of the Conventual Pietro Ridolfi da Tossigano in 1586 and of the Observant Francesco Gonzaga in 1587.[37]

For his narration of Francis's life, Mark of Lisbon's principal source is Bartholomew of Pisa's *De conformitate*, which he accepts without the slightest reticence, Protestant polemics notwithstanding.[38] In his version of the saint's voyage to Egypt, he closely follows Bartholomew, who (as we have seen) draws mostly on Bonaventure and the *Actus*. But Mark elaborates on the contents of Francis's sermon to the sultan. The saint explains that he has come at God's bidding. Since the sultan and all his people have wandered from the path of natural reason (*razaõ natural*), God wished that Francis teach them the holy law which alone allows salvation. Francis insists that baptism is indispensable to be reborn in Christ and to be freed from the devil:

> Great Soldan, open the eares and eyes of thin understanding: misprise not the Embassadge which thine omnipotent eternall king sendeth thee, permit his grace to enter into thy hart, and by his holy light he will give thee instant knowledge of the greate blindes wherein till this day thou hast lived: and consider attentively how much thou art bound unto his divine majesty, letting thee now understand that he can give thee a kingdome in heaven much greater then this which he hath given thee here on earth.

If you persist in your errors, Francis continues, God will hold you responsible: beware the punishment that awaits you. Far more than his sources (the *Conformities* and the *Actus*), Mark gives a sort of model, relating *in extenso* the sermon that Francis preached to the sultan (a sermon which is longer in the French and English versions than in the original Portuguese). Where early sources portray an inimitable saint, Mark presents Francis as a model for Franciscan missionaries to the infidels. The sultan listens eagerly, but hesitates to convert. Francis then proposes the trial by fire which the sultan refuses, as in Bonaventure's *Legenda major*. Mark, following Bartholomew, affirms that the sultan granted Francis and his friars the right to preach throughout his kingdom; he relates the story of the woman in the inn and the deathbed baptism of the sultan.[39] These conversions show that mission to infidels can be crowned with success; this impression is confirmed by another conversion which follows that of the woman in the inn: following the *Conformities*, Mark relates that a Moor, seeing the poverty of Francis and his companions, offered them alms. When they refused, explaining that for the love of God they refused money, the Moor was so moved he offered to sell all that he had in order to provide them with what they needed. The English translator underlines the anti-Protestant message of the episode: 'The worthy example of their life was so admirable, that they who could not be converted by their doctrine, were converted by meane of their vertuous worckes, which indeed are of much more efficacie: they mollified the most fierce and barbarous nations, mortall enemies of the Christian name, making them compassionate and pitiful.'[40] While Luther affirms that one is saved by faith and not works, the actions of Franciscan missionaries prove the contrary. The voyage to Egypt is not a minor episode in the saint's life; on the contrary, it is the founding act of the Franciscan missions to the infidels, which were flourishing in the second half of the sixteenth century.

Mark comes back to this point in the fourth book of his *Chronicles*, when he narrates the adventures of the martyrs of Marrakech in 1220 and attributes to Francis a vision of militant Christendom confronted by the Moorish peril. Regarding the General Chapter of 1219, Mark declares:

> In this chapter, it was revealed unto S. Francis, that he should againe send his Religious over the world, to preach the faith of Jesus Christ, as well amongst Christians as Pagans. After this, the most capable Religious of the Order were chosen for Provincials, S. Francis applied himselfe to obey the holy will of God. And because the rage of the Mores was spred over three partes of the world, Asia, Africa, and Europe; he resolved to send his Religious into those partes to preach the truth of the faith of Jesus Christ, to reduce the Pagans from their damnable errours: And to make a beginning, he chose Asia for himselfe, whither he went with eleven of his Brethren, and preached to the Soldan and the Mores of his kingdome. He sent Brother Giles into Africa with Religious of like fervour and devotion who thincking to preach to the Mores; were apprehended by Christians and very unwillingly brought back to into Italy. He sent six Italian Religious of very perfect life, into Spaine, where the Emperour Miramolin of Marocco persecuted the Christians.[41]

There is not the slightest mention here of the apostolic life, nor of thirst for martyrdom: Mark's Francis is more concerned about geopolitics, about 'the rage of the Mores' (*a sanha dos Mouros*) which is dangerously spreading through three continents. A veritable general, he splits his troops into three parts, keeping Asia for himself (Egypt is apparently in Asia, for Mark) and assigning Africa and Europe to his faithful missionary friars. Mark is the first author, as far as I know, to affirm that the Moroccan mission of 1220 was part of a coherent missionary movement directed by Francis himself, whose goal was the conversion of 'pagans'. His interpretation corresponds with the considerable missionary activity of the sixteenth-century Franciscans; these missions will continue to multiply in the following centuries, from Canada to the Philippines.[42]

Irish friar Luke Wadding published his *Annales minorum*, a Franciscan chronicle in eight volumes, between 1625 and 1654. While he covers the same territory as his Portuguese predecessor Mark of Lisbon (whom he frequently cites), his approach is different. First, he pays closer attention to the development of the order and is less interested in the biography or hagiography of its key figures. Second, he shows a greater scepticism towards some of his sources; in particular, he avoids citing Bartholomew of Pisa's *Conformities*, which he perhaps thought had been discredited by Protestant attacks. In the preface of his chronicle, Wadding fulminates against the 'crimes' of Erasmus Alber, the blasphemy which he proffered against Francis; he admiringly cites Henri Sedulius who, thanks to his 'genius', had easily refuted the accusations of the heretic Alber.[43] But where Sedulius defended Bartholomew's work, Wadding says nothing. Wadding tries to answer not only the criticisms coming from Protestants, but also those of Catholic rivals, such as the Dominicans.

Wadding's description of the Franciscan missions of 1219–20 provides a good example of his method. Like Mark, he links the Egyptian and Moroccan missions; indeed the link is stronger, since he places his description of the saint's journey to Egypt immediately after his narration of the martyrs of Marrakech. Like Mark, Wadding affirms that, after the General Chapter of 1219, Francis sends friars 'to the kingdom of the Miramolin, so that he himself in the East and they in the West might preach the Gospel for the salvation of the Mohammedan people, and that they might in this way win people for Christ'.[44]

When he describes Francis's mission, Wadding scrupulously cites his sources: Mark of Lisbon, Bonaventure, Jacques de Vitry, and Marino Sanudo, among others. He first follows Bonaventure's version: the crossing to the enemy camp, the preaching to the sultan, the proposition of a trial by fire. He next inserts Jacques de Vitry's description from the *Historia occidentalis*, then adds 'it was thus neither in vain, nor without fruit that Francis sowed the seeds of faith in the sultan's heart. He preached not fruitlessly to him whose soul he softened and modified, for before he was ferocious and inhuman, but immediately afterwards became very benevolent and gentle towards the Christians.'[45] As proof, Wadding, citing Jacques de Vitry and Matthew Paris, recalls the sultan's clemency, generosity, and love of justice, in particular when he signed a truce at the end of the crusade (p. 361). Moreover, he says, we know, based on the authority of Mark of Lisbon, Ugolino, and others (here again he avoids citing Bartholomew of Pisa), that Francis succeeded in converting the sultan in secret. And he again cites Jacques de Vitry, who speaks of a sultan of Iconium who was baptized (whom Wadding confuses with the sultan of Egypt) (p. 362). Wadding seeks to provide a solid base to Franciscan erudition, according to the new norms of seventeenth-century textual criticism. Despite the differences in style and method which distinguish him from Mark of Lisbon, his vision of Franciscan mission is essentially the same: in 1219–20, Francis and his friars establish a missionary strategy which remains the model for the European Christian missionaries of the sixteenth and seventeenth centuries.

The advent of printing allowed the production and diffusion of images of devotion or of propaganda. In response to the caricature of the saint disseminated by Protestants, the Franciscans promoted the traditional image of the saint. In 1594, Andreas de Puttis published in Rome his *S. Francisci historia cum iconibus in aere excusis ad Illm. et Rm. D. Dominum Constantium S.R.E. Presb. Cardin. Sarnanum.* It is a book of forty-nine engravings by Francesco Villamena, portraying the saint's life and miracles. Each engraving takes up a full page (11 × 7.5 cm), accompanied by a brief caption (in two lines) in Latin with an Italian translation.[46] The book enjoyed a wide distribution: it was republished in Rome in 1608, then again in 1649—this time, with a caption in Castilian added to the Latin and Italian one. The cardinal named in the dedication of the 1594 edition is Costanzo Boccafuoco da Sarnano, a partisan of the Friars Minor Conventual, and indeed it is the conventual habit that Francis and his friars wear on the engravings.

The forty-nine illustrations give a traditional image of Francis. They are inspired principally by the *Legenda maior*, the *Actus*, and Bartholomew of Pisa. Francesco Villamena perhaps also drew inspiration from the frescos that Dono Doni painted *c.*1564 in the cloister of the convent of Assisi.[47] The depiction of the trial by fire resembles many of those we looked at in the previous chapter: Francis advances towards the fire which he points to with a sweep of his hand; with the other hand, he points heavenward. The sultan, enthroned under a tent, leans towards the saint. Around him, two turbaned clerics raise their hands in astonishment and glance worriedly towards the sultan. Behind, we see armed soldiers. Francis boldly confronts the fire before the dumbfounded Turks.

But it is the image of the sultan's conversion *in extremis* (Fig. 24) that proves the success of the saint's preaching. In the background the saint, emerging from the clouds, appears to two kneeling friars. In the foreground is the sultan's bedchamber. The dying sultan joins his hands in prayer while the two friars pour the baptismal waters over his head. Shorn of his turban and of all other sign of his worldly power, the sultan no longer looks oriental, but instead resembles the friars who baptize him, and who are distinguished from him only by their habit and their tonsure. These images,

FRATRIBVS APPARENS FRANC⁹ TALIA FATVS
SOLDANI ITE SACRO SPARGITE FONTE CAPVT
STANDO S·FRANC.º INITALIA APPARSE ADVA FRATI NEL
EGITTO AMONENDOGLI CHE ANDASSERO A BATTEZZARE
IL SOLDANO CHE STAVA P MORIRE

Fig. 24. Andreas de Puttis, *San Francisci historia* (1594), pl. 16: 'Francis appeared
to two friars in Egypt, ordering them to go baptize the sultan who was dying.'

destined to be widely diffused, show that the optimistic and heroic vision
of Franciscan mission is still possible at the end of the sixteenth century.

Other images circulated in new printed editions of Bonaventure's *Legenda
maior*. Engraver Martin van den Enden gives a polemical slant to the
encounter, taking up in a single engraving (Fig. 25) a number of traditional

Seldani munera sprrrat, paratus igné subire pro asserené fid.

Fig. 25. Martin van den Enden, the trial by fire.

stereotypes of the Saracen infidel. The sultan, enthroned, wears a turban topped with a crown; he holds his left hand out towards the fire and Francis. The saint does not walk through the fire, but he holds a crucifix in the flames: neither the crucifix nor his hand are burnt. Around him are the mocking, ugly faces of the infidels. One offers the saint an open box which Francis, his eyes fixed on the fire, does not acknowledge. On the left, a bald and nearly naked man with a deformed head presents an amphora overflowing with treasure. But the most striking element is no doubt the statue of Jupiter, thunderbolt in hand, perched on a pedestal behind the sultan's throne. The engraving illustrates the artist's incomprehension and disdain of the barbarous world of the Turks.

Jacques Corbin published in 1634, with the privilege of King Louis XIII and with the approbation of the professors of theology of the University of Paris, an epic poem in twelve cantos entitled *La Saincte Franciade*.[48] Against 'those who hold that fables are the only proper subject of heroic poems' (p. ii) he proposes an epic Francis. We will not tarry over his presentation of the life of the *poverello*, essentially drawn from Mark of Lisbon's *Chronicle*. His version of the saint's voyage to Egypt holds no surprises: Francis arrives in the crusader camp, predicts the terrible defeat of 29 August 1219, meets the sultan, preaches the Gospel truth to him, and proposes the trial by fire. The sultan, impressed, does not dare convert to Christianity, fearing the consequences. The saint consoles him:

> The saint obtained from God that he not be punished;
> And he will not die without being washed with baptismal waters.
> The sultan takes consolation and permits him
> To preach in all the places washed by the Nile
> May his voice spread forth and be fertile,
> Be enriched by a harvest acquired by his speaking
> In all the territory where his empire extends.
> And as a mark of grace he liberates all the Christians
> Captive in his kingdom, without having to pay
> The price of their ransom, and for an honest price
> He furnishes them victuals for man and beast.
> Thirty thousand captives are liberated by the saint.

(p. 126)

Corbin then relates, in detail, the story of 'a lady who, compelling him with a lewd flame, said that she wanted to lie with him' (p. 127). Corbin claims that this happened twice to the saint: first in Egypt and later in Sicily, at the court of Frederick II. Francis cooled the ardor of these lascivious women by lying in the burning coals of the fireplace. In this presentation of the saint as an epic hero, there is no place for failure. Francis and his friars are 'all burning for martyrdom' (p. 124), but nothing suggests that the fact that they do not obtain this goal represents failure. On the contrary, the saint succeeds in converting the Egyptians, including their sultan, and obtains freedom for 30,000 prisoners. It is only much later, in the presence of the seraph, just before receiving the stigmata, that Francis again invokes his desire for martyrdom:

> He [Francis] says: O, my Lord, I gave all my efforts,
> Crossed over the seas, to suffer martyrdom,
> But your grace always denied it to me.
> I am still ready to attack Mahomet
> To obtain the cross that your voice promises me.
> Then he said to Leo: Leave me alone, my brother,
> To speak with God of our common affair.
> Perhaps God wishes that you and I go
> To Egypt or to Fez, and there we will suffer.

(pp. 298–9)

Francis still hopes for martyrdom at the hands of the infidels, but Christ has something else in store for him: 'The arrow is drawn and near are the shots' announces the seraph, who then inflicts the five wounds on Francis. Corbin makes the active search for martyrdom an essential element of Francis's sanctity: as with Bonaventure, it is only at the stigmatization that his thirst for martyrdom is quenched—in a unique way which proves his singular sanctity.

Barbarians Too Humane? Bossuet's Version of the Encounter

The search for martyrdom is the key to Francis's mission for Jacques Bénigne Bossuet, the best-known Catholic preacher of Louis XIV's France, in his *Panégyrique de St. François d'Assise* (1652). The reign of the Sun King witnessed the slow but implacable erosion of the religious freedom that Henry IV had granted to French Protestants through the Edict of Nantes in 1598; Louis XIV would eventually revoke the edict in 1685. Bossuet never encouraged this impingement on Protestants' rights, but nor did he ever criticize it. He was no stranger to conflict with Protestants; he had several bitter debates with the Protestants of Metz, where he was archdeacon from 1652 to 1659.[49] Nothing indicates that he had read Protestant pamphlets such as the *Alcoran of the Franciscans*, but it may well be that his defence of Francis is inspired, at least in part, by the Protestant attacks on the saint.

Bossuet preached his *Panégyrique de St. François* in Metz on 4 October 1652, the saint's feast day.[50] He presents the saint as the epitome of divine folly in face of the wisdom of the world. Jews, gentiles, and heretics have rejected the Saviour, he says. The Jews, who awaited a Messiah crowned with royal dignity, did not deign to recognize him in Jesus, a man living in poor simplicity. The gentiles, impressed by their own erudition, had only disdain for this man who lived miserably and died ignominiously. The heretics sought to praise Christ by denying that he suffered the shameful trials which are attributed to him, from his birth in a stable to his death on the cross. But Bossuet holds that it is precisely this folly in the eyes of the world which marks the true Christian. Those of this world esteem three values above all: material riches, human wisdom, and worldly fame. Christ's message rejects all three, overturning the wisdom of this world. None of the saints prove it better than Francis.

Bossuet presents to his flock a Francis *alter Christus*, even if he avoids using the term: he is no doubt aware of the Protestant accusations that the Catholics adore Francis instead of Christ. Francis overturned the wisdom of this world by pursuing poverty (this is the first of the three points of the panegyric), by searching out physical suffering even unto death (second point), and by rejecting the honours of this world when he refused to be ordained priest (third point). In conclusion, the orator insists on the difficulty for the rich to enter heaven and on the grace that they can merit by giving their riches to the poor, who are so to speak the Lord's accountants.

It is during his exposition of the second point, Francis's mortification of the flesh, that Bossuet discusses his mission to the 'barbarians'. Not content simply to live in exemplary poverty, Francis throws himself naked onto the snow, wears a hair shirt, wears himself down with vigils and fasting. In what seems folly to us, wise men of this world, the saint delights in his supplications: 'after all, "what greater delight for a Christian than to despise delights?"', the orator exclaims, quoting Tertullian.[51] The panegyrist then addresses the 'hard but indubitable truths': 'it is you who have made inimitable Francis, the happy madman; it is you who have enflamed him with a violent desire for martyrdom, who make him search everywhere an infidel who thirsts for his blood'.[52] Just as the love that Christ holds for us inspired him with a burning desire to shed his blood for our redemption, Bossuet continues, for true Christians, inflamed with love for their Lord, nothing is sweeter or more desirable than to shed their blood for him, in order to be able to join him in eternity. Here again, what seems folly in the eyes of the world is supreme wisdom. It is indeed this fervent desire which drives Francis to seek out martyrdom:

> I cannot, then, wonder that St Francis longed so passionately for martyrdom, he who always had before his eyes his Saviour nailed to the Cross, and who drew continually from those Adorable Wounds that heavenly water of the love of God which springs up into the life eternal. Intoxicated with this Divine drink, he seeks martyrdom with the eager, unreasoning impetuosity of a madman; neither rivers, nor mountains, nor the wide expanse of seas can stop him. He passes into Asia, into Africa, into whatever place he thinks likely to be most hostile to the name of Jesus. He preaches openly to those people the glories of the Gospel; he unmasks the impostures of their false prophet, Muhammad. Strange to say, these vehement invectives do not stir up the anger and indignation of the infidels against Francis! On the contrary, they admire his indefatigable zeal, his unconquerable resolution and steadfastness, his measureless contempt for the things of this world; they pay him all sorts of honours. Francis, indignant at finding himself treated with respect by the enemies of his Master, redoubles the vehemence of his attacks upon their monstrous religion; but, marvelous though it seems, they show him no less deference; and this brave athlete of Jesus Christ, seeing that he may not merit a martyr's death at their hands, says to his companion: 'Come away from here; let us quit this place where the inhabitants, barbarous though they may be, are too humane for us, since we cannot compel them either to adore our Master or to persecute us who are His servants. O God! when shall we merit the triumph of martyrdom, if even among the most blinded and hardened infidels we meet with such honourable treatment? Since God does not consider us worthy of such a grace, or of sharing the glory of His shame, let us go, dear brother, to end our lives in the martyrdom of penance; or let us seek some spot on earth where we may drink to the very dregs the ignominy of the Cross.'[53]

Bossuet is no doubt familiar with Bonaventure's *Legenda maior* and per-haps with other texts we have examined, such as the *Actus*. But he follows none of these texts in describing Francis's search for martyrdom. He is not of course writing a biography of the saint, but he seeks to present the quest for martyrdom as the highest degree of love. Bossuet does not mention the crusade: it does not interest him. He feels no need to evoke the geographical or chronological details of Francis's three attempts: it suffices to say that his ardour propelled him over moun-tains, rivers, and seas, unto Asia and Africa. The sultan disappears totally from the story: Francis preaches to 'barbarians' who hate Jesus' name; he expounds the Gospel and attacks 'the impostures of their false prophet, Muhammad'.

Bossuet denounces Muhammad in the same terms in other texts. In his *Panegyric of Saint Peter Nolasco* (1665), founder of the Mercedarians, an order devoted to the redemption of captives, the orator laments the cruel destiny of captives 'in the prisons of the Mohammadans', bemoans 'the great and terrifying progress of this monstrous religion'. Satan, he affirms, pushed Muhammad to call himself a prophet. 'And this monstrous religion, which contradicts itself, exists only through its ignorance; it persuades through its violence and its tyranny; its only miracles are its arms, redoubtable and victorious, which make the world tremble and which establish by force the empire of Satan in all the Universe.' Until when, he asks Jesus, will you permit your enemy to sit on the throne of Constantine and to 'maintain with such arms the blasphemies of Muhammad'?[54] Yet against this redoubtable might, the Christians have a weapon of astonishing power: charity. During a voyage of Peter Nolasco to the court of a 'Moorish king of Andalusia', a relative of the king, astrologer and physician, was shaken by the saint's example, when he saw how he had devoted his life to the redemption of captives. Suddenly, this 'Mohammedan' professed his faith in Christ and wished to be baptized and enter into the Mercedarian order.[55] Against the power and violence of the 'Mohammedans', the panegyrist opposes Christian charity. Not that he discourages the use of military force: in his funeral oration for Queen Marie-Thérèse (1683), Bossuet praises the royal grandeur of the queen's spouse. Among other accomplishments, Louis XIV had rebuilt the French navy, covered the sea with his victorious ships which, he predicts, will soon capture Algiers 'rich in Christendom's booty', already shelled by Duquesne.[56] In his *Discours sur l'histoire universelle*, written for the Dauphin in the 1670s (and reworked until 1704), Bossuet caricatures Islam once again: it is a heresy founded by a false prophet.[57]

In his later writings we again find the stereotypical image of the 'Mohammedan', bitter enemy of Christendom, who opposes Christian 'reason' with violence. From Constantinople and Algiers, he makes ignorance rule through the force of arms. But this is not the image that we find in the *Panegyric of St. Francis*, where, on the contrary, the saint cannot find violent men ready to spill his blood for the Lord. Even when he insults Muhammad and attacks the tenets of Islam, he is unable to provoke their hatred. The defect of these 'barbarians' is not their violence, but on the contrary the fact that they are 'too humane'. In what does this weakness consist? The 'enemies of Christ' refuse to recognize Jesus as Saviour, but at the same time show great deference towards Francis, whose ascesis they admire and to whose sermons they gladly listen.

These 'too humane' barbarians perhaps reflect the orator's audience, who claim to admire Francis but refuse to follow his example. Indeed, these barbarians resemble the Jews, gentiles, and heretics that Bossuet censures at the beginning of his panegyric: too much enamoured of the riches, pleasures, and glory of this world to accept the message of poverty, mortification, and humility proposed first by Christ, then by Francis. In his conclusion, as we have seen, Bossuet addresses his audience directly, reproaching them for their love of the riches of this world, a love incompatible with the love of Christ. These wealthy men and women, who claim to be Christians, profess (like the 'barbarians' to whom Francis preached) an admiration for the *poverello*'s poverty and sanctity. But neither Bossuet's listeners nor Francis's follow in the saint's footsteps: they are, alas, 'too human'.

The seventeenth century witnesses the gradual pacification of the major conflicts that had plagued Europe: the peace of Westphalia installs a *modus vivendi* between Protestants and Catholic states, even if (as we have seen) sources of conflict and recrimination, such as the revocation of the Edict of Nantes in 1685, remain numerous. In central Europe, the failed Ottoman siege of Vienna in 1683 marks the beginning of the decline of Ottoman power in Europe; as a result, the 'Turk' inspires considerably less fear. But in the eighteenth century the Franciscans face a new menace: the scepticism of the Enlightenment.

12

Saint and Sultan Seen by
Philosophes and Traditionalists

Eighteenth Century

The Enlightenment *philosophes* vehemently criticized the role played by the religious orders in European societies. For them, the religious 'fanatics', led by the Franciscans and Jesuits, were a dead weight on intellectual life and in particular on university teaching; they drained the financial resources of the state; they encouraged Europe's youth to lead a life of leisure and chastity instead of working and founding families. The suppression of the Jesuits in many European kingdoms (including France in 1764) gave hope that Franciscans and the other monastic orders would disappear in turn, that they would be relegated to the dustbin of history. These *philosophes* wrote polemics about the history of these orders, painting their lives of their founders in dark colours: Francis was one of their favourite targets. Their tracts provoked strong reactions from Catholic authors, Franciscans and others, who staunchly defended the *poverello*'s sanctity.

It is not always easy to distinguish the criticisms of the *philosophes* from those of the Protestants: all the more so since Protestant authors continued to attack Francis and the friars minor in works which were carefully read by the *philosophes*. In 1701, Jean-Baptiste Renoult published, in Amsterdam, *The adventures of the Madonna and of Francis of Assisi, gathered from diverse works of the Roman Doctors, written in a recreational style yet at the same time capable of showing the ridiculousness of Papism beyond any doubt.*[1] The author, a former Franciscan converted to Calvinism and established in London, presents himself as a Protestant pastor persecuted along with the many other exiles after the revocation of the Edict of Nantes in 1685. He affirms that his goal is to inspire in his Protestant readers 'a righteous aversion to papism, so that nothing will be able to shake their faith'. The fables that the 'papists' tell are much worse than those found in the 'Alcoran of Mahomet', says the author who claims to have read the latter (pp. 117–18). Renoult, a much better storyteller than Erasmus Alber, instead of attacking the *Conformities* mockingly narrates Francis's biography. When, for example, Francis receives the divine order to restore the church, Renoult ironizes: the church, which today claims to be infallible, at the time needed repair. The polemicist sardonically relates how Francis strips naked 'without shame or confusion', before his father and his fellow citizens. He takes a particular pleasure in relating the legend of the Francis's snow woman:

> Sometimes one imagines that the frock quenches the flames of lust; but this is in fact far from the truth. The great saint Francis himself would have been consumed a thousand times by these flames if he had not invented a novel remedy for the temptations of the flesh. ... By a very clever trick, he fell in love with mistresses whose complexion is indeed the fairest in the world, but who nevertheless tempted no one before him. At least we read that the friars accepted this. This lover, rushing out of his cell all aflame, dives in a pile of snow; from this snow he makes women, some are his wives, others his sisters, his daughters, his servants. He lay with all of them and loved them unstintingly. This act pleased the Holy Mother Church so much that, though it has proclaimed rigorous laws against the marriage of priests and monks, nevertheless, in consideration for saint Francis, has never prohibited and will never prohibit them from sleeping with snow women.   (pp. 94–5)

This passage illustrates Renoult's tone: while he follows in the footsteps of Protestant polemicists like Erasmus Alber, his ironic humour resembles that of the eighteenth-century free-thinkers. Renoult does not speak of Francis's mission to the sultan.

The Protestant polemics against Francis and the Franciscans continue in the eighteenth century.[2] The French version of the *Alcoran des cordeliers* is republished in Amsterdam in 1734,[3] along with engravings of key moments in the saint's life. One of these scenes shows the woman in the inn: Francis lies naked in a fireplace, in the midst of a roaring fire, his habit lies strewn on the floor; an astonished woman stares at him. Nothing here suggests the Orient: on the contrary, the scene takes place in a room with a window and a fireplace that look northern European; the woman also looks European, in her face and in her clothing. As we saw with the illustrations of Protestant tracts of the sixteenth and seventeenth centuries, only the fact that these images are printed in polemical works indicates that they are meant to inspire derision and not devotion.

Between the Protestant polemicists against Francis and his stalwart Catholic defenders, there are a few more balanced assessments. Pierre Bayle, in the article that he devotes to Francis in his *Dictionnaire historique et critique* (1697), rejects many of the accusations that the *Alcoran des cordeliers* proffered against Francis: for example, that he received the stigmata during a fight with Dominic, who pierced him repeatedly with a skewer. But Bayle affirms that the Franciscans, in defending the *Conformities* which contain so many absurdities, have only succeeded in 'inspiring in the Protestants this thought, that the monks, willing to abandon nothing, still believe today in the highest excess of superstition born in the centuries of ignorance'.[4]

For other authors, Francis becomes a favourite object of derision, no doubt for several reasons. First, he was the founder of orders which continued to play an important role in European society, in particular French society. Second, he inspired tremendous popular devotion, far beyond that of other founding saints of orders (such as Dominic or Ignatius Loyola). Finally, his unique life was easy to caricature. For Johann Jakob Zimmermann (1695–1756), Francis was 'stupid and inept', an illiterate and ignorant man haunted by absurd visions, who spoke with animals, 'spreading old wives' tales without the slightest shadow of reason falling on his spirit'.[5] He reproaches him for having turned a multitude of monks from the cult of the Lord in order to worship him as a saint. Other authors, in the same way, present Francis as the antithesis of the *Aufklärung*: uncouth, illiterate, superstitious, or, better yet, crazy. For Ludwig Timotheus von Spittler (1752–1810), Francis is an enthusiast (*Schwärmer*) who must have 'fallen on his head' (*im Kopfe gefehlt*).[6]

The French *philosophes* were equally acerbic towards the Franciscans. The *Encyclopédie* mockingly notes that the 'hood was once the occasion for a war among the Franciscans' and presents this dispute as worse than 'Scotism': one more example of churchmen's penchant for arguing bitterly over superfluous matters rather than taking care of their flocks.[7] For the *Encyclopédie d'Yverdon*, edited by the ex-Franciscan Fortuné Barthélémy de Félice, the order's successes prove the 'force of fanaticism'. The friars live under the banner of mendicancy, synonym of laziness:

This order today is so well established in Europe and in Spanish America today that we find more than 150 thousand combatants under the banner of Saint Francis of Assisi: so many arms taken from agriculture and the arts! So many layabouts on the dole for working citizens! So many celibates to the detriment of those who obey the laws of nature![8]

Rebellious against the laws of nature which require man to work for his bread and to procreate to assure the survival of humanity, the Franciscans are a dead weight on society.

Sacro Monte di Orta, Lago di Orta (Orta San Giulio, Piedmont): 1750–1756

In the face of these attacks, Catholic authors and artists defended Francis and the Friars Minor. Around 1750, a chapel dedicated to the encounter between Francis and the sultan was built on the Sacro Monte di Orta on the shores of the Lago di Orta in Piedmont. In a veritable rococo diorama stand life-size statues representing the principal figures: in the midst of a crowd of armed, turbaned soldiers, Francis preaches to the sultan and proposes to confront the flames, while dumbfounded Muslims contemplate the scene. On the walls of the chapel, frescos depict Saracen soldiers capturing Francis and Illuminatus, the fall of Damietta, Francis predicting the crusaders' imminent defeat, angels expressing their joy at the saint's mission, and Christ preaching in the temple. This chapel is today the fourteenth in a series of twenty chapels on the Sacro Monte di Orta, but it was chronologically the last one constructed. The pilgrim climbs the hill and contemplates scenes from the life of the saint, from his birth in a stable (in the first chapel) to his canonization by Gregory IX (in the twentieth).[9]

This is one of many *sacri monti* in Italy. The first *sacro monte* was built at the initiative of Bernardino Caimi, Observant friar, who was *custos* of the holy sites in Jerusalem in 1477. When he returned to Italy in 1478, he conceived the plan of reconstructing Mount Zion in Italy, of creating an opportunity for Christians to make the pilgrimage to the Holy City, as it were, without leaving Italy, avoiding the expense and dangers of the voyage and not paying tribute to the Mamluks. There had previously been numerous churches in Europe which claimed to be replicas of the Holy Sepulchre and which welcomed pilgrims. In the fifteenth century, the Franciscans promoted the establishment of stations of the cross, corresponding to the stages of Christ's crucifixion. But Bernardino's project was more ambitious: he wanted to build a series of forty-three chapels on Mount Varallo in Piedmont, where the pilgrim could relive the principal events in Christ's life, culminating with an exact copy of his sepulchre. The first chapels were built under Bernardino's supervision, the others after his death, until the seventeenth century. Other *sacri monti*, dedicated to Christ or the Virgin, followed Varallo, forming what one author described as a chain of fortresses at the foot of the Alps to protect Italy against the 'Protestant pestilence'.[10]

In 1583, the commune of Orta decided to build a *sacro monte* devoted to Francis's life. This was the first *sacro monte* devoted to a saint, just as the Franciscan altarpieces of the thirteenth century were the first to depict the life of a saint (an honour previously reserved for Christ). *Alter Christus*, Francis becomes the object of a kind of veneration previously reserved to Jesus and his mother. The establishment of the iconographical programme was entrusted to the Capuchins. Nineteen of the twenty chapels were built between 1597 and 1660; the final chapel built, as we have seen, was devoted to the preaching to the sultan.

Orta offers a baroque staging, in three dimensions, of the life of the *poverello*. Each of the twenty chapels illustrates an episode from his life. Let us take the example of the first chapel, devoted to his birth in a stable. On the floor of the chapel are statues: the midwife holding the infant Francis, the wet-nurse offering him her breast, the new mother, exhausted, in the arms of a servant woman, while another woman offers her a cup. The frescos on the walls portray other women looking on. Other frescos show scenes from the life of the young Francis, before his conversion. In another fresco, Joachim of Fiore predicts the coming of two reformers of the church, Francis and Dominic. This chapel presents Francis's birth as a sort of remake of Christ's, an idea absent from the *Legenda maior* but present in other iconographic cycles beginning in the fifteenth century (for example, as we have seen, in the frescos by Benozzo Gozzoli in Montefalco). The pilgrim thus realizes, from the beginning of his ascent of the hill, that the saint is the image of Christ. The other chapels are built on the same model: a scene in three dimensions, with life-size polychrome statues, and scenes from the life of Francis painted on the walls. A number of chapels also have frescos depicting scenes from Christ's life, prototypes of episodes in Francis's life, to underline the parallels between the two.

Orta's iconographical programme is Capuchin. We see this in the pointed hoods that Francis and his friars wear: it is clearly that of the Capuchins, which provides the order with its name. We also see it in the choice of scenes: while most of them are well established in Franciscan iconography, some of them are unusual. In the fourth scene, for example, Francis, inspired by the Gospel, renounces all his possessions and puts on his Franciscan habit; this scene echoes the Bardi altarpiece, but was rarely represented in the convents of Conventuals or Observant friars. The subject of the tenth chapel is totally new: Francis resists the attacks of demons and the temptations of this world (women and riches) by throwing himself in a briar patch in order to mortify his flesh: this is a Franciscan adaptation of a motif that we find in the lives of the early hermits, such as Anthony or Benedict. On the walls are painted the trials that the devil inflicted on Job and Christ. All this underlines the extreme abnegation that is the Franciscan life. One could say the same for the thirteenth chapel, representing the penitence that the saint inflicted on himself for having eaten chicken (a scene which we encountered on the Bardi altarpiece): a friar leads Francis, in his underpants, hands tied, to a column in a square in Assisi, where he will be punished. Just in case the pilgrim does not see the parallel, a fresco shows Christ being led naked before Pontius Pilate.

The twelfth chapel most clearly shows Capuchin apologetics: it depicts the confirmation of the Franciscan Rule by Christ himself. Three friars come to see Francis to ask him to water down the Rule, which for them is too harsh: Christ appears in person to confirm that he himself is the author of the Rule and to castigate the friars for their laxity. This scene is taken from Angelo Clareno's *Chronicle or History of the Seven Tribulations of the Order of Brothers Minor.*[11] The Capuchins embrace the spiritual friar's polemical vision and present themselves as the true heirs of Francis, the only ones who respect the Rule which Jesus revealed to Francis. A fresco depicts the revolt of the Jews during their exile in the desert, an analogy also borrowed from Angelo, for whom the Franciscans rejected the Rule just as the idolatrous Jews rejected the law that God revealed to Moses.

Almost a century separates the completion of the penultimate chapel from the construction of the chapel devoted to the preaching to the sultan. Why this hiatus? No doubt the Capuchins of the sixteenth and seventeenth centuries did not consider it one of the most important episodes in the saint's life. It is difficult to know why, in the middle of the eighteenth century, the friars deem it worthy of commemoration. The wars between the Ottomans and the European powers (in particular Austria and Russia) may have played a role, but the war against the Turks had been a much more present menace in Italy in the sixteenth century. In any case, the chapel was built around 1750. The Milanese sculptor Carlo Beretta made the wooden polychrome statues in 1756: fifty-two persons witness the trial by fire. In the same year, Milanese painter Federico Ferrari painted the frescos.

Fig. 26. The friars disembark, with an American Indian in the foreground. Federico Ferrari, fresco from chapel XIV, Sacro Monte d'Orta.

On the walls, the frescos depict the arrival of the friars in the crusader camp: they are captured and beaten by the soldiers, then dragged by their rope belts before the sultan; Ferrari, like Nicolás Francés or Jacopino de' Scipioni, places the accent on the violence of the Muslim soldiers. In the foreground of the landing scene (Fig. 26), Ferrari paints an American Indian, to show that the voyage to Damietta is the founding act of the Franciscan missions which will take the order, in the eighteenth century, to the shores of the Pacific in California.[12] In the background, we see the crusaders capturing Damietta. Above the city, angels contemplate, with satisfaction, the missionary work of the saint. In a medallion, Jesus preaches in the temple, to underline the analogy between Francis's mission to Egypt and this episode in Christ's life: just as Jesus preaches to the Jews, Francis goes to the sultan's court to preach the Gospel.

Fig. 27. Before the sultan, chapel XIV, Sacro Monte d'Orta.

On the floor of the chapel stand Carlo Baretta's fifty-two sculptures. In the centre of the scene, against the wall of the chapel, sits the enthroned sultan (Fig. 27). Before him is the trial by fire: Francis prepares to confront the flames as he pushes away a dish filled with gold pieces offered by one of the sultan's servants. On the right, one of the infidel priests, dressed in a long white robe and wearing a yellow hat, turns and walks away, a huge book under his arm. Other Muslims, clerics and soldiers, look on: some seem indifferent, others astonished: one falls to his knees. Francis is accompanied by other friars; one holds a book in his hand which he offers to his Muslim adversaries.

Baretta's and Ferrari's message is quite traditional. They insist on the Muslims' violence, their refusal to confront the flames or respond to the book that the friar offers them: a refusal embodied in the priests who turn away and walk off. Yet all hope is not lost: the sultan contemplates the scene and seems open to the friars' message; some of the soldiers are also well-disposed, especially those who fall on their knees. Franciscan mission is arduous but not useless; success is possible, even if it is a long process. The Indian that Baretta paints on the chapel wall announces both the longevity and the universality of Franciscan mission.

Voltaire and Francis

It was also in 1756, the year that Carlo Beretta and Federico Ferrari depicted the confrontation between Francis and the sultan, that Voltaire published his *Essai sur les mœurs*, in which we find a very different rendering of the encounter. For the *philosophe*, the meeting of Francis and the sultan highlights the gulf between the fanaticism that characterizes medieval Europe and the justice and tolerance of the dynasty of Saladin. Voltaire denounces the religious orders and the nefarious consequences of their propagation: by belonging to these orders, thousands of men and women become foreigners in their own countries, subjects of the pope. While these contemplatives, instead of leading a productive life, live on the dole of their compatriots, the countryside lacks inhabitants and the colonies lack settlers. He reviews the different monastic orders and lambasts their founders:

> It seems difficult to allow reason to judge the children of Loyola without giving its advice on that extravagant Francis of Assisi and that energumen Dominic and that insolent Norbert, and all those instructors of the papal militia, all at the expense of the citizens and always dangerous for governments.[13]

Voltaire disdains the *poverello* because he represents for him a model that should not be followed. He warns his readers not to venerate poverty and ascesis:

> Above all, avoid establishing a cult for scoundrels who have no merits other than those of ignorance, enthusiasm and filth; who have taken on the duty and the glory of laziness and begging: do those who were useless during their lives deserve apotheosis after their deaths?[14]

Voltaire takes up the criticism of Franciscans that he found in the *Alcoran des cordeliers*. He presents Bartholomew of Pisa's *Conformities* (written, as we have seen, at the end of the fourteenth century) as a work contemporary with Francis: he ridicules the legends of the wolf of Gubbio and the snow woman. But what most irks him is the success of the order: 5,000 friars already in 1219, he says, and then laments:

> Today, even though the Protestants have taken away a prodigious number of their convents, they still have seven thousand male convents under different names and more than nine hundred women's convents. In their most recent chapters there were 115 000 men and roughly 29 000 women: this is an intolerable error in a country where the human species is visibly lacking.[15]

It is understandable that Francis provoked such admiration and so many followers in thirteenth-century Europe, when the power and riches of the clergy provoked widespread revulsion. But Francis represents the opposite extreme, fanaticism: he is 'a demented fanatic who walks around naked, who talks to animals, who catechizes a wolf, who makes a wife of snow'.[16] Voltaire, indeed, never misses a chance to make fun of the snow woman.[17]

It is in his sweeping historical narrative, the *Essai sur les mœurs et l'esprit des nations*, that Voltaire discusses Francis's preaching to the sultan, whom he calls 'Mélédin'. Voltaire has great disdain for the crusades and the crusaders, the embodiment of the worst of the vices, fanaticism.

> We Christians, we must admit, have too often imitated the barbarous anathemas recommended by the Jews: from this fanaticism sprang the crusades which depopulated Europe to sacrifice Turks and Arabs to Jesus Christ in Syria; this fanaticism gave birth to the crusades against our innocent brothers called *heretics*; this fanaticism stained with blood produced the infernal day of Saint Bartholomew.[18]

The crusade, bitter fruit of fanaticism, inspires only disgust and spite in Voltaire, as we clearly see in the narration tinged with disdain and irony that he provides of the crusades in the *Essai sur les mœurs*. The character who comes out best is no doubt Saladin, whom he presents as all that the fanatical crusading leaders were not: 'he never persecuted anyone for his religion: he was at the same time conqueror, humane, and a philosopher.'[19] In his will, Saladin gave alms to poor Jews, Christians, and Muslims, 'wishing to make known by this disposition that all men are brothers, and that to help them one must enquire about not what they believe, but what they suffer.

Few of our Christian princes displayed such magnificence, and few of the chroniclers with which Europe is overloaded knew how to do him justice.'[20]

It is in a similar positive light that Voltaire presents Saladin's nephew, al-Kâmil, or rather 'Mélédin', who 'was reputed for loving law, science and leisure rather than war'. Having related how the crusaders debarked in Egypt and lay siege to Damietta, Voltaire continues:

> Saint Francis of Assisi, who was then establishing his order, himself arrived in the camp of the besiegers. Having imagined that he could easily convert the Sultan Mélédin, he advanced with his companion, friar Illuminatus, towards the Egyptian camp. They were seized and brought to the sultan. Francis preached to him in Italian. He proposed to Mélédin to light a great fire in which his imams on one side and Francis and Illuminatus on the other would throw themselves to see which was the true religion. Mélédin, to whom an interpreter explained this singular proposition, responded with a laugh that his priests were not the kind of men who would cast themselves in a fire for their faith. Francis then proposed to throw himself alone into the flames. Mélédin told him that if he accepted such a proposition, he would seem to doubt his religion. He then sent Francis off graciously, seeing that he was not a dangerous man.[21]

The sultan Mélédin, known for his goodness and his love of law and science, bravely confronts the fanatical crusaders and vanquishes them. Here he is up against another kind of fanatic, whom he judges not to be dangerous. Everything, in this brief passage, mocks Francis's endeavour: he naïvely imagined that he could easily convert the sultan; he preaches in Italian. The proposition of a trial by fire provokes the sultan's laughter. Confronted by the blind fanaticism of the Christians of Europe, the goodness and sagacity of Mélédin, like that of his uncle Saladin, shine all the more brilliantly.

But Voltaire has not finished; his narration continues:

> Such is the force of enthusiasm that Francis, not having succeeded in throwing himself on a pyre in Egypt to make the sultan Christian, wanted to try this adventure in Morocco. He got on a ship for Spain, but, having fallen ill, he had friar Gilles and four of his companions go off to convert the Moroccans. Friar Gilles and the four friars sailed to Tetuan, arrived in Morrocco, and preached in Italian from a horse-cart. The Miramolin, taking pity with them, had them shipped off to Spain; they came back a second time and were again sent back. They came back a third time: the emperor, exasperated, condemned them to death from his couch, and he himself decapitated them.[22]

Voltaire has confused the chronology, deliberately or not. Thomas of Celano, followed by Bonaventure, as we have seen, placed Francis's aborted trip to Morocco well before the trip to Egypt. Here Voltaire places it after and combines it with the story of the five martyrs of Marrakech (1220). These martyrs, like their master, are the embodiment of fanaticism; the *philosophe* emphasizes their ridiculousness: they preach in a cart, in Italian, which at first only inspires pity in the 'Miramolin' (i.e. the Almohad caliph of Marrakech), who sends them back to Spain. It is only on the third attempt that the friars succeed in exasperating the Miramolin who kills them with his own hand. Voltaire's source, no doubt, is a Franciscan chronicler, probably Luke Wadding or Mark of Lisbon.

Voltaire then adds that 'the death of these five companions of Francis of Assisi is still celebrated annually at Coimbra, in a procession as singular as their adventure'. He explains that the bodies of the friars are buried in this city in Portugal, in Santa Croce church, and that each year, to commemorate the arrival of their relics, the youth of the city make a solemn, night-time procession. 'The boys are only covered by small briefs that only go down to their upper thighs; the women and girls have equally short skirts. The walk is long; they often stop to rest.' What sorts of things happen during the frequent pauses in this nocturnal procession of near-naked youths? Voltaire lets the reader imagine what he will. The fanatical Franciscans and those who venerate them deserve only mockery, for Voltaire.

Trop est trop: Jean Henri Maubert de Gouvest

In the midst of the same context of controversy and polemics concerning the monastic orders, in 1767, Jean Henri Maubert de Gouvest (1721–67) published anonymously, in The Hague, a pamphlet entitled *Trop est trop: Capitulation de la France avec ses moines & religieux de toutes les livrées, avec la revue générale de leurs patriarches*.[23] The author's goal is clearly summarized in the Gospel passage he cites on the title-page: 'Every tree that does not bear good fruit is cut down and thrown into the fire' (Matt. 7: 19). The trees that Maubert wants to cut down are the monastic orders, which have too long taken root in France. The tract is addressed to the 'Lord commissaries' of the royal commission 'established for the examination of the monastic and religious institutions in the kingdom' (p. iii). In the tradition of Voltaire, Maubert affirms that 'the welfare of the state requires that we reduce this multitude of houses where generations will suffocate and bury themselves, that we destroy the nests of these wasps who devour the honey of the industrious bees' (p. v). There is no point in asking the monks to combat corruption and to reform themselves, for the result of such a reform would be the expansion of the monastic orders, which would then weigh even more heavily on society and would take away more men and women from an active and productive life. In the name of progress we must abolish these orders (just as we have abolished other obsolete practices, such as the judicial duel), or at least constrain them. The Jesuits had been abolished in France three years earlier, in 1764: many free-thinkers hoped that the remaining orders would also be banned. For example, Simon-Nicolas-Henri Linguet, whose *Histoire impartiale des Jésuites* (1768), despite its title, seeks above all to show that the remaining orders, in particular the Franciscans, are as dangerous as the Jesuits. In order to do this, he attacks Francis and the *Conformities*.[24]

But it is above all Maubert who forges a polemical biography of the *poverello*. Maubert divides his tract into two parts: in the first, the 'review of the founders', he relates, in high polemic style, the lives of the founders of the principal monastic orders and the history of these orders. In the second part, the 'capitulation' proper, he presents a plan to rationally dispose of the goods of the monastic orders in France. He proposes to close the houses of the canons regular by prohibiting them from accepting novices and by transferring their property and persons to the parochial churches. As for the other orders, Maubert would authorize only four: 'that of St. Benedict, which we could call the Hospital of the Feverish, that of St. Francis of Assisi, which will be the Hospital of Foolish Idiots, that of St. Bernard the Trappist, which will be the Hospital of the Fanatical Lunatics, and that of St. Bruno, which will be the Hospital of the Desperate' (pp. 158–9). The other orders will be disbanded; their members will be allowed to join one of the four authorized orders. The members of these orders will be obliged to lead an active and useful life: the Benedictine monasteries will be transformed into rural infirmaries (and the monks and nuns into nurses and educators); the Trappist and Carthusian convents will become prisons (pp. 238–44). What about the Franciscans? For Maubert they weigh heavily on the public fisc: 'there are roughly thirty thousand of these nurslings of the begging bowl in the kingdom: they represent a surcharge of fifteen million on the taille. Should there be any hesitation to uproot without pity these bad trees that bear no fruit, or that only bear bad fruit?' (p. 233). He proposes to reduce the various mendicant orders to one, the Capuchins, and to require them to follow Francis's Rule or to be held as perjurers. They will be required, in particular, to live on alms alone.

To argue his case, Maubert insists on the leisure, the laziness, and the insanity of the monks, defects which date from the foundation of their orders—this is the point of his first part, where the reader learns 'how the monks of the desert went insane' (p. 12), or that Bernard of Clairvaux 'was a man of boundless ambition ... His ambition was vainglory, he wanted to be a great person, to delve into everything, and to appear a superior man in all things' (p. 31). Robert d'Arbrissel was 'a crazy master' (p. 35). St Bruno, 'his brains overturned by the fear of hell' (p. 37), founded the Carthusians, 'whose hierarchy is sustained by fanaticism and stupidity' (p. 47). Dominic is a fanatic who obtained for his friars preachers 'the monstrous privilege of torturing and burning alive the heretics that they were unable to persuade and convince' (p. 55).

But it is Francis and the Franciscans who most interest Maubert; he devotes forty pages to them, more than a third of his first part. His Francis is a 'venerable madman, whose distinctive quality is his supreme idiocy' (p. 61); 'he was all his life a fanatic, but a fanatic as imbecilic as he wished to appear' (p. 62). Maubert thus sets the tone of his life of Francis, model of anti-hagiography. An unworthy son, Francis rebels against his father who, because of the son's insanity, naturally wanted to keep him at home, away from the mocking crowds. When Francis took off his clothes and 'stood in the middle of the assembly as naked as he was when he emerged from the womb of his mother', the bishop, had he been a sensible man, would have 'immediately sent this insolent son to the house of correction with instructions to give him a good whipping' (p. 70). But the bishop covered him with his coat and only encouraged his folly. Francis then 'continued to dry out his brain through fasting and night prayers' (pp. 72–3). Maubert, contrary to many Protestant polemicists, affirms that 'Francis was not a scoundrel' (p. 71), that he 'was in good faith in the visions that he had and in the foolish things he said' (pp. 72–3). He never had the idea of founding an order or establishing a rule: this was the project of Friar Elias.

Elias plays, for Maubert, as in the long tradition that begins with spiritual Franciscans like Angelo Clareno, the role of scheming and ambitious author of the institutionalization of the friars minor. Elias had no difficulty in joining Francis and his first fanatical companions, nor in obtaining Francis's confidence, nor, subsequently, in convincing him to found an order with a rule. Granted, the Rule was not exactly what Elias would have wanted; Francis managed to mark it with his 'hatred of money and his love of ignorance and filth'. Once the Rule was approved, Elias managed to get himself named general of the order, which he cleverly continued to call Franciscan, taking advantage of the devotion which the friars and the populace showed to the *poverello*. But the order was in fact now Elias's, not Francis's. He needed now only to rid himself of the founding saint to have free reign over the order. And for that he had an idea: send him to Egypt to be killed by the Saracens! This then is the context in which Maubert presents the mission to the sultan:

> He [Elias] is violently suspected of having wanted to get rid of Francis for good, having not dared yet to do so. He is suspected of having put into the imbecile's head the idea of going to convert the sultan of Egypt to the Christian faith. At any rate, Francis made the voyage. Elias did not know that for the Mohammedans the insane are considered worthy of respect and compassion. Francis was admitted into the presence of the sultan, who had the patience to listen to him preach and the generosity to order that he be escorted out of his land, for fear that ill might befall him. The new Apostle returned as he had left, angry that the Mamluks had not done him the favor of impaling him. He interpreted the failure of his expedition as a message from Heaven that he should stay in his province and martyrize himself. (pp. 82–3)

Elias, meanwhile, had gone to Rome to obtain from the pope the right of perjury, to permit the friars to have money even as they swear they will have none. He was still in Rome when he was surprised by Francis's 'unexpected return from Egypt' (p. 84), but this does not faze him for long. Knowing that Francis's reputation for sanctity brings no small benefit to the order, he inflicted the stigmata on him, and subsequently poked the wounds from time to time so that they bled continuously. The saint, unaware of Elias's ruse, thought the wounds were truly miraculous. He retired to Mount Alverno and had hallucinatory visions inspired by his extreme ascesis, while Elias held the reins of the order. He was indeed opposed by a few zealous ascetics: Elias got rid of them by shipping them off to obtain martyrdom from the infidels. Francis, sensing that his end was drawing near, had himself transported to the Portiuncula where 'his love of poverty being stronger than his modesty, he stripped as naked as a hand; and in this simplicity, he heroically awaited death' (p. 91).

The purpose of this polemical presentation is double: Maubert seeks first to ridicule Francis, who produced no true miracles, who did not lead a life worthy of admiration, and who hence is not worthy of veneration. At the same time, he affirms that the order of friars minor was not founded by Francis, but by Elias, a scheming, dishonest, ambitious man. In the chapters following the death of Francis, Maubert presents a brief history of the order, which only confirms that the Franciscans have almost never followed the severe lifestyle of their supposed founder. They had become so dissolute by the fourteenth century that the Observants broke off from the primitive order. But these Observants, or Cordeliers, soon lost their original fervour: the cords which give them their name are now most often made of silk. Only the Capuchins follow, more or less, a respectable ascetic life, for Maubert. We should let them live in strict obedience to the Franciscan Rule, but the state should not subsidize them. The denigration of Francis is an integral part of the attack against the Franciscans' privileges in France.

Constantin Suyskens: Francis in the *Acta Sanctorum* (1768)

In the face of such attacks, Catholic authors, in particular members of the monastic orders, defended the role of these orders in European society and tried to show that the cult of their founding saints rested on solid bases. It was probably in 1768 that Constantin Suyskens (d. 1771), Bollandist and Jesuit, wrote the article on Francis for the fifth volume of the *Acta Sanctorum*, published after his death, in 1780. The Bollandists, Jesuit scholars, had begun in the sixteenth century a monumental project of erudition: the narration and documentation of the saints of the church, based on the in-depth study of all the documents available. The two first volumes of the *Acta Sanctorum* were published in 1643. They were devoted to the saints whose feast days fell in the first days of January. The project was enthusiastically received at the Vatican and in general in Catholic circles; some Protestant scholars also praised the project for its rigour. This enterprise should be understood, in part, as a reaction against Protestants' and free-thinkers' criticisms of the cult of the Catholic saints. In relying on respected authorities and in banning doubtful legends, the Bollandist fathers tried to ground hagiography on the bedrock of textual erudition. But not all were happy about this: when, for example, in 1675, Father Daniel von Papenbroeck rejected the traditional story that the prophet Elias had founded the Carmelites, the Carmelites responded with a salvo of pamphlets denouncing the affront to their order. This concluded in a trial in which Papenbroeck and his writings were found heretical. Caught between Catholics like the Carmelites who looked askance at this assault on their traditions, Protestants hostile to the cult of the saints, and increasing numbers of *philosophes* and free-thinkers, the Bollandists nevertheless continued to publish the *Acta*, until the suppression of the Jesuits stopped the project for over sixty years. The fourth volume for the month of October, in which Suyskens published his article on Francis, was one of the last volumes published before this interruption.

Constantin Suyskens gives a detailed and well-documented narration of Francis's life. He begins by presenting his sources and assessing them, expressing his preference for Thomas of Celano's *Vita prima* and for Bonaventure's *Legenda maior*. He keeps his distance from later texts, particularly those which contain elements that he deems legendary, especially Bartholomew of Pisa's *Conformities*. Even as he lambasts Erasmus Alber and the other 'Lutheran heretics' who had attacked Bartholomew with 'lies and slander', he affirms that the *Conformities* mix the true and the dubious without properly distinguishing between the two.[25] What Suyskens proposes, on the contrary, is to critically sift through his sources in order to establish a 'certain' or 'probable' version of the saint's life. This strategy is clear in his presentation of the 'Voyage of Saint Francis to Syria and to Egypt' (pp. 611–17). He begins by relating, *in extenso*, Thomas of Celano's version. Then he gives Bonaventure's. He qualifies the information given by the two hagiographers as 'sure'. Then he affirms that Wadding had added elements gathered from less reliable sources, in particular from Bartholomew of Pisa. He cites other authors (Marino Sanudo, Jacques de Vitry, the pseudo-Ernoul *Chronicle*) which, for him, confirm or complement Celano and Bonaventure. Then he rejects a number of legends as not worthy of credence. He qualifies as 'false' the idea that the sultan Mélédin let Francis preach throughout his territories and gave him a *signaculum* guaranteeing this right. The 'fabulous' story of the Saracen beauty in the inn is equally rejected, as is the sultan's promise that he would convert ('magis improbabilia', p. 616) and the story that Francis, after his death, sent two friars to baptize the sultan ('Verum ego cogor eadem omnia pro fabulosis habere', p. 616). These are the same opinions that Jesuit scholar Louis Maimbourg had expressed in his *Histoire des Croisades* published in 1675–6.[26]

The result, for the mission to Egypt as for the rest of Francis's life, is that Suyskens confirms the traditional versions of the saint's life (in particular that of Thomas and of Bonaventure), cleansed of more recent legendary accretions, and grounds his judgements on the best practices of modern erudition. But despite all their 'scientific' pretensions, the Bollandists' point of view of course remained Catholic and traditional. It was not likely to convince sceptics and free-thinkers.

Joseph-Romain Joly, *L'Égyptiade* (1786)

Joseph-Romain Joly employs a quite different strategy to defend Francis against the attacks of the *philosophes*: he composes an epic poem in twelve cantos, *L'Égyptiade* (1786), which amplifies and glorifies the saint's exploits in the Orient.[27] At the outset of the poem, Francis decides to go and convert the sultan of Egypt; he embarks in Italy with his companions. While heaven approves of his endeavour, the demons are angry: Belphégor, 'one of the chiefs of the Empire of the dead' (p. 10), leads the ship astray, sends storms against it, but the saint's prayers calm the elements and the ship finally arrives in the port of Alexandria. In Egypt, Francis is present when the crusaders take Damietta. But Belphégor succeeds in rallying the Muslim troops, then in infiltrating the Christian ranks and sowing discord there; the result is the defeat of the crusader army. The papal legate Pelagius flees the battlefield and leaves Egypt, but Francis stays on, determined to meet the sultan. The sultan sees the saint in a dream and then asks one of his prisoners, Pierre de Nemours, bishop of Paris, about Francis. The bishop relates the life and holiness of the *poverello*, from his birth in a stable to the granting of the Portiuncula indulgence: this narration takes up of five of the poem's twelve cantos. Mélédin listens patiently; he seems well-disposed towards Christianity and says that he had read the Gospel. For his part, Pierre de Nemours knows enough about the Qur'ân to affirm that it contains praises of Jesus.

The sultan is thus prepared when, in the eighth canto, Francis arrives at the castle of Tanis. The sultan, 'wise philosopher', contemplates the holy man in admiration; Francis declares that he has come to bring the truth to the sultan to save his soul:

> 'What! You think, he [the sultan] says, that I am in error;
> The law of Muhammad disgusts you!
> He recognizes the God that your sect adores.
> He claims to honor the Christ whom you serve.
> Let us not quibble over difficult details;

There is more than one path to climb to heaven.'
'Prince,' Francis responds, 'your reason leads you astray.'

(pp. 247–8)

The sultan, like the philosophers who denigrate Christianity, is poorly
served by his reason; how can we try to approach divine power, which
created heaven and earth, with our feeble reason? Francis launches a lengthy
lesson of catechism, explaining the history of the relations between God
and man, from Abraham to Christ. He then attacks Muhammad and his
doctrine:

> By what right did Mahomet against Christ's priesthood
> Concoct a plan for a hideous enterprise?
> Who sent him? Whence comes his credibility?
> Look in the holy books: no one predicted him.
> In Jesus' favor a thousand oracles were produced,
> Joining their brilliance to the renown of his miracles.
> Show me one sole action of your chief
> Where Divine aid proved his mission:
> On the contrary, we see that the scandal of his moeurs
> Infects the Qur'ân, even unto its moral teachings.

(pp. 251–2)

This invective provokes the anger of the 'Muslim priests and the grandees
of the kingdom', but has the desired effect on the sultan: the Qur'ân is 'a
horrible amalgam whose hideous recital | Obliges Mélédin to turn away'
(253). The saint's sermon makes the demons sigh in despair. Francis then
proposes the trial by fire, which sends the terrified muftis packing. He then
asks Mélédin to light a fire in the hippodrome which he will traverse in
sight of all; the sultan hesitates and tells Francis that he will give his response
the following day.

The wise monarch has a weak point that the demon Belphégor knows
well: his love for his favourite, the sultana. She accuses her husband of
wishing to become Christian and warns him of an unpleasant consequence
of his conversion: monogamy, which would require him to keep only his
first wife, now old, and to no longer share his bed with the sultana. With this
argument, she convinces the sultan to send Francis away; as a farewell gift,
he frees over one thousand Christian prisoners. The saint, saddened, bids
farewell to the sultan and warns him that he loves too much the pleasures
of this world. During the return trip, Belphégor again attacks the saint's
ship, causing a shipwreck in Crete. Then there is a celestial battle between

Belphégor and the archangel Gabriel, who finally vanquishes the demon and chains him; he announces to Francis that his voyage was not in vain:

> For twenty months he [the sultan] will remain a feeble catechumen,
> Held back by pride or by human fear.
> Finally the dropsy in his side
> Having converted his blood into raw lymph,
> He will receive the living waters from the hands of Quintaval
> Freeing man's captive nature ...
> The tomb of the Lord, which every Christian reveres,
> Which was visited without fear under Calvary
> Until the reign of Omar and since Godfrey
> Will be the mortgage and the price of his faith.
> This prince, before his death, from the sultan of Syria
> For your order will obtain this blessed grotto.
> From the hands of infidels who sully the Holy Places
> Your children will save this precious relic!
>
> (pp. 355–6)

The sultan will convert to Christianity and give the holy places to the Franciscans; the angel adds that Francis will soon receive the singular marks of a sublime martyrdom: the stigmata.

The poet is not unpretentious: in his preface, he bewails the lack of great epic poets in French (a lack which he of course hopes to make up), deplores the rarity of epic poems on Christian themes, as he denigrates the efforts of Camoens, Tasso (who resorted too often to magic in a poem whose theme, the liberation of the Holy Sepulchre, required more *gravitas*), Milton (the story of the fall should have been the object of a tragedy, says Joly, rather than an epic). But his true adversaries are the Protestants and the *philosophes* who attack the church and its saints, whom he will defend with his verse:

> Since several years the monks have fallen considerably in the esteem of a certain public. Have they deserved this discredit? This is a question which I will not answer. It is nonetheless unlucky for my work to appear in an age where all Europe seems rabidly hostile towards religion. What good fortune can I hope for, in bringing to light a founder of an order and a saint so revolting to the eyes of a frivolous world as Francis of Assisi?

He rarely cites the anti-Franciscan works that we have examined, other than a brief mention, in a note, of the *Histoire impartiale des Jésuites*, which had questioned the authenticity of the stigmata (pp. 357–62). He does not express his opinion on whether or not contemporary criticisms of the

Franciscan order were legitimate. But his ambition is clear: to present to his non-'frivolous' Catholic readers a Christian hero, founder of an order which is still present in the Orient (in the holy places, as we will see in the next chapter) and which continues to send its missions to the infidels throughout the world.

Fig. 28. Engraving from the end of the eighteenth century, frontispiece of a German life of Francis.

Joly's Francis triumphs over the dark forces of Belphégor. This image of his preaching before the sultan echoes that of the inimitable orator of Henry of Avranches, a veritable doctor of theology who leaves his Saracen adversaries speechless. An engraving from the end of the eighteenth century also celebrates Francis's courage and his victory over the Muslim clerics. It is a frontispiece from a German life of the saint (Fig. 28).[28] At first glance, it seems a classic depiction of the trial by fire, like those we have seen many times: the turbaned sultan sits enthroned in the middle of the scene: he is surrounded by armed men; Francis, in Capuchin habit, walks boldly towards the fire which burns in the foreground; on the right we see three dumbfounded imams: one of them turns away. But there is a new element here: the black smoke, symbol of blindness, which seems to chase the imams from the scene: even the imam who has his face turned towards Francis cannot see the miracle taking place before him. The sultan, however, sees clearly: he contemplates the saint's radiant face and the brilliant light of the fire. This is an affirmation, at the heart of the *Aufklärung*, that Francis and the Catholic Church are on the side of true enlightenment.

At the dawn of the nineteenth century, the birth of romanticism gives a fresh image of the Middle Ages and of Francis. Where the Enlightenment saw only superstition and violence, the romantics discern spirituality and idealism. A new portrait of the saint emerges, notably in 1826, when Jean-Joseph Görres publishes his *Saint Francis of Assisi, a troubadour*.[29] For Johann August Wilhelm Neander (1789–1850), Francis's visions make him unique; his love of poverty and his compassion for the poor are his and his companions' chief virtues.

Some nineteenth-century Protestants began to see Francis no longer as a henchman of the Antichrist, but rather as a reformer, a precursor of Luther. Friedrich Böhringer (1812–79) compares Francis and Peter Waldo and concludes that the two were similar: they preached poverty, criticized the wealth of the church.[30] Ludwig Flathe makes Francis a Luther *avant la lettre*. He takes up the historiography of the spirituals and concludes that Francis and the spirituals attempted to reform the church: the spirituals' persecution marked the failure of this attempt, but gave them the honour of being Protestant proto-martyrs.[31]

Historian Jules Michelet also compares Francis and Luther: Francis 'cried, as Luther after him: "the law is dead, long live grace!" '.[32] But the comparison stops there: nothing else in the life of the Italian mystic evokes that of the austere German reformer. While Michelet avoids the term 'fanaticism' to describe the lives of Francis and his companions, he presents them under the sign of excess: laughing at Christmas, weeping on Good Friday, giving themselves over to 'frenzied austerities'. For Michelet, there was a theatrical dimension to Franciscan life which was analogous to that of the ancient bacchanals, even if the excesses, of course, are not the same: 'The all-powerful dramatic genius that pushed Saint Francis to imitate Jesus in everything did not limit itself to his birth and his life; it required also his passion. In the final years of his life he was carried around on a cart, through the streets and intersections, bleeding from his side and imitating, through the stigmata, those of the Lord' (p. 362).

Michelet combines the disdain of the Enlightenment with the admiration of the romantics. He only briefly mentions Francis's voyage to Egypt. Having decided that the Franciscan life should be preached everywhere, the saint 'shared out the world with his companions, keeping for himself Egypt where he hoped to obtain martyrdom; but in spite of his efforts, the sultan stubbornly refused and sent him back' (p. 361). This failure is a proof of Francis's excessive and naïve zeal.

But for other nineteenth-century authors, Francis's mission was far from a failure. On the contrary, it established the basis for the Franciscan presence in the Holy Land, in particular at the Holy Sepulchre, a presence which France was ready to defend with its warships, as it showed in the Crimean War.

13

Francis in Jerusalem

Però chi d'esso loco fa parole
    Non dica Ascesi, che direbbe corto
    Ma Oriente, se proprio dir vuole.

Wherefore, who speaks of that place speaks amiss
    Saying *Ascesi* [Assisi]—a falling short that were—
    But *Orient* would truly name what it is.

(Dante, Paradiso, XI. 52–4)

When, in the Crimean War, France, allied with the Ottomans and English, fought Russia, one of the main pretexts was the protection of the rights of the Franciscans to guard the holy places of Jerusalem. For more than five centuries, European monarchs had lobbied and negotiated with the Mamluks, then the Ottomans, to establish and maintain a Franciscan presence in the Holy Land. This presence, along with the good or bad treatment of the friars at the hands of the Muslim rulers, became a pretext either to oppose projects for crusades and wars of conquest (so as not to poison the good relations that the friars entertained with the Muslim sovereigns) or on the contrary to argue for their urgency (to fly to the aid of the persecuted friars).

For various Franciscan authors in the Holy Land, Francis's mission to the Orient was the founding act that legitimized the Franciscan presence at the holy places. The saint is supposed to have visited the Holy Sepulchre, the Cenacle, and the other holy sites; he predicted that his disciples would obtain custodianship (*custodia*) of them; for some, the saint himself obtained them from the sultan. From the sixteenth century, when the privileged role of the Franciscans was threatened by Greek and Western rivals, the friars defend their rights by invoking this now-mythic past. Other European authors, from the nineteenth century, celebrated the heroic renunciation

of the friars and the persecutions that they suffered at the hands of the
Ottomans and called for new crusades to take back the Holy Land. For
some of them, Francis's voyage to the Orient was a civilizing mission to
the barbarians, precursor of the colonial movement of the nineteenth and
twentieth centuries.

The Franciscans in Mamluk Jerusalem: 1333–1517

In 1333, al-Nâsir Muhammad, Mamluk sultan of Egypt, granted the
Franciscans a presence in the Church of the Holy Sepulchre, two chapels on
the Mount of Olives, and a part of the Church of the Nativity in Bethlehem.
The possession and control of these sites was not complete: other Christians,
subjects of the sultan—Georgians, Copts, Melkites, and others—claimed
similar privileges. European pilgrims in the early fourteenth century speak
of Georgian clerics present in the holy places.[1] Other European orders—in
particular the Dominicans—tried to obtain rights as well. On 21 November
1342, Pope Clement VI, in his bull *Gratias agimus*, confirms the Franciscan
privileges in the Holy Land. They are the fruit of long negotiations
between the Mamluk sultans of Egypt and Christian princes. James II, King
of Aragon (1291–1327) had obtained similar rights for the Dominicans
in 1323, then for the Franciscans in 1327: after the king's death in 1327,
these concessions were never realized. It was the king of Naples, Robert
of Anjou, who obtained new privileges for the friars minor in 1333.

This 1333 concession was a major achievement for the Franciscans, but
it must have seemed a precarious one. It depended on the goodwill of the
Sultan al-Nâsir (and subsequently of his successors), who could withdraw
it as easily as he had granted it. Any new crusade, in particular, could
change the situation. One of the principal motives for the sultan, no doubt,
was to establish good relations with the Angevin kingdom of Naples,
whose traditional ally, French King Philip VI, was considering a crusade
against Egypt.[2] Before obtaining the Angevins' aid in these negotiations, the
Franciscans, like the Dominicans before them, had sought the intervention
of James II of Aragon. These two rival dynasties, Aragonese and Angevin,
had been fighting for dominance in the Mediterranean since the 'Sicilian
Vespers' of 1282.

Robert d'Anjou was born in 1277, the same year that his grandfather
Charles I of Anjou, king of Sicily and brother of Louis IX of France, bought

the title of king of Jerusalem from Mary of Antioch, great grand-daughter of King Amaury I of Jerusalem and claimant to the throne. In 1288, at the age of 12, Robert was sent as a hostage to the king of Aragon along with his brothers Louis and Raymond, in exchange for the liberation of their father, the new King Charles II, who had been the prisoner of the Aragonese king for four years. The three brothers stayed in Catalonia until 1295: Aragonese King Alfonso III entrusted their education to Franciscan friars. Hence the interest in the friars minor shown by Robert and especially by his older brother Louis, who wished to become Franciscan and who apparently corresponded with Peter John Olivi.[3] His father Charles II at first opposed these plans, in particular since Charles's eldest son, Charles Martel, died in 1295, and Louis became his heir. In 1296 Louis renounced his inheritance in favour of his brother Robert; the same year he entered the friars minor and was named bishop of Toulouse. But the new bishop died the following year, in 1297, at the age of 23.[4]

On the death of Charles II in 1309, Robert of Anjou became king of Naples and of Jerusalem. Robert and his wife Sancia showed a keen interest in the friars minor. Sancia entertained the idea of abandoning her husband to enter into a convent of Poor Clares; when she spoke to the pope of her desire, he reminded her of her duties as queen and wife (she became Franciscan in 1344, a year after her husband's death). The royal couple presided over the General Chapter of the order, held in their capital of Naples, in 1316.[5] The following year, John XXII announced the canonization of Louis of Toulouse. Robert had wished for his brother to be declared a saint, in part to reinforce the idea that the Angevin dynasty enjoyed a *beata stirps*, sacred lineage: Robert now had an uncle (St Louis of France) and a brother among the saints. This was all the more useful as his rule was contested by rivals: the Aragonese in Sicily and his nephew Carobert (king of Hungary and son of his deceased brother, Charles Martel). We see this concern for legitimation in the altarpiece that Simone Martini painted soon after Louis's canonization: the saint, seated, places a crown on the head of his brother, kneeling on the right of the image. The message is clear: during his life, Louis renounced his royal title in favour of his brother; his canonization confers a divine sanction on this investiture. Simone takes up a *topos*, that of a king crowned by Jesus or a saint, and gives it a historical reference. Louis is wearing the Franciscan habit underneath his episcopal robes; he carries the crosier, ring, and mitre which show his status of bishop. Two angels place a crown on his head, symbol of his sanctity and superior to the crown that he confers upon his brother.[6]

Robert was not the only one to try to benefit from Louis's canonization: the friars minor did the same. In the year of his canonization, in 1317, as we have seen, John XXII attacked the spirituals and imprisoned several of them (including Angelo Clareno).[7] The division in the order was now flagrant and the two factions did their best to posthumously recruit the new saint to their cause. The spirituals insisted on the humility and love of poverty that animated the saint as well as on his connection (in fact, rather tenuous) with their hero Peter John Olivi. The conventuals for their part were delighted to add a new name to the growing pantheon of Franciscan saints: chapels, frescos, and altarpieces in his honour are found in many Franciscan churches.[8] But Louis had in fact been neither a 'conventual' nor a 'spiritual'; he died twenty years before the rupture between the two factions. His canonization reaffirmed the strong links between the Franciscans and the royal couple of Naples who both ended up donning the Franciscan habit: Robert in January 1343, just eighteen days before his death, which allows him to be represented in Franciscan habit on his funerary monument in Naples;[9] and Sancia, as we have seen, entered a Franciscan convent after her husband's death.

Some historians have been too quick to follow the apologists of the spirituals and to make Louis a spiritual *avant la lettre*. Others have in the same way depicted Robert as friend and protector of the spirituals. But as Samantha Kelly has shown, Robert never took up their defence. He had close links with Pope John XXII who had been his chancellor before being elected (with Robert's help) to the papacy; from 1319 to 1324, while the pope persecuted the spirituals, Robert held court in Avignon. It is true that the relations between the two men chilled and that John briefly allied himself with Robert's enemy, Louis of Bavaria. Queen Sancia, from 1329, welcomed spirituals who continued to affirm the evangelical poverty rejected by the pope in his bulls *Ad conditorem canonum* (1322) and *Cum inter nonnullos* (1323). Between 1331 and 1333, the tensions mounted: the minister general came to Naples to organize a trial against Franciscans close to Sancia, and the pope sent a letter to the queen, whom he reproached for spreading 'the contagious virus' of heresy. But between 1333 and 1334, calm returned: the Franciscans were acquitted by an ecclesiastical court and the pope spoke of absolving the *fraticelli* in the kingdom of Naples who had returned to obedience. This conflict may reflect more the political tension between the pope and Robert than the heretical predilections of his queen.[10] But it is clear that the queen sympathized with the Franciscan dissidents. Angelo Clareno had written seven letters to Sancia's brother Philip, who subsequently founded a spiritual convent in Naples under the tutelage of the queen.[11]

It was in this context of tension that Friar Roger Guérin convinced Sancia and Robert to negotiate with al-Nâsir Muhammad.[12] Protector of the Franciscans, king of Jerusalem, who better than Robert could intervene with the sultan? If the royal couple found the timing propitious, it is no doubt because the obtaining of the holy places for the Franciscans would be advantageous in their confrontation with the pope. Frederick II, excommunicated by Gregory IX, had obtained Jerusalem from al-Kâmil; now Robert, in conflict with the Pope, would obtain a place for the friars minor in the Holy Land. Al-Nâsir Muhammad was well disposed for these negotiations; he had sent, in 1331, a message to Pope John XXII and to King Philip VI of France, via the pontifical legate Pierre de La Palu, patriarch of Jerusalem, declaring his 'will to concede wider exemptions to merchants, full liberty of cult to priests, to Christians, and to the pilgrims who come to the places of the Holy Land, and even the possession of the Holy Places, under the condition that the pope abolishes all prohibitions of commerce between Europe and Egypt'. Concerning the restitution of the Holy Land, the sultan had affirmed that 'neither prayers nor threats would ever compel him to grant to the Christians an inch of land'.[13] Robert, king of Jerusalem, had indeed been asked to lead a new crusade to recover his holy heritage. One of the most fervent partisans of crusade, Marino Sanudo, came to find him in Naples around 1330; Robert received him politely but promised nothing. Too prudent to embark on such an adventure, Robert preferred to negotiate rights to the holy places.[14] The negotiations were long and complex, in particular because the sultan had to balance the privileges of the Franciscans with those already granted to the different Eastern churches. He granted to the Franciscans full possession of the Cenacle (the sanctuary at the site of the Last Supper) and important rights in three other places: the Basilica of the Nativity in Bethlehem, the tomb of the Virgin Mary, and the Holy Sepulchre. The Franciscans shared these last three sites with clergy from the Oriental churches; the keys were entrusted to Mamluk officers. The Franciscans also obtained the right to repair and restore these buildings, though in practice this was difficult, for in general they had to obtain the agreement of the other Christian communities and the local authorities.

Various authors testify to the presence of Franciscans in the Holy Land in the years following the Mamluk concession. A document in Arabic, dated 21 Ramadan 735 (15 May 1335), mentions the purchase, by a Frankish Christian named Marguerite, accompanied by a brother Roger (no doubt Roger Guérin) and other friars, of land on Mount Zion worth 1,000 silver dirhams. Other purchases followed and the friars took possession of the ruined Cenacle and built a convent there.[15] Pilgrims' accounts confirm the presence of the friars. Ludolf von Sudheim made a pilgrimage from 1336 to 1341. He relates his visit to the Church of St Mary on Mount Zion and adds:

> Now the Friars Minor stay in this monastery. In my day they received from the queen Sancia, wife of King Robert, what was necessary for their sustenance. There they celebrate the divine office devoutly and openly, except that they may not preach publicly to the Saracens nor bury their dead without the permission of the authorities of the city. In my day, the friars were very valiant men. The pilgrims, merchants and even the Saracens praised them, for they did good works for everyone.[16]

Franciscan friar Niccolò da Poggibonsi, in his *Libro d'Oltramare*, describes his pilgrimage to the Holy Land from 1346 to 1350. Poggibonsi counted twenty altars in the Church of the Holy Sepulchre in Jerusalem: the principal altar is held by the Greeks, he says, while the other communities have their altars: the Armenians, the Jacobites, the 'Indians', the Ethiopians, the Nubians, the Georgians, the Nestorians. The Franciscans have the altar of St Mary Magdalene. This catalogue confirms that the friars minor indeed benefited from their privileges in Christendom's holiest church, but they were only one group among many, and that their privileges depended on the goodwill of the sovereign and the relations between the Holy City's various Christian communities.[17] Poggibonsi also visited his Franciscan brothers in their church on Mount Zion; he was in Jerusalem when the friars took possession of the 'Church of Bethlehem' granted to them by 'Medephar, sultan of Babylon'.[18] When he subsequently passed through Damietta, he recalled that St Louis had taken the city in 1248, but says nothing about the fifth crusade or about the encounter between Francis and al-Kâmil.[19]

Various testimonies, including that of Ludolf von Sudheim, show the importance of the financial donations of Sancia and Robert for the reconstruction and maintenance of the Cenacle and for the material needs of the Franciscans in the Holy Land. The friars took the precaution of having their privileges confirmed by successive Mamluk sultans: Queen Joanna I, grand-daughter and successor of Robert and Sancia, wrote to the new sultan Sha'ban II in 1363 to ask him to confirm the Franciscan privileges. In the preceding year, 1362, Pope Urban V had granted the Franciscans money to repair their convent at the Cenacle and to found a new one in the valley of Jehoshaphat.[20] Queen Isabel of Castile became queen of Sicily in 1479 when her husband, Ferdinand, inherited the kingdoms of Aragon and Sicily. In 1489, she promised to give an annual donation of a thousand golden ducats from the Sicilian treasury to the friars minor in the Holy Land, for the upkeep of their convent; her husband Ferdinand apparently also promised a thousand ducats. Various sources from the sixteenth and seventeenth century show that the Sicilian monarchs continued to make this annual donation.[21] Other European princes also gave to the Franciscans in the Holy Land: in 1486, an anonymous pilgrim stayed in a house in Jerusalem that Philip the Good, Duke of Burgundy (1419–67), had built for the pilgrims on Mount Zion; the duke also donated funds for the pilgrims' meals.[22]

It is in this context that, starting in the fourteenth century, some authors affirm that Francis himself obtained privileges in the Holy Land from the sultan. Angelo of Clareno, writing around 1326, affirms, as we have seen, that the sultan 'ordered that Francis and his companions be allowed to go freely to the Holy Sepulchre, without paying any tribute'. He relates that Francis himself visited Christ's tomb before returning to Italy.[23] Angelo, a century after the saint's death, is the first person to claim that he had made a pilgrimage to Jerusalem. At the very moment when Franciscans and Dominicans were trying to obtain access to the Holy Sepulchre, Angelo claimed not only that the founding saint of his order had been there, but that the sultan had granted him specific rights; not the possession of the holy places, but at least the right to visit them freely.

Ugolino da Montegiorgio, in his *Actus Beati Francisci et sociorum eius* (more or less contemporary with the negotiations between Mamluks and Angevins), says that the sultan 'freely granted to [Francis] and his companions the right to preach wherever they wished. And he gave them a sign, thanks to which no one could bother them.'[24] Ugolino's reference to a sign (*signaculum*) from the sultan, probably means a safe-conduct or laissez-passer. He says nothing, however, about Francis's possible presence in the holy places.

It is also in the 1330s that we first read of unusual relics which supposedly testify to Francis's preaching to the Muslims. These consist of an ivory horn adorned with silver and two wooden sticks attached with chains. These objects are now in the treasury of the basilica of Assisi. On the silver rings along the edges of the horn is an inscription that reads: 'with this bell [sic] Saint Francis convoked the people to his preaching and with these sticks, in beating them one against the others, he imposed silence upon them. John Nicholuti de Senis made me.'[25] In 1338, a catalogue of the relics of the basilica of St Francis at Assisi mentions these objects and transcribes the inscription; we find a similar notice in the second inventory, dated 1385. While these inventories and the inscription associate the objects with Francis, they contain no mention of either his preaching in the Orient, nor of the sultan. The ivory horn clearly comes from the East and the sticks are reminiscent of simanders, wooden percussion instruments used in various Eastern churches to call the faithful to prayer, whether they indeed belonged to Francis or were brought back by Franciscans in the fourteenth century.

In the legend underneath the fresco of the trial by fire by Jacopini de' Scipioni in Bergamo (1506) we read that 'Francis accepted from him [the sultan] a horn and two sticks as a security.'[26] The sultan himself is supposed to have given them to Francis. This is what the Franciscan scholar Luke Wadding affirms in the seventeenth century.[27] These objects are concrete proofs of the respect and friendship that the sultan showed to Francis and of the permission he gave the saint to preach in his territories.

Various authors of the fourteenth century follow the *Actus* and affirm that Francis succeeded in converting the sultan and that he gave a *signaculum* guaranteeing free access to the holy places and the right to preach: Bartholemew of Pisa, for example, in his *Opus de conformitate vitae beati Francisci ad vitam Domini Iesu Christi* (1385).[28] Around 1480, Friar Mariano da Firenze, in his *Libro delle vite de Sancti Frati Minori*, mixes the versions of Jacques de Vitry, Bonaventure, and the *Actus*, affirming that the sultan had given permission to the saint to preach everywhere in his lands.[29] But no one claimed that al-Kâmil gave the holy places to Francis.

During the Mamluk period (until 1517) the Franciscans maintained their prerogatives in the Holy Land. Numerous narratives by European travellers and pilgrims confirm this; the friars kept a hospice for pilgrims.[30] One could cite, for example, Bertrandon de la Broquière, a Burgundian spy who travelled to the Holy Land in 1432–3, who mentions Franciscans present in Beirut, in the Church of the Nativity in Bethlehem, at Jehoshaphat, at the Holy Sepulchre, and especially at the Mount Zion convent just outside the Holy City.[31] We could multiply the testimonies of pilgrims who stayed with the Franciscans in the Holy Land: Englishwoman Margery Kemp in 1414, or German Hans Tucher in 1479.[32] No other order succeeded in establishing itself permanently in the Holy Land; the Dominicans' attempts were in vain.[33] Even the excessive zeal of some of the friars did not endanger the order's privileges: in 1391, four friars minor from the convent of the Cenacle went onto the Haram al-Sharif and preached, in Arabic and Italian (according to their hagiographers) against Muhammad and the Qur'ân. They sought out the qâdî of Jerusalem and invited him to accept baptism, which earned them the death sentence. But the following year, the Franciscans tried to obtain new privileges from the Mamluks in the valley of Jehoshaphat.[34] The Franciscans acted as hosts and tourist guides for European pilgrims: we can cite the testimony of Louis de Rochechouart, bishop of Saintes, who explains the role that the friars played during his pilgrimage in 1461: the Franciscans obtain mules for the pilgrims landing in Jaffa; they house them in Ramlah and on Mount Zion; they act as guides for their visits to sites around Jerusalem. We find the same scenario in the narration of an anonymous pilgrim in 1486. Rochechouart, curious, fires questions at the friars and often relates their responses, especially those of a certain 'friar Laurent the Sicilian'. This pilgrim studied in the Franciscan library at Mount Zion, where he read (among other things), Jacques de Vitry's *Historia orientalis*.[35]

Some European knights who arrived at the Holy Sepulchre as humble pilgrims, paying tribute to the Mamluk guards to enter, dreamt of conquering it as crusaders. Nompar de Caumont, a Gascon lord, describes how he was dubbed in the Church of the Holy Sepulchre on 8 July 1419. He listened to a mass in honour of St George, took communion, then received 'the order of knighthood' at the hands of a knight and in the presence of a Franciscan who had celebrated the mass. His sword, placed on the altar of the Holy Sepulchre and blessed by the Franciscan friar, was then given to him by the knight who had first slapped him six times ('five slaps in honour of the five wounds of Our Lord and one in honour of my lord saint George', Caumont explains). Then the new knight pronounced the 'promises which the knights make at the Holy Sepulchre of Our Lord in Jerusalem'. These promises include the respect of fidelity in marriage, the refusal of treason, and the protection of widows, orphans, and the 'Holy church'. What is more, Caumont and the other knights promised 'to aid with all our might the conquest of the Holy Land'.[36] The Holy Sepulchre was also the royal pantheon of the crusader kings of Jerusalem; Nompar and his companions no doubt contemplated their tombs with reverence and nostalgia.[37] While the Mamluks had granted privileges to the Franciscans in part to discourage crusades, some friars did not hesitate to perpetuate these rites, imbued both with the hope of a Christian reconquest of the Holy City and at the same time nostalgia for a heroic epoch long lost.

Franciscans and Ottomans, Sixteenth–Nineteenth Centuries

The Franciscans succeeded in maintaining their presence in Jerusalem and Bethlehem under the Egyptian sultans until 1517, when Ottoman sultan Selim I conquered the Mamluk sultanate and Palestine came under the sway of Istanbul. Henceforth, the Greek Orthodox Church tired to affirm its rights in the Holy Land. For the first time in centuries, there was a Greek patriarch in Jerusalem, Germanos, who tried, without success, to obtain the exclusive custody of the holy places. In 1551, the Franciscans were expelled from the Cenacle; they established a new headquarters in the Convent of the Holy Saviour. In 1605, the French ambassador De Brèves obtained the confirmation of the Franciscans' privileges; Louis XIII sent Louis Deshayes de Courmenin to Constantinople and the Holy Land in 1621; Deshayes subsequently published a *Voiage de Levant*. At the Holy Sepulchre he found Franciscans who, he says, were under the protection of the king of France.[38] The 'Cordeliers' were the representatives of the Latins, one of the eight nations present at the Sepulchre, alongside the Greeks, Abyssinians, 'Kophites' (Copts), Armenians, Nestorians, Georgians, and Maronites (pp. 358–9). Deshayes mentions a Franciscan convent in Bethlehem (pp. 372–3) and complains that the Turks took possession of the Franciscan monastery of the Cenacle and converted it into a mosque prohibited to Christians (p. 369). 'The poor religious who serve [these sanctuaries] are hence sometimes reduced to such extremities, since no help comes from Christendom, that their condition is deplorable' (p. 371).

At the accession of sultan Murat IV (1623–40), the Greek patriarch of Jerusalem, Theophanes (1608–44), succeeded in gaining privileges to the detriment of the Franciscans. Without delving into all the details (the intrigues of the Greeks and the Franciscans, the bribes paid to the sultan, the intervention of the foreign allies on each side), let us simply note that, between 1630 and 1637, various holy places changed hands seven times.[39] For Murat, the conflict among the Christians was a fine opportunity to raise funds for the Ottoman state. In 1740, Louis XV, in his negotiation of new accords with the Sublime Porte, obtained the confirmation of the privileges of the Latin clerics and the promise that they would not be bothered. The Franciscans greeted this French protection with mixed sentiments; at times they were in conflict with the French consul in Jerusalem—especially when he tried to introduce the Jesuits into the Holy Land, endangering the friars' monopoly among European clerics.[40]

Greeks and Franciscans battled on the field of history. The Greeks showed to the Sublime Porte *firmans* or charters to justify their privileges: a first document from the Prophet Muhammad himself, guaranteeing the rights of the Christians who submit to his power; a second charter issued by the Caliph 'Umar when he conquered Jerusalem in 638, granting the eternal possession of the holy places to the Greek patriarch and declaring that all the Christians who went there as pilgrims (Armenians, Nestorians, Copts, Franks, etc.) were subject to the patriarch's authority. Other privileges were signed by the Ummayad Caliph Muawiya I and by Ottoman sultans Mehmet II, Selim I, and Suleyman II. All these documents are forgeries, most of them written in the sixteenth and seventeenth centuries to justify the claims of the church of Constantinople.[41] For the Greek Patriarch Dositheos (d. 1707), his Franciscan adversaries are the 'precursors of the Antichrist'.[42]

In the face of these Greek claims, the Franciscans obviously could not pretend to have received privileges from Muhammad, 'Umar, or Muawiya. They could not go further back than the life of their founding saint. But they knew that Francis had come to the Holy Land and had spoken with the Egyptian sultan. Since they were preoccupied with the control of the holy sites, it seemed natural to them that Francis had the same concerns. Why shouldn't Francis himself have obtained the custody of the holy places from al-Kâmil? After all, the friars minor had a venerable tradition of attributing to their founder the establishment of convents actually founded well after his death.[43] Not all friars were ready to make such an affirmation: Franciscan scholar Francis Quaresmius, who published his monumental *Historica theologica et moralis Terrae Sanctae elucidatio* in 1635, does not claim that Francis received the holy places from the sultan. He simply relates the *poverello*'s pilgrimage to the Holy Land, affirming that his presence prefigured that of his friars who were destined to receive the custody of these sites.[44]

Other Franciscans of the seventeenth and eighteenth centuries declare that Francis himself established the convent of the Cenacle on Mount Zion, thanks to privileges that he obtained directly from the sultan. Mariano Morone da Maleo, *custos* of the Holy Land, published in 1669–70 his *Terra Santa nuovamente illustrata*, a history of the Holy Land from biblical times to his own travels in the region in the middle of the seventeenth century.[45] Morone relates Francis's mission, following Mark of Lisbon's narrative. But he affirms that Francis went twice to the holy places in Jerusalem: first before going to Egypt, then again after his return from the court of the sultan, who had granted him full possession of the Cenacle. Hence Francis founded in person this convent along with others in the region. The chronicles do not mention the saint's presence in Jerusalem. This didn't matter; it is unthinkable that a man of Francis's piety would not make the pilgrimage when he was so close.[46]

Another Franciscan who took up his pen to defend the rights of his order in the Holy City in the face of the 'schismatics' and the 'Saracens' was Juan de Calahorra, in his *Chrónica de la provincia de Syria y tierra santa de Gerusalen*.[47] The good friar relates, in over 750 pages, the history of the Franciscan province from Francis's arrival in 1219 until the year 1632. The second half of the *Chrónica* (the final four of his eight books) narrates the tribulations that the Franciscans had suffered in the Holy Land since the Ottoman conquest of 1517: the scheming of the Greek and Armenian schismatics (and sometimes of non-Franciscan Europeans) who plotted to usurp the privileges of the good friars; the expulsion of the friars from their convent on Mount Zion; the physical persecution and financial exploitation that they endured at the hands of the Ottoman authorities. But the final chapters of the eighth and final book of his *Chrónica* are less pessimistic: the 'Great Turk' orders that the privileges unduly usurped by the Greeks and Armenians be restored to the Franciscans. The author then recalls the rights of the friars and the indulgences accorded to friars and pilgrims. He closes his chronicle by giving the convent's expense account (which includes tributes paid to the Great Turk) in order to insist on the friars' penury; the disciples of the *poverello* need the financial assistance of European Christians.

The heroes of this chronicle, of course, are the valorous friars, always ready to suffer hunger, misery, insults, and injury—unto martyrdom, if necessary—in order to keep the holy places and to serve the pilgrims from Europe. Francis's voyage East is the subject of the first of Calahorra's eight books; it legitimizes the presence of his disciples in the Holy Land. Calahorra opens his *Chrónica* with the fall of Jerusalem to Saladin: the cause of this calamity was the ingratitude and the many sins of the city's Christian inhabitants. Just as God had the pagan Romans destroy the Holy City to punish the unworthy Jews, he later snatched it from the hands of the ungrateful Christians. This catastrophe incites the popes to call for new crusades. Calahorra then relates the crusade from 1217 until 1219: the battles in Syria, the arrival of the troops in Damietta, the conflicts between John of Brienne and Pelagius, the capture of the Chain Tower and the death of al-ʿAdil. At this point, he says, the 'tyrant Coradin', prince of Syria (al-Muʿazzam), decides to destroy the city of Jerusalem to draw the Christian army away from Egypt. He succeeds in knocking down the walls, but when he wants to demolish the Church of the Holy Sepulchre, his own Muslim subjects prevent him: they do not want to sully the tomb of a holy prophet. Calahorra explains to his readers that the Muslims venerate Jesus as a great prophet born from the Holy Virgin, even though they do not accept his divinity.

Calahorra next narrates Francis's voyage. He explains that a 'volcano of love' burnt in the saint's heart, pushing him to seek salvation for all. The Spanish friar follows Luke Wadding and Mark of Lisbon, whom he cites by name. He relates the saint's crossing with eleven companions to Acre, then his trip to Damietta with Illuminatus, his preaching to the crusaders and his prediction of the Christian defeat at the hands of the sultan's troops. Then he tells of how the two friars crossed enemy lines and were led to the sultan. Francis preached to the sultan and his court 'in the Saracen tongue', by divine grace (p. 18). The sultan was touched by his preaching, and his men recognized 'the influence of a superior virtue'. The saint proposed the trial by fire that the sultan refused. The sultan offered presents to the saint and, when Francis refused, granted him the right to preach everywhere in his lands. Next comes the story of the woman in the inn and her conversion. Yet the saint, discouraged by the 'hardness and obstinacy of the Egyptians' (p. 21), decided to go to Jerusalem.

Calahorra describes in detail the *poverello*'s itinerary: he visited the sites associated with the flight into Egypt, went to Gaza, then visited the holy places of Jerusalem, Bethlehem, Nazareth, and Galilee. But his pilgrimage was interrupted by the arrival of a friar from Italy who told him how Brother

Elias had modified the rule to make it less austere. Francis understood that he needed to return to Italy, but first he made his way back to Egypt, where the sultan gave him the ivory horn. Calahorra then relates how the saint promised to send friars to baptize the sultan and how, nine years later, on his deathbed, the sultan indeed received baptism at the hands of two friars. The fact that the sultan was well disposed towards the Christians in 1219 explains why he was so generous with them after the debacle of the crusade in 1221, explains Calahorra; this is thanks to the saint's preaching.

But what most interests Calahorra is Francis's presence in Jerusalem, which cannot be reduced to a simple private pilgrimage. The saint understood that destiny pushed him towards the Holy City. Francis is moved to walk in Jesus' footsteps, but saddened by the catastrophic state of the holy sites: everywhere, churches have been transformed into stables for the horses of the Saracen oppressor. At the moment of Francis's arrival in the Holy City, Calahorra inserts a chapter on a dream that Francis had before his conversion; this dream is related by Thomas of Celano and then Bonaventure and is subsequently well-represented in Franciscan iconography. According to Celano, Francis dreamt that he saw a palace full of weapons; he thought that this meant that he would have a brilliant career as a knight, but, says Celano, he was wrong; in fact this meant that, like a new David, Francis would liberate Israel from the hands of its enemies (1C 5). Bonaventure simply explains that God reserved for the saint a glory far superior to that hoped for by the young Francis (*LM* 6). Calahorra gives a completely different interpretation of this vision; for him, the young Francis thought that the dream meant that he would conquer the Holy Land by armed force. In fact, continues the friar, God revealed to him that the Franciscans would peacefully conquer the holy sites. In this way, God announced to the saint the providential role that the order would play in the protection of the holy sites, and it was only when he arrived in Jerusalem that Francis finally understood his dream. God hence willed that the friars take these places from the sacrilegious hands of the Saracens and that they humbly watch over them. The duty of seventeenth-century Christians was to help (politically, morally, and financially) Francis's successors preserve the holy sites.

Francisco Jesús María de San Juan del Puerto, a Spanish Franciscan missionary in Morocco, also published, in 1724, a chronicle of the Franciscan Holy Land.[48] For del Puerto, as for Calahorra and Morone, the Franciscan custody of the holy sites was God's will: the three authors affirm that God revealed this to Francis through the dream of the palace of weapons.[49] But del Puerto goes further: by renouncing his biological father and by rejecting worldly riches, Francis revealed himself to be the true son of Abraham, the worthy heir of the Promised Land. Joachim of Fiore had predicted in the twelfth century that God would put the Holy Land in the hands of Francis and his sons.

The Spanish friar takes up the classic texts to narrate the saint's travels, citing (among others) Bonaventure, Francis Quaresmius, Juan de Calahorra, and Morone da Maleo. But he gives free reign to his imagination—or rather to his will to associate the saint with all the holy places in Palestine. Page after page, we follow Francis across Palestine: he visits Jaffa, Jerusalem (whose principal sanctuaries del Puerto describes in detail), the Mount of Olives, Bethlehem, all the sanctuaries in Egypt, then (after his return from Egypt), Mount Sinai, the Jordan, Nazareth, Mount Tabor, etc. Francis goes to preach to the sultan, hoping to illuminate the 'infidel men' (*hombres infieles*) 'so blind in their filthy sect' (*tan ciengos en su inmundissima secta*). He relates Francis's and Illuminatus' departure from the crusader camp, the encounter with the Saracen guards who take them to the sultan, then their preaching. According to all the chroniclers, Francis did not speak through an interpreter, says del Puerto, who thinks that Francis received the gift of tongues; it is nevertheless difficult to decide if Francis spoke Arabic by divine grace or if on the contrary he spoke in Italian and everyone understood him as if he spoke in his own language (p. 93). Next is the long sermon in which Francis explains the Trinity, the Creation, the Fall, the Incarnation, the crucifixion, and the sacraments (pp. 93–5). This sermon moves the sultan but leaves him uncertain; Francis proposes the trial by fire which the sultan refuses, but he grants the saint and his disciples the right to preach anywhere in his lands. This preaching inspires the admiration of the Egyptians and a certain number of conversions (including the 'Mora' of the inn). But the principal fruit of this preaching, for del Puerto, is the miraculous transformation of the sultan, who becomes a model of justice, protector of the Christians in his lands, generous even with his defeated enemies, who gives the Holy City of Jerusalem to his friend the emperor Frederick II. Del Puerto follows Morone and attributes the foundation of the Cenacle to Francis himself (pp. 47, 145). He recognizes that there are no documents that prove this and that Father Calahorra himself doubted that Francis would have wished to establish a convent in infidel lands. But for del Puerto, on the contrary, the saint who had sent so many friars to preach in Egypt and the Maghreb must have ardently desired to establish a Franciscan presence in the lands of Islam. He is hence convinced that Francis himself founded the Cenacle convent.

Numerous other authors, Franciscans or not, subsequently affirm that al-Kâmil granted the possession of the holy places to Francis. We have seen that poet Joseph-Romain Joly claimed, in 1786, that the sultan 'Mélédin' had given the custody of the holy places to the Franciscans after the saint's mission to Egypt.[50]

European pilgrims in Jerusalem continued to describe the sad state of the holy sites and of their Franciscan guardians. They asked their readers to show their solidarity with these brothers, either by giving them the financial means necessary to surmount their penury, or by urging their rulers to intervene to protect them from the Turk. François de Chateaubriand, in his *Itinéraire de Paris à Jérusalem* (1811), abundantly and appreciatingly cites Deshayes de Courmenin's *Voiage de Levant*. For Chateaubriand, who visited Jerusalem in 1806 and 1807 and stayed at the Franciscan convent, things had not changed since the seventeenth century: 'We see, then, the unfortunate Fathers, the guardians of the tomb of Christ, solely occupied for several centuries in defending themselves day by day against every species of tyrany and insult.'[51] Chateaubriand had sifted through a trunk containing *firmans*, granted by the Turkish authorities, guaranteeing the friars' privileges. He noted proudly that the French king's ambassador was often mentioned in these documents, which showed that he had played an important role in obtaining these guarantees. The friars do not understand, he says, the value of these documents.[52]

In Jerusalem, Chateaubriand feels nostalgia for the golden days of Godfrey of Bouillon. He lambasts the eighteenth-century writers who 'have taken pains to represent the Crusades in an odious light' (p. 54). For Chateaubriand, on the contrary, the crusaders, despite their shortcomings, were imbued with an admirable idealism that pushed them to abandon wives and children, lands and material riches, to wrest the Sepulchre from the grasp of the Muslims.

> The point in question was not merely the deliverance of that sacred tomb, but likewise to decide which of the two should predominate in the world, a religion hostile to civilization, systematically favourable to ignorance, despotism, and slavery, or a religion which has revived among the moderns the spirit of learned antiquity and abolished servitude. ... The spirit of Islamism

is persecution and conquest; the Gospel, on the contrary, inculcates only toleration and peace. (p. 55)

The recollection of the crusaders and the tribulations of the modern friars are mixed with the hopes of future glory, for Chateaubriand and for his Franciscan hosts. The friars gave the French pilgrim 'an honour which I had neither solicited nor deserved. ... they requested me to accept the Order of the Holy Sepluchre' (p. 156); he was dubbed in a rite similar to that in which Nompar de Caumont took part in 1419. Chateaubriand claims that this order is 'of high antiquity in Christendom', even if it does not date, as some claim, to the age of St Helen. Only the Franciscan guardian of the holy sites has the right to induct new members into the order, by dubbing them, in the Church of the Holy Sepulchre, with Godfrey of Bouillon's sword. The new knight of the order is moved. In his *Mémoires d'outre-tombe*, Chateaubriand often evokes Francis, 'my patron in France and my hotelier at the Holy Sepulchre'.[53] 'My patron also visited the Holy Sepulchre', he affirms.[54]

Other pilgrims contemplate Godfrey of Bouillon's sword and spurs, or are initiated into the order of the Knights of the Holy Sepulchre; the British consul mentions these rites in 1856 and asks ironically if the *effendis* of the adjacent café, calmly smoking their hookahs, could possibly imagine the strange rite that was taking place in the church next to them, one of the Europeans' many bizarre rituals.[55] Some of these travellers, like Chateaubriand, depict the Franciscans in the Holy Land as new martyrs groaning under the weight of Turkish oppression. Abbé Grand publishes in 1837 the account of his travels to the Holy Land; he approvingly cites long passages of Chateaubriand's *Itinéraire*. He says that the Ottoman authorities tax the Christians of Jerusalem at every occasion, making them pay for holding processions, for pilgrims' entry into the city, for the right of repairing their convents: 'The little tyrant of Jerusalem, lodged in Pontius Pilate's palace, still exercises his arbitrary power.' And the good abbot adds: 'all the governments of Europe should make free' the city of Jerusalem.[56]

The conflict between Franciscans and the Greeks was one of the causes of the Crimean War (1854–6)—or at least one of the pretexts from the point of view of two of the belligerents, France and Russia. Napoleon III wanted to reaffirm French influence in the Holy Land, which had been lost since the Revolution (except, briefly, during Napoleon I's Palestine expedition in 1799). By presenting himself as the protector of the Vatican and the friars minor in the Holy Land, the emperor no doubt hoped to win the allegiance of the French church. He knew that this line risked provoking a conflict with Russia, which defended the Orthodox Church. For Napoleon, this was in fact a good way to stir up trouble between the Russians and their new allies, the Catholic Austrians. The diplomatic missives from the Quai d'Orsay were sent not only to the Sublime Porte, but also the Austrians, in order to obtain their allegiance. In 1852, when the Ottomans seemed to be leaning towards Russia and the Orthodox, France sent its new steamship, the *Charlemagne*, to Constantinople. Turkish officers were invited to tour the gunboat. The Sublime Porte understood the message and judged in favour of the Franciscans.[57] Russia declared war against the Ottomans in 1853 and seized Wallachia and Moldavia; the Ottomans, the French, and the English invaded Crimea. At the end of the war, the treaty of Paris (1856) marked the victory of the Ottomans and their allies. For the Franciscans, this meant the confirmation of their privileges in the Holy Land.

In the following year, 1857, Brother Marcellino da Civezza published the first of eleven volumes of his *Universal History of the Franciscan Missions*.[58] He presents the missionary friars not only as luminous witnesses to the truth in the lands of darkness, but also as representatives of reason and civilization among savage barbarians. He paints a portrait of the contemporary Holy Land not unlike those of Chateaubriand and Abbé Grand:

> Whoever now sees Palestine, all of Syria and Egypt—and even, we could say, all Asia and the coasts of Africa, and in general all of that country that from the Mediterranean, to the East and to the South of our hemisphere, it is not possible that he recognize that world which history tells us had once flourished, for long centuries.... The populace is everywhere vulgar, ignorant, less than savage, displaying a disgusting barbarity that has lost all impetus and audaciousness. It is as if these people, who have lost not only their civilization, but even their humanity, were condemned to the most horrible punishment we could imagine: inept and filthy stupidity.[59]

These are sentiments that we often find in nineteenth-century Europe, where the notion of European superiority over the savages of Asia and Africa is used to justify conquest and colonization. Civezza claims that Palestine is 'an extremely desolated country' (pp. 44–5), but that it bears the marks of its ancient glory, which might some day be revived. The current desolation is due to the 'bestial torpor' of its inhabitants: 'If these lands came into the hands of industrious people, they would show their admirable fecundity.'[60] This is a classic argument, found for instance in the writings of John Locke, for whom those who work the land and improve it (for example, European settlers) become the legitimate owners of the land, to the detriment of those who are less 'industrious' (American Indians).[61] Civezza's purpose is not to call for the conquest and colonization of the Holy Land, but we sense that he would not be opposed to the idea: in the following pages he briefly relates the history of the crusades which he presents, in the romantic point of view, as a noble ideal that was not always well respected.

While the crusaders ultimately failed, God granted a major victory to the friars minor during the crusade of 1219–21:

> The Friars minor obtained, thanks to a long peaceful mission of sweat, tribulations and all sorts of sacrifices, preaching Jesus Christ by word and by example, what the princes, the knights and the Christian nations had not been able to obtain through the terrible wars that they had waged so long, with such heroism, against the enemies of Christ's faith. There is no doubt that Francis of Assisi—the saint whose fundamental trait is gentleness and Christian love towards humanity, the saint who set out for Palestine to promote the crusade of peace, suffering and love for the conversion of these barbarous and bestial people and for the protection of the holy places of our redemption—on this occasion more than ever appears crowned with a divine halo that far outshines that of Peter the Hermit.[62]

Francis's glory surpasses that of Peter the Hermit because the saint's 'crusade of peace' was a lasting success, contrary to the expedition initiated by the hermit. In Damietta, Francis undertook a new sort of war, a war that is still ongoing, says Civezza, during which the friars minor shed their blood, showing an example of fortitude and patience against the barbaric fury of the enemy.[63] Civezza praises the fortitude of the sons of Francis who for centuries have, with courage and patience, watched over the holy places that Europe's princes have been unable to defend with their arms. Civezza's version of Francis's meeting with al-Kâmil carries no surprises: he follows well-marked tracks, using primarily Bonaventure, but also Marino Sanudo. He cites at length, with approbation, Bossuet's version according to which (as we have seen) Francis's attacks against the 'imposture of Muhammad' provoke the admiration of his infidel listeners.

What were the fruits of this audacious mission? First, the secret conversion of the sultan. Civezza relates the story from the *Actus*, which he considers trustworthy since no one has proved the contrary ('è fama non contradetta da nessuno', p. 68). As for the story of the woman of the inn and the flaming bed, he recognizes that it is probably a legend, but for him it is yet another testimony of the impression that Francis left among the peoples of the Orient. As for the traditions according to which Francis personally founded Franciscan convents and hospices at Mount Zion, the Holy Sepulchre, Bethlehem, and Nazareth, Civezza says that there is no reason to doubt their truth.[64]

Indeed, these traditions are still widespread. We find them in an article that *La Grande Encyclopédie* devotes to Francis in 1893:

> [The saint] went to Damietta, to the crusader camp, and witnessed their defeat, which he had predicted. Hoping to obtain by miracle that which one could no longer hope for from victory, and taken with a desire for martyrdom, he managed to go see the sultan Meledin. To prove the truth of what he preached, he proposed to enter into a flaming fire. Meledin refused but, touched by his faith, treated him kindly and granted him the custody of the Holy Sepulchre, entrusted ever since to the Franciscans. Having given up hope of converting the infidels or of obtaining martyrdom from them, Francis returned to the Portiuncula.[65]

In the following year, 1894, Alphonse Couret relates a legend which attributes the acquisition of the Cenacle to the saint.[66] Francis and a companion arrived in Jerusalem on a hot summer afternoon and entered the city through a breach in the walls, then went to the Church of the Holy Sepulchre. The Muslim officers who guarded the entrance to the church, woken from their nap, demanded a payment of 18 gold sequins; Francis (described as an old man) explained that he has no money. The guards took him to the Wali whom they wakened from his nap, which contributed to his ill humour. He doubled the tribute, demanding 36 sequins immediately, then threatened to behead them. At this point Francis pulled from his pocket a letter of safe-conduct signed by the sultan, and the Wali, pale and trembling, profusely apologized and offered gifts and money to the two friars. Francis of course refused, but asks for the Church of the Cenacle, in ruins. The Wali gladly granted this request and drew up the papers on the spot, adding the custody of the Holy Sepulchre. Francis himself founded the Franciscan convent in Jerusalem. The defeat of the crusaders was followed by the arrival of 'this phalange of heroic monks who, for five hundred years, in the midst of the silence of an indifferent Europe, preserved the Holy Sepulchre and conserved it for the tearful love of the faithful and the pilgrims' (p. 118). While Couret presents this story as a legend, other authors continue to claim that al-Kâmil himself granted the holy sites to Francis and his brothers. We find this assertion in the twenty-first century, for example from Patrick Ryan, Jesuit and president of Loyola Jesuit College of Abuja, Nigeria.[67]

Franciscan Mission to the Infidels and European Colonialism

We have seen that the discourse of Civezza, Chateaubriand, and Abbé Grand is 'orientalist', in Edward Said's sense of the word: it affirms the superiority of Europeans over the peoples of the Orient in a manner that justifies, implicitly or explicitly, the power of the former over the latter.[68] Such sentiments are frequent in the writings of European authors contemporary with the French and English conquests in the Maghreb and the Middle East in the nineteenth and twentieth centuries. For authors like Civezza, Francis's voyage founded not only the Franciscan presence in Jerusalem, but also a missionary movement that was both evangelical and civilizing to 'barbarians' all over the world. Already in 1634, Jacques Corbin, in his *Saincte Franciade*, affirms that God revealed to Francis the providential role that the Capuchin missionaries would play in Asia, Africa, and America.[69] We have seen how Federico Ferrari, in a fresco at the Sacro Monte di Orta (*c.*1750), put an American Indian in the foreground of Francis's arrival in Egypt.[70] The message is clear: Francis, landing in Egypt, founds the Franciscan mission movement which is destined to bring Christianity to America. Indeed, in the mid-eighteenth century, Franciscan friars founded missions in California. Surprisingly, the Franciscan authors who describe the deeds of these missionaries say nothing about their founding saint's mission to the sultan.

In Jerusalem, the friars were at times bothered by the colonial appetites of the European powers. On 19 May 1799, an Anglo-Turkish coalition succeeded in defending Acre against Napoleon, making the emperor lift the siege and crushing his dreams of the conquest of the Near East. The Franciscan guardian of the holy sites thanked Sir Sidney Smith, captain of the English fleet, in the name of all the Christians of the Holy City that he thus saved from the 'pitiless hands of Bonaparte'.[71]

It is primarily among historians of the crusade that we see an orientalist vision of Francis's encounter with al-Kâmil. In France, in particular, the memory of the crusade is mobilized and manipulated to justify France's colonial enterprises in the Arab world. The criticisms of Voltaire or Diderot are swept aside; the crusades become historical embodiments of the French civilizing mission. The principal architect of this revision was Joseph-François Michaud (1767–1839) who, like his friend Chateaubriand, sought to rehabilitate the crusades in the face of Enlightenment criticism. Michaud was also inducted into the Order of the Holy Sepulchre during a voyage to the Holy Land in 1830–2. He published the seven volumes of his *Histoire des Croisades* between 1812 and 1822 and subsequently reworked them; the fifth edition was published in 1838, one year before his death.[72]

Michaud's vision of the crusades is neither Voltaire's scorn nor Chateaubriand's romantic revalorization. Like the *philosophe*, Michaud bewails the expressions of the crusaders' 'fanaticism', in particular the massacres during the capture of Jerusalem in 1099.[73] But he shares with Chateaubriand the conviction that the crusades were nevertheless a heroic adventure in which the French in particular gained everlasting glory. At the end of the first volume of his *Histoire*, Michaud sums up the positive and negative effects of the crusades on Europe, the Orient, and Byzantium. The overall balance sheet is positive: 'Knowledge, laws, morals, power, all must proceed together. This is what has happened in France; therefore must France one day become the model and centre of civilization in Europe. The holy wars contributed much to this happy revolution, which may be seen even in the first crusade.'[74]

For his narration of the fifth crusade, Michaud uses the French chronicles and some of the Arab chronicles (translated by his collaborators) and, for Francis's mission, Bonaventure. He presents Francis as a holy man and relates with enthusiasm his life of evangelical poverty. For Michaud, Francis was led into Egypt by the fame of the crusade, and by the hope of there effecting some great conversion. Distressed by the defeat of 29 August which he had predicted, 'Dissatisfied with the crusaders, and devoured by the zeal of a mission from God, he then conceived the project of securing the triumph of the faith by his eloquence and the arms of the Gospel alone.' Francis went to the Saracen camp, found the sultan, and delivered his message of salvation. He challenged the 'doctors of the law', proposed 'to confound imposture and prove the truth of the Christian religion, offered to cast himself into the midst of a burning funeral-pile'. The sultan, astonished, sent the saint away; he 'obtained neither of the objects of his wishes, for he did not convert the sultan, nor did he gather the palm of martyrdom'.[75] For Michaud, as for the French chronicles which are his principal sources, this mission demonstrated the saint's courage and piety, but proved to be futile. The sultan's role is minimized; he shows neither admiration nor aversion towards the saint, only surprise. There is no suggestion that the sultan, at the conclusion of this encounter, would be any more open towards Christianity or more clement towards Christians.

Following this description, Michaud presents Franciscan preaching as part of a civilizing mission. He relates that Francis, when he returned to Italy, founded their order of the friars minor, which the historian describes briefly, then adds:

> The disciples of St. Francis sometimes carried the word of God among savage nations; some went into Africa and Asia, seeking, as their master had done, errors to confute and evils to endure; they frequently planted the cross of Christ upon the lands of the infidels, and in their harmless pilgrimages, constantly repeated the scriptural words, *Peace be with you*; they were only armed with their prayers, and aspired to no glory but that of dying for the faith.[76]

While Francis's voyage to Egypt bore no fruit in the Orient, it caused the saint to found a civilizing missionary movement. This new 'crusade' launched by Francis is 'innocent'. This innocence is both admirable and naïve: alas, real military crusades (that were far from innocent) were necessary to make these 'savage people' understand Christian reason. Michaud also insists on the message of peace that the missionary friars bear: they carry only the Gospel and the cross; their only arms are the words of the Gospel and prayers; they are always ready to suffer martyrdom. This is a defence of Franciscan mission in response to the numerous criticisms formulated in the eighteenth and nineteen centuries; they were criticized (they and other missionaries, in particular the Jesuits) for having acquired land and riches, for exploiting natives, for indoctrinating them. Michaud's missionaries are far above all these criticisms. Francis and his friars bring a message of peace, but they preach it not to the crusaders, but to their enemies: the crusade, far from being antithetical to mission, seems to be a prerequisite for it.

The *Histoire des Croisades* enjoyed an enormous popularity in France and throughout Europe: German, English, Spanish, and Italian translations were published in the nineteenth century. The European powers had begun to undertake conquests in Muslim lands that were often presented as new crusades. Michaud was in the entourage of Charles X when he was preparing his expedition against Algiers in 1830; he compared the king to his illustrious predecessor, St Louis. This flattery was perhaps not disinterested: the king granted Michaud and his collaborator, Arabist Jean-Joseph Poujoulat, significant funds to finance a research trip to the Near East. For Charles X, as subsequently for Louis-Philippe (and for men in the entourages of the two kings), the Algerian adventure was indeed a new crusade, through which the monarch revived the glorious tradition of his medieval predecessors. The crusades were an essential element in the historical reconstruction that Louis-Philippe undertook in order to present himself as the legitimate sovereign of the French: the clearest expression of this is the Salle des Croisades at Versailles.[77] Jean-Joseph Poujoulat notes, in the preface to his *Abrégé de l'histoire des croisades, à l'usage de la jeunesse* (*Abbreviated version of the History of the Crusades, for the use of the young,* 1838), that 'the conquest of Algiers in 1830 and our recent campaigns in Africa are nothing other than crusades. If Saint Louis's crusade against Tunis had succeeded, Charles X would not have needed to send his armies into Africa.'[78] The youth who might be sent off to Algeria should know that they were following in the footsteps of St Louis and many other glorious French heroes of yesteryear. 'The narration of the great events of olden times shall serve as lessons of patriotism for our youth' (p. xvii). When Napoleon III addressed the troops ready to set off for Lebanon in 1860, he exhorted them to be 'the worthy children of those heroes who gloriously carried Christ's banner into those countries'.[79]

The *Histoire des croisades* was republished in 1877 in a luxury edition, with 100 engravings by Gustave Doré.[80] Doré presents the crusades as a vast epic, from the preaching of Peter the Hermit who launched the first crusade until the battle of Lepanto. One of these engravings, as we saw in the Introduction, presents Francis preaching to the sultan in a Moorish palace reminiscent of the Alhambra in Granada. Francis, standing, dominates the sultan who looks down and does not seem to listen to the saint. This sultan is no longer the powerful and imposing figure that he was at the end of the sixteenth century (for example, in the Gesù church in Rome) and sometimes still in the eighteenth (Sacro Monte di Orta). While once the powerful sultan, eyes aflame, surrounded by armed soldiers, lorded over a small and weak Francis who stood timidly at the foot of his throne, for Doré Francis stands over a solitary sultan whose position (seated on a comfortable couch) and whose expression suggest passivity rather than violence. His is a romantic and orientalist vision of the encounter of Damietta, which complement's Michaud's text. The reader can appreciate the energy and the audacity of the founding saint of Franciscan mission as he notes the indolence, passivity, and inscrutability of the Oriental monarch. When the Turks were colonizing Europe in the sixteenth and seventeenth century, the enthroned sultan lorded over Francis; now, in the nineteenth and twentieth centuries, various artists, like Doré, show a confident Francis standing over a seated, passive sultan.

If 1830 marked the beginning of the French colonial era in the Maghreb, it was the First World War which opened the Near East to the French and British. In 1917, Edmund Allenby took Jerusalem for the English; during his ceremonial entry into the Holy City, on 11 December, two Franciscans read, in French and Italian, the proclamation of the British government imposing martial law and proclaiming respect for the three religions and their holy places.[81] The privileged role of the friars was confirmed, but in the following decades the Franciscans had to negotiate new pressures from different European nations (especially England, France, and Italy) who sought to affirm their influence in the Holy City.

It is in this context that we must situate one of the most imposing monuments of Franciscan erudition of the twentieth century. Chateaubriand, we have seen, had gone through the Franciscan archives in Jerusalem and affirmed that the friars did not understand the value of the documents which they possessed, which proved the long-standing legitimacy of their possessions in the Holy Land. At the end of the nineteenth and the beginning of the twentieth century, one Franciscan friar in Jerusalem, Girolamo Golubovich, fully appreciated their value; he undertook to publish these documents, along with all sorts of information gathered in European libraries concerning the presence of the Franciscans in the Holy Land. In 1898 he published the first results of his research under the title, *Serie chronologica dei reverendissimi superiori di Terra Santa*.[82] Then, between 1906 and 1939, he published twenty thick volumes of his *Biblioteca bio-bibliografica della terra santa e dell' oriente francescano*, a magisterial and meticulous catalogue of the Franciscan presence in the Orient from 1217 until the beginning of the fifteenth century. This work, indispensable for anyone interested in the subject, has been cited frequently here. The considerable erudition of the polyglot friar is employed for an apologetic purpose: he sought to give the friars in the Holy Land an exhaustive documentation of their history, a history which could then be used to affirm the solid foundation on which their privileges rested. Hence the Ottomans, and then the new British masters of Palestine, would know that the Franciscans, far from being parvenus or European colonizers, had put down roots in the Holy Land centuries before, and that their rights were better documented than those of the 'heterodox' Greeks. Their proper place, in the face of the claims of rival Christians, Oriental and European, could be staunchly defended.

Golubovich rejects the Greek claims which were founded on forged documents, as he shows exhaustively: the diplomas in favour of the Greeks, ostensibly from the chanceries of Muhammad or 'Umar, were forged in the sixteenth century. The Franciscan friar tries to examine the Franciscan legends with the same rigour, rejecting for example the notion that al-Kâmil himself granted the holy places to Francis. But he is wedded to the idea that Francis had visited the holy places, though he admits that only late sources affirm this. The saint's pilgrimage to Jerusalem remained a founding myth of the Franciscan presence in Orient. Even Pope Benedict XV declared, on Francis's feast day in 1918, that the *poverello* had gone to Jerusalem to pray at the Holy Sepulchre.[83]

Fig. 29. Paolo Gaidano, Francis before the sultan, Jerusalem, Holy Saviour Convent.

In 1898, the year that Golubovich published the first part of his massive work, Paolo Gaidano gave visual expression to a similar vision of Franciscan history.[84] This artist from Turin painted a series of ten canvases for the Holy Saviour Convent, the seat of the friars minor in the Holy Land. In the first painting, we see the front of the Portiuncula church; in the background we see Assisi, over which looms the Citadella de la Rocca (little does it matter to the artist that it had been destroyed in 1198). The scene is the 'chapter of the mats' (the meeting of the General Chapter of the order in 1219): Francis raises his hands to bless his brothers as he sends them to evangelize the four corners of the earth. Next are three canvases representing Francis's voyage to the Orient. We first see him boarding a boat at Ancona, bidding farewell to his brothers with a gesture of benediction; a sailor pulls vigorously on the oars of the skiff that takes the saint and his companions to the ship waiting in the background. Next comes the meeting in sultan's tent (Fig. 29). Through the entrance to the tent, we see the faces of curious Arab soldiers, behind them other tents and, in the background, the city of Damietta. Inside the tent, the sultan, dressed in white, a sword belted around his waist, sits on a pouf, a tiger-skin rug at his feet, and looks at the saint. The meeting between the two men echoes that of Gustave Doré: the saint, standing, speaks to a seated sultan who passively looks at him. But for Gaidano the threat of violence is much more immediate: each of the Arabs in the tent has one or two weapons; outside, from the group of soldiers crowded outside the tent, emerge a series of spears. Granted, this is not the formidable, disciplined army that we found in the Chiesa del Gesù, whose sultan was the incarnation of power and owner of immense riches. Gaidano's sultan, collapsed on his pouf, could not make Europe tremble; he seems more of a petty Bedouin chief than a great sultan. But we sense real danger for Francis, whose fate could be the same as that of the tiger at the chief's feet. The saint nevertheless succeeds in being heard out not only by the sultan, but also by other Muslims, as we see in the following painting: he preaches to a group of Muslims, men, women, and children, who listen to him humbly and attentively. Some kneel or lower their gaze in testimony of their humility; they are receptive to the saint's message. The men, sporting fezzes, look much more like the nineteenth-century inhabitants of the Ottoman Empire than those of the Ayyubid sultanate of the thirteenth century. Is this anachronism involuntary (like that of the Rocca) or deliberate? In any case, it underlines the continuity between Francis's preaching mission and that of his friars in the Holy Land in the nineteenth century.

For Gaidano, in the tradition of so many Franciscan authors since the seventeenth century, presents Francis's preaching to the sultan as the founding act of the Franciscan presence in the Orient, a courageous mission to barbarous savages, along the lines of Civezza's portrayal. The other episodes that Gaidano painted for the convent, now the Franciscan headquarters in the Holy Land, confirm this reading. In these paintings, Gaidano portrays the saint's disciples in the Orient, either to show them at the service of its inhabitants (as they give aid to plague victims in Jerusalem) or to underline the central role of Jerusalem in Franciscan mission (we see the fourteenth-century Franciscan missionary Odorico da Pordenone stop to pray at the Holy Sepulchre before setting off on a missionary expedition that will take him to China). Gaidano also commemorates the violent death of friars at the hand of the Muslims: the 1391 martyrs of Jerusalem or the 1860 martyrs of Damascus. Martyrdom is a constant danger for the friars in the Orient, from Francis's preaching in the thirteenth century to the nineteenth-century Ottoman era.

While the sultan is a mere petty Bedouin sheikh for Gaidano, he is an imposing figure in the series of four bas-reliefs sculpted by Arnoldo Zocchi for the Church of St Joseph in Cairo, built between 1904 and 1909 by the Franciscan province of the Holy Land.[85] The dedication of the church to Joseph evokes the saint's presence in Egypt with the Virgin Mary and the Christ child, thus stressing that Egypt has been Christian territory since Jesus' childhood. Zocchi's sculptures recall Francis's presence, to show as it were that Egypt has also been Franciscan territory ever since the saint came to speak with the sultan. Zocchi, like Gaidano, presents the mission to the sultan as the founding act of Franciscan mission in the Orient, though here the emphasis is on a founding presence in Egypt. Three of the four scenes that Zocchi devotes to Francis take place in Egypt. In the first, Francis takes leave of the legate Pelagius: the scene takes place in the midst of the crusader camp, before rows of soldiers and the tents of the army, with the solid ramparts of a city in the background. In the second scene (Fig. 30), Francis and Illuminatus, having crossed to the enemy camp, present themselves to the Egyptian soldiers. Francis speaks to the soldiers and gestures with his right hand; in his left hand, he carries the Gospel. Illuminatus waits humbly behind, his arms crossed and his head bowed. Here we are not before Damietta, for in the background, behind the Egyptians' tents, rise the Giza pyramids, flanked by a large mosque. It is apparently more important for Zocchi to stress the fact that the encounter

Fig. 30. Arnoldo Zocchi, Francis before the Egyptian soldiers, bas-relief, St Joseph Square, Cairo.

Fig. 31. Arnoldo Zocchi, Francis before the sultan, St Joseph Square, Cairo.

took place in Egypt than to represent the surroundings of Damietta; in this way he brings the saint closer to Cairo. Nothing in the expression of the soldiers betrays the slightest hostility towards the friars; this is all the more striking when we compare this image to those of other artists (Nicolás Francés, the illuminators of Bonaventure manuscripts, or Jacopino de' Scipione) who stress (following Bonaventure) the soldiers' brutality towards the two friars. Here, on this square in the Egyptian capital, Zocchi avoids suggesting any violence towards the Franciscans. The friars are the heralds of evangelical peace, listened to and respected by all, even in the midst of a war opposing European and Egyptian armies. The message to the viewer, European or Egyptian, Christian or Muslim, is clear: the Franciscans have been in Egypt since the days of Francis himself and they are here to stay, in spite of wars and upheavals.

The following bas-relief (Fig. 31) portrays Francis preaching to the sultan and his army in the midst of the tents of his camp. A large crowd looks on and seems to listen attentively to the saint: well-ordered ranks of bearded turbaned men stand; behind are ranks of men on horseback. The sultan, seated on a high throne, his right arm extended, leans towards Francis and stares at him, though it is not clear whether his look expresses anger or astonishment. The saint, standing before the throne, his head slightly higher than the sultan's, looks him in the eye. While the sultan's expression remains ambiguous, Francis, strong and confident before the Egyptian ruler, intrepid in the midst of his army, is a model for the Franciscans in Egypt in the twentieth century. A fourth bas-relief shows Francis and his friars on the Mount of Olives, with the city of Jerusalem at their feet. The saint, standing, raises his hands in prayer; his companions prostrate themselves at the sight of the Holy City. This is a now-classic evocation of the saint's pilgrimage to the Holy City as a founding act of Franciscan mission to the Orient; Zocchi echoes this tradition and inserts it into his cycle which insists above all on the saint's presence in Egypt as a precursor to the order's presence, embodied in the Church of St Joseph.

The sultan progressively shrinks under Doré's pencil and Gaidano's brush; José Benlliure Gil (1855–1937) makes him disappear completely. This Valencian artist, who often travelled in the Maghreb and who greatly admired the orientalist painters, painted a series of seventy-four gouaches on the life of the *poverello*, based for the most part on episodes from the *Fioretti*, for a book published by the Franciscans of Valencia to commemorate the seventh centenary of the saint's death in 1926.[86] In the image of the preaching to the Saracens, we see neither the city of Damietta, nor any tents, nor the slightest suggestion of an army (none of the Arabs seems to be carrying any weapons). The scene is a barren desert where a few prickly pears grow, where fourteen Bedouins sit on the ground; it is impossible to say who their leader is. All seem to listen passively to the saint. Francis is no longer in the court of a powerful monarch, but at the world's end, amongst Bedouins who seem to have neither power nor wealth and who are devoid of any outward signs of civilization.

In the following year, 1927, Friar Ferdinando Diotallevi describes Francis's voyage to the Orient, using the sources gathered by Golubovich to relate (following mostly Celano and Bonaventure) his travels to Egypt and his meeting with al-Kâmil.[87] But this is not what interests him. He understands nothing about the crusade; he even says that it was the sultan who was attacking Damietta and who captured it on 5 November 1219. Diotallevi is only interested in Francis's presence at the holy sites. He affirms that the sultan gave him the ivory horn and that his brother Coradin granted him a safe-conduct to visit the holy places. He then describes (without citing any source), the saint's travels, with a companion, through the desert to Jerusalem: walking in the footsteps of the Holy Family (on their return from Egypt), clambering up dunes, eating dates that he picked from the palms. He relates the arrival at the Mount of Olives, where the two friars in ecstasy contemplate the Holy City. Diotallevi then imagines their prayers at Christ's tomb and in the other holy places and relates the legend (which he identifies as such) of the Wali who granted the Cenacle to the saint. Diotallevi dates the Franciscan presence in the Holy Land to this initiatory voyage. He concludes his exposition by evoking the Franciscan presence in 1926, seven centuries after the death of the order's founding saint: 'Saint Francis is now more than ever alive in the Holy Land, in the blessed land of Jesus, of whom the *poverello* was an enamored lover, a perfect imitator.'[88]

Other Franciscan authors insist on Francis's presence in the holy places to legitimate the order's place in the Holy Land. We have seen how Girolamo Golubovich, so adept at exposing unfounded legends, nevertheless clings to the legend of Francis's pilgrimage to Jerusalem, in spite of a total absence of contemporary sources. In the same way, Bernard d'Andermatt, in a biography of the saint written in 1901, claims that the saint's presence is affirmed by 'a very ancient tradition' which should be believed a priori, since no document proves the contrary. Indeed, since no thirteenth-century author specifically denies that Francis visited Jerusalem, the Franciscan scholar can conclude that the tradition is authentic.[89] Paul Sabatier declares that Francis 'set off for Syria and the Holy Places'; he recognizes that there is no textual basis for this trip, but imagines Francis in Bethlehem for Christmas.[90] An even more peculiar assertion is that of Franciscan Martiniano Roncaglia, for whom 'It can be admitted, for psychological reasons, that St. Francis visited the Holy Sepulchre. What causes perplexity is that so interesting an item has escaped the first biographers.'[91] The good friar does not say whether the psychological needs are those of the saint or those of his twentieth-century adepts. He celebrates the fact that the friars succeeded in obtaining the holy places where the flower of European chivalry had failed. He proclaims:

> After the massacre of the Last Crusaders, everything seemed practically lost, and forever. But, by a historical law of Providence, well known to one who treats of the theology of history, the seed transplanted by the medieval Crusader to the land of the Orient had begun to fructify without his being aware of it. The Friars Minor, with daring dynamism born of new strength, reaped the inheritance of the Crusaders: not their territories, but their purest idealism, that is, the custody of the Holy Places, which had determined the first Franks to cross the Mediterranean. In a relatively short time and in a peaceful manner, the West was able to accomplish in part what two centuries of indescribable sufferings, of constant and fruitless wars, were unable to do. ...
>
> Replacing the haughty Crusaders, armed sentinels of the Shrines, came the poor and unarmed sons of St. Francis; in lieu of the cuirass and the sword, their armor consisted of trust in God, and it was only in the name of the Lord that they resisted their enemies.[92]

Roncaglia, in the tradition of the romantics, presents the crusades in an ambiguous light: violent, useless, but imbued with a religious idealism which confers on the crusaders, in spite of everything, a heroic aura. Yet the 'military crusades', he continues, were 'corrupted' by the crusaders themselves (often more interested in their own material gain and personal glory than in the success of the enterprise) and by the lack of political unity among Europe's princes. But 'St. Francis of Assisi [was] the idealizer of a new type of Crusade' that was never corrupted: evangelical mission to the Muslims.[93] Yes, Roncaglia admits, Francis failed to convert the sultan, but that did not discourage him: he gave mission to Muslims an important place in his first Rule and many other friars followed in his footsteps, setting off to preach to Muslims. And this Franciscan mission was crowned with a singular success: 'The Custody of the Holy Places, maintained in perpetual peril of death, constitutes the greatest glory of the Franciscan Order.'[94]

Various twentieth-century authors nevertheless expressed doubt that Francis had ever visited the holy places. Giulio Basetti-Sani noted that in 1217 Honorius III had prohibited pilgrims from going to Jerusalem, in order to deprive the Ayyubids of tribute during the crusade; the pope excommunicated anyone who transgressed this prohibition. It is unlikely that Francis disobeyed this papal order.[95] This is also the opinion of historian Franco Cardini, who thinks it unlikely that al-Kâmil gave Francis permission to go to Jerusalem. Moreover, for Cardini, Francis showed the futility of the ideal of crusading and even of pilgrimage: Christ is everywhere; there is no need to seek him on pilgrimage or to recover the places where he lived. Francis imported Bethlehem to Italy, by making the first Nativity scene at Greccio; he also brought Calvary to Mount Alverno through his stigmatization. Why go to Palestine?[96] Yet many twentieth-century authors continued to imagine the *poverello* at the Holy Sepulchre. Alain Absire, who devoted a novel, *Le Pauvre d'Orient* (2000), to Francis's mission to al-Kâmil, imagined that Francis went there, and that in that church, the holiest in Christendom, Christ first appeared to him in the form of a seraph.[97]

But denying the saint's voyage to Jerusalem does not mean rejecting the idea that he undertook a civilizing mission in barbarous lands, a pacific crusade that was a precursor to European colonization in the nineteenth and twentieth centuries. Novelist and essayist Gilbert Keith Chesterton published, in 1924, two years after his conversion to Catholicism, a series of meditations on Francis. He recognizes that the principal motivation which sent Francis to Syria was the quest for martyrdom. But it was not the only one.

> He was full of the sentiment that he had not suffered enough to be worthy even to be a distant follower of his suffering God. And this passage in his history may really be roughly summarized as the Search for Martyrdom.
>
> This was the ultimate idea in the remarkable business of his expedition among the Saracens in Syria. ... His idea, of course, was to bring the Crusades in a double sense to their end; that is, to reach their conclusion and to achieve their purpose. Only he wished to do it by conversion and not by conquest; that is, by intellectual and not material means. The modern mind is hard to please; and it generally calls the way of Godfrey ferocious and the way of Francis fanatical. That is, it calls any moral method unpractical, when it has just called any practical method immoral. But the idea of St. Francis was far from being a fanatical or even an unpractical idea. ...
>
> The way he approached the matter was indeed highly personal and peculiar; but that was true of almost everything he did. It was in one way a simple idea, as most of his ideas were simple ideas. But it was not a silly idea; there was a great deal to be said for it and it might have succeeded. It was, of course, simply the idea that it is better to create Christians than to destroy Moslems. If Islam had been converted, the world would have been immeasurably more united and happy; for one thing, three-quarters of the wars of modern history would never have taken place.[98]

Chesterton contrasts Francis's strategy to that of the crusaders, presenting it as an alternative: the accomplishment of the crusades through peaceful means. This idea is dear to many twentieth-century authors, as we will see in the following chapter. For Chesterton, his goal is noble: if we had been able to make Islam disappear through crusades or, even better, through Franciscan preaching, that would have saved the world most of its modern wars, says, without irony, a subject of an empire that had conquered a quarter of the planet. The eradication of the great rival religion and the expansion of Christianity could only be salutary.

Chesterton relates the legend of the meeting between saints Francis and Dominic at the chapter of the mats, at the Portiuncula, just before the saint's departure for the Orient. Dominic, with the 'mind of a soldier', and Francis, peaceful and gentle, are of course quite different. But both were prepared to defend Christendom with arms, if necessary. 'While it is probable that St. Francis would have reluctantly agreed with St. Dominic that war for the truth was right in the last resort, it is certain that St. Dominic did enthusiastically agree with St. Francis that it was far better to prevail by persuasion and enlightenment if it were possible' (p. 150).

Chesterton relates Francis's journey to the sultan's court and their meeting, where he proposes to throw himself into the fire. While he expresses some doubt as to the literal truth of this traditional version of the story, he affirms that the saint was impetuous and, after all, perfectly capable of throwing himself into a fire. He was not afraid of the Muslims' weapons; why should he fear mere flames? What is certain, he says, is that Francis was courteously received by the sultan and was unable to obtain his goal, martyrdom. It was 'a sort of ironic tragedy and comedy called The Man Who Could Not Get Killed. Men liked him too much for himself to let him die for his faith' (p. 153). But while the man was welcomed, the message was not. This heroic attempt represents 'one of the great might-have-beens of history'. In other terms, it seems, if al-Kâmil had listened to the saint's message, if he had converted to Christianity, an important 'bridge' would have been established. One suspects that for the English essayist it was a one-way bridge: the Muslims would have converted to Christianity and would have let the Europeans have the Holy Land. If Francis had succeeded, in other words, the British would not have needed Allenby.

Muriel Jaeger has a similar vision in her *Experimental Lives*, a series of five essays; the second, 'The Christian', gives a brief biography of Francis. Like many other twentieth-century authors, she presents the saint as a pacifist horrified by the fervour of crusading that inflamed all Europe. His idea was to convert the Muslims by more peaceful means, or failing that to receive the martyr's crown. But when Francis succeeded in arriving in the sultan's presence, 'he received the half-humorous, half-reverential treatment which semi-barbarous races extend to those "touched by God" '.[99] She relates the proposed trial by fire and the sultan's refusal. For Jaeger, Francis did not impress the sultan. She wonders in what language their dialogue took place and concludes that communication between them must not have been easy. The fact that the sultan tried to shower Francis with gifts proves, for her, that he understood nothing of the *poverello*'s message.

While for Voltaire and some of his contemporaries Francis was a fanatic who strayed into the court of an enlightened sultan, various nineteenth- and twentieth-century authors saw things quite differently. Bernard d'Andermatt affirms that the sultan refused the trial by fire because he 'feared an uprising among his subjects, who were prone to fanaticism'; now the Muslims are the fanatics, not Francis and his friars.[100]

This confrontation between European enlightenment and Arab or African obscurity is found in a painting by Dutch artist Alex Asperlagh, *St Francis at the Sultan's Court*, dated 1927 (Fig. 32). The saint, crucifix in hand, is bathed in the light emanating from his halo. His habit, tied at the waist with a rope, has the form of that of the Friars Minor, but it is brilliant white, a whiteness that contrasts with the black skin of the Egyptian sultan. As shown by Doré or Gaidano, Francis is standing; he points heavenwards and energetically preaches, while the seated sultan does not look at the saint. Here the sultan is accompanied by two veiled women whose large eyes stare blankly. Francis is a bearer of light to a shadowy realm where polygamy shows how far the inhabitants are from the spiritual values incarnated by the saint.

The end of European colonialism in the Near East after the Second World War did not mark the end of this image of Oriental barbarism as a backdrop for a saint who incarnated the values of the Christian West. In 2001, American novelist Valerie Martin wrote a life of the *poverello* in the form of thirty-one fictionalized tableaux, more or less inspired by the frescos of Assisi, Montefalco, and other Franciscan churches. One of these scenes takes place in the crusader camp the evening of the crushing defeat of 29 August 1219: 'The dark towers of Damietta brood over the scene, and in the evenings when the muezzins call their faithful to their unholy prayers, the shrill cry makes the wounded shield their eyes, imagining they

Fig. 32. Alex Asperlagh, *Sint Franciscus aan het hof van den Sultan*.

hear the screams of carrion birds gathering over their heads.'[101] The Arabic language, heard at the muezzin's call, is compared to bestial sounds; later she calls the language 'harsh', softened only when its sounds are pronounced by the French renegade who serves as interpreter. In this hostile world reigned a benevolent sultan who, when the friars arrived, offered them sherbet. The sultan had heard about the saint and received him joyously. Francis proposed the trial by fire, which shocked the sultan: 'No, no, Brother Francesco,' he exclaimed. 'Surely your God does not require this.'[102] Francis preached, with the help of the interpreter, relating Christ's life, his death, the promise of eternal life for those who follow him; the sultan listened patiently and at the end exclaimed that it was a lovely story, then offered gifts to the friars (after numerous refusals, they finally accepted the ivory horn) and sent them back to the crusader camp. This mission accomplished nothing, but it was less the fault of Francis or the sultan than that of the legate Pelagius who refused the sultan's generous offer to return Jerusalem to the crusaders in exchange for their departure from Egypt. For this American novelist, Egypt is an exotic and hostile land where the inhabitants speak a bestial tongue. Only al-Kâmil is ambiguous: he states his admiration for Francis, but his response to his preaching is strange. Why does he exclaim that it was a nice 'story'? Because he knew nothing of Jesus? Because he considered it a mere fable, a pleasant divertissement agreeable to listen to? But both of these interpretations contradict what Martin earlier affirmed, that the sultan had heard of Francis and was impatient to speak with him. Why then did he show so little interest in what he had to say? She qualifies the meeting as a 'mission of peace', but in her version of Francis's sermon he says nothing about peace.

Martin's novel is but a recent avatar of a long and venerable tradition in the West: one imagines the Muslim Orient as a violent and barbarous land that the saint attempts to convert to peace, to Christianity, and to civilization. Other twentieth-century authors, much less hostile towards Islam, will present the encounter between Francis and al-Kâmil as the embodiments of ecumenical dialogue.

14

Francis, Apostle of Peace

While some twentieth-century authors continued to see, in the encounter between Francis and al-Kâmil, the manifestation of Western superiority, most, on the contrary, presented the two as men of peace far above the fray between fanatical crusader and jihadists. The conversation in the sultan's tent becomes a friendly chat during which Francis preached peace, the two men discovered the common roots of their spirituality, the beginning of a true friendship, or even the occasion for Francis to be initiated into Sufism. In the often bloody context of decolonization in the Middle East and the Maghreb, Arab nationalists often charged Western imperialists—English, French, and subsequently American—with being the heirs of the fanatical crusaders. Some Western authors dreamt of a peaceful alternative: if the crusaders were the precursors of the imperialists, Francis becomes a sort of spiritual forebear to the European pacifists of the twentieth century, to those who oppose colonial violence and war in the Middle East—up to and including the two Iraq wars of George Bush father and son.

The *Badal* of Assisi: Louis Massignon

In Damietta on 9 February 1934, Louis Massignon and Mary Kahil (an Egyptian Melkite Christian) offered themselves up to God for the conversion of the Muslims. They established the 'Badaliya Foundation'. *Badaliya* means 'substitution', from the Arabic *badal* (plural *abdâl*), 'substitute'. For the Sufis, the *abdâl* are one of the hierarchical orders of saints. Thanks to their merits and their intercession come the spring rains, victory over one's enemies, and the avoidance of diverse calamites. For Massignon, the mystics and ascetics, through prayer and privation, can become 'substitutes' who obtain grace in God's eyes, not only to their own benefit, but to that of those around them. Hallâj, the Sufi to whom Massignon devoted his dissertation (1922), who was executed for heresy in Bagdad in 922, is an example of a *badal*. Hallâj had declared that his burning love for God filled him with the desire for martyrdom. For Massignon, Hallâj is a Christ figure within Islam, who suffers death to testify to Muslims that God is love and that Christ died as a *badal* for all men. In a prayer published in 1921, Massignon expresses his hope that Hallâj might one day be canonized by the Catholic Church.[1]

Massignon's writings about Hallâj are a strange mix of remarkable erudition, profound appreciation of Muslim piety and mysticism, and a polemical vision of Islam as an imperfect expression of Christianity. This singular vision of Islam has already been the object of numerous studies, in particular those of Jacques Waardenburg and Edward Said.[2] What interests us here has received little attention: it is the prominent role that Massignon gives to Francis of Assisi in his pantheon of *abdâl*. This professor at the Collège de France accepts as true Bonaventure's version of Francis's preaching to al-Kâmil, in particular the proposed trial by fire. Massignon combed through the Arabic sources and found what he thought was proof of the saint's sojourn. According to Ibn al-Zayyât's *Kawâkib*, Fakhr al-Dîn al-Fârisi, spiritual counsellor to al-Kâmil, had a *hikâya mashhûra* (memorable adventure) with a *râhib* (Christian monk). For Massignon, this *râhib* had to be Francis, even if there were plenty of other candidates: for example, the Coptic patriarch of Alexandria, who participated in a debate with Muslim scholars in al-Kâmil's presence in 1221, or perhaps the Copt put to death for blasphemy in Cairo in 1209.[3] But Massignon is looking for a confirmation of Bonaventure's version; he goes so far as to identify this Fakhr al-Dîn with the old Saracen sage who, according to Bonaventure (followed by many authors and artists), fled the trial by fire.

Massignon's career is brilliant and unique. A fervent Catholic, he owed his profound faith to Muslim friends in Baghdad who saved his life in 1908. He had arrived in Ottoman Mesopotamia the previous year to engage in archaeological prospection. The young scholar of Arabic avoided Europeans, lived in a working-class neighbourhood of Baghdad, and dressed in Arab clothing. It was a time of sharp tensions between France and the Ottoman Empire, and during one of his archaeological expeditions in the desert, he was suspected of being a spy. Arrested on a boat on the Tigris during his return trip to Baghdad, he was chained to a bed and threatened with death. Once in Baghdad, he was imprisoned and waited in fear. At this point, his Muslim friends in Baghdad intervened, despite the danger this represented for them, bore witness to his innocence, had him released from prison, and took him into their homes. This generosity and this profound hospitality coming from friends who he knew only slightly, a hospitality anchored in their Muslim faith, profoundly shook the young man. Previously an atheist, Massignon became a fervent Catholic at the same time as he developed a profound admiration for Islam and for his Muslim friends. For the rest of his life, he tried to put his considerable erudition to work to reconcile these two elements: his Catholic faith and his admiration for the faith of his Muslim hosts. He came to see himself as a *badal* ready to substitute himself for his Muslim friends, to intervene on their behalf for Christ. He devoted a good part of his career to retracing the history of other *abdâl* that preceded him.

In his dissertation on Hallâj, completed in 1922 but published only in 1975, Massignon presents the Muslim mystic in the guise of a Christian martyr. His Hallâj, when sentenced to death, says to the vizier who condemned him 'I will die attached to the Cross'. The vizier replies: 'Do you think you are taking up the *mubâhala* of the Christians of Najrân?'[4] Various *hadîths* relate that Muhammad proposed to the Christians of Najrân, who refused to recognize in him a prophet, a trial by fire (*mubâhala*).[5] The Christians were frightened and refused, accepting Muhammad as a prophet. In putting this declaration in the mouth of the Hallâj's persecutor, Massignon underlines what is for him the Christlike character of the Muslim saint: through his martyrdom, he is a sort of substitute (*badal*) for the Christians of Najrân who had not dared to confront the trial by fire.

Massignon places Francis's mission in the context of the philosophical and cultural *rapprochement* between Islam and Christianity.[6] For Massignon as for Bonaventure, Francis's burning desire for martyrdom is love of the highest degree. His will to confront the flames to testify to the truth of Christianity before the sultan proves that he is indeed a *badal*, ready to offer himself up (unto death, if necessary), as a substitute in order to save the Muslims. For Massignon, Francis in 1219 proposed as it were to take up the 'dialogue' with Islam where the Christians of Najrân had left it; he would prove the superiority of Christianity by fire. But in Damietta, it is now the Muslims who refuse this confrontation.

Massignon became a Franciscan tertiary in 1932, taking the name Ibrahim—the Arabic version of Abraham, spiritual father of the three monotheistic religions.[7] Having by chance met up with Mary Kahil in Cairo, where he had known her twenty years before, he took her with him to Damietta in 1934 to establish the Badaliya foundation: 'May you be blessed', he later wrote to his friend, 'for having called me back to the desire for martyrdom. My heart is once more aflame and I have sworn to God to tear myself away from everything, gradually, gently, but implacably, so that I may be judged worthy of martyrdom in a Muslim land, if God is willing.'[8] The new Franciscan tertiary considers himself the spiritual heir to Francis and Hallâj. On 18 July 1934, Massignon and Kahil were received by Pope Pius XI, who blessed their 'offering' at Damietta.

The following year, in his *Hégire d'Ismaël*, Massignon returns to the theme of substitution.[9] He cites (pp. 115–16) the Mercedarians' fourth vow: 'I promise to go place myself in the power of the Saracens, to make myself a prisoner, if necessary, for the redemption of Christ's faithful.' By accepting captivity at the hands of the infidels, the Mercedarian friars, whose purpose was the ransoming of captives, were an example of substitution: Massignon proposed that he and his adepts be ready for the same sort of self-sacrifice in order to liberate the souls of their Muslim hosts. He invokes Francis as the initiator of this type of *badaliya* towards Muslims:

> On the evening of a defeat (August 30th, 1219) at Damietta from the crusader camp, Francis set out from the crusader camp and went to the Muslim camp to offer to affront a trial by fire, for the love of one muslim soul, the Ayyubid sultan Muhammad ibn Abî Bakr al-Malik al-Kâmil.
>
> Denied the martyrdom he had sought, he learned through a vision that upon his return to Italy he would obtain another death of love: this was his stigmatization, at Alverno, on the day of the Exaltation of the Holy Cross. His compassion for Islam, this true spiritual crusade, which Louis IX would later imitate in Carthage, earned him the right to become the first visible co-sufferer with the crucified Christ, 'ascending from the rising of the sun, having the sign of the living God.' [Ap. 7: 2] Thus began, seven centuries ago, the long procession of the standard-bearers of the Passion.
>
> Since Saint Francis's visit to Damietta, the sceptical eyes of a jaded world have seen, with surprise, hundreds of stigmatized men and women—and have been able to touch the supernatural wounds through which the bleeding Christ, suffering his Passion for them, shows them how much he has loved them. If this bloody proof of his love, surpassing the proof of tears, has been dispensed to the church, let it remember the day when the burning seal

of the faith of Ishmael ... found itself called, through the body of Francis, marked with the five wounds of Jesus; and the Church will rediscover, with the lance-wound, the holy pain which the abandonment by Islam inflicts on the heart of its spouse.   (pp. 117–18)

For Massignon, as for the other Franciscan hagiographers since Celano and Bonaventure, God refused to make a martyr of Francis at Damietta because he had in store for him a greater glory, the stigmata. But for the two thirteenth-century hagiographers, the sultan and his Saracens are forgotten by the time we get to the theophany on Mount Alverno. Not for Massignon: the stigmata are the fruit of the 'true spiritual crusade' that the saint leads, a crusade of love. And it is this love which burns the saint, marking him with the signs of Christ.

In 1947, Massignon wrote the statutes of his Badaliya confraternity: he explained its genesis and its purpose.[10] 'We [members of the Badaliya] offer and engage our lives, from this moment, as hostages.' The purpose of this engagement is to favour the 'manifestation of Christ in Islam', not only as a prophet recognized by the Qur'ân, but as 'true God and true Man'. The Muslims who do not yet recognize Christ are 'this marginalized people, long ago cut off from the promise of the Messiah as descendants of Hagar'. The members of the confraternity work for the 'reconciliation of these dear souls, for whom we wish to substitute ourselves *"fil badaliya"*, by paying their ransom in their stead and at our cost.' Massignon once more evokes the trial by fire rejected by the Christians of Najrân, then proposed by Francis and rejected by al-Kâmil. The new *abdâl* promised to continue the *shahâda* or testimony of their forebears: Francis, St Louis, and the Père de Foucauld.

Massignon often returns to the place of Francis and Damietta in his theology of substitution. Damietta became, according to his friend Denise Barrat, 'his favourite city'.[11] He wrote in 1957:

> At Damietta, where Saint Francis of Assisi offered himself up to the trial by fire, in 1219, in order to touch the heart of one Muslim, the sultan al-Mâlik al-Kâmil, God showed him that He had reserved for him another martyrdom, that of the stigmatization and the lance-blow of love, that he would receive two years later, at Alverno, *nel crudo sasso*. ... This wound made Saint Francis the herald and the standard-bearer of the supreme crusade, in which the lance of divine transcendence, of the Muslim holy war, wounded Christendom with love and compassion, through the first of the lovers stigmatized by God's heart.[12]

The voyage to Damietta, supreme act of substitution, provokes the stigmatisation and shows the way to the reintegration of Islam into the church. This singular view of the relations between Islam and Christianity displeased many: Muslims who could not accept to see Islam relegated to a sort of preparatory stage before Christianity; many Christians upset by what they saw as a troubling syncretism; his lay colleagues, who, while recognizing his formidable erudition, could not accept the mystical and apologetic aspects of his work. But the members of his little confraternity, the Badaliya, in particular Franciscan scholars, took up the torch after their master's death in 1962 and continued to develop his singular vision of the encounter between Francis and al-Kâmil.

Francis and al-Kâmil According to Massignon's Franciscan Disciples

Giulio Basetti-Sani was one of the members of the Badaliya foundation, and one of Massignon's most fervent disciples. When this Franciscan friar began to take interest in Islam and to study the Qur'ân, he saw Muhammad as an impostor inspired by Satan and Islam as a profane deviation from the true faith. But in his conversations with Massignon, his ideas changed; he describes this transformation in a book he devoted to Massignon, published in 1971.[13] Basetti-Sani concludes that Muhammad was divinely inspired and that Islam plays a positive role in the history of redemption. This role, for Basetti-Sani as for Massignon, is one that would have scarcely pleased Muhammad or his followers, a sort of phase in preparation for their ultimate integration into the Catholic Church: if Islam is positive, it is never more than an imperfect expression of the ultimate truth, Christianity. In his *Koran in the Light of Christ,* Basetti-Sani gives a Christian reading of the Qur'ân that, while devoid of polemics, passes over in silence the Qur'ân's rejection of Christian doctrines and practice and places the accent on the elements in the Muslim holy book that are in harmony with Christian doctrine, in particular concerning Jesus.[14] The goal, as expressed in the title of another of his books is to find 'Jesus Christ hidden in the Qur'ân'.[15]

The Italian friar's numerous books and articles revolve around the same themes and try to show that Francis had a special mission to show to Muslims the path that leads to Christ. In his *Muhammad and Saint Francis*, published in 1959, he presents a Massignonian Francis who proposes a trial by fire to take up the *mubâhala* that had been refused by the Christians of Najrân.[16] His saint is a pacifist in open conflict with the church's promotion of the crusade. This book was fiercely attacked by various traditionalist Catholics who looked askance at this gesture of accommodation towards Islam. The author relates how a fellow friar branded the book a historical and doctrinal fraud.[17] But Basetti-Sani remained convinced that the encounter between Francis and al-Kâmil presented a new model of ecumenical dialogue for the twentieth-century church. He developed this idea in other books, in particular his *Per un dialogo cristiano-musulmano: Mohammed, Damietta et La Verna* (1969), then in his *L'Islam e Francesco d'Assisi: La missione profetica per il dialogo* (1975).[18] For Basetti-Sani, Francis understood that the crusades were contrary to the love that the Gospels preached; he did all he could to stop them. True, we find no trace of this idea in the thirteenth-century sources, but that is because his contemporaries, convinced of the justice and necessity of the crusades, in despite of all their admiration for the saint, did not take his utopian dreams seriously. If the *poverello*'s companions could not understand him, those of the twentieth century—in particular Massignon and Basetti-Sani—could appreciate his vision.

For Basetti-Sani, Francis understood that God did not want crusades. That was why he made Innocent III die before he could realize his plan of setting off for the East at the head of a crusader army. God sent Francis to show an alternative path, the path of dialogue and peace, to Europe's Christians, but they were deaf to his message. Basetti-Sani imagines, on several occasions, Francis in colloquy with the pope—Innocent III, then Honorius III—vainly trying to dissuade him from launching a new crusade. Seeing that his efforts were fruitless, he found a clever ploy: he obtained the privilege of the Portiuncula, which offered the same indulgence to those who visited the church in Assisi as to those who went to Jerusalem. Surely, he thought, this would discourage people from going off on a crusade. In 1217, Francis, having heard that in France there was opposition to the crusade, decided to go and join the pacifist movement; but he was intercepted in Florence by Ugolino who sent him back to Assisi. Finally, seeing that the crusaders were leaving for Egypt, Francis decided that he had no choice but to go to discourage them from fighting.

Basetti-Sani employs all the principal sources for Francis's trip to Egypt, but clearly prefers Bonaventure since, he explains, the Seraphic doctor had spoken with the 'sole eye witness, Illuminatus'. As soon as he arrived in the crusader camp, Francis began to preach against the war: not just against engaging in battle on one unlucky day, as Celano claimed (he had not understood Francis's prophetic mission to Islam), but against the entire crusading enterprise. His sermons sowed doubt in the hearts of many crusaders and provoked the hostility of Pelagius and the other leaders. Then came the crushing defeat of 29 August 1219; some began to think that Francis was right. Al-Kâmil proposed peace to the crusaders: he would give them Jerusalem if they left Egypt. It is at this point that Francis and Illuminatus cross over to speak with the sultan. Basetti-Sani closely follows Massignon, for whom (as we have seen) Francis proposed a trial by fire modelled on the *mubâhala* of Najrân. Of course Francis knew nothing of the Muslim traditions concerning Najrân, but he was divinely inspired. The sultan refused the trial by fire but showed great respect for the saint, whom he told, as Bonaventure related, 'I believe that your religion is good and true.' But Bonaventure, Basetti-Sani explains, had misunderstood this; the sultan was simply expressing the respect that any educated Muslim has for the two other religions of the book, Judaism and Christianity; these words do not imply that he was prepared to convert.

Seeing that there was no point staying with the crusaders after Pelagius had refused the sultan's generous peace offer, Francis returned to Italy; he did not go to the holy sites of Jerusalem (if he had, Basetti-Sani says, Celano and Bonaventure would have said so). The saint never forgot his special mission towards the Muslims. He is a prophet who announces 'a new program for the salvation of Islam' (p. 187). His own sons did not understand him: the five martyrs of Marrakech, who attacked the Prophet and the Qur'ân, show this: Francis did not approve of their deeds. The saint's hagiographers, starting with Celano and Bonaventure, presented the stigmatization as God's response to his ardent desire for martyrdom. Basetti-Sani goes further: the stigmata are a message to the Muslim world: they 'prove to Islam the reality of Jesus Christ's crucifixion' (p. 247). Francis is an 'intercessor for the Muslim world' (p. 249); 'Francis's wounds will help the Muslims discover the crucified and risen Christ' (p. 254).

Numerous Franciscan authors follow Basetti-Sani in claiming that Francis preached energetically against crusading. Francis de Beer affirms, 'As soon as he arrived in Damietta, Francis discouraged the crusaders from fighting; he does not want to take part in the attack. But the crusaders paid him no heed, and it is the sultan who will listen to him!' 'Against the extravagance of the crusade, Islam needed a radical witness who would be the radical counter-example. Martyrdom is conscientious objection against all those who identify with the intolerance of holy war: it is anti-crusade.'[19] Another friar, Isaac Vázquez Janeiro, affirms that 'According to Celano, Francis preached before the Christian army against the crusade'.[20] Cornelio Del Zotto qualifies Francis's trip to Egypt as 'an itinerary of peace in the midst of war'. The saint 'sowed thoughts of peace and built the deep foundations of a future of pacification'. He tried to dissuade the crusaders from fighting; he sought out the sultan for a 'mediation of peace'. In the sultan's presence, Francis managed 'to pass over insurmountable obstacles and to destroy the ponderous and ancient barriers to open the serene path of dialogue and of reciprocal comprehension'.[21]

In the same way, conventual friar Michael Robson claims that Francis 'hints that he was displeased by the crusaders' conduct'. This is of course possible, but it does not meant that he was opposed to crusading (as Robson insinuates) any more than the well-documented fact that he was 'displeased' by the conduct of some Franciscan friars meant that he was hostile to the order of friars minor.[22] If thirteenth-century authors did not clearly say that Francis was opposed to the crusades, it is because their 'understanding of the saint was found to be limited'; Robson affirms that Francis, through his conversion, obtained a more objective vision of society than his contemporaries.[23] For Robson, a 'hagiographical veil' covered Francis's opposition to the crusades. But the problem which Robson refuses to face is that, once one lifts that veil, there is no source for Francis's supposed opposition to the crusades. This has not prevented other Franciscans from making even more audacious declarations than Robson. For J. Hoeberichts, 'Francis occupied an exceptional position among his contemporaries with regard to the crusades. ... There was a small, insignificant man from Assisi who dared to oppose this church policy.'[24] Sister Kathleen Warren claims that 'Francis went to Egypt to actively oppose the Crusades.'[25]

While these authors walk in the footsteps of Massignon and Basetti-Sani, they do not follow them to the end: in general, they reject Bonaventure's claim that Francis proposed a trial by fire. Neither dramatic confrontation with Islam nor thirst for martyrdom fits the new image of a pacifist saint. Cornelio Del Zotto, for example, even as he affirms the trustworthiness of Bonaventure's version, makes no mention of the proposed trial by fire, since it would no doubt tarnish his idealized portrait of Francis.[26] Thomas and Bonaventure had claimed that Francis went to Egypt in search of martyrdom, but Warren has doubts: 'I do not think that Francis was motivated by this desire'; she relegates the discussion of this issue to a footnote, where it cannot nuance her portrait of a pacifist saint.[27] Various authors have compared Francis to Gandhi.[28] Gwenolé Jeusset, a Franciscan who lived many years in Côte d'Ivoire, is more circumspect. He is not convinced by Massignon's arguments about the trial by fire, nor does he believe that Francis went to preach peace. It was only once he was with the sultan that the saint discovered a Muslim piety which surprised him and led him to reflect about his faith; if he subsequently said nothing about his experiences in Egypt, it is perhaps because he was no longer convinced of the inferiority of Islam compared to Christianity.[29] Yet other Franciscan writers make their founding saint into a militant pacifist.

The Counter-Crusader

The Franciscans of the twentieth century did not invent this image of the apostle of peace. Some of the romantics of the preceding century already posited an opposition between a militant church that preached crusades and Francis, visionary man of peace. Friedrich Böhringer contrasted the church policy of opposition through armed force with that of Francis, who tried to win over the 'Mohammedans' to Christ through pacific means. Francis practised peace, the Church preached war.[30]

Various twentieth-century non-Franciscan authors also imagined that Francis had been hostile to the crusades and that his preaching to the sultan was a sort of pacifist alternative to war. We have encountered this idea in Chesterton in 1927 and Muriel Jaeger in 1932.[31] Nikos Kazantzakis published a hagiographical novel in 1954: *Ho phtochoules tou Theou,* published in English translation in 1962 under the title *God's Pauper: St. Francis of Assisi.*[32] For the Greek novelist, Francis was at the outset in favour of crusading: when the ship on which he travelled along with crusaders was shaken by a violent storm, he begged God to calm the seas, so that the soldiers might be able to give his sepulchre back to him. But Francis was then shocked by the crusaders' behaviour in their camp, and even more so by the pillaging, thefts, and murder during the capture of Damietta. For Kazantzakis, the sultan shows no admiration for Francis, only a mix of contempt and amusement; he is a man with no spirituality, being obsessed with thirst for power and the pleasures of the flesh. After this misadventure, Francis understood that the 'true sepulchre' which we have to liberate is not in the Holy Land, but in our hearts.

Many authors underline the role that Francis's voyage played, or rather that his absence played, in the institutionalization of the order. English playwright Julian Mitchell imagines a meeting between Cardinal Ugolino and friars John Parenti and Elias.[33] The three agree that they need to reform the order and to establish clear rules for it, in particular to permit the order to have common property for the material needs of the friars. There is only one obstacle—'the brother', in other words Francis, who would be opposed. But Elias has an idea: to let 'the brother' go to the Orient as he wished; Ugolino, who had prohibited Francis from leaving Italy, quickly authorized his mission. Francis, delighted, sets off. Mitchell does not stage the meeting with al-Kâmil, but after having spoken with him Francis finds that 'the infidels are more Christian than the crusaders', which makes him cry. In Mitchell's play, as for Angelo Clareno in the fourteenth century, Jean-Henri Maubert de Gouvest in the eighteenth, or Paul Sabatier and others in the twentieth, Francis's trip East allowed the 'bad' Franciscans to take over the order: at the beginning of the second act of the play, a friar arrives from Italy to warn Francis, who leaves immediately. We find essentially the same scenario in *Francisco de Asís, Obra en 14 cuadros* by Mexican playwright Maruxa Vilalta: the trip to Egypt gives the worldly friars the chance to take over the order.[34]

For Mitchell, the voyage East opens Francis's eyes, inspiring both disgust with the crusaders and respect for the Muslims. For Morris Bishop, who wrote a biography of the saint in 1974, the saint's ideal was 'fundamentally opposed' to that of the crusaders. The failure of his mission, unable to succeed in the midst of war's barbarity, explains why Francis never spoke afterwards of his voyage to the Orient.[35] For Henri Queffélec, Francis's mission of peace, underestimated both by his contemporaries and by historians, was as important as the voyage of Anwar Sadat to Israel in 1977.[36] For novelist Alain Absire, Francis is a pacifist visionary who formed a profound friendship with al-Kâmil; only the blind opposition of Cardinal Pelagius prevented the realization of peace.[37] For some authors, particularly Franciscans, the friars minor embodied a peaceful crusade opposed to the bloody crusade of the church, the protection of the holy places instead of the armed struggle to recover them.

We find similar ideas expressed by some historians of the crusades. Stephen Runciman shows a disdain for Francis similar to that of Voltaire or Michelet. The Muslims, seeing him arrive, 'soon decided that anyone so simple, so gentle and so dirty must be mad, and treated him with the respect due to a man touched by God'. But, contrary to Voltaire or Michelet, for Runciman Francis's principal motivation is to establish peace: 'He had come to the East believing, as so many good and unwise persons before and after him have believed, that a peace-mission can bring about peace.'[38] He was politely received by the sultan, but his utopian mission was superfluous: al-Kâmil was already well-disposed towards peace; the bellicosity was in the crusader camp, especially in Cardinal Pelagius's heart.

James Powell, historian of the fifth crusade, presents Francis's endeavour as a 'mission of peace'. He claims that Francis 'was opposed to the Christian militarism that characterized the crusading movement'. His mission East would mark 'the beginning of a quest for a peaceful alternative'. 'The opposition to the crusades will serve to promote the missionary alternative which developed during the saint's live and came directly from his ideals.'[39] Powell and others can cite many Franciscan sources which present the saint's love of peace.[40] Francis himself, in his first Rule, exhorted his friars, just as Christ had in the Gospel of Matthew (10: 13), to wish peace upon every house they entered. Francis indeed is part of a long ascetic tradition that rejects war just as it rejects riches and sexuality. Francis was never a preacher of crusading as Bernard of Clairvaux, for example, had been, or as were numerous later Franciscans. But nor does anything indicate any particular hostility towards crusading: in his writings, it is money and women who inspire disgust in him, far more than war.

How then can one show that Francis was hostile to crusading? Powell, like many Franciscan authors before him, relies on the passage in Thomas of Celano's *Vita secunda* where Francis warns the crusaders not to fight against the sultan's troops. In so doing, Powell has to misrepresent Celano's text, composed at a late date (1247), a sort of collection, as we have seen, of various sayings and deeds of the saint, stories which Thomas gathered in earlier texts and from oral testimonies of the saint's companions. In a series of stories about Francis's gift of prophesy, Thomas relates that Francis predicted the crusaders' defeat in a particularly bloody battle (traditionally identified with that of 29 August 1219). For Thomas, Francis spoke out not against crusading, nor against war in general, but against fighting on one specific day, a day (as God revealed to him) that was particularly unlucky. But for Powell, Francis preached against crusading in general and Thomas, so as not to offend the church authorities, modified his warnings.

The episode from the *Vita secunda* does not lend itself to this interpretation. Thomas claims that during the defeat Francis cried hot tears for the crusaders who fell in battle, particularly for the Spaniards, who had fought ferociously. He does not seem to have shed a single tear for the Muslim dead. One might answer that Thomas saw the incident through hagiographical lenses, that he modified the story to present an image of the saint acceptable to the church hierarchy; but in this case, why would he include this detail? How can we suppose, along with Powell, Basetti-Sani, and others, that Francis actively preached against the crusades in the midst of the crusader camp, and did so until the capture of Damietta, yet that no chronicler mentions this? Powell and the others have a strange method: they form an idea of Francis, a pacifist like those of the twentieth century, then affirm that Thomas of Celano hid this reality so as not to offend papal sensibilities.

Other historians follow in Powell's footsteps. Chiara Frugoni affirms that Francis, 'in silent disagreement with the Church, which had taken the side of the armed crusaders, championed the peaceful conversion of the infidels'.[41] Since this dissention is 'silent', Frugoni does not need to offer proof of it. Francis had 'tried in vain to dissuade the crusaders from fighting'; the fact that he went to see the sultan, risking his life, shows his great 'comprehension of the other'.[42] Instead of the pointless violence of arms, Francis proposed dialogue and persuasion. Frugoni hesitates between Thomas's and Bonaventure's versions of the mission. In 1993, she criticized Bonaventure who, in claiming that Francis had proposed a trial by fire, makes the saint 'authoritarian and vindictive', while Thomas presents him, in a more authentic manner, as humble and pacifistic. But in 1995, she followed Massignon, Basetti-Sani, and Gabrieli, who preferred Bonaventure's version.[43] Gabrieli and Frugoni claim that Fakhr al-Dîn was the frightened old man of Bonaventure's version. For Gabrieli, Francis could not have been aware of the story of the *mubâhala* of Najrân. Frugoni, on the contrary, claims that Francis knew of it and wished to take up the 'dialogue' by proposing a trial 'which was part of their culture', even if the ordeal is more a part of European culture than of that of the Arab world.[44] The saint went East to 'bring peace where the crusaders and the infidels were fighting over the possession of the holy places. ... How could the Christians think to come to the aid of the Holy Land with violence and war? But no one listened to him.'[45]

Other historians have shown the weakness of such arguments. Randolph Daniel emphasized that desire for martyrdom was the driving force of Franciscan missions from the beginning, in Damietta as in Marrakech.[46]

Franco Cardini, in an article published in 1974, shows how the idea that Francis represented a passage from the age of crusading to the age of mission rests on a false dichotomy. The two coexisted in the thirteenth century and were in no way incompatible. Francis perhaps criticized the actions of some crusaders, but he was in rupture neither with the fifth crusade nor with the idea of crusading.[47] For Kasper Elm, the voyage to Egypt and Franciscan mission to Muslims comprise a sort of pilgrimage where Francis pursues *imitatio Christi* by preaching to infidels. The dangers and trials, far from being superfluous, make Franciscan mission into an ideal penitential exercise.[48]

Benjamin Kedar, in his *Crusade and Mission: European Approaches to the Muslims* (1984), shows how in the thirteenth century there is no incompatibility between crusading and missionary preaching: the two are seen as complementary rather than contradictory. He rejects the idea that Francis was opposed to the crusades, since there is no source to prove it. 'Francis's attitude to the armed struggle against the Muslims must remain a moot point, since none of his scanty writings bears on the issue.'[49] Bert Roest has recently shown how the pacifist conception of mission, involving respect for the Muslim other, is an invention of Franciscan historiography of the twentieth century and has no basis in medieval sources.[50]

The Sufi of Assisi

Idries Shah presents Francis as a novice mystic who learnt Sufism in al-Kâmil's tent. Shah's books, in particular *The Sufis*, published in 1964 with a preface by Robert Graves, introduced Sufism to a wide Anglophone readership.[51] The book and its author were the object of criticism and polemics: Shah was criticized for usurping the title of Sufi *shaykh*, for claiming to be a direct descendant of the Prophet Muhammad, and for presenting a brand of Sufism which reflected his own idiosyncratic mystical ideas rather than those of traditional Sufism. For Shah, Sufism was not a purely Muslim phenomenon: it existed before the Qur'ân and is found well beyond the Muslim world. To demonstrate Sufism's universal nature, Shah devotes several chapters to its occult European forms, from the foundation of the Order of the Garter to traditional English morris dancing to the obscure rites of the Templars.

Shah devotes a chapter to Francis, a veritable European Sufi who discovers in Damietta the profound sources of spirituality. Francis was exposed young to Sufism, without realizing it: before his conversion, the songs which he had on his lips came from a venerable troubadour tradition which bore the marks of Arabic poetry. Francis's poetry strangely resembles that of the Sufi poet Rumi. Shah briefly narrates the *poverello*'s life, noting various parallels with Sufi traditions.

Why then did Francis want to go to the Orient, or to Spain and Morocco? No doubt because he sought to establish contacts with dervishes in Asia Minor or Sufi poets in Andalusia. He is a 'troubadour looking for his roots'.[52] Little does it matter that the contemporary sources speak of his desires to convert or obtain martyrdom: his companions could not understand him; they were puzzled. There is no doubt, Shah continues, that in the court and the army of the sultan Francis found what he sought: Sufi adepts who could speak with him of their discipline and their wisdom. Francis did not try to convert anyone; on the contrary, when he returned to the Christian camp he tried to dissuade the crusaders from fighting.

Shah does not go into the details of the conversations between the Italian novice and his Muslim hosts, but for him Francis's subsequent life shows how much he learnt from them. Upon returning from Damietta, he established the rule of his order: 'The atmosphere and setting of the Franciscan Order is closer to a dervish organization than anything else.'[53] Everything in the order recalls Sufism, for Shah, from the way of praying to the symbolism of the six-winged seraph. The Franciscan habit is a copy of the robes of Sufi dervishes. The Franciscan salutation, invoking peace, is nothing more than the translation of *salam aleykum*, which he heard on the lips of his Arab hosts. But alas, mixed with these Sufi elements are Christian ones: this awkward amalgam explains the problems that perturbed the order as soon as the saint died.

James Cowan, in his biography of the saint (2001), follows in Shah's footsteps. Cowan acknowledged that at the outset Francis was persuaded of the superiority of Christianity over Islam: the desire to convert the other, or to obtain martyrdom, pushed him East. But the Australian novelist has no patience with the medieval versions of his mission; he feels that his biographers never understood him.[54] Francis, impatient with the nitpicking distinctions of the scholastic theologians, wanted to drink from the well-springs of Christian spirituality, in the East: to visit the land where Christ lived, of course, but also to confront the religious other, Oriental Christian and Muslim. Setting aside the medieval texts, Cowan imagines Francis in animated but relaxed discussion with al-Kâmil and his theologians and

Sufis. They certainly spoke of their religious differences, but that was not the essence of their discussion. While the two armies were camped against each other, in the sultan's tent a friendly conversation about Sufism took place. The fruits of these conversations, for Francis, were numerous: Cowan reiterates Shah's list, emphasizing the Franciscan habit and the salutation of peace. Francis's spirituality, which for Cowan is only clearly expressed after his return from Egypt, is a mix of Western and Oriental elements. If the longing to convert Muslims or to be martyred had pushed Francis from Italy to al-Kâmil's camp, he seems to have forgotten these ambitions as soon as he entered his tent, becoming a mystical apprentice in search of Sufi wisdom.

From Damietta to Jaffa (1229): A Glimmer of Hope to a Violent World

We have seen how various authors, from the thirteenth century on, tried to attenuate or deny the notion that Francis's mission was a failure, since he succeeded neither in converting the sultan nor in obtaining martyrdom. Some twentieth-century authors found a new answer to this problem: for them, when in 1229 al-Kâmil granted Jerusalem to Emperor Frederick II, it was the fruit of the message of peace that Francis had sown in the sultan's heart ten years before. It may seem surprising that none of Francis's ardent defenders had previously thought of this. But many of them were unaware that it was the same sultan al-Kâmil (who is almost never named in Franciscan sources) who signed the treaty of Jaffa with Frederick. Let us add that the emperor's action was harshly criticized and that the treaty of Jaffa obtained Jerusalem for only fifteen years, and we see why medieval Franciscans would not particularly want to associate the treaty with their founding saint. In the eighteenth century, Friar Francisco del Puerto saw in the treaty of Jaffa the saint's good influence;[55] nevertheless few authors before the twentieth century follow suit. But from the perspective of the twentieth century, when al-Kâmil and Frederick can be seen as visionary men of peace in the midst of fanatics who preached crusade and jihad, the idea has a certain success.

Julien Green published his *Frère François*, a sort of novelized hagiography, in 1983. Like so many others before him, he placed Francis's mission in the context of the growing divisions within the order.[56] The saint, tired and frustrated, impulsively decided to go East, as he had long dreamt of doing, in search of martyrdom. To his surprise, no one tried to dissuade him, Green adds. Ugolino, also tired of the conflict, still revered the saint's purity of life and his inspiration that was the origin of the order. But for the cardinal, the age of original inspiration had passed: the hour of organization and consolidation had come, and for these tasks the opinionated and intransigent saint was more an obstacle than anything else. Let him go East, with the blessing of the cardinal protector of the order.

For Green, Francis was not hostile to the crusade at the outset. But when he arrived in the crusader camp, he was dumbfounded by the spectacle he discovered:

> When he saw the motley swarm of humanity that bore the name of Christian army, he must have been momentarily stupefied. *That* was the Crusade—the magic word that had haunted the years of his youth? As he would soon discover, there was a little of everything in that crowd: Mixed together with the soldiers in hopeless disorder was a menagerie of suspect creatures, thieving, criminal tramps, the low rascals, male and female, who followed the troops, right behind the commissariat. Illuminati and seers moved amidst that were Frenchmen, Germans, Italians, Englishmen, believers who wanted to fight for Christ alongside atheists with blasphemy in their mouths and profit on their minds.
>
> One look was enough to show Francis that he had to begin by converting the Christians. The Saracens would come later.   (p. 201)

Francis's voice rang out in the midst of the multicoloured tents; he obtained conversions 'In this place ridden with boredom and despair' (p. 202). Francis was troubled when he learnt of an ill-prepared attack planned against Damietta. He vainly tried to dissuade the crusaders, who called him a coward. Then came the crushing defeat of 29 August. Francis, dumbfounded, 'had but one idea: to bring peace by any means possible. Upon reflection the only way was to go straight to the sultan. The plan was crazy, but Francis's mind worked simply' (p. 202).

Three motivations are mixed, for Green, in the saint's spirit: the conversion of the sultan, the quest for martyrdom, and, now, peace. Green presents al-Kâmil as the perfect antithesis of the crusaders: educated, interested in religious poetry, curious, learned in science, a patron of poets and intellectuals. Tired of the wars which impoverished Egypt, the sultan longed for peace, to permit the Egyptian peasants to till their fields and to permit the lucrative exchanges with foreign (particularly Venetian) merchants to resume. When Francis and Illuminatus arrived before the sultan, he welcomed the opportunity for a philosophical and theological discussion. 'Francis's expression radiated intelligence, and an immediate sympathy sprang up between the two men' (p. 204). Al-Kâmil kept him several days in his palace.

Francis understood that he could not convert his new friend, who showed him respect and generosity and who called him 'Brother Francis'. Francis perhaps accompanied his new friend to a mosque where the two men prayed together to the One God. Al-Kâmil granted Francis a *laissez-passer* for the holy places and had him escorted back to the crusader camp.

Green concluded that this encounter, 'apparently unsuccessful' (p. 205), in fact bore fruit. First, Francis came away with a new esteem for Islam: a faith in the One God that should be respected. 'This broad view of the problem of religion had an enormous, almost revolutionary, force' (p. 205). His confidence in the crusading enterprise was shaken: how could they be justified against a man like his friend the sultan? Francis was subsequently witness to massacres in Christ's name during the capture of Damietta. Revolted, he abandoned the crusader army. The encounter bore fruit for al-Kâmil as well: ten years later he gave Jerusalem to Frederick II. Green recognizes that political calculation played a role in the treaty of Jaffa: none the less, it represented a 'victory of wisdom and tolerance' (p. 205). For other authors, too, such as novelist Alain Absire, the treaty of Jaffa was at least in part due to Francis's good influence on al-Kâmil.[57]

The image of Francis as a peace emissary is solidly established. We find it in the work of Carlo Carretto, an Italian Catholic who, inspired by the example of the French hermit known as the Père de Foucauld, in 1954 joined the Petits frères de Jésus in the Algerian desert to lead a life of evangelical poverty. His *Letters from the Desert*, his best-known work, draw spiritual lessons from these years of ascesis and contemplation. Carretto was fascinated by Francis; in 1965 he founded, in Spello, a few kilometres from Assisi, the Little Brothers of the Gospel. In 1980 he published *Io, Francesco* (*I, Francis*), where he wrote in the first person, taking the voice of Francis contemplating a twentieth-century world ravaged by pollution, corruption, and materialism and haunted by the fear of thermonuclear apocalypse.[58] Caretto's Francis does not like what he sees in Europe in 1980; he would no doubt have been more at ease in the Algerian desert. Francis has plenty of ideas to solve the century's problems: as he relates his own biography, Caretto's Francis gives advice to his twentieth-century readers. Caretto explains in his introduction that if we put into action Francis's project, we can escape atomic Armageddon. Francis's lessons are simple and clear: love and generosity towards the poor, respect for nature and, above all, rejection of violence. Francis relates how he tamed the wolf of Gubbio not with knives and hatchets, but with bread and broth.

> I tell you this, and I tell you most emphatically: Speak of non violence, be apostles of nonviolence, become non-violent.
> Now is the hour to do so, in fact it may be the last hour, in as much as you are all sitting on top of a stockpile of bombs, and you can blow up at any moment now.   (p. 75)

Francis, a true Christian witness to Jesus' tenderness, went to his death like a lamb, without bleating. But around him in Italy, Francis saw men sharpening their spears to defend the church, in preparation for a crusade.

> And my nonviolent ideal, my dream of going forth to meet human beings like lambs, was being shattered.
> I had even managed, in the midst of such chaos, to make a voyage to Egypt, and actually to meet with Sultan Malek-el-kamel—if only to show myself and others that there was no need to be afraid to go out to meet the enemy unarmed. But my mission did not succeed.
> The Sultan treated me well, and I returned home without a scratch. But I did not care. I wanted peace. And instead…I felt beaten, defeated, conquered.   (p. 86)

Francis's mission of peace in Damietta was a failure because the crusaders were deaf to the saint's call to stop the war. Caretto's Francis warns his twentieth-century readers that, if they refuse like the crusaders to heed his call to peace, they risk annihilation.

Thirteen years later, in 1996, Albert Jacquard is also haunted by concerns of the moment. It is no longer the cold war with its nuclear sword of Damocles that worries him, but the cultural, political, and economic relations between North and South. Like Caretto, he sees Francis as a model who can inspire solutions to our current problems, though Jacquard does so in a secular vein. Francis, he calls, 'help us become men'.[59] Why Francis? Jacquard explains that among history's great revolutionaries, who blazed new trails instead of following well-worn paths, three stand out: 'Akhenaton, the Pharaoh who affirmed the unity of God, Jesus, the prophet who suggested founding relations between men on love, and Francis, the son of a merchant who proposed poverty as an ideal of life, profoundly shook people's assumptions. After them, everything changed.'[60] What are Francis's lessons for us? Poverty, first of all: the inhabitants of the rich world must reduce their boundless consumption in solidarity with the poor. Ecology: Francis, in his *Canticle*, recognized that we are all brothers and sisters: not just people, but also animals, plants, even 'my sister water'. This is the respect that we need to have for our planet.

The mission to Damietta inspires a long chapter on Islam and Christianity. Jacquard relates that Francis wished to convert the sultan 'or be punished for his audaciousness and suffer martyrdom' (p. 77). The saint presented himself at the gates of Damietta and was taken to the palace. The sultan attentively listened to Francis for two days, then granted him a *laissez-passer* to go to the holy places. When he returned to the Christian camp, he was witness to bloody massacres at the capture of Damietta. But his journey was not in vain:

> It seems that the sultan did not forget Francis's smile, his gentleness and the expression of a limitless faith. Perhaps this memory was decisive when he decided, ten years later, even though nothing obliged him to do so, to return Jerusalem to the Christians. What the armies from Europe had not been able to obtain, the intelligence and tolerance of Malik al-Kâmil permitted Islam to offer. No doubt the radiant aspect of Francis, who died three years before and had just been canonized by the Church, had pursued its gradual work in the conscience of this man, open as he was to the thought of others. (pp. 78–9)

What lessons can be drawn from this encounter for the end of the twentieth century? 'This episode, seven centuries old, can help us find ways to avoid a confrontation provoked by the demographic evolution of the coming decades' (p. 79). The growing economic disparities between North and South are accompanied by important demographic inequalities: the possibilities of a crisis between an overpopulated, poor South and a rich, underpopulated North are real. But Francis and al-Kâmil have shown that the supposed breach between the Muslim and Western worlds does not have to be. Cultural cooperation and dialogue are essential. Jacquard suggests the establishment of a 'Mediterranean Cultural Community', an organization which would build bridges in order to lay the foundations of a real common Mediterranean culture, while respecting national and local cultures. For Jacquard, we must avoid making the same mistakes as we did with the European Union, built on economic cooperation, which had difficulty creating a common culture. With the MCC, let us build the cultural foundations first: economics and politics will follow. Where should we place the headquarters of this new organization? In Damietta, of course!

The Spirit of Assisi: Promotion of Ecumenical Dialogue

Pope John Paul II promoted, more than anyone, Assisi and St Francis as emblems of ecumenical dialogue. In November 1978, for his first trip outside of Rome after his election, the new pope went to Assisi. It was also in Assisi, on 27 October 1986, that he inaugurated the first world day of prayer for peace, bringing together representatives of the Catholic Church, of Protestant and Eastern Churches, and Muslim, Buddhist, Jewish, and other religious leaders. The images of these men (and a few women) praying together under the pope's leadership was meant to present a model of peaceful understanding and harmony to a world where religious divisions often provoked violence. In January 1993, in the midst of war in the former Yugoslavia, the pope called a new meeting in Assisi, to pray for peace in the Balkans. John-Paul II wanted to make Assisi a symbol of reconciliation and peace between religions, as interethnic and interreligious warfare plagued a part of Europe. The pope declared:

> Each of us knows that his religious belief is for life and not for death. It is for the respect for every human being, and not for man's oppression of man. It is for peaceful conviviality of nations, peoples, and religions, and not for violent confrontation or war.[61]

It is in this context that different Franciscan authors presented the encounter between Francis and al-Kâmil as a model for ecumenical dialogue. For Capuchin Anton Rotzetter, Francis is a 'Bridge to Islam'.[62] Isaac Vázquez Janeiro affirms that Francis tried neither to convert the sultan nor to obtain martyrdom: he simply wished to have access to the holy places and to respect the beliefs and religious practices of others: 'Francis and Damietta seem to dictate the theme of our seminar on the liberty of conscience as a factor of pacification.'[63] Michael Robson places the encounter under the rubric of 'ecumenical reconciliation': 'In the midst of a simmering violence he sought dialogue and gentle persuasion. This courteous and respectful attitude towards those who did not share his Christian faith is one of the reasons why Francis is held in such admiration and affection in ecumenical circles.' The goal of the encounter was 'pursuit of Truth in a peaceful and respectful manner'.[64] For many Franciscans, starting in the 1980s, the encounter between Francis and al-Kâmil, along with the chapter on mission in the *Regula non bullata*, offer a model of ecumenical dialogue which we should follow, whose purpose is not the conversion of the other, but peaceful cohabitation and mutual understanding.[65]

To present Francis as an apostle of peace does not necessarily imply any knowledge or respect of Islam. A group of Franciscan friars prepared a series of twenty-six prayers for the eighth centenary of the saint's birth (in 1982): among them, a prayer entitled: 'Damietta: prayer for justice and peace'. They affirm that at Damietta Francis contemplated in horror the senseless massacre committed, on both sides, in the name of God. 'He decided to take things into his own hands, and went into Muslim territory to try to find and talk to the Sultan. He knew the danger because of the Muslim belief at that time that to kill a Christian was to guarantee salvation.' Francis made a positive impression on the sultan but did not succeed in converting him. He declared: 'If all Christians were as you, there would be no war between us.'[66] There follows a long prayer calling for peace and reiterating biblical passages concerning peace. These Franciscans present themselves as pacifists in the image of their founder. In their ignorance of Islam, however, they succeed in insulting more severely than most medieval polemicists: they affirm that it was 'a Muslim belief' apparently widespread 'at that time' that to kill a Christian was a sure path to salvation. It is unnecessary to insist that such an idea has never been a 'Muslim belief' and that numerous Christians lived under al-Kâmil's rule, as under the rule of many other Muslim princes. These authors seem to think that the Orient contains only Muslims, unaware that millions of Christians live there. The barbarity of both sides, who think that it is pious to kill infidels, only more dramatically highlights the saint's qualities. We find a similar ignorance with other twentieth-century authors. Peggy Schultz claims that Francis 'met with al-Kâmil, a meeting believed to be the first between a Westerner and a Muslim leader'.[67]

Ecumenism also has its critics in Catholic circles, as we clearly see in some of the reaction to the meetings of Assisi, in particular the first one in 1986. The prayer meetings mixing Catholic, Protestant, and Orthodox priests, Muslim imams, Jewish rabbis, and Buddhist monks did not please everyone. Nor did the temporary transformation of some of the city's churches into mosques or Buddhist temples; in the Church of St Claire, reported some Italian journalists, African animists sacrificed chickens on the altar containing the saint's relics while Native Americans performed ritual dances.[68] Among those absent from the festivities was Cardinal Joseph Ratzinger (the current Pope Benedict XVI), who subsequently expressed his misgivings about the event, urging Catholics to avoid 'relativism' or 'syncretism'.

These same traditional Catholics discovered this sin of relativism in the writings of some Catholic theologians. One of the books which provoked unease in the church was called *Toward a Christian Theology of Religious Pluralism* (1997) by Jacques Dupuis, professor of theology at the Gregorian University in Rome.[69] This Jesuit theologian tries to understand, from a Catholic point of view, the positive role that non-Christian religions play in God's plan. He concludes that these religions can lead to salvation and criticizes those who argue for Christian exclusivism. Once more, Francis's attitude towards Muslims is presented as exemplary:

> In the context of a Church tormented with fear of the Muslim world, Saint Francis of Assisi (1182–1226) was committed from the start to a peaceful approach to the Muslims. He wished to enter into friendship with them and to show that he considered them not enemies but friends. This attitude to the Muslims seems to go back to the time of Francis's conversion and to have been well present in his mind before the Fourth Lateran Council (1215). For the first time in the history of the Church a method of approach to the Muslim world, fully inspired by the Gospel spirit, was being clearly formulated; never before had the Christian, anti-Muslim apologetics taken a similar attitude. For the first time too, in the 'rule' of a religious order, a special chapter was included which dealt with the evangelization of Muslims and the way of approaching them. Francis's voice was truly prophetic in calling for mutual understanding and reconciliation between Christians and their 'Muslim brothers', which would bear fruit later, not least in Vatican II.[70]

He cites *in extenso* the sixteenth chapter of the *Regula non bullata*, which for him shows that Francis considered Muslims as his brothers and friends, not as infidels or enemies of the cross. But alas, this ecumenical spirit, which presaged that of Vatican II more than seven centuries later, was too advanced for the spirit of the times.

> The Gospel spirit of Francis in approaching the Saracens appeared a great innovation; for his contemporaries the Muslims were the wolves that tore to

pieces the flock of Christ. This explains how the text from the 'Early Rule' quoted above came to be substantially altered in the 'Later Rule' (*Regula bullata*), composed under the direction of Cardinal Ugolini and approved by Innocent II (1223). To Francis's great dismay the new text eliminated entirely the irenic program which he had devised for treating the Saracens. The author of the new text did not share the saint's ideas concerning the evangelization of Muslims, which he viewed as utopic, and decided to leave them out.[71]

In other words, Francis created a new strategy of *rapprochement* with his 'Muslim brothers', but the institutional church stifled him, since for it Muslims were bitter enemies. Dupuis's ecumenism is an exercise in squaring a circle: as a Catholic and Jesuit, he must affirm the unique salvific role of the church and of Jesus Christ. But he also wants to recognize the positive role of other religions without reducing them to the status of imperfect expressions of Christianity. He says that those outside the church can find grace through the path of 'baptism of desire'. The ultimate goal of ecumenical dialogue is not conversion from one religion to another, but the ultimate convergence of all religions, at the end of time, in the recognition of the Unique Truth.

This book by a Jesuit, professor of theology in one of the principal universities of the Catholic Church, did not please the Vatican hierarchy. The Congregation for the Doctrine of the Faith, under the direction of Cardinal Ratzinger, opened an inquiry into the orthodoxy of the book in 1998. The Gregorian University announced that Professor Dupuis would be relieved of his teaching duties in order to have time to prepare his response. In 2001, after these investigations, the Congregation published a 'Notification' which saluted the book's erudition and spirit of ecumenical dialogue, but which warned the faithful against its 'ambiguous formulation and insufficient explanations' susceptible, it was feared, to 'provoke confusion and misunderstanding'. The Congregation recalled the unique and role of Christ in the church and for salvation. This decision was seen as a warning against those inside the church who promoted religious 'relativism'.

This warning was confirmed on 19 November 2005, when the same Ratzinger, now Pope Benedict XVI, took from the Franciscans their autonomy within the church, placing them under the joint control of the bishop of Assisi, of Cardinal Camillo Ruini, and of the Italian episcopate. How should one interpret this decision? Vittorio Messori, close to both Popes John-Paul II and Benedict XVI, explains that 'Ratzinger never forgave the Franciscan community for the excesses of the days of prayer in Assisi'. Among other things, the manipulation of the Franciscan legend rankled. Messori reproaches the Franciscans for having made their founder into 'a sort of village idiot who spoke to wolves and birds. In fact, he was not a pacifist. He was a son of the Church of the crusades!' When the journalist asked Messori if Francis had not been a pacifist, he responded:

> Absolutely not. Francis participated in the fifth crusade as a chaplain to the troops and not as a man of peace. He sought by all means to obtain martyrdom in order to reconquer the Holy Land and fell into a depression when the crusaders lost. He did not go see the sultan to dialogue but to convert him and he defied him to walk on burning coals to see who was the more powerful, Christ or Muhammad.[72]

But Francis the pacifist is increasingly evoked in a troubled world in the aftermath of 11 September 2001. While some Cassandras predicted a new world war, a 'Clash of Civilizations' between two monolithic entities called 'Islam' and the 'West', a clash which would be a resuming of age-old hostilities born in the age of the crusades, some more optimistic and ecumenical souls evoked the encounter between Francis and al-Kâmil to show that a *rapprochement* between religions and cultures is possible for those who have an open mind. Authors like the Jesuit Patrick Ryan present Francis and al-Kâmil as role models for those who seek peace and wish to avoid the clash of civilizations.[73] A few weeks after the terrorist attacks on New York and Washington, from 29 September to 27 October 2001, the tenth Ordinary General Assembly of Bishops met in Rome. The recent attacks and their uncertain consequences were no doubt on the minds of the bishops when Giacomo Bini, minister general of the order of Friars Minor, addressed the conference:

> The Bishop, sign of hope, has the task of animating the life of the religious communities of his diocese in the direction of creativity, the acceptance of the risk of new types of presence and new ministries; of encouraging and undertaking paths along which only truly evangelical charity can move; and of stimulating religious to be present in areas of conflict, tension and division, as when Francis of Assisi went unarmed to meet Sultan Malik al-Kâmil and managed to dialogue with him while the crusader armies of all Europe were only concerned with overcoming the enemy. A prophetic gesture like this is a sign of hope for everyone in all times, since it does not offer a definitive or simplistic solution to a problem, but rather opens up new horizons which may become new paths of dialogue and reconciliation.[74]

According to the minister general of the friars minor, Francis is a role model
for twenty-first-century bishops. Francis succeeded in 'dialoguing' with al-
Kâmil. This assertion supposes that the purpose of Francis's enterprise was
dialogue and not the sultan's conversion or the quest for martyrdom. This
unarmed dialogue was in contrast with the crusaders' bellicosity, which
was assuredly not an example to follow. Far from being a mere anecdote or
historical detail, Francis's mission is a 'prophetic gesture', a 'sign of hope'
which should urge the bishops to pursue dialogue and reconciliation when
they are confronted with problems instead of trying (like the crusaders) to
impose a 'definitive or simplistic solution'.

On 29 September 2001 Orianna Fallaci published in the Milanese
newspaper *Il Corriere della sera,* a vicious diatribe against Islam under the
title 'La Rabbia e l'Orgoglio', 'Rage and pride'. This rambling essay is
peppered with invectives not only against the terrorists, but against all those
in Europe who had not realized that the attacks of 9/11 were part of a war
against the West, a war of which Muslim immigration into Europe, which
she presents as a clandestine invasion, is an even more dangerous dimension.
Fallaci affirms the superiority of the West over Islam, of cathedrals over
mosques, of Dante over Umar Khayyâm, etc.

Among the many reactions to the rambling invective of the Italian
pamphleteer was that of journalist Tiziano Terzani, titled 'Il Sultano e San
Francesco' (The Sultan and St Francis), published in *Il Corriere della sera* on
8 October 2001. As the title indicates, Terzani proposes, over and against
the violence of a Bin Laden and the hatred of a Fallaci, the mutual respect
which Francis and al-Kâmil showed for each other. Terzani addresses Fallaci
as an old friend disappointed and bewildered by the unthinking hatred in
'Rage and Pride':

> I'm also writing, publicly, for those of your readers who, perhaps like me,
> were almost as stunned by your outburst as they were by the collapse of
> the towers. I'm writing to let them know they're not alone. Thousands of
> people perished in those towers and with them our sense of security. What
> seemed to die in your words is reason, the noblest part of the human mind,
> and compassion, the noblest sentiment of the human heart.[75]

He reproaches Fallaci for having embarked on a new crusade. We can never
wipe out terrorism through war, affirms Terzani; we should instead try to
understand its causes and resolve them. The causes of Muslim resentment
towards the USA are numerous: favour shown to Israel, thirst for oil,

propping up corrupt governments in the Muslim world, etc. We need new visionaries, sighs Terzani.

Francis and al-Kâmil once more show us the path to follow:

> A phrase of Toynbee's keeps going round in my mind: 'The works of artists and writers live longer than the deeds of soldiers, statesmen and businessmen. Poets and philosophers go further than historians. But the saints and the prophets are worth more than the rest put together.'
>
> Where are the saints and prophets today? We could certainly do with at least one! We need a St. Francis. There were crusades in his day, too, but he was concerned with the others, the ones the crusaders were fighting against. He did all he could to go and find them. The first time he tried, the ship he was sailing on was wrecked, and he only just survived. He tried again, but fell ill on the way and had to turn back. Then, in the siege of Damietta in Egypt during the fifth crusade, embittered by the crusaders' behavior ('he saw evil and sin'), but deeply moved by the sight of the dead on the battlefield, he finally crossed the front line. He was taken prisoner, chained and brought before the Sultan. It's a shame CNN didn't exist in 1219, because it would have been fascinating to see this meeting on television. It must have been remarkable, because after a conversation which doubtless lasted deep into the night, the Sultan allowed St. Francis to return unharmed to the crusaders' encampment the next morning.
>
> I like to imagine each putting his viewpoint to the other, St. Francis speaking of Christ, the Sultan reading passages from the Koran, and them ultimately agreeing with each other on the message that the poor friar of Assisi repeated wherever he went: 'Love your neighbor as yourself'. I also like to imagine there was no aggression between them, given that the friar knew how to laugh as well as preach, and that they parted on good terms in the knowledge that they couldn't stop the course of history anyway.[76]

Francis and al-Kâmil have all the qualities that Fallaci lacks: gentleness, modesty, critical distance. In the midst of a bloody conflict, they found time (one evening, until the wee hours of the morning) to speak with each other. Terziani's Francis seems hostile to the crusade: he takes interest in the crusaders' enemies; he is shocked by the sight of the dead. Terzani does not claim to know what the two men said to each other, but he likes to imagine a relaxed and friendly dialogue. The two men know that they have no power to divert the forces of history: there is no mention either of conversion or of a peaceful end to the war. His Francis wanted above all to 'go see' the enemies of the crusaders, to try to understand them. This is the attitude that Terzani recommends to young Italians: avoid being blinded by hatred and intolerance like Fallaci; go and see the Muslim other, learn his languages, read his literature, study his religion. And do so with modesty and peaceful circumspection, knowing that we cannot stop history, that we will not be able to prevent the violence of the new fanatics of crusade and jihad.

Francis and al-Kâmil were on the minds of those who got together for the third encounter of Assisi, a day of prayer for peace in the world, on 24 January 2002. As the US and its allies were engaged in war in Afghanistan in response to the attacks of 9/11, John-Paul II called together clerics of all confessions to pray for peace. Here is how several enthusiastic participants, five women from the Foundation for a Healing among Nations, describe the pope's endeavour:

> Some say that he is doing what St. Francis did on the battlefield, inviting peace with defenseless hands. Almost eight hundred years ago, the Middle East was under siege of the fifth Crusade and St. Francis made his way to Egypt and miraculously impressed the Sultan al Kamil, a Muslim, with his humble and loving presence. St. Francis asked the Sultan to choose peace.
>
> What is significant to address is that this action which St. Francis initiated almost eight centuries ago was now realizing the fruit of its efforts so tangibly experienced by the meeting of the Mideast religious leaders in Egypt and their agreement for peace declared as the First Alexandria Declaration of the Religious leaders of the Holy Land. This meeting was taking place at the same time the Day of Prayer for Peace was occurring in Assisi on January 21, 2002.[77]

The pope made no direct mention of Francis's encounter with al-Kâmil in his welcoming speech, though he invoked Francis as 'a singular prophet of peace', loved not only by Christians, but by believers of various religions.[78] At a time when fanatical voices were calling for jihad or crusade, the pope presented Francis as a symbol of peace and denounced all violence in the name of religion.[79]

To avoid accusations of syncretism or relativism concerning this encounter, Cardinal Ratzinger (who, as we have seen, expressed misgivings about the 1986 encounter) was brought to Assisi. He subsequently wrote an article about the event for the Catholic monthly *30 giorni*. He explains that the encounter of Assisi implies no lack of differentiation or quality among religions. It is, rather, a very positive sign of a real desire for peace among the faithful of all religions, proof that when one is far from peace, one is far from God. He describes the crowds in the streets of Assisi that applauded the pope when he walked in their midst. This is testimony not only of the respect and love they feel for him, but above all of their admiration for this man who has done so much for justice and peace in the world: 'by the force of his personality, the depth of his faith, and his passion for peace and reconciliation, by the charisma of his office, he succeeded in doing the impossible: calling together, in a pilgrimage for peace, the representatives of a divided Christianity and the representatives of various religions'.[80]

The pope convoked this encounter in Assisi because he had before his eyes a model, Francis who, like him, knew how to pursue peace and reconcile people. The cardinal recalls that Francis was a warrior until his conversion, which occurred in a prison cell in Perugia: it was then 'that he began to think of Christianity in a new way'. His mission to the sultan is the fruit of this new way of thinking:

> And only then did he truly know Christ and understand, too, that the crusades were not the way to defend the rights of Christians in the Holy Land. He saw, rather, that one had to take the message literally in imitation of the Crucified One.
>   This man, Francis, who responded totally to the call of the crucified Christ, continues today to glow with the splendor of the same peace that convinced the sultan, the peace that truly demolishes any wall. If we as Christians embark on the journey to peace following Saint Francis's example, we cannot fear any loss of our identity. For, it will be only then that we find it.[81]

Ratzinger's Francis is above all a man of peace; he rejects the crusades. The fruit of his mission was a 'peace that convinced the sultan': is the cardinal referring to the generous terms that al-Kâmil accorded to the defeated crusaders in 1221 or to the treaty of Jaffa in 1229? In any case, for him the mission was not a failure; Francis's peace convinced the sultan. And Francis and the Orient constitute a model for the Christian who takes the path of peace.

This image of Francis as a 'peaceful crusader' lives on. This was the title given to an Op-Ed piece in the *New York Times* on Christmas Day 2006, by Thomas Cahill, for whom Francis provides a model for us today, an antidote to the clash of civilizations.[82] This idea is expressed artistically by Franciscan iconographer Robert Lentz in 2006, in a painting *St Francis and the Sultan* (Fig. 33). In a mix of Western, Byzantine, and Islamic artistic traditions, Lentz presents the two men in a fraternal embrace. They are both holy men: their golden haloes blend together, doubled by the surrounding flames, the equivalent of haloes in the Persian miniature tradition, and Lentz's response to the legend (which he rejects) of the proposed trial by fire. The name of each is given in Arabic, with, underneath a Qur'ânic adage: 'Praise to God, Lord of the worlds!'[83]

The twentieth century, like the preceding centuries, forged a Francis in its own image, a saint whose actions in Damietta correspond to the needs of his faithful and his admirers. Massignon's and Basetti-Sani's *poverello* sought

Fig. 33. Robert Lentz, *St Francis and the Sultan.*

to bring clear proofs of Christ's love to the Muslims, whom he loved as brothers. For Idries Shah, on the contrary, Francis was a Christian Sufi who came to the East to sit at the feet of those whom he recognized as the true spiritual masters of the day. Other authors are unable to imagine that their hero sought death at the hands of the sultan or even conversion of the Muslims: his adventure was a mission of peace, or the quest for evangelical dialogue. In a world haunted by interreligious violence and apocalyptic predictions of new clashes of civilizations, I may seem pedantic when I stress the fragility of the historical basis for this image of an ecumenical saint hostile to the crusading movement. But the authors of the twentieth and twenty-first centuries do nothing more or less than their predecessors: create a saint that fits their ideological needs.

Epilogue

What is there left to say about this peculiar encounter between two men, in an armed camp pitched in the sands of the Nile delta? Is this meeting, which has fascinated and perplexed many authors and artists from the thirteenth century to the twenty-first, any more comprehensible at the end of this book than it was at the outset? Or is it rather a distant mirror in which, over the centuries, each observer perceives only the fleeting reflection of his own fears and hopes? Once we strip away the prejudice and the polemical or apologetical agendas of each writer, from crusading bishop Jacques de Vitry to Pope Benedict XVI, via Bossuet and Voltaire, what is left of the event itself, the dialogue in al-Kâmil's tent? Not much, one is tempted to reply.

This brings us to a classic problem that confronts every historian, whose sources are inevitably subjective and incomplete. After all, what in fact do we know about other events which have come to be seen as milestones, watersheds, or *lieux de mémoire*: Christopher Columbus's first encounter with Native Americans, the conversion of Constantine, or the lives of great religious leaders (Buddha, Jesus, Muhammad)? A few scraps of information, incomplete and problematic texts, most of them written well after the fact for specific ideological purposes, then reworked and elaborated upon over the centuries. Some have tried to go back to these sources, to scrape away the layers of additions and commentaries to find the pristine original text. But beyond these fragmentary sources, the historian gazes into emptiness and admits his ignorance.

Michel de Certeau aptly described the difficult and paradoxical position of the historian of religion. In a society in which religion is no longer the dominant force which it once was, it becomes an object of curiosity and erudition. Our chronological and cultural distance from the Christian or

Muslim Middle Ages, or from the age of the wars of religion (Certeau's field of study) permits us to see clearly, more objectively than those who lived though the events in question. Yet we remain, whether or not we admit it, prisoners of our sources: 'antiquated polemics unconsciously shape scholarly research' in the twentieth century, as Certeau remarked in regard to the history of Jansenism.[1] We have seen that the same is true of Franciscan history: the writings concerning Francis's life and the beginnings of the order are indelibly marked by the problems and conflicts that shook the order during its first two centuries. When we try to perceive Francis, we always see him through the deforming lenses of the sources.

Rather than try to find Francis and al-Kâmil behind the multiple deforming mirrors, I have studied the play of light, of reflections between these mirrors. Why have so many authors and artists been fascinated by this encounter? Because for them, it was not merely a curiosity, or a footnote to the history of a crusade which failed on the banks of the Nile. It was much more: an emblematic encounter or confrontation between East and West. Emblematic in what way? Here, of course, the image was ever shifting. For Franciscan authors, from the thirteenth century to the twenty-first, Francis is the supreme model of sanctity. His trip to Egypt, like so many other events in his life, becomes an additional proof of his holiness. It also becomes the act of foundation of activities central to the order: quest for martyrdom, mission, guardianship of the holy sites or (more recently) pursuit of ecumenical dialogue.

The successes of the friars minor make Francis into the favourite target of the order's enemies, especially the Protestants and free-thinkers who, from Erasmus Alber to Voltaire and Jean Henri Maubert de Gouvest, paint the *poverello* as a fanatic hoping to die at the hands a wise and generous sultan who refuses to harm him. As a symbol of the rejection of the world, founder of a powerful order of the Catholic Church, Francis was an object of attack and mockery from those who fought against the church's power. This of course provoked traditional Catholics, in particular Franciscans, to staunchly defend their patron saint.

Yet since the nineteenth and especially twentieth centuries, the saint's popularity is not confined to Catholic circles. This man who rejected his family's riches to lead a life of poverty and simplicity, who praises nature and speaks to birds and wolves, continues to inspire admiration and fascination well beyond the Catholic Church. Lay and Catholic authors of the twentieth century invoke him as a model and a source of inspiration for solidarity with the poor, for the search for simpler lifestyles, for the respect for the environment, or (in our case) as a model of dialogue with the 'Other'. No saint of the Catholic Church, one is tempted to say, can rival the *poverello*'s popularity. Why take interest in a little Umbrian who has been dead for almost eight centuries? Why this continuous fascination? Even the attacks of an Erasmus Alber or a Jean Henri Maubert de Gouvest only attest to the ubiquity of a devotion they decry, for a person who fascinates even his most staunch opponents. Francis leaves no one indifferent.

At the heart of this study is the problem of the relationship between history and memory. As Pierre Nora has said, 'Memory is an absolute and history only knows the relative'.[2] The encounter at Damietta is a *lieu de mémoire*, an event which has become a lesson and example, which one develops in accordance with one's purposes (encouraging devotion for the saint, promoting the crusades, affirming the superiority of Europe over the Arab world, etc.). This begs the question of the utility and necessity of historical memory. Why do we need to identify, in the course of history, model men and women whom we hold up as examples to follow? If we think that we must launch a new crusade or, on the contrary, that Europe should be more open to the Muslim world, why do we need to recruit to our cause, posthumously, this little Umbrian from the thirteenth century?

These are, of course, questions without answers. Having deconstructed the ideological prejudices and assumptions of artists and writers from Jacques de Vitry to Tiziano Terzani, I cannot proffer a 'true' or 'objective' version of the encounter at Damietta. I can only observe that modesty behooves the historian who, in gazing into the murky waters of the past, may see above all his own reflection, the image of his hopes and fears. I simply hope that, through this presentation of the game of mirrors concerning the *lieu de mémoire* of the meeting at Damietta, I have been able to shed a bit of light.

Notes

INTRODUCTION

1. Joseph-François Michaud, *Histoire des Croisades* (2nd edn. Paris: Ponthier, 1826), iii. 466–7.
2. Cardinal Joseph Ratzinger, 'Lo splendore della pace di Francesco', *30 Giorni*, 20/1 (Jan. 2002).
3. Thomas Cahill, 'The Peaceful Crusader', *New York Times*, 25 Dec. 2006.
4. For a political and military biography of al-Kâmil, see Hans Gottschalk, *Al-Malik al-Kâmil von Egypten und seine Zeit: Eine Studie zur Geschichte Vorderasiens und Egyptens in der ersten Hälfte des 7./13. Jahrhunderts* (Wiesbaden: Harrassowitz, 1958). To situate his reign in its historical context, see Carl Petry (ed.), *The Cambridge History of Egypt*, i. *Islamic Egypt, 640–1517* (Cambridge: CUP, 1998).
5. 2C 30; see Ch. 3 below.
6. Oliver of Paderborn, *Historia damiatina*, §31, in *Die Schriften des Kölner Domscholasters, spätern Bischofs von Paderborn und Kardinal-Bischofs von S. Sabina Oliverus*, ed. O. Hoogeweg (Bibliothek des literarischen Vereins in Stuttgart, 202; Stuttgart, 1894), 159–280.
7. On the status of *dhimmi* in general, see Claude Cahen, 'Dhimmi', EI². On Egypt, see Terry Wilfong, 'The Non-Muslim Communities: Christian Communities', in Petry (ed.), *Cambridge History of Egypt*, i. 175–97; Norman Stillman, 'The Non-Muslim Communities: The Jewish Community', ibid. 198–210.
8. One of the Monophysite clerics, Butrus al-Sadamantî, apparently composed a summary (now lost) of these debates. See Benjamin Kedar, *Crusade and Mission: European Approaches to the Muslims* (Princeton: Princeton University Press, 1984), 123; Georg Graf, *Geschichte der christlichen arabischen Literatur* (5 vols. Vatican: Biblioteca Apostolica Vaticana, 1944–53), ii. 357, 365.
9. Theodore I Lascaris's initiative is known only through the response to it, which the sultan delegated to a certain Sâlih ibn al-Husayn al-Ja'farî. Erdmann Fritsch, *Islam und Christentum im Mittelalter: Beiträge zur Geschichte der muslimischen Polemik gegen das Christentum in arabischer Sprache* (Breslau: Müller & Seiffert, 1930), 17. The Arabic text is published as *Disputatio pro religione Muhammedanorum adversus Christianos: Testum arabicum e codice leidensi,*

ed. F. J. Van den Ham (Leiden: Brill, 1877–90). Oliver of Paderborn, *Epistola*, 5, in *Schriften*, 296–307; on this letter, see Anna-Dorothee von den Brincken, 'Islam und Oriens Christianus in den Schriften des Kölner Domscholasters Oliver (+1227)', in Albert Zimmerman and Ingrid Craemer-Ruegenberg (eds.), *Orientalische Kultur und europäisches Mittelalter* (Berlin: Walter de Gruyter, 1985), 86–102; John Tolan, *Saracens: Islam in the Medieval European Imagination* (New York: Columbia University Press, 2002), 199–202.

10. These texts, with those concerning the martyrs of 1227, are partially edited in *AASS*, 16 Jan., ii. 426–35. Several Franciscan chronicles of the Middle Ages relate the history of the martyrs; see the *Chronica XXIV Generalium ministrorum ordinis fratrum minorum*, in *AF* iii. 15–33, 579–96, and 613–16. This chronicle was written by Franciscan friar Arnaud de Sarrant *c*.1370; on this text, see Maria Teresa Dolso, *La Chronica XXIV generalium: Il difficile percorso dell'unità nella storia francescana* (Padua: Centro Studi Antoniani, 2003). On the texts about these martyrs, see Isabelle Heullant-Donat, 'La Perception des premiers martyrs franciscains à l'intérieur de l'Ordre au XIIIe siècle', in S. Cassagnes-Brouquet, A. Chauou, D. Pichot, and L. Rousselot, *Religion et mentalités au moyen âge: Mélanges en l'honneur d'Hervé Martin* (Rennes: Presses Universitaires de Rennes, 2003), 211–20; Tolan, *Saracens*, 336 n. 9; James D. Ryan, 'Missionary Saints of the High Middle Ages: Martyrdom, Popular Veneration, and Canonization', *Catholic Historical Review*, 90 (2004), 1–28.

11. Arnauld de Sarrant, *Chronica XXIV Generalium Ordinis Minorum*, in *AF* iii (1897), 593.

12. Giordano di Giano, *Chronica Fratris Jordani*, §8, H. Boehmer (ed.), *Collection d'études et de documents sur l'histoire religieuse et littéraire du moyen âge*, 6 (Paris, 1908).

13. Heullant-Donat, 'La Perception des martyrs'.

14. *RNB* 16, tr. in *ED* 74–5.

15. For David Flood, chs. 14–17 were written shortly before the fourth Lateran council (1215) and were at this time added to the primitive rule. But no 13th-cent. source confirms this hypothesis. See Flood, *Die Regula non bullata der Minderbruder* (Werl in Westfalen: Dietrich-Coelde-Verlag, 1967), 125, 129.

16. *RB* 12; tr. *ED* 106.

17. Honorius III adressed his bull *Vinee Domini custodes* to 'dilectis filiis fratribus predicatoribus et minoribus in regno Miramolini', to whom he enjoins: 'convertatis incredulos, erigatis lapsos, sustentetis debiles, pusillanimes consolemini et fortis nihilominus confortetis', *BF* i. 24; T. Ripoll and A. Bremond (eds.), *Bullarium ordinis fratrum praedicatorum* (8 vols. Rome, 1729–49), i. 16. See Kedar, *Crusade and Mission*, 143–4.

18. *BF* i.26; republ. with corrections by I. Vázquez Janeiro, 'Conciencia eclesial e interpretación de la Regla francescana', *Spicilegium Pontificii Athenaei Antoniani*,

24 (Rome, 1983), 27–8; see Vázquez Janeiro, 'I Francescani et il dialogo con gli ebrei e saraceni nei secoli XIII–XV', *Antonianum*, 65 (1990), 533–49, esp. pp. 542–3.

19. See Tolan, *Saracens*, 218–19; Tolan, 'Taking Gratian to Africa: Raymond de Penyafort's Legal Advice to the Dominicans and Franciscans in Tunis (1234)', in Adnan Husain and Katherine Fleming (eds.), *A Faithful Sea: The Religious Cultures of the Mediterranean, 1200–1700* (Oxford: One World, 2007), 47–63.

CHAPTER 1

1. Jacques de Vitry, in *Lettres de Jacques de Vitry 1160/70–1240, évêque de Saint-Jean d'Acre*, ed. R. B. C. Huygens (Leiden: Brill, 1960); tr. from *ED* i. 580–1.

2. Jacques de Vitry, *Historia occidentalis*, ed. J. F. Hinnebusch (Fribourg: Schweiz Universitätsverlag, 1972), ch. 22, pp. 161–2; I have reproduced the tr. from *ED* i. 580–1, with corrections.

3. J. Benton, 'Qui étaient les parents de Jacques de Vitry?', *Le Moyen Age*, 70 (1964), 39–47; Philipp Funk, *Jakob von Vitry: Leben une Werke* (Leipzig: Teubner, 1909; repr. Hildesheim: Gerstenberg, 1973); John Hinnebusch, 'Extant Manuscripts of the Writings of Jacques de Vitry', *Scriptorium*, 51 (1997), 156–64.

4. See John Baldwin, *Masters, Princes and Merchants: The Social Views of Peter the Chanter and his Circle* (2 vols. Princeton: Princeton University Press, 1970); Franco Morenzoni, *Des écoles aux paroisses: Thomas de Chobham et la promotion de la prédication au début du XIIIe siècle* (Paris: Institut d'études augustiniennes, 1995); Nicole Bériou, *L'Avènement des maîtres de la Parole: La Prédication à Paris au XIIIe siècle* (Paris: Institut d'études augustiniennes, 1998).

5. Jacques de Vitry, *Vita Mariae oigniacensis*, in *AASS* xxiv (23 June), 542–88; English tr. Margot H. King, *Life of Mary of Oignies* (Toronto: Peregrina Publishing Co., 1993), here p. 99.

6. Jacques de Vitry, *Life of Mary of Oignies*, 81.

7. Ibid. 60.

8. Ibid. 107.

9. Ibid. 108.

10. The date of the bishop's approbation is uncertain, but it is probably in June 1215, according to William Hinnebusch, *The History of the Dominican Order* (New York: Alba House, 1966), 40–2.

11. Petrus Vallium Sarnaii Monachus (Pierre des Vaux de Cernay), *Hystoria albigensis*, ed. P. Guébin and E. Lyon (3 vols. Paris: Honoré Champion, 1926–9), §285 (Latin text, i. 281–3; 13th-cent. French tr., iii. 99), §105 (Latin text, ii. 7; 13th-cent. French tr., iii. 105).

12. Jacques de Vitry, *Life of Mary of Oignies*, p. 156.

13. Petrus Vallium Sarnaii Monachus, *Hystoria albigensis*, §508 (Latin text, ii. 202; 13th-cent. French tr., iii. 161).

14. On this crusade, see James Powell, *Anatomy of a Crusade, 1213–1221* (Philadelphia: University of Pennsylvania Press, 1994). The principal Latin chronicle is Oliver of Paderborn, *Historia damiatina*, in *Die Schriften des Kölner Domscholasters, spätern Bischofs von Paderborn und Kardinal-Bischofs von S. Sabina Oliverus*, ed. O. Hoogeweg (Bibliothek des literarischen Vereins in Stuttgart, 202; Stuttgart, 1894), 159–280; Jacques de Vitry's are an important source for the crusade. On the principal Arab chroniclers for the Ayyubid period, see Donald Little, 'Historiography of the Ayyûbid and Mamlûk epochs', in Petry (ed.), *Cambridge History of Egypt*, i. 412–44 (esp. 414–20); Hans Gottschalk, *Al-Malik al-Kâmil von Egypten und seine Zeit: Eine Studie zur Geschichte Vorderasiens und Egyptens in der ersten Hälfte des 7./13. Jahrhunderts* (Wiesbaden: Harrassowitz, 1958), 6–16. On the Coptic sources, see Johannes den Heijer, 'Coptic Historiography in the Fâtimid, Ayyûbid and Early Mamlûk Periods', *Medieval Encounters*, 2 (1996), 67–98. Three important chronicles are available in French or English trs.: Al-Makîn ibn al-'Amîd, *Chronique des Ayyoubides*, tr. Anne-Marie Eddé and Françoise Micheau, *Documents relatifs à l'histoire des croisades*, xvi (Paris: Académie des Inscriptions et Belles-Lettres, 1994); *History of the Patriarchs of the Egyptian Church, Known as the History of the Holy Church*, edn. of the Arabic text and English tr. by Antoine Khater and Oswald Burmester (4 vols. Cairo: Société d'archéologie copte, 1943–74); Ahmad ibn 'Ali al-Maqrîzî (15th-cent. chronicler), *A History of the Ayyubid Sultans of Egypt*, tr. R. J. C. Broadhurst (Boston: Twayne, 1980).

15. Humbert de Romans, *De Dono timoris*, Paris, Bibliothèque Nationale MS Latin 15953, cited by Jean Welter, *L'Exemplum dans la littérature religieuse et didactique du moyen âge* (Paris and Toulouse: Occitania, 1927; repr. Genève: Slatkine, 1973), 118.

16. Jacques de Vitry, *Sermo ad crucesignatos vel -signandos* 2. 37, ed. and English tr. Christoph Maier, *Crusade Propaganda and Ideology: Model Sermons for the Preaching of the Cross* (Cambridge: CUP, 2000), 120–1. On these sermons, see Maier, *Preaching the Crusades: Mendicant Friars and the Cross in the Thirteenth Century* (Cambridge: CUP, 1994); Penny Cole, *The Preaching of the Crusades to the Holy Land, 1095–1270* (Cambridge, Mass.: Medieval Academy of America, 1991); Jeannine Horowitz, 'Les *exempla* au service de la prédication de la croisade au XIIIᵉ siècle', *Revue d'Histoire Ecclésiastique*, 92 (1997), 367–94.

17. 'Il ot en France. 1. bon clerc, qui preeça de le crois, qui ot à non maistres Jakes de Viteri. Cil en croisa moult, là ou il estoit en predication. L'eslirent il cannone d'Acre et manderent a l'apostole qu'il lor envoiast par lui faire evesque. Et saciés vous bien de voir, s'il n'en eust le commandement de l'apostole, il ne l'eust mie recueillie; mais toutes eures passa il outre mer et fu vesques, grant piece. Et si fist moult de bien ne le tiere; mais puis le resigna il, et revint arriere en France, et pui le fist il apostoles cardenal de Rome.' *Chronique d'Ernoul et de Bernard le Trésorier*, ed. L. de Mas-Latrie (Paris, 1871), ch. 35, p. 410. On this text, see the following chapter.

18. The critical edn. contains seven letters, but the third, which is extant in only two manuscripts, does not seem to have been written by Jacques. See Huygens, introd. to his edn. of the *Lettres,* 528–30. On the dating of the letters, ibid. 534–7.

19. Jacques de Vitry, *Lettres,* i. 120–49; tr. in *ED* i. 579–80.

20. Pia Gemelli, 'Giacomo da Vitry e le origini del movimento francescano', *Aevum,* 39 (1965), 474–86; R. Huygens, 'Les Passages des lettres de Jacques de Vitry relatifs à saint François d'Assise et à ses premiers disciples', *Hommage à Léon Hermann* (Collection Latomus, 44; Brussels, 1960), 446–53.

21. J. Dalarun, *François d'Assise ou le pouvoir en question: Principes et modalités du gouvernement dans l'ordre des Frères mineurs* (Brussels: De Boeck, 1999), 24, 30.

22. Bernard Vollot, 'La Règle des frères mineurs de 1216', *Franciscana* 2 (2000); *ED* i. 87–96.

23. John Pryor, 'The Voyage of Jacques de Vitry from Genoa to Acre, 1216: Juridical and Economical Problems in Medieval Navigation', in M. Peláez (ed.), *Derecho de la navegación in Europa* (Barcelona: Promociones Publicaciones Universitarias, 1987), 1689–1714.

24. See *History of the Patriarchs of the Egyptian Church,* 4. 41; Mackenzie, *Ayyubid Cairo: A Topographical Study* (Cairo: American University in Cairo Press, 1992), 57–8.

25. On the topography, see the map in Powell, *Anatomy,* 139; that of Jonathan Riley-Smith, *Atlas of the Crusades* (New York: Facts on File, 1991), 95, is inexact, since it indicates the current coastline (whereas Powell's shows the coastline as it was, in theory, in the thirteenth century).

26. Al-Maqrîzî, *History,* 167.

27. On the dating, see Huygens, introd. to Jacques de Vitry, *Lettres,* 534–7; the third letter of the collection is probably not in fact by Jacques (ibid. 528–30).

28. Jacques de Vitry, *Historia orientalis,* ed. F. Moschus (Douai, 1597; repr. Westmead, 1971), §15; *Lettres de Jacques de Vitry 1160/70–1240, évêque de Saint-Jean d'Acre,* ed. R. B. C. Huygens (Leiden: Brill, 1960 and 2000) §5. 5–43.

29. See *Gesta obsidionis Damiate,* in Reinholdus Röhricht (ed.), *Quinti belli sacri scriptores minores sumptibus* (Geneva: J. G. Fick, 1879), 73–115 (here 111–15); Sibt Ibn al-Jawzî, *Mir'ât al-zamân,* passage tr. Anne-Marie Eddé in H. Bresc *et al.* (eds.), *La Méditerranée entre pays d'Islam et monde latin (milieu X^e–milieu XIIIe siècle): Textes et documents* (Paris: Sedes, 2001), 62–4; Powell, *Anatomy,* 162.

30. *Letter* 6. 11–13; Ps. 106: 16 (Vulgate, 107) and 46: 3 (47).

31. This information is confirmed by Oliver of Paderborn, ch. 33; Oliver affirms that Jacques also baptized children captured during a raid on Mount Tabor in Syria (ch. 3).

32. The other hypothesis, put forward by Huygens (Jacques de Vitry, *Lettres,* 621–2 n.), is that this passage was included in the letter sent to the pope but then removed by a pro-Franciscan scribe—the scribe of MS A or of its

exemplar. I find this less plausible: why would a pro-Franciscan scribe remove the whole passage, and not simply the parts critical of the Franciscans?

33. Dalarun, *François d'Assise*, 34.

34. Golubovich, i. 7; Martiniano Roncaglia, *St. Francis and the Middle East* (Cairo: Mondial Press, 1957), 23 n. 38; Huygens, note to Jacques de Vitry, *Lettres,* 621–2 n.

35. In this context, 'Henricus' seems to be the same as 'Henricus senescalcus ecclesie nostre' mentioned previously in the same letter (6. 270b).

36. Oliver of Paderborn, *Historia damiatina*, §56; a similar book, according to Oliver, was discovered just before the capture of the city (see §35); cf. Jacques de Vitry, *Lettres,* 7. On these texts, see Jean Richard, 'The Mongols and Franks', *Journal of Asian History*, 3 (1969), 45–57, repr. in J. Richard, *Orient et Occident au moyen âge: Contacts et relations, XIIe–XVe s.* (London: Variorum, 1976), esp. p. 45; Richard, 'L'Extrême-Orient légendaire au moyen âge: Roi David et Prêtre Jean', *Annales d'Éthiopie*, 2 (1957), 225–42; repr. in Richard, *Orient et Occident*, esp. pp. 228 and 230; François de Medeiros, *L'Occident et l'Afrique*, 193–203; Charles Beckingham and Bernard Hamilton (eds.), *Prester John, the Mongols, and the Ten Lost Tribes* (Aldershot: Variorum, 1996); Powell, *Anatomy*, 178–80; Tolan, *Saracens*, 199–201.

37. Oliver of Paderborn, *Historia damiatina*, §35, here quoted from the English tr. by John J. Gavigan, *The Capture of Damietta* (Philadelphia: University of Pennsylvania Press, 1948; repr. New York, 1980), 89–90. On this passage, see Tolan, *Sons of Ishmael: Muslims through European Eyes in the Middle Ages* (Gainesville, Fla.: University Press of Florida, 2008), ch. 2.

38. Oliver of Paderborn, *Historia damiatina*, §48.

39. Sibt Ibn al-Jawzî, *Mir'ât al-zamân*, passage tr. into French by Anne-Marie Eddé in Bresc *et al.* (eds.), *La Méditerranée*, 63.

40. Oliver of Paderborn, *Historia damiatina*, §§79–80.

41. Christian Cannuyer, 'La Date de rédaction de l'*Historia Orientalis* de Jacques de Vitry (1160/70–1240), évêque d'Acre', *Revue d'Histoire Ecclésiastique*, 78 (1983), 65–72. For a French tr. of this text, see Jacques de Vitry, *Histoire orientale*, tr. Marie-Geneviève Grossel (Paris: Honoré-Champion, 2005).

42. *Chronique d'Ernoul et de Bernard le Trésorier*, ch. 38, pp. 444–6; on this text, see Ch. 2 below.

43. On the dating of the work, see Hinnebusch's introduction to his edn. of the *Historia occidentalis*, pp. 16–20.

44. Jacques de Vitry, *Historia occidentalis* 77.

45. Ibid. 92.

46. Ibid. 107.

47. Ibid. 158–9; tr. *ED* i. 582.

48. Jacques de Vitry, *Historia occidentalis* 162; tr. *ED* i. 585.

49. Jacques de Vitry, *Historia occidentalis* 159; tr. *ED* i. 583; Matt. 10: 9–10; Luke 10: 4.

CHAPTER 2

1. *Chronique d'Ernoul et de Bernard le Trésorier*, ed. L. de Mas-Latrie (Paris, 1871), ch. 37, pp. 431–5; tr. from *ED* i. 605–7 (tr. slightly modified).

2. See John Pryor, 'The *Eracles* and William of Tyre: An Interim Report', in Benjamin Z. Kedar (ed.), *The Horns of Hattin* (Jerusalem: Jerusalem: Yad Izhak Ben-Zvi and London: Variorum, 1992), 270–93; J. Folda, 'Manuscripts of the History of Outremer by William of Tyre: A Handlist', *Scriptorium*, 27 (1973), 90–5.

3. 'Dont fist descendre un sien vallet qui avoit non Ernous. Ce fu cil qui ceste conte fist metre en escrit.' *Chronique d'Ernoul et de Bernard le Trésorier*, 149; cf. Margaret Morgan, *The Chronicle of Ernoul and the Continuations of William of Tyre* (Oxford: OUP, 1973), 41. On this chronicle, see also Catherine Croizy-Naquet, 'La Description de Jérusalem in *La Chronique d'Ernoul*', *Romania*, 115 (1997), 69–89.

4. 'Ceste conte de la terre d'outre mer fist faire le tresoriers Bernars, de sant piere de Corbie. En l'ancanacion. millo. ccxxxij.', cited by Morgan, *Chronicle of Ernoul*, 46.

5. Morgan, *Chronicle of Ernoul*, ch. 4.

6. See Tolan, *Sons of Ishmael*, ch. 8.

7. *RNB* 3. 8; *RB* 3. 4.

8. *Chronique d'Ernoul et de Bernard le Trésorier*, 421. The idea that the Caliph is the 'Saracens' Pope' is found in other 12th- and 13th-cent. texts. The *Diversitate Saracenorum et hostium Christianitatis et sectis et civitatibus eorum*, which gives a description of Saladin's troops at the siege of Acre in 1189–91, affirms 'Calyphus vero de Baldac, qui est princeps et pontifex legis saracenice, per totum Orientem suos predicatores direxit et, facta venia peccatorum secundum legem Maometh, ingentes populos et plurima regna adversus Dominum et adversus Christum eius commovit' (ed. Benjamin Kedar, 'A Western Survey of Saladin's Forces at the Siege of Acre', in B. Kedar and J. Riley-Smith (eds.), *Montjoie: Studies in Crusader History in Honor of Hans Eberhard Meyer* (Aldershot: Variorum, 1997), 113–22, here 122). In a similar fashion, the patriarch of Jerusalem and the Templar and Hospitaler masters explain to Pope Innocent III that in Baghdad is 'papa Sarracenorum Caliphius, qui colitur, timetur et adoratur tamquam Romanus pontifex in lege eorum' (Ryccardus de Sancto Germano, *Chronica*, ed. C. A. Garufi, *Rerum Italicarum Scriptores* NS 7/2: 56, cited by Kedar, 'Western Survey', 117 n. 20). Thanks to Benjamin Kedar for having brought these texts to my attention.

9. See Tolan, *Sons of Ishmael*, ch. 6; Margaret A. Jubb, *The Legend of Saladin in Western Literature and Historiography* (Lewiston, NY: Edwin Mellen Press, 2000); Anne-Marie Eddé, *Saladin* (Paris: Flammarion, 2008).

10. Oliver of Paderborn, *Historia damiatina*, §§82–3.

11. Anonymous continuation to the *Ernoul*, in *RHC occ.* ii. 348; the tr. in *ED* i. 609 is defective.

12. *RHC occ.* ii. 348. A few pages later, after the final defeat, the same chronicle gives a different assessment: 'Ensi fu perdue la noble cité de Damiate par peché et par folie et par l'orgueil et la malice dou clergé et des religions' (*RHC occ.* ii. 352).

13. BN Ms Fr. 352, fo. 169b: 'Il y avoit ii. clers en Damiete qui alerent par conduit au soudant et li disent quil venoient a lui pour lui sauver sarme sil les voloit bien croire. Li souin lor dist quil avoit de boins clers de sa loy que il manderoit. Mandés furent; si distrent au soudant: "Sire, tu es expiex de la loi, si la dois garder. Nous te commandons de par Mahomet que tu a ces ii. faces les testes cauper. Car ensi l'ensaigne la lois." Il respondi que non feroit, mes dist as clers: "Ou cas que vous estes venus pour mame sauver, se voles demourer o moi, ie vous donrre grans possessions." Cil disent que non, ne il ne vaudrent prendre nus presens que on lor vout faire. Lors les fist raconduire en lost des crestiens.' I have slightly corrected, from the manuscript, the text given by Röhricht, *Testimonia minora de quinto bello sacro e cronheres occientalibus* (Geneva: Fick, 1882), 133, and repr. by Golubovich, 40–1.

14. Brussels, Bibl. royale, ms. 11142, fo. 120; see Mas-Latrie, 'descriptions des manuscrits', *Chronique d'Ernoul*, pp. xxxvii–xxxviii). On this illumination, see Fanny Caroff, 'L'Adversaire, l'autre, l'Oriental: L'Iconographie du monde musulman in le contexte des croisades. Manuscrits enluminés en France du Nord, en Flandre et in les États latins d'Orient entre le XIIIe et le XVe siècle' (3 vols., thèse de doctorat, Université de Paris I, 2002), i. 223–32; iii. 640. I thank Fanny Caroff for having brought this manuscript to my attention.

15. *Conti di Antichi Cavalieri*, ed. A. Del Monte (Milan: Cisalpino-Goliardica, 1972); Italian text with French tr. and introd. by Gérard Genot and Paul Larivaille in *Novellino, suivi de Contes de chevaliers du temps jadis* (Paris, 1988), tale number 16, p. 302.

16. On the image of Saladin in the *Conti*, see Tolan, *Sons of Ishmael*, 92, 94, 96, 98–9.

CHAPTER 3

1. 1C 57, tr. *ED* i. 231.

2. Giordano, *Chronica*, §§19, 30, and 31.

3. Ibid., §59.

4. See Jacques Dalarun, *La Malaventure de François d'Assise: Pour un usage historique des légendes franciscaines* (Paris: Éditions Franciscaines, 2002), 91–2.

5. Gregory IX, *Mira circa nos* (Perugia, 19 July 1228), *BF* i. 42–5; See R. Armstrong, '*Mira circa nos*: Gregory IX's View of St Francis of Assisi', *Greyfriars Review*, 4 (1990), 75–100 (repr. in *Laurentianum*, 25 (1984), 385–414); Ruth Wolff, *Der heilige Franziskus in Schriften und Bildern des 13. Jahrhunderts* (Berlin: Gebr. Mann, 1996), 37–59.

6. David Abulafia, *Frederick II: A Medieval Emperor* (London: Penguin, 1988).

7. David Abulafia, *Frederick II: A Medieval Emperor* 152.

8. Ibid. 164–9.

9. Al-Makîn ibn Al-'Amîd, *Chronique des Ayyoubides*, 38–9. Cf. al-Maqrîzî, *Histoire d'Egypte*, in *Revue de l'Orient Latin* 9:509 ff; Badr al-Dîn, '*Iqd al-jamân, RHC or.* ii. 185–94. On these negotiations and on Frederic's crusade, see R. Stephen Humphreys, *From Saladin to the Mongols: The Ayyubids of Damascus, 1193–1260* (Albany, NY: State University of New York Press, 1977), 183–204; Thomas Van Cleve, 'The Crusade of Frederick II', in Kenneth Setton (ed.), *History of the Crusades* (6 vols. Madison: University of Wisconsin Press, 1969–89), ii. 429–62; Abulafia, *Frederick II*, 164–201.

10. Ibn Wâsil, *Mufarrij al-kurûb*, passage tr. into French by Thierry Bianquis and Pierre Guichard, in *Pays d'Islam et monde latin, X^e–XIIIe siècle: Textes et documents* (Lyon: Presses Universitaires de Lyon, 2000), 232; Abulafia, *Frederick II*, 170–1; Joshua Prawer, *Histoire du royaume latin de Jérusalem* (2 vols. Paris: CNRS, 1969–70), ii. 176.

11. Celano says that one king was present at the canonization, without naming him; it was probably Jean de Brienne (1C 124).

12. *BF* i. 40–1.

13. G. Barone, 'L'azione degli Ordini Mendicanti', in Pierre Toubert and Agostino Paravicini Bagliani (eds.), *Federico II e le città italiane* (Palermo: Selerio, 1994), 278–89.

14. *BF* i. 45. See Rona Goffen, *Spirituality in Conflict: Saint Francis and Giotto's Bardi Chapel* (University Park, Pa.: Pennsylvania State University Press, 1988), 2.

15. See Ch. 7 below.

16. Le Goff, *St. François d'Assise* (Paris: Gallimard, 1999), 70; John Moorman, *A History of the Franciscan Order: From its Origins to the Year 1517* (Oxford: OUP, 1968), 47; André Callebaut, 'Autour de la rencontre à Florence de Saint François et du Cardinal Hugolin en été 1217', *Archivum Franciscanum Historicum,* 19 (1926), 530–58.

17. For the different versions of Francis's last benediction, see J. Dalarun, *François d'Assise ou le pouvoir en question* (Brussels: De Boeck, 1999), 50–65.

18. See Dalarun, *Malaventure*, 22–6, 86.

19. Ibid.; on the structure of the *Vita prima*, see Dalarun, 'Les Prologues des légendes franciscaines', in Ludovico Gatto et Paola Supino Martin (eds.), *Studi sulle società e le culture del Medioevo per Girolamo Arnaldi* (Florence: All'Insegna del Giglio, 2002), 157–81 (esp. pp. 158–60).

20. N. Tammassia, *S. Francesco d'Assisi e la sua leggenda* (Padua and Verona, 1906), 73, 81, cited by Wolff, *Der heilige Franziskus*, 92.

21. 1C 112; see Wolff, *Der heilige Franziskus*, 92.

22. Jacques Le Goff, *Saint Louis* (Paris: Gallimard, 1996).

23. Gregory the Great, *De vitis patrum liber tertius sive verba seniorum*, 67 (PL 73. 772); Wolff, *Der heiliege Franziskus*, 151.

24. See John Moorman, *A History of the Franciscan Order* (Oxford: Clarendon Press, 1968 and 1998), 21–31; Grado Merlo, *Nel nome di San Francesco: Storia dei frati minori e del francescanesimo sino agli inizi del 16. secolo* (Padua: Editrici francescane, 2003), 19–28.

25. See Tolan, *Saracens*, ch. 5.

26. 'Sed nimirum in his omnibus suum vir beatus desiderium non implevit cui mirabilius in singularis gratiae praerogativam gerenda suorum dominus insignia stigmatum reservavit.' Julien de Spire, *Vita sancti Francisci*, in *Analecta Franciscana*, 10 (1926–41), 333–71.

27. Honorius III, *Cum dilecti filii*, BF i. 2; Moorman, *History*, 50.

28. Honorius III, *Cum secundum consilium*, BF i. 6; Merlo, *Nel nome di San Francesco*, 40; Moorman, *History*, 50.

29. *Rule of Saint Benedict*, ch. 58.

30. Giordano, *Chronica*, §15; Moorman, *History*, 50.

31. Giordano, *Chronica*, §§12–14; Moorman, *History*, 50.

32. According to Paul Sabatier (*Vie de Saint François d'Assise* (Paris, 1894), 278), Francis returned in June or July 1220. For G. Golubovich (*Biblioteca*, i. 96–7), he returned in spring 1221. F. Cuthbert, *Saint Francis of Assisi* (London, 1912 and 1921), and Moorman, *History,* 50 n. 5, think that the most probable date for their return was autumn 1220.

33. 2C 58; see Merlo, *Nel nome di San Francesco*, 61–3; Moorman, *History*, 50–1.

34. Moorman, *History*, 51.

35. *Compilatio assisiensis*, 105; 2C 143, 151. See Dalarun, *François d'Assise*, 56–65; see also Dalarun, 'Répondre', *Rivista di storia e letteratura religiosa*, 34 (1998), 175–81; Dalarun, *François d'Assise*, 71.

36. Dalarun, *François d'Assise*, 67, 70–2.

37. Giordano, *Chronica*, §17. See Dalarun, *François d'Assise*, 67, 70–2.

38. Chiara Frugoni, *Francesco e l'invenzione delle stimatte* (Turin: Einaudi, 1993), 56; Dalarun, *Malaventure*, 120.

39. Thomas de Celano, *Legenda ad usum chori* in *Legendae S. Francisci Assisiensis saeculis XIII et XIV conscriptae*, ed. PP. Collegii S. Bonaventurae, in *Analecta Franciscana*, 10 (1926–41), 119–26.

40. Julien de Spire, *Vita sancti Francisci*, in *Analecta Franciscana*, 10 (1926–41), 333–71. On Julian's text, see Jason Miskuly, 'Julian of Speyer: Life of St. Francis', *Franciscan Studies*, 49 (1989), 93–117.

41. See Golubovich, 30–1.

42. Giordano, *Chronica*, §10.

43. *Laetabundus* xi (*AF* x. 400–1); tr. *ED* i. 353–4.

44. The *Compilatio assisiensis* is often called the *Legenda Perusina*, since the manuscript which contains it is in Perugia; on these texts, see the introductory notices in *FF* and *ED*. See also the analysis of their prologues in Dalarun, 'Les Prologues', 160–6.

45. See Ch. 14 below.

CHAPTER 4

1. Henricus Abricensis, *Legenda Sancti Francisci versificata*, 8. 90–180, in *Analecta Francescana*, 10 (1926–41), 405–21, repr. in *FF* 1125–1206; Henry of Avranches, *The Versified Life of Saint Francis*, tr. Gregory Shanahan, in 'Henry of Avranches: Poem on the Life of St. Francis *(Legenda Sancit Francisci versificata)*', *Franciscan Studies*, 48 (1988), 125–212; repr. in *ED* i. 421–520.

2. The poem is 'the *magnum opus* of the generation's most successful Latin poet' according to David Townsend, 'From the *Vita beati Francisci* of Henry of Avranches: A Likeness in Verse', in *Anglo Latin and its Heritage: Essays in honour of A.G. Rigg on his 64th Birthday* (Turnhout: Brepols, 2001), 149–62 (here 149). See also Michael Bihl, 'De *Legenda versificata s. Francisci* auctore Henryco Abrincensi', *Archivum Franciscanum Historicum*, 22 (1929), 3–53; Raoul Manselli, 'Henry d'Avranches e l'islam: S. Francesco in Terra Santa', *Studi in onore di Francesco Gabrieli nel suo ottantesimo compleanno* (Rome: Università di Roma 'La Sapienza', Dipartimento di studi orientali, 1984), 459–67; Hester Goodenough Gelber, 'Revisiting the Theater of Virtue', *Franciscan Studies*, 58 (2000), 19–36; Giuseppe Cremascoli, 'I classici nella Legenda sancti Francisci versificata di Enrico di Avranches', *Studi medievali*, 3rd ser. 40 (1999), 523–34.

3. On Henry's biography, I follow Konrad Bund, 'Studien zu Magister Heinrich von Avranches. I. Zur künftigen Edition seiner Werke', *Deutsches Archiv für Erforschung des Mittelalters*, 56 (2000), 127–69. On his poetic œuvre, see also A. G. Rigg, *A History of Anglo-Latin Literature, 1066–1422* (Cambridge: CUP, 1992), 179–93.

4. In J. C. Russell and J. P. Heironimus (eds.), *The Shorter Latin Poems of Master Henry of Avranches Relating to England* (Cambridge, Mass.: Medieval Academy of America, 1935), 33.

5. Henry of Avranches, *Querimonia de pirore Cantuariensi, eo quod non favorabilem se prebuit carmini*, vv. 22–5, 33, in *Shorter Latin Poems*, 92.

6. See Russell and Heironimus, *Shorter Poems*; Bund, 'Studien', 134–5.

7. See Bund, 'Studien', 139.

8. 'Cum tua sic alios premat excellencia reges, | Sumque poesis ego supremus in orbe professor, | Dicendi, licet equiuoce, sumus ambo monarchi.' Cited by Josiah C. Russell, 'Master Henry of Avranches as an International Poet', *Speculum*, 3 (1928), 34–63 (here 40), after the edn. of E. Winkelman, 'Drei Gedichte Heinrichs von Avranches an Kaiser Friedrich II', *Forschungen zur deutschen Geschichte*, 18 (1878), 482–92.

9. These documents are reproduced by Russell, 'Master Henry', 55–8; see also Bund, 'Studien', 144–7.

10. John of Garland, *Exempla honestae vitae*, cited by Rigg, *A History of Anglo-Latin Literature*, 166, from E. Habel (ed.), 'Die *Exempla honestae vitae* des Johannes de Garlandia, eine lateinische Poetik des 13. Jahrhunderts', *Romanische Forschungen*, 29 (1911), 131–54.

11. A. Rigg and P. Binkley, 'Two Poetic Debates by Henry of Avranches', *Mediaeval Studies*, 62 (2000), 29–67.

12. Michael of Cornwall's poems are edited by Alfons Hilka, 'Eine mittellateinische Dichterfehde: Versus Michaelis Cornubiensis contra Henrycum Abrincensem', in A. Börner and J. Kirchner (eds.), *Mittelalterliche Handschriften: Paläographische, kunsthistorische, literarische und bibliotheksgeschichtliche Untersuchungen; Festgabe zum 60. Geburtstage von Hermann Degering* (Leipzig: Hiersemann, 1926; repr. Hildesheim and New York: Georg Olms, 1973). See Peter Binkley, 'The Date and Setting of Michael of Cornwall's *Versus contra Henrycum Abrincensem*', *Medium Aevum*, 59 (1990), 76–84.

13. Binkley, 'Date and Setting', 78–9.

14. Henry of Avranches, *Bordo-Siler*, vv. 5–10, in Rigg and Binkley, 'Two Poetic Debates', 37; on the sexual transmission of leprosy, see vv. 395–400 (p. 48).

15. On the dating of the text, see Townsend, 'From the *Vita beati Francisci*', 151. Chiara Frugoni places the text in 1237 at the earliest; at this point Gregory IX confirms for the first time that he accepts the stigmata (Frugoni, *Francesco e l'invenzione delle stimmate*, 94 n. 74). I am not convinced. After all, the *Vita prima*, Henry's sole written source, affirms the existence of the stigmata, despite the pope's possible reticence. Nothing would be more normal for Henry than to follow his source.

16. Cambridge, University Library MS. Dd. 11.78, fos. 200^r–238^r. This manuscript is described by Bihl, 'De *Legenda versificata*', 7–8. See appendix I ('Additiones et variationes codicis C') of the edn. of the *Legenda versificata*, in *Analecta Francescana*, 10 (1926–41), 489–91. On this manuscript, see David Townsend and A. G. Rigg, 'Medieval Latin Poetic Anthologies (V): Matthew Paris' Anthology of Henry of Avranches' (Cambridge, University Library MS. Dd. 11.78)', *Mediaeval Studies*, 49 (1987), 352–90.

17. Versailles, Bibliothèque municipale, MS 8. This manuscript is described by Bihl, 'De *Legenda versificata*', 8–10. See appendix II ('Additiones et variationes codicis V') of the edn. of the *Legenda versificata*, in *Analecta Francescana*, 10 (1926–41), 492–521.

18. 1C 73–5, 99–101, 121–6; Henry, *Legenda*, 10. 31–61, 13. 22, 14. 40–81.

19. Russell, 'Master Henry', 54.

20. *FF* 302–3; *ED* i. 207.

21. See 1C 74–5, Henry of Avranches, *Legenda*, 10. 37–51 and Ch. 3 above. The *Compilatio assisiensis* (108) has the Cardinal pronounce sharp criticism of the practice of sending friars abroad: 'Cur mimisti fratres tuos tam longe ad moriendum fame et ad tantas alias tribulationes?' To this Francis responds: 'Dominus elegit et misit fratres propter profectum et salutem animarum omnium hominum totius mundi, et non solum recipientur in terra fidelium, sed etiam infidelium.'

22. Cremascoli, 'I classici'.

CHAPTER 5

1. Miklós Boskovits, *The Origins of Florentine Painting: 1100–1270* = Richard Offner, Klara Steinweg, Miklós Boskovits, and Mina Gregori, *A Critical and Historical Corpus of Florentine Painting* (Florence: Giunti Barbèra, 1993), i/1. 112–23, 147–50, 470–507.

2. *Regula non bullata*, prologue 2. This principle is confirmed by Pope Nicolas III in 1279, in his bull *Exiit qui seminat*: 'Hii sunt illius sancte regule professores, que evangelico fundatur eloquio, vite Christi roboratur exemplo, fondatorum militantis Ecclesie apostolorum ejus sermonibus actibusque firmatur.'

3. Chiara Frugoni, *Francesco: un'altra storia* (Genoa: Marietti, 1988); Frugoni, *Francesco e l'invenzione delle stimmate: Una storia per parole e immagini fino a Bonaventura e Giotto* (Turin: G. Einaudi, 1993), esp. pp. 357–98; Eamon Duffy, 'Finding St. Francis: Early Images, Early Lives', in P. Biller and A. Minnis (eds.), *Medieval Theology and the Natural Body* (York Studies in Medieval Theology, 1; York: York Medieval Press, 1997), 193–236, here p. 205. For examples of other altarpieces from the 13th cent. that illustrate the lives of saints, see Boskovits, *Origins of Florentine Painting*, fig. 50 (St Catherine dossal, with eight scenes of her life, which Boskovits dates to the 1220s); fig. 55 (San Verano dossal, mid-13th cent.); pl. XIV, pp. 292–303 (St Zenobius dossal, mid-13th cent.).

4. The passage is Matt. 10: 9–10, as found in both 1C 22 and *LM* 3. 1, but the artist indicates, in the open book that the priest holds, 'Sequentia sancti evangeli secundum Lucam', referring no doubt to the similar passage in Luke 10: 4.

5. 1C 52; *LM* 6. 2; Duffy, 'Finding St. Francis', 226–7.

6. For Duffy (ibid. 227–8), the source of the scene is *LM* 14. 5.

7. See Pietro Scarpellini, 'Iconografia francescana nei secoli XIII e XIV', in *Francesco d'Assisi: Storia e arte* (Milan: Electa, 1982), 91–126; Dieter Blume, *Wandermalerei als Ordenspropaganda: Bildprogramme im Chorbereich franziskanischer Konvente Italiens bis zur Mitte des 14 Jahrhunderts* (Worms: Werner'sche Verlagsgesellschaft, 1983); Klaus Krüger, *Der frühe Bildkult des Franziskus in Italien: Gestalt- und Funktionswandel des Tafelbildes im 13. und 14. Jahrhundert* (Berlin : Mann, 1992); Michel Feuillet, *Les Visages de François d'Assise* (Paris: Desclée de Brouwer, 1997).

8. On this images, see Feuillet, *Les Visages*, 89–93.

9. 1C 127.

10. 1C 138.

11. 1C 135.

12. Frugoni, *Francesco e l'invenzione delle stimmate*, 321ss. For examples of Italian historified crucifixes, see Boskovits, *Origins of Florentine Painting*, figs. 5/6 (Pisan example from the beginning of the 12th cent.), 18 (second half of 13th cent.), 30 (*c.*1200), and pl. VII (pp. 245–59, end of 12th or beginning of 13th cent.).

13. See Frugoni, *Francesco e l'invenzione delle stimmate*, 321–3 and pl. 129.

14. Hellmut Hager, *Die Anfänge des italienischen Altarbildes: Untersuchungen zur Entstehungsgeschichte des toskanischen Hochaltarretabels* (Munich: A. Schroll, 1962), 9, cited by André Chastel, *La Pala, ou le retable italien des origines à 1500* (Paris: Liana Levi, 1993), 72.

15. Chastel, *La Pala*, 72.

16. Wolff, *Der heilige Franziskus*, 141.

17. See Boskovits, *Origins of Florentine Painting*, 501–7.

18. Benvenuto Bughetti, 'Vita e miracoli di S. Francesco nelle tavole istoriate dei secc. XIII e XIV', *Achivum franciscanum historicum*, 19 (1926), 636–732.

19. William Miller, 'The Franciscan Legend in Italian Painting in the Thirteenth Century' (dissertation, Columbia University, 1961), 79–85; Judith Stein, 'Dating the Bardi St. Francis Master Dossal: Text and Image', *Franciscan Studies*, 36 (1976), 271–97; Frugoni, *Francesco: Un'altra storia*, 8–9.

20. See Ch. 6, below, on Bonaventure.

21. See below, Chapter 10.

22. Eamon Duffy, 'Finding St. Francis: Early Images, Early Lives', in P. Biller and A. J. Minnis (eds.), *Medieval Theology and the Natural Body* (York: York Medieval Press, 1997), 193–236.

23. Particularly scenes 3, 11, 14; see Duffy, 'Finding St. Francis'.

24. See esp. Ch. 8 below, on Angelo Clareno.

25. *LM* 2. 4; Duffy, 'Finding St. Francis', 220–1.

26. *LM* 6. 2; Duffy, 'Finding St. Francis', 226–7.

27. This suggestion is made by Miller, 'Franciscan Legend', 82.

28. Krüger, *Der frühe Bildkult des Franziskus*, 199–201.

29. Ibid.; Frugoni, *Francesco e l'invenzione delle stimmate*, 337–45; Boskovits, *Origins of Florentine Painting*, 112–16.

30. Boskovits, *Origins of Florentine Painting*, 112–23, 147–50, 470–507.

31. Krüger, *Der frühe Bildkult des Franziskus*, 119–28.

32. Blume, *Wandermalerei als Ordenspropaganda*, 100–1.

33. Frugoni, *Francesco: Un'altra storia*, 21–2.

34. 'Le immagini, una voce a parte', the title of ch. 5 in Frugoni, *Francesco e l'invenzione delle stimmate*.

35. Ibid. 216–22.

CHAPTER 6

1. *AF* 10: 557–652; tr. *ED* ii. 602–4.

2. Bonaventure, *Sermones de S. Francisco*, 2, in *Sermonis de diversis*, ed. Jacques Bougerol (2 vols. Paris: Éditions Franciscaines, 1993), 762; *Opera omnia*, ix. 579; tr. *ED* ii. 757.

3. Bonaventure, *Collationes in Hexaemeron* 19. 14, in *Opera omnia*, v. 422.

4. On these dates, see Dalarun, *Malaventure*, 17–18, 223–5.

5. On the chronology of his life, see Jacques Guy Bougerol, *Introduction à Saint Bonaventure* (Paris: J. Vrin, 1988), 3–11.

6. Ibid. 15–16.

7. *Legenda minor* 7. 8 (*AF* 10: 678), tr. in *ED* ii. 717.

8. The documents on these disputes are in the *Chartularium Universitatis parisiensis*, ed. H. Denifle and É. Chatelaun (4 vols. Paris: 1889–97; repr. Brussels: Culture et Civilisation, 1964), i. 226–7, 242–3, 252, 258 (nn. 200, 219, 230, 231). See Andrew Traver, *The Opuscula of William of Saint-Amour: The Minor Works of 1255–1256*, Beiträge zur Geschichte des Philosophie und Theologie des Mittelalters, 63 (Münster, 2003), 1–6; Bougerol, *Introduction à Saint Bonaventure*, 210; M. Dufeil, *Guillaume de Saint-Amour et la polémique universitaire parisienne, 1250–1259* (Paris: Picard, 1972), 94–100.

9. A. G. Traver, 'Rewriting History? The Parisian Secular Masters' *Apologia* of 1254', *History of Universities*, 15 (1997–9), 9–45.

10. Thomas of Eccleston, *De Adventu Fratrum Minorum in Angliam* (1258–9), ed. A. Little (Manchester: MUP, 1951), §15; tr. Leo Shirley-Price: *The Coming of the Franciscans* (Oxford: Mowbray, 1964), 74–5.

11. Thomas de Cantimpré, *De Apibus*, p. 175, cited by R. P. Mortier, *Histoire des maîtres généraux de l'Ordre des Frères Prêcheurs*, i (Paris: Alphonse Picard & Fils, 1903), 452; Salimbene of Adam, *Cronica*, CCCM 125 (1999), 634.

12. *Chartularium Universitatis parisiensis*, 1. 272–5 n. 243; see Traver, *Opuscula*, 5.

13. This question is taken up as the first article of the second question of his *De Perfectione Evangelica*, in *Opera omnia*, v. 124–8.

14. William of Saint-Amour, *De Quantitate Eleemosyne*, ed. A. Traver: 'William of Saint-Amour's Two Disputed Questions *De quantitate eleemosyne* and *De valido mendicante*', *Archives d'histoire doctrinale et littéraire du moyen âge*, 62 (1995), 323–32; see Traver, *Opuscula*, 7–10; M. Dufeil, *Guillaume de Saint-Amour*, 102–3.

15. *Chartularium Universitatis pariensis*, 1. 339 n. 293, cited by Bougerol, *Introduction à Saint Bonaventure*, 6 n. 15.

16. Salimbene de Adam, *Cronica*, ed. Giuseppe Scalia, CCCM 125, 462–3. On this episode, and on this particular passage, see David Burr, *The Spiritual Franciscans: From Protest to Persecution in the Century After Saint Francis* (University Park, Pa.: Pennsylvania State University Press, 2001), 29–41. Thomas of Eccleston relates John's resignation but says nothing of the scandal, simply saying that 'at length his health could no longer sustain the burden of the Minister General's office, and he obtained leave from Pope Alexander IV to resign'. (Thomas of Eccleston, *De Adventu Fratrum Minorum in Angliam*, §13; tr. Shirley-Price: *Coming of the Franciscans*, 57).

17. Salimbene de Adam, *Cronica*, 472–3.

18. Bonaventure, *Licet Infufficientiam Meam*, in *Opera*, v. 468–9; see passage tr. Bougerol, *Introduction à Saint Bonaventure*, 256–7. See Dalarun, *François d'Assise ou le pouvoir en question*, 98.

19. Bonaventure, *Itinerarium Mentis in Deum*, in *Opera Omnia S. Bonaventurae*, v. 295–316, here prol. 1, p. 295.

20. Ibid., prol. 4, p. 296; English tr. (2005) from the Franciscan Archive, http://www.franciscan-archive.org/bonaventura/opera/bon05295.html.

21. Raoul Manselli, 'La cericalizazione dei Minori e san Bonaventura', in *San Bonaventura,* cited by Le Goff, *Saint François*, 181.

22. Dalarun, *François d'Assise ou le pouvoir en question*, 102.

23. *AF* 10:379; I have not followed the translation at *ED* i. 370.

24. *Contitutiones Narbonenses*, in Bonaventure, *Opera omnia*, viii. 465, cited by Wolff, *Der heilige Franziskus*, 101.

25. Frugoni, *Francesco e l'invenzione delle stimmate*, 25–8.

26. Dalarun, *Malaventure*; idem, 'Les Prologues des légendes franciscaines', *Studi sulle società e le culture del Medioevo per Girolamo Arnaldi*, ed. Ludovico Gatto and Paola Supino Martin (Florence: All'Insegna del Giglio, 2002), 157–81.

27. On *captatio benevolentiae* in hagiography, see Wolff, *Der heilige Franziskus*, 88–90; on the prologue of the *Legenda*, see Dalarun, 'Les Prologues', 171–3.

28. See Dalarun, *Malaventure*, 227.

29. 1C 74–5; see Ch. 3 above.

30. Henri d'Avranches, *Legenda*, 7. 152–76; see Ch. 4 above.

31. *LM* 1. 1. On this passage, see Dalarun, *Malaventure*, 232–3.

32. *LM* 4. 11; see Dalarun, *Malaventure*, 229–30.

33. 2C 24, taken from L3C 63.

34. Dalarun, *Malaventure*, 237–46.

35. *L3C* 1; *ED* ii. 67. A 14th-cent. manuscript contains an anthology of Franciscan *exempla*, including a testimony attributed to Illuminatus: ed. Livarius Oliger, 'Liber exemplorum fratrum minorum saeculi XIII', *Antonianum*, 2 (1927), 204–76, §§98–9, pp. 250–1; see Golubovich, 36–7.

36. See Ch. 5 above.

37. See n. 35 above.

38. See Robert Bartlett, *Trial by Fire and Water: The Medieval Judicial Ordeal* (Oxford: Clarendon Press, 1986); Dominique Barthélemy, 'Diversité des ordalies médiévales', *Revue historique*, 280 (1988), 3–25; idem, 'Les Ordalies de l'an mil', *La Justice en l'an mil* (Collection Histoire de la Justice, 15; Paris: Association Française pour l'Histoire de la Justice, 2003), 81–92; idem, *Chevaliers et miracles: La Violence et le sacré dans la société féodale* (Paris: Armand Colin, 2004), 225–60.

39. Grégoire de Tours, *De gloria martyrum*, c. 80, ed. Bruno Kisch, MGH *Scriptores rerum merovingicarum* 1 (Hanover, 1885), 542–3; see Bartlett, *Trial by Fire and Water*, 4, 20–1, 71.

40. Bartlett, *Trial by Fire and Water*, 21.

41. Guibert of Nogent, *Tractatus de incarnatione contra Iudaeos* 3. 11, PL 156. 528; see Bartlett, *Trial by Fire and Water*, 21.

42. Petrus Damianus, *Vita Beati Romualdi*, ed. Giovanni Tabacco, Fonti per la storia d'Italia, 94; Rome: Istituto Storico Italiano, 1957), 59. See Bartlett, *Trial by Fire and Water*, 21.

43. Roger Bacon, *Opus majus*, ed. J. Bridges (3 vols. Oxford: Williams & Norgate, 1900); see Jeremiah Hackett (ed.), *Roger Bacon and the Sciences* (Leiden: Brill, 1997).

44. Richard Lemay, 'Latin Translattions and Translators', in Hackett (ed.), *Roger Bacon and the Sciences,* 25–47 (here 40); Hackett, 'Roger Bacon on Rhetoric and Poetics', ibid. 133–49 (here 141); Camille Bérubé, 'Le Dialogue de S. Bonaventure et de Roger Bacon', *Collectanea franciscana*, 39 (1969), 61–3.

45. Bonaventure *Collationes in Hexaemeron*, in *Opera omnia*, 5 (Quaracchi: Colegium S. Bonaventurae, 1891).

46. See Bougerol, *Introduction à Saint Bonaventure*, 235–41.

47. *Collationes in Hexaemeron*, I. 11 (p. 331).

48. 'Omnes veri philosophi unum Deum coluerunt. Unde etiam Socrates, quia prohibebat sacrificium fieri Apollini, interfectus fuit, cum coleret unum Deum' (*Collationes in Hexaemeron* 5. 15 (p. 356)).

49. Here is the complete title of the *Collatio*: 'De tertia visione tratatio septima et ultima, quae agit de recta via et ratione, qua fructus Scripturae percipiantur, sive qua per scientiam et sanctitatem ad sapientiam perveniatur' (p. 419).

50. *Collationes*, 19. 10–12, pp. 421–2.

CHAPTER 7

1. For a brief history of the arguments for and against the attribution to Giotto, see Giorgio Bonsanti (ed.), *La basilica di San Francesco ad Assisi/The Basilica of St. Francis in Assisi* (4 vols. Modena: F. C. Panini, 2002), iv. *Schede*, 518–21.

2. For a complete photographic documentation with description and studies, ibid. See also Elvio Lunghi, *La Basilique de Saint François à Assise* (tr. L. Meijer, Florence: Hazan, 2000); Serena Romano, *La basilica di San Francesco ad Assisi: Pittori, botteghe, strategie narrative* (Rome: Viella, 2001), esp. ch. 7, 'La redazione del programma e lo svolgimento del cantiere della navata', pp. 179–206.

3. For a reproduction of the document and an analysis, see Silvestro Nessi, *La Basilica di San Francesco in Assisi e la sua documentazione storica* (Assisi: Casa Editrice Franciscana, 1982 and 1994), 25.

4. 'Fratri Heliae recipienti pro domino Gregorio papa', cited by Moorman, *History*, using Ed Lempp, *Frère Élie de Cortone* (Paris, 1901), 170–1, and S. Attal, *Frate Elia, Compagno di San Francesco* (Rome, 1936), 121.

5. *BF* i. 40–1, reproduced in Nessi, *La Basilica*, 44.

6. *BF* i. 49.

7. Nessi, *La Basilica*, 45. As Moorman has noted (*History*, 88), the *Speculum perfectionis* (14th cent.) affirms that Francis himself designated the Portiuncula as 'caput et mater'; this probably reflects the disapproval of 14th-cent. spirituals for the basilica more than the saint's true feelings.

8. Lempp, *Frère Élie*, 163; Giordano, *Chronica*, §61; Nessi, *La Basilica*, 46.

9. See Alistair Smart, *The Assisi Problem and the Art of Giotto* (Oxford: Clarendon Press, 1971), 3–6.

10. Henry James, *Italian Hours* (New York: Grove Press, 1959), 233 (original edn. Boston: Houghton Mifflin, 1909).

11. Le Goff, *Saint François*, caption to pl. 1.

12. Moorman, *History*, 88–9. Thomas of Eccleston, *De Adventu Fratrum Minorum in Angliam*, §13; tr. Shirley-Price, *Coming of the Franciscans*, 50–1. On the other sources, see Richard C. Trexler, 'The Stigmatized Body of Francis of Assisi: Conceived, Processed, Disappeared', in Klaus Schreiner and Marc Müntz (eds.), *Frömmigkeit im Mittelalter: Politisch-soziale Kontexte, visuelle Praxis, körperliche Ausdrucksformen* (Munich: Fink, 2002), 463–97, esp. pp. 490–6. On the discovery of 1818, see Bonsanti (ed.), *La basilica di San Francesco*, iv. 343.

13. Giordano di Giano, in 1262, affirms 'Blessed Father Francis had expressed the desire to be buried in Saint Mary of the Portiuncula', *Chronica*, §61.

14. Trexler, 'Stigmatized Body', 490–6.

15. Nessi, *La Basilica*, 52–4; the bull of 10 July is reproduced by Romano, *La basilica*, 229.

16. See Lunghi, *La Basilique*, 26–43; Charles Mitchell, 'The Imagery of the Upper Church at Assisi', in *Giotto e il suo tempo* (Rome: De Luca, 1971), 113–34, repr. in Andrew Ladis (ed.), *Franciscanism, the Papacy, and Art in the Age of Giotto* (New York: Garland, 1998), 201–27; Hans Belting, 'Assisi e Roma: Risultati, problemi, prospettive', in *Roma anno 1300: Atti dell IV settimana di stui di storia dell'arte medievale dell'Università di Roma 'La Sapienza'* (Rome: L'Erma di Bretschneider, 1983), 93–101, repr. in Ladis, *Franciscanism*, 243–51.

17. Measurements given by Bruno Zanardi, *Il cantiere di Giotto: Le storie di san Francesco ad Assisi* (Milan: Skira, 1996), 176.

18. On this cycle, the bibliography is considerable. One can begin with Bonsanti (ed.), *La basilica di San Francesco*, ii. 832–89 (for the reproduction of the frescos) and iv. 511–46 (for the description and analysis of the scenes, with bibliographical references).

19. A *terminus post quem* is given in the fresco of Innocent III's dream (scene 6), where there is a colonnade constructed by Nicholas IV in 1291. It has also been noted that the three popes depicted in the frescos (Innocent III, Honorius III, and Gregory IX) are identical and correspond closely to the portrait of Pope Boniface VIII, which suggests a *terminus post quem* of Dec. 1294 (date of his election) and a *terminus ante quem* of 1305 (date of his death). Another *terminus ante quem* is furnished by the first fresco, set in the main square of Assisi, where one sees the tower of the Captain's Palace which does not yet have the modifications made in 1305. It seems that the artists who painted the frescos in the Palace of Priors in Perugia (completed in

1299) knew the Assisi cycle. All of this suggests that the frescos were painted between 1295 and 1299. See Lunghi, *La Basilique*, 66.

20. For the texts of these legends, see Bonsanti (ed.), *La basilica di San Francesco,* iv. 521–45.

21. This analysis is inspired in part by the paper given by Jérôme Baschet to the seminar 'Histoire comparée de phénomènes de conversion' to the École des Hautes Études en Sciences Sociales, Paris (Feb. 1996). See also Umberto Milizia, *Il ciclo di Giotto ad Assisi: Struttura di una leggenda* (Anzio: De Rubeis, 1994), 57–60.

22. 'The great reality of Giotto's designs adds to the helpless wonderment with which we feel the passionate pluck of the Hero, the sense of being separated from it by an impassable gulf.' Henry James, *Italian Hours*, 233.

23. 'One last question, perhaps, may be asked. Do the Assisi frescos faithfully depict St. Francis himself? Physically, of course, the man we see on the walls can hardly look like the *poverello* as his companions saw him. The paintings portray him, a sturdy peasant type, like a Roman hero in action. But do the stories truly portray his mind? Did St. Francis's personal contemplation actually take the Christian Platonic mystical form which St. Bonaventure attributes to it in the *Legenda Major*? The probability—prima facie—is that it did. … If any one, in that day, could discern the mentality of the saint, it was St. Bonaventure.' Mitchell, 'Imagery of the Upper Church', 133.

24. 'Weniger ein Triumph des historischen Franziskus als veilmehr ein Triumph *über* diesen Franziskus', Hans Belting, *Die Oberkirche von San Francesco in Assisi: Ihre Dekoration als Aufgabe und die Genese einer neuen Wandmalerei* (Berlin: Mann, 1977), 9; see Wolff, *Der Heilige Franziskus*, 13.

25. Dieter Blume, *Wandermalerei als Ordenspropaganda* (Worms: Werner'sche Verlagsgesellschaft, 1983), 42ss.

26. Henry Thode, *Franz von Assisi und die Anfänge des Kunst der Renaissance in Italien* (Berlin: G. Grote'sche, 1904); French tr. by Gaston Lefèvre, *Saint François d'Assise et les origines de l'Art de la Renaissance en Italie* (2 vols. Paris: Renouard, n.d.).

27. See Tolan, *Saracens*, ch. 5.

28. Bonsanti (ed.), *La basilica di San Francesco*, iv. 530–1, who gives a detailed description of the scene with bibliographical references.

29. Thode, *Franz von Assisi*, 262–3.

30. Bonsanti (ed.), *La basilica di San Francesco*, iv. 530–1, who cites Pietro Toesca, *Giotto* (Turin: Unione tipografico, 1941), 57; Cesare Gnudi, *Giotto* (Milan: Martello, 1958), 79; Bruno Zanardi, *Il cantiere di Giotto*, 59; Luciano Bellosi, *La Pecora di Giotto* (Turin: Einaudi, 1985), 154.

31. Francesca Flores d'Arcais, *Giotto* (Arles: Actes Sud, 2001), 86.

32. 'Cum beatus Franciscus ob Christi fidem voluit intrare in ignem magnum cum sacerdotibus Soldani Babilonie, sed nullus eorum voluit intrare cum eo,

sed statim de suis conspectibus aufugerunt', cited by Bonsanti (ed.), *La basilica di San Francesco*, iv. 530.

33. For Chiara Frugoni, 'L'affresco stravolge totalmente il significato dell'invito di Francesco' by making a simple proposition into a real confrontation. Frugoni, 'Analisi delle singole scene (note strorico-iconografiche)', in Zanardi, *Il cantiere di Giotto*, 174.

CHAPTER 8

1. Angelo Clareno, *A Chronicle or History of the Seven Tribulations of the Order of Brothers Minor*, tr. David Burr and E. Randolph Daniel (St Bonaventure, NY: Franciscan Institute Publications, 2005), 28–33. For the Latin text, see Angelo Clareno, *Opera*, ii. *Historia septum tribulationum ordinis minorum*, ed. Orietta Rossini (Rome: Istituto storico italiano per il medio evo, 1999), books 1–2, pp. 78–83; Angelo Clareno, *Liber chronicarum sive tribulationum ordinis minorum*, ed. Giovanni Boccali, with Italian tr. by Marino Bigaroni (Assisi: Edizioni Porziuncola, 1999), 164–75.

2. Gian Luca Potestà, *Angelo Clareno, dai poveri eremiti ai fraticelli* (Rome: Istituto Palazzo Borromini, 1990); David Burr, *The Spiritual Franciscans* (University Park, Pa.: Pennsylvania State University Press, 2001). See also Felice Accrocca, *Francesco e le sue immagini: Momenti della evoluzione della coscienza storica dei frati Minori (secoli XIII–XVI)* (Padua: Centro Stuii Antoniani, 1997), 93–160; Barone, *Da frate Elia agli spirituali* (Milan: Biblioteca francescana, 1999).

3. See David Burr, *The Spiritual Franciscans: From Protest to Persecution in the Century after Saint Francis* (University Park, Pa.: Pennsylvania State University Press, 2001), 353–4 n. 5.

4. Angelo Clareno, *Chronicle*, 153. See Burr, *Spiritual Franciscans*, 43–5.

5. On his stay in Armenia, see Raoul Manselli, 'Spirituali missionari: L'azione in Armenia e in Grecia. Angelo Clarno', in *Espansione del francescanesimo tra Occidente e Oriente nel secolo XIII: Atti del VI Convegno internazionale di studi francescani* (Assisi, 1979), 271–91.

6. Potestà, *Angelo Clareno*, 27–9. Angelo describes these events in *Chronicle*, §§156–7.

7. Potestà, *Angelo Clareno*, 29–32.

8. Ibid. 33.

9. Ibid. 61–4; *RNB*, c. 1.

10. Potestà, *Angelo Clareno*, 65–7.

11. Ibid. 78–91. 'Nullus enim ad discipulatum Christi, nec regulariter, nec canonice intrat vel recipitur, nisi ille qui ad ipsum sicut ad martyrium ingreditur.' Angelo Clareno, *Letter* 26, cited by Potestà, *Angelo Clareno*, 89 n. 92. 'Tota vita stadium est, cursus est, martirium est, transitus est; qui servaverit Regulam coronam accipiet sicut martyr.' Angelo Clareno, *Letter* 5, cited by Potestà, *Angelo Clareno*, 89 n. 93.

12. Ibid. 95–121; see Burr, *Spiritual Franciscans*, 161–7.

13. Potestà, *Angelo Clareno*, 98–100.

14. *Letter* 49, in *Opera*, i: *Epistole*, ed. Lydia von Auw (Rome: Istituto Storico Italiano per il Medio Evo, 1980), reproduced in the appendix of the *Liber chronicarum* (ed. Boccali), 771–84.

15. Potestà, *Angelo Clareno*, 123–6.

16. Ibid. 123.

17. *Letter* 14; see Potestà, *Angelo Clareno*, 134–5.

18. Potestà, *Angelo Clareno*, 143.

19. Angelo Clareno, *Expositio regulae fratrum Minorum*, ed. L. Oliger (Karachi, 1912); on this text, see Potestà, *Angelo Clareno*, 153–67.

20. Angelo Clareno, *Expositio regulae fratrum Minorum*, 45–8; Potestà, *Angelo Clareno*, 159–60.

21. Angelo Clareno, *Chronicle*, §1. On the identity of John of Celano (or of Ceprano), author of a lost life, cited twice by Angelo, see the notes to this passage in the two Latin edns.; also see Accrocca, *Francesco e le sue immagini*, 37–56.

22. Angelo Clareno, *Chronicle*, §§47–9. This episode is reminiscent of the council of demons at the beginning of Robert de Boron, *Merlin, roman du XIIIe siècle*, ed. Alexandre Micha (Geneva: Droz, 1979), 18–23.

23. Angelo Clareno, *Chronicle*, §3.

24. Ibid., §5.

25. See e.g. ibid., §12.

26. Ibid., §14.

27. Ibid., §28.

28. See e.g. ibid., §§53–8, 71–87.

29. Ibid., §56. See *Compilatio assisiensis*, 17; Accrocca, *Francesco et le sue immagini*, 168–9.

30. *LM* 4. 11. See Ch. 6 above.

31. Angelo Clareno, *Chronicle*, §58; *Compilatio assisiensis* 17.

32. He attributes to Angelo a 'roller-coaster view of Franciscan reform prospects—relaxation under Crescentius followed by a brief Prague Spring under John, which in turn gives way to the Warsaw Pact tanks rolling in under Bonaventure' (Burr, *Spiritual Franciscans*, 34).

33. Angelo Clareno, *Chronicle*, §§94–6.

34. Ibid., §104.

35. Ibid., §104.

36. Ibid., §114.

37. Ibid., §§116–17.

38. Ibid., §119.

39. Ibid., §. 120; on this vision, see Burr, *Spiritual Franciscans*, 33–4. This story is also found in the *Actus beati Franciscus et sociorum eius,* as we will see in the next chapter.

40. Angelo Clareno, *Chronicle*, §§126–7.

41. Burr, *Spiritual Franciscans*, 32–9.

42. Angelo Clareno, *Chronicle*, § 129.
43. Ibid., §§151–2; tr. slightly modified, based on the Latin text of Angelo, *Historia* (ed. Rossini), pp. 222–3.
44. Angelo Clareno, *Chronicle*, §§175–6.
45. See Ch. 13 below.
46. 'ad partes fidelium divina revelatione praemonitus remeavit'; see Ch. 6 above.
47. Giordano, *Chronica*, §§11–14, tr. Laureilhe, pp. 31–3.

CHAPTER 9

1. Ugolino da Montegiorgio, *The Deeds of Blessed Francis and his Companions*, *ED* iii. 490–2. For the Latin text, see *Actus beati francisci et sociorum eius*, ed. Marino Bigaroni and Jacques Cambell (Assisi: Edizioni Porziuncola, 1988), 314–22; reprinted in *FF* 2085–2219.
2. For the following, see Enrico Menestò, 'Introduzione', *FF* 2057–84; 'Introduction', *Francis of Assisi: Early Documents*, iii. 429–34; Cambell, introduction to the *Actus*, 40–8.
3. 'Ego, frater Hugolinus de Monte Santa Marie, steti ibidem tribus annis et vidi...' *Actus*, 55. 18; 'Et omnia predicta retulit michi Hugolino ipse fr. Iohannes', 58. 21; 'Hanc ystoriam habuit fr. Iacobus de Massa abore fr. Leonis; et fr. Hugolinus de Monte S. Marie ab ore dicti fr. Iacobi; et ego qui scribo ab ore fr. Hugolini, viri fide digni et boni.' 9. 71.
4. The date of composition of the *Actus* is later than the closing of the Franciscan convent of Brunforte in 1327 (event mentioned in the text) and prior to 1337, date of the establishment of the feast of the stigmatization of Saint Francis; see Cambell, introduction to the *Actus*, 36–7.
5. *Actus*, 48. 1; *ED* iii. 526.
6. In particular John of La Verna (*Actus*, 56. 8) and John of Penna (57. 26 and 58. 21).
7. *Actus*, 64; Angelo Clareno, *Chronicle*, §§117–20. See Ch. 8 above. For other borrowings from Angelo, see Cambell, introduction to the *Actus*, 31–5.
8. *Actus*, 25; Angelo Clareno, *Chronicle*, §§22–4; Thomas of Celano gives a very different version of the vision (2Cel 82).
9. *Actus*, 60.
10. Ibid. 3, 5, and 62.
11. Ibid. 62.
12. Ibid. 17.
13. Ibid. 47. 29.
14. Ibid. 2. 18.
15. Ibid. 12 and 15.
16. Ibid. 16.
17. For visions of dead friars, ibid. 22, 29, 46, 52; for the revelation to Francis of his own salvation, ibid. 18. On these visions of the dead in the Middle

Ages, see Jean-Claude Schmitt, *Les Revenants: Les Vivants et les morts dans la société médiévale* (Paris: Gallimard, 1994), tr. Teresa Fagan as *Ghosts in the Middle Ages: The Living and the Dead in Medieval Society* (Chicago: University of Chicago Press, 1998).

18. See *Actus*, 1.

19. See Ch. 1 above.

20. *Actus*, 13.

21. See Ch. 13 below.

CHAPTER 10

1. Arnaud de Sarrant, *Chronicle of the Twenty-Four Generals*, in *AF* 3: 22–3.

2. Goffen, *Spirituality in Conflict*, 1; see Alberto Busigani and Raffaello Bencini, *Le chiese di Florence: Quartiere di Santa Croce* (Florence: Sansoni, 1982), 23–100.

3. See Ch. 7 above.

4. Goffen, *Spirituality in Conflict*, 5; the text of the bull is reproduced by Busigani & Bencini, *Le chiese di Florence*, 25.

5. See Ch. 8 above.

6. Goffen, *Spirituality in Conflict*, 6.

7. Ibid. 8–11.

8. See Ch. 13.

9. Goffen, *Spirituality in Conflict*, 51–4; Jane Long, 'Bardi Patronage at Santa Croce in Florence, ca. 1320–1343' (dissertation: Columbia University, 1988), chs. 3 and 4.

10. This is the dating that Goffen proposes, *Spirituality in Conflict*, 55–7; Long prefers a date after 1317 (Long, 'Bardi Patronage', chs. 3 and 4). See also Jane Long, 'The Program of Giotto's Saint Francis Cycle at Santa Croce in Florence', *Franciscan Studies*, 52 (1992), 85–133. For a detailed comparison of the Bardi and Assisi cycles, see James Stubblebine, 'The Relation of the Assisi Cycle to Giotto's Santa Croce Frescos', in *Assisi and the Rise of Vernacular Art* (New York: Harper & Row, 1985), 16–40, taken up in Ladis, *Franciscanism*, 252–76. For Stubblebine, Giotto's frescos in Florence were painted *before* those of Assisi; the latter were not by Giotto, but by a far inferior artist who imitated, not altogether successfully, Giotto's Florentine fresco. Few art historians have been convinced by Stubblebine's arguments, yet his comparison of the frescos remains interesting and insightful.

11. Long, 'Program', 91.

12. Dante, *Paradiso*, XI. 124.

13. Long, 'Program', 124.

14. Ibid. 99–101.

15. See Tolan, *Saracens*, introd. and ch. 10; Tolan, *Sons of Ishmael*, ch. 8.

16. Andrew Ladis, *Taddeo Gaddi: Critical Reappraisal and Catalogue Raisonné* (Columbia, Mo.: University of Missouri Press, 1982), 114–26.

17. Blume, *Wandermalerei als Ordenspropaganda*; Louise Bourdua, *The Franciscans and Art Patronage in Late Medieval Italy* (Cambridge: CUP, 2004).

18. Blume, *Wandermalerei als Ordenspropaganda*, 49–54, 161–3, tafel 39, illus. 111.

19. Silvia Mazzini, *La* Legenda maior *figurate nel MS. 411 della Biblioteca Nazionale di Roma* (Rome: Istituto Storico dei Cappucini, 2000), 11–18 and pls. 1, 9, 14, 17. Thanks to Dominique Donadieu-Rigaut for drawing my attention to this manuscript.

20. See Moorman, *History*, 376–83, 441–500; Stanislao da Campagnola, *Le origini francescane come problema storiografico* (2nd edn. Perugia: Università degli studi, 1979), 77–86; Merlo, *Nel nome di San Francesco,* 324–81; Duncan Nimmo, *Reform and Division in the Medieval Franciscan Order: From Saint Francis to the Foundation of the Capuchins* (Rome: Capuchin Historical Institute, 1987), 364–429 and *passim*.

21. Jürgen Werinhard Einhorn, 'Das grosse Franziskusleben des Hl. Bonaventura in zwei illuminaten Handschriften in Rom und Madrid', *Collectanea Francescana,* 62 (1992), 5–61. The Roman manuscript has been published in a facsimile edn.: Servus Gieben (ed.), *Francesco d'Assisi attraverso l'immagine: Roma, Museo francescano, Codice inv. nr. 1266* (Rome: Istituto storico dei cappuccini, 1992). The illustrations here are from the Roman manuscript. I have not been able to consult the images from the Madrid manuscript, other than the 26 reproduced by Einhorn, or to confirm the current location of the manuscript.

22. Illustration 3 MS M (Madrid) 4r, MS R (Rome) fo. 9r; see Einhorn, 'Das grosse Franziskusleben', 32–44; cf. illustrations 19, 89, 97.

23. Illustrations 12, 13, 14, 18.

24. G. E. Solberg, 'Taddeo di Bartolo, His Life and Work' (dissertation: Columbia Univ., 1991), 153–56, 438–54, figs. 92–114; Sibilla Symeonides, *Taddeo di Bartolo* (Sienna: Accademia Senese degli Intronati, 1965), 100–3, 214–17, pls. XXXVIII–XXXIX, XLI–XLIII. Symeonides (p. 101) is in error when he identifies the saint to the right of Francis as 'Saint Louis de France'; it is in fact St Louis de Toulouse.

25. See Ch. 6 above.

26. James Banker, 'The Program for the Sassetta Altarpiece in the Church of S. Francesco in Borgo S. Sepolcro', *I Tatti Studies: Essays in the Renaissance*, 4 (1991), 11–58; Chastel, *La Pala*, 126–7, 267–8.

27. Banker, 'Program for Sassetta Altarpiece', 54.

28. On Fra Angelico and his work, see Gabriele Bartz, *Guido di Piero, Known as Fra Angelico (ca. 1395–1455)* (Cologne: Könemann Verlagsgesellschaft, 1998); Bartz does not discuss this image. See also U. Baldini, *L'opera completa dell'Angelico* (Milan: Rizzoli, 1970).

29. On this artist, see John Pope-Hennessy, *Giovanni di Paolo, 1403–1483* (New York: OUP, 1938).

30. John of Brienne became Franciscan at the end of his life, according to the Franciscan chronicler Salimbène (see Golubovich, i. 179–80).

31. Diane Ahl, *Benozzo Gozzoli* (New Haven, Conn.: Yale University Press, 1996), 59, pl. 61 (Olivi); 57, pl. 60 (John of Brienne and Robert d'Anjou); 60 (for Louis de Toulouse, whose portrait was painted by one of Gozzoli's assistants, according to Ahl).

32. Gal. 6: 17; *LM* 13. 9; Ahl, *Benozzo Gozzoli,* 49. Bonaventure, in fact, takes up the citation that Thomas of Celano had used and which became a Franciscan *locus classicus*; see *ED* iv (index), 209.

33. Ahl, *Benozzo Gozzoli*, 48–62, 230–1; Ahl, 'Benozzo Gozzoli's Cycle of the Life of Saint Francis in Montefalco: Hagiography and Homily', in Sandro Sticca (ed.), *Saints: Studies in Hagiography* (Binghamton, NY: Medieval and Renaissance Texts and Studies, 1996), 191–213.

34. 'Quando soldanus misit unam puellam ad tentandum B. F. et ipse intravit in ignem et omnes estupuerunt'; transcription in Ahl, *Benozzo Gozzoli*, 230.

35. *Actus beati francisci et sociorum eius*, ch. 27; see Ch. 9 above.

36. Ronald Kecks, *Ghirlandaio* (Paris: Éditions du Félin, 1996); Jean Cadogan, *Domenico Ghirlandaio: Artist and Artisan* (New Haven, Conn.: Yale University Press, 2000), 230–6. The complete cycle of frescos may be viewed online: http://www.wga.hu/frames-e.html?/html/g/ghirland/domenico/5sassett/frescoes/.

37. The cycle may be viewed online: http://www.legambientepadova.it:8080/salvalarte/sfranc_img.htm. The date is found on the image of Pope Nicholas IV before Francis.

38. See Wolfgang H. Savelsberg, *Die Darstellung des hl. Franziskus von Assisi in der Flämischen Malerei und Graphik des späten 16. und des 17. Jahrhunderts* (Rome: Istituto Storico dei Cappuccini, 1992).

39. J. W. Einhorn, 'Franziskus und der "Edle Heide"', in C. Meier and U. Ruberg (eds.), *Text und Bild: Aspekte des Zusammenwirkens zweier Künste in Mittelalter* (Weisbaden: Reichert Verlag, 1980), 630–50; Einhorn, 'Die Holzschnitte des Wolf Traut zur "Legend des heyligen vatters Francisci" nach Bonaventura, Nürenberg 1512: Ihre Vorlagen und ihr Fortwirken', *Franziskanische Studien,* 60 (1978), 1–24; Virgilio Bermejo Vega, 'La Difusión de la iconografía franciscana a fines de la Edad Media: "Il poverello" de Asís en la entalladura del siglo XV', *Espiritualidad y Franciscanismo: VI Semana de Estudios Medievales* (Logroño: Instituto de Estudios Riojanos, 1996).

40. Einhorn, 'Franziskus und der "Edle Heide"', pls. 1, 2, and 4.

41. Doris Carl, 'Franziskanischer Märtyrerkult als Kreuzzugspropaganda an der Kanzel von Benedetto da Maiano in Santa Croce in Florenz', *Mitteilungen des Kunsthistorischen Instituts in Florenz*, 39 (1995), 69–91.

42. Mustafa Soykut, *Image of the Turk in Italy: A History of the 'Other' in Early Modern Europe: 1453–1683* (Berlin: K. Schwarz, 2001); Nancy Bisaha, Creating

East and West: Renaissance Humanists and the Ottoman Turks (Philadelphia: University of Pennsylvania Press, 2004).

43. See Carl, 'Franziskanischer Märtyrerkult', 72–7.

CHAPTER II

1. 'el Soldan dixole [to François] vete a buena ventura, que no te quiero facer mártir, que te fagan fiesta después los christianos', Pedro Pascual, *Sobre la seta Mahometana*, in *Obras de San Pedro Pascual*, ed. P. Armegon Valenzuela (4 vols. Rome, 1906–8), iv. 1–357 (here 204).

2. Riccoldo da Montecroce, *Epistolae V de perditione Acconis 1291*, ed. R. Röhricht, *Archives de l'orient latin*, 2 (1884), 258–96 (here 278).

3. Marinus Sanutus dictus Torsellus, Patricius Venetus, *Liber Secretorum Fidelium crucis super Terrae Sanctae recuperatione et conservatione quo et Terrae Sanctae historia ab Origine et eiusdem vicinarumque prouinciarum geographica descriptio continetur*, vol. i of *Gesta dei per Francos*, ed. Bongars (Hanover: Wechelianis, 1611); repr. with introd. by Joshua Prawer (Toronto: University of Toronto Press, 1972). On Marino Sanudo (or Sanuto) 'the elder' (not to be confused with Marino Sanuto the 'younger', 1466–1536), see David Jacoby, 'Catalans, Turcs et Vénitiens en Romanie (1305–1332): Un nouveau témoignage de Marino Sanudo Torsello', *Studi medievali*, 3rd ser. 15 (1974), 217–61; Christopher Tyerman, 'Marino Sanudo Torsello and the Lost Crusade: Lobbying in the Fourteenth Century', *Transactions of the Royal Historical Society*, 5th ser. 32 (1982), 57–73; Gloria Allaire, 'Sanudo, Marino [the Elder, also called Marino Sanudo Torsello] [c.1270–c. 1343]', *Trade, Travel, and Exploration in the Middle Ages: An Encyclopedia* (New York: Garland, 2000), 535–6; Sylvia Schein, *Fideles Crucis: The Papacy, the West, and the Recovery of the Holy Land, 1274–1314* (Oxford: Clarendon Press, 1991); Evelyn Edson, 'Reviving the Crusade: Sanudo's Schemes and Vesconte's Maps', in Rosamund Allen (ed.), *Eastward Bound: Travel and Travelers, 1050–1550* (Manchester: MUP, 2004), 131–55.

4. Marino Sanudo, *Liber Secretorum Fidelium*, 208–9; for the text of the continuation of the *Eracle*, see *RHC occ.* ii. 348 and Ch. 2 above.

5. *Tractatus de martyrio sanctorum* (Basel: Jacobus Wolff de Pforzheim, 1492). See E. Randolph Daniel, *The Franciscan Concept of Mission in the High Middle Ages* (Louisville, Ky.: University Press of Kentucky, 1975; repr. St Bonaventure, NY: Franciscan Institute, 1992), 118–27.

6. F. J. Sanchez Canton, *Maestre Nicolas Frances* (Madrid: Instituto Diego Velázquez, 1964), 21–5.

7. We find e.g. a Moor's head on the shield of King Baligant in the *Grandes Chroniques de France*, Paris, Bibliothèque Ste Geneviève MS 783, fo. 117.

8. See e.g. the fresco of the flagellation which Giotto painted *c.*1305 in the Cappella Scrovegni of Padua, or, at the end of the 15th cent., the painting

of Christ crowned with thorns by Hieronymus Bosch, London, National Gallery (NG 4744).

9. See Ana Echevarria, *Fortress of Faith: The Attitude towards Muslims in Fifteenth-Century Spain* (Leiden: Brill, 1999), 13–17.

10. *Immagini di un ritorno: Gli antichi affreschi francescani di Santa Maria delle Grazie a Bergamo*, ed. Fernando Noris (Bergamo: Bolis, 2004).

11. See Ch. 10 above.

12. The caption underneath the fresco is: 'Come S. Francisco per desiderio de martirio andando al Soldano se incontro in doy pecorelle et tuto per cio realmente [?] disse a frate illuminato suo compagno quello ditto del evangelio esse adimplito in loro "ecce ego mitto vos sicut oves in medio luporum".' Transcription in *Immagini di un ritorno*, 25, which I have completed from the photo, p. 58.

13. 'Come S. Francesco … el Soldano et havendoli predicato Dio trino et uno volse intrare nel fogo … piglio uno cornetto da luy con doy bachette per securità. rifutando dinari.' Transcription in *Immagini di un ritorno*, 25, which I have completed from the photo, p. 58; the ellipses indicate illegible passages.

14. Erasmus Alber, *Der Barfusser Münche Eulenspiegel und Alcoran, mit einer Vorrede D. Martini Luther* (Wittemberg: Hans Lufft, 1542). Erasmus Alber, *Alcoranus Franciscanorum. Id est, Blasphemiarum & nugarum Lerna, de stigmatisato idolo quod Franciscum uocant, ex Libro conformitatum* (Frankfurt: Peter Brubach, 1543). Erasmus Alber, *The alcaron of the barefote friers, that is to say, an heape or numbre of the blasphemous and trifling doctrines of the wounded idole Saint Frances taken out of the boke of his rules, called in latin, Liber conformitatum* (London: R. Grafton, 1550). Citations are from the following edn.: *The Alcoran of the Franciscans, or a Sink of Lyes and Blasphemies. Collected out of a Blasphemous Book belonging to that Order, called The Book of the Conformities. With the Epistles of Dr. Martin Luther, and Erasmus Alberus, detecting the same. Formerly printed in Latine, and now made English, for the discovery of the Blasphemies of the Franciscans, a considerable order of Regulars amongst the Papists* (London: Printed for L. Curtise in Goat Court on Ludgate Hill, 1679). On this text, see Klaus Reblin, *Freund und Feind: Franziskus von Assisi im Spiegel der protestantischen Theologiegeschichte* (Göttingen: Vandenhoek & Ruprecht, 1988), 71–8.

15. Bartholomew of Pisa, *De conformitate vitae Beati Francesci ad vitam Domini Iesu*, in *AF* 4–5 (1906–12). On this text, see Carolly Erickson, 'Bartholomew of Pisa, Francis Exalted: *De conformitate*', *Mediaeval Studies*, 34 (1972), 253–74; Stanislao da Campagnola, *Le origini francescane come problema storiografico* (2nd edn. Perugia: Università degli studi, 1979), 64–7; Mariano d'Alatri, 'L'immagine di San Francesco nel "De Conformitate" di Bartolomoe da Pisa', in *Francesco d'Assisi nella storia: Secoli XIII–XV*, i (Rome: Istituto storico dei cappuccini, 1983), 227–37.

16. See Ch. 10 above.

17. *AF* 4: 480–3; 5: 467–8.

18. *Alcoran of the Franciscans*, frontispiece, p. 151.

19. Ibid. 134.

20. Ibid. 141–2.

21. The story of the snow woman is found for the first time in 2C 117.

22. Martin Luther, *On Monastic Vows* (1521), in *D. Martin Luthers werke: Kritische Gesamtausgabe* (Weimar, 1883–), viii. 573–669; English tr. in *Luther's works*, ed. Jaroslav Pelikan and Helmut Lehman (55 vols. Philadelphia: Fortress Press, 1955–86), xliv. 255–6.

23. Martin Luther, *Readings on Genesis*, in *D. Martin Luthers werke*, xlii. 264–549; *Luther's works*, ii. 327–8.

24. Martin Luther, *Commentary on Isaiah*, ch. 42, in *D. Martin Luthers werke*, xxx. 261–585.

25. Martin Luther, *Commentary on Psalm 45*, in *D. Martin Luthers werke*, xl. 472–610; *Luther's works*, xii. 284.

26. Reblin, *Freund und Feind*, 99–102.

27. Matthias Flacius Illyricus, *Ecclesiastica historia congesta per aliquot iuros in urbe Magdeburgica XIII centuriae* (Basel: Oporini, 1564); See Reblin, *Freund und Feind*, 79–87.

28. Nicolas de Vignier, *Légende dorée ou sommaire de l'histoire des frères mendiants de l'ordre de S. Dominique et de S. François* (Leiden: Jean le Maire, 1608); this 1st edn. is anonymous; the edn. published in Amsterdam in 1734 bears his name. On this text see Damien Vorreux, *François d'Assise dans les lettres françaises* (Paris: Desclée de Brouwer, 1988), 186–7.

29. Pierre Du Moulin, *Le Capucin: Traitté auquel est descrite l'origine des Capucins, & leurs voeux, reigles, & disciplines examinees* (Sedan: Pierre Jannon, 1641); On this text see Vorreux, *François dans les lettres françaises*, 187–9.

30. Rafaele Russo, *Il ciclo francescano nella chiesa del Gesù in Roma* (Rome: Istituto Storico dei Cappucini, 2001).

31. Da Campagnola, *Le origini francescane*, 87–107.

32. The bibliography devoted to the Gesù is considerable; see in particular Gauvin Bailey, *Between Renaissance and Baroque: Jesuit Art in Rome, 1565–1610* (Toronto: University of Toronto Press, 2003), 187–260; Howard Hibbard, 'Ut Picturae Sermones: The First Painted decorations of the Gesù', in Rudolf Wittkower and Irma Jaffe (eds.), *Baroque Art: The Jesuit Contribution* (New York: Fordham University Press, 1972), 29–49.

33. The cycle has been attributed to Paolo Bril, to Maarten Pepijn and to Joseph Heintz; it is possible that the three painters collaborated on it; see Bailey, *Between Renaissance and Baroque*, 201, 216. On the iconography of the cycle, see Russo, *Il ciclo*; Bailey, *Between Renaissance and Baroque*, 252–3.

34. See Cristina Degli'Innocenti, *Il Pomarancio: Nicolò Cirgignani* (Fucecchio: Edizioni dell'Erba, 1997). Bailey, *Between Renaissance and Baroque*, pls. 87–89 (for the frescos in the Gesù); on the frescos of martyrs in other Roman churches (esp. San Stefano Rotondo) see pls. 37–52, 55, 68–71.

35. Marcos de Lisboa, *Crónicas da Ordem dos Frades Menores* (Porto: Faculdade de Letras da Universidade do Porto, 2001: photostatic reproduction of the 1557 edn., with introduction and notes by José Adriano de Freitas Carvalho). *The chronicle and institution of the Order of the seraphicall father S. Francis: conteyning his life, his death, and his miracles, and of all his holie disciples and companions, set foorth first in the Portugall, next in the Spanish, then in the Italian, lastlie in the French, and now in the English tongue* (St. Omer: John Heigham, 1618). See da Campagnola, *Le origini francescane*, 107–9; Felice Accroca, '"Non sai tu che S. Francesco è in terra un angelo del cielo?": L'immagine di san Francesco nelle *Croniche* di Marco da Lisbona', in *Frei Marcos de Lisboa: Cronista franciscano e bispo do Porto* (Porto: Faculdade de Letras, 2002), 225–45.

36. Bernard Dompnier, 'Les Enjeux de l'édition française des *Chroniques* de Frère Marc de Lisbonne', in *Frei Marcos de Lisboa*, 185–209.

37. Da Campagnola, *Le origini francescane*, 107–11.

38. Accroca, 'Non sai tu', 240.

39. Marcos de Lisboa, *Crónicas*, part 1, cc. 55–8, fos. 39–41; English tr., book 1, chs. 69–71, pp. 123–7.

40. Marcos de Lisboa, *Crónicas*, part 1, c. 57, fo. 40^v; English tr., book 1, c. 70, p. 126.

41. Marcos de Lisboa, *Crónicas*, part 1, book 4, c. 1, p. 127; English tr., book 4, vol. 2, ch. 1, pp. 420–1.

42. The Récollets were established in Montreal by 1615; see Marcel Trudel, *Histoire de la nouvelle France*, i. *Les Vaines Tentatives: 1524–1603* (Montreal: Fidès, 1971). See also the narration by Récollet Gabriel Sagard of his voyage to Canada in 1623–4: Gabriel Sagard, *Le Grand Voyage du pays des Hurons* (Montreal: Presses de l'Université de Montréal, 1998). A friar named Marcos de Lisboa (not the same person as our author) sent a letter to the king of Portugal *c*.1612, mentioning 52 Franciscan convents in the Philippines (see Emma Blair (ed.), *The Philippine Islands, 1493–1803* (55 vols. Cleveland, Ohio: A. H. Clark, 1903–9), xvii. 209–10.

43. Lucas Waddingus, *Annales minorum seu trium ordinum a S. Francisco institutorum*, i (Karachi, 1931), 36. On Wadding, see *Father Luke Wadding: Commemorative Volume* (Dublin: Clonmore & Reynolds, 1957); da Campagnola, *Le origini francescane*, 111–20.

44. 'ad Miramolini Regnum, ipse Orientis, illi Occidentis populis Mahumeticis salutare preadicarent Evangelium, et undique quas possent gentes Christo lucrifacerent', Wadding, *Annales minorum*, i. 352.

45. 'Non ergo inaniter, nec penitus infructuose in Soldani corde fidei semina jecit Franciscus, neque inutiliter praedicavit, cujus animum adeo flexit et mutavit, ut ante ferocem et inhumanum, mox mansuetissimum et benignum reddiderit in Christianos.' Wadding, *Annales minorum*, i. 360.

46. See Simonetta Prosperi Valenti Rodinò, 'La diffusione dell'iconografia francescana attraverso l'incisione', in *L'immagine di San Francesco nella Controriforma* (Rome: Quasar, 1982), 159–223 (esp. pp. 166, 176–8); pl. 112 reproduces the 49 engravings. There is also a reprint of the 1594 edn., publ. 1981: *Ottavo centenario della nascita di San Francesco: Tutta la vita del Santo di Assisi raccontata in quarantanove immagine incise in Roma da Anrea de' Putti ristampata in 500 esemplari sur carta per incisione da citta di Florence 1978.*

47. This is the suggestion of A. Cristofani, *Le Storie d'Assisi* (Assisi: 1886), 491, cited Rodinò, 'La diffusione', 176. On the frescos (now damaged) see Pasquale Magro, *La Basilica sepocrale di San Francesco in Assisi* (Assisi: Casa editrici francescana, 1991), 61–2.

48. Jacques Corbin, *La Saincte Franciade contenant la vie, gestes et miracles du bien heureux patriarche Sainct-Francois* (Paris: Nicolas Rousset, 1634); on this text, see Vorreux, *François dans les lettres françaises*, 124–9.

49. See Georges Minois, *Bossuet: Entre Dieu et le Soleil* (Paris: Perrin, 2003), 88–98.

50. Bossuet, *Panégyrique de St. François d'Assise*, in *Œuvres*, ed. Abbé Velat and Yvonne Champailler (Paris: Pléiade, 1961), 235–58; English tr. Louis Bourdaloue and Denis O'Mahony, *Panegyrics of the Saints* (London: K. Paul, Trench, Trubner & Co., 1924). On this text, see Vorreux, *François dans les lettres françaises*, 177–80.

51. Bossuet, *Panégyrique de St. François*, 250.

52. Ibid.

53. Ibid. 252–3; English tr., 126–7.

54. Bossuet, *Panégyrique de Saint Pierre Nolasque*, in *Œuvres*, 539–55 (passages cited 544–5). On Pierre Nolasque (Père Nolasc in Catalan), see James Brodman, *Ransoming Captives in Crusader Spain: The Order of Merced on the Christian–Islamic Frontier* (Philadelphia: University of Pennsylvania Press, 1986), 15–25.

55. Bossuet, *Panégyrique de Saint Pierre Nolasque*, 552–3.

56. Bossuet, *Oraison funèbre de Marie-Thérèse d'Autriche*, in *Œuvres*, 107–33 (passages cied 114–15). On the war between France and Algiers, see Moulay Belhamissi, *Alger, l'Europe et la guerre secrète (1518–1830)* (Alger: Dahlab, 1999).

57. Bossuet, *Discours sur l'histoire universelle*, in *Œuvres*, 665–1027 (here 942–3).

CHAPTER 12

1. Jean-Baptiste Renoult, *Les avantures de la Madona et de François d'Assise, Recueillies de plusieurs ouvrages des Docteurs Romains, écrites d'un stile récreatif en même temps capable de faire see le ridicule du Papisme sans aucune controverse* (Amsterdam: Daniel la Feuille, 1701). This pamphlet was reprinted in 1745,

then in 1882, under the title *Les aventures galantes de la Madone avec ses dévots, suivies de celles de François d'Assise* (Paris: Pairault, 1882); the references here are to this edn. On this text, see Vorreux, *François dans les lettres françaises*, 235–9. Renoult also wrote a *Réponse de Monsieur Renoult, ministre, à son père pour se justifier d'hérésie: Nouvelle édition augmentée d'une dispute entre le même auteur et un missionnaire papiste sur le retranchement de la coupe* (London: D. Du Chemin, 1735).

2. Reblin, *Freund und Feind*, 112–61.

3. See above, Ch. 2.

4. Pierre Bayle, *Dictionnaire historique et critique* (4th edn. Amsterdam: chez P. Brunel, 1730), ii. 492–8. For an introd. to the considerable bibliography on Pierre Bayle, see Isabelle Delpla and Philippe de Robert (eds.), *La Raison corrosive: Etudes sur la pensée critique de Pierre Bayle* (Paris: Champion, 2003); Antony McKenna and Gianni Paganini (eds.), *Pierre Bayle dans la République des Lettres: Philosophie, religion, critique* (Paris: Champion, 2004); Ruth Whelan, *The Anatomy of Superstition: A Study of the Historical Theory and Practice of Pierre Bayle* (Oxford: Voltaire Foundation, 1989). On his views on Francis, see Reblin, *Freund und Feind*, 124–8.

5. Reblin, *Freund und Feind*, 128–32 (citation p. 130 n. 3).

6. Ibid. 144.

7. Art. 'Capuchon', in *Encyclopédie ou Dictionnaire raisonne des sciences, des arts et des métiers* (Paris: 1751–65; repr. Stuttgart-Bad Cannstatt, Frommann, 1966–7), ii. 640. 'Scotism', a term of abuse for 18th-cent. *philosophes,* refers to the speculative theology of Franciscan John Duns Scotus (1266–1308) and his followers.

8. Art. 'Franciscains', in Fortuné Barthélémy de Félice, *Encyclopédie ou Diction-naire universel raisonné des connoissances humaines* (42 vols. Yverdon-les-Bains, 1770–80), xx. 553; electronic edn. by Claude Blum (Paris: Champion électronique, 2003). See Vorreux, *François dans les lettres françaises*, 198–9.

9. Gianni Guadalupi (ed.), *Hortus conclusus: San Giulio, Orta e il sacro monte* (Milan: F. M. Ricci, 1996); *Isola San Giulio e il sacro monte d'Orta*, ed. G. Dell'Acqua (Turin: Istituto Bancario San Paolo di Torino, 1977); Luigi Mallè, *Il Sacro Monte di Orta* (Rome: Cassa di Risparmio di Roma, 1963); *Il Sacro Monte d'Orta e San Francesco nella storia e nell'arte della controriforma: Atti del Convegno Orta San Giulio, 4–6 giugno 1982* (Turin: Pubblicazione a cura della Regione Piemonte, 1985). Thanks to Manuela Ciri for bringing Monte d'Orta to my attention.

10. Guadalupi (ed.), *Hortus conclusus,* 33.

11. On the role played by the works of Angelo Clareno in the Capuchin vision of Franciscan history, see Ch. 8 above.

12. See next chapter.

13. Voltaire, letter to Louis René de Caradeuc de La Chatolais, 21 Mar. 1763, in *Voltaire's Correspondence*, ed. Theodore Besterman (Geneva: Institut et Musée Voltaire, 1959), 269–70.

14. Voltaire, 'Superstition', in *Dictionnaire philosophique* (1764; Paris: Flammarion, 1964), 358.

15. Voltaire, *Essai sur les mœurs et l'esprit des nations et sur les principaux faits de l'histoire depuis Charlemagne jusqu'à Louis XIII* (2 vols. Paris: Bordas, 1990), ii. 284. On Voltaire as historian, see Karen O'Brien, *Narratives of Enlightenment: Cosmopolitan History from Voltaire to Gibbon* (Cambridge: CUP, 1997), 21–55.

16. Voltaire, second *Homélie sur la superstition*, in *Œuvres complètes*, xliii. 361, cited by Vorreux, *François dans les lettres françaises*, 198.

17. See *Voltaire's Correspondence*, 63 (1961), 75; 74 (1962), 85, 125; Vorreux, *François dans les lettres françaises*, 198.

18. Voltaire, *Profession de foi des Théistes*, in *Œuvres complètes*, xxv (Paris: Gagniard, 1830), 411–36 (here 422); on this text, see the article by J. Seban in Raymond Trousson and Jeroom Vercruysse (eds.), *Dictionnaire générale de Voltaire* (Paris: Champion, 2003), 994–6.

19. Voltaire, *Essai sur les mœurs*, i. 862.

20. Ibid. i. 580. See Tolan, *Sons of Ishmael*, ch. 6.

21. Voltaire, *Essai sur les moeurs*, i. 587.

22. Ibid. i. 587–8.

23. *Trop est trop: Capitulation de la France avec ses moines & religieux de toutes les livrées, avec la revue générale de leurs patriarches* (The Hague: Frédéric Staatman, 1767). See Vorreux, *François dans les lettres françaises*, 239–43; Cardinal George Grente (ed.), *Dictionnaire des Lettres Françaises: Le XVIIIe siècle* (Paris: Fayard, 1995), 868.

24. Simon-Nicolas-Henri Linguet, *Histoire impartiale des Jésuites: Depuis leur établissement jusqu'à leur première expulsion* (n.pl., 1768; electronic version at http://gallica.bnf.fr/).

25. *AASS* Oct. ii. 534.

26. Louis Maimbourg, *Histoire des Croisades pour la délivrance de la Terre Sainte* (2 vols. Paris: Sébastien Mabre-Cramoisy, imprimeur du Roy, 1675–6). I consulted the 1686 edn.; see ii. 233–4.

27. Joseph-Romain Joly, *L'Égyptiade, ou le voyage de Saint François d'Assise à la cour du Roi d'Egypte: Poème en douze chants* (Paris: Jombert le jeune, 1786); it is a revised version of a poem publ. 1776 under the title of *L'Egyptienne*. See Vorreux, *François dans les lettres françaises*, 235–9.

28. *Das Leben dess heiligen seraphischen Vatters Francisic, Stiffters dess Ordens mer minderen Bruder.* See Einhorn, 'Franziskus und der "edle Heide"', p. 636 and pl 5.

29. Jean-Joseph Görres, 'Der heilige Franziskus von Assisi: ein Troubadour', *Der Katholik*, 5 (1826), 14–53. French tr., 'Saint François d'Assise, un troubadour', *Revue européenne*, 7 (1833), no. 25, pp. 65–87 and no. 27, pp. 325–47. A brief mention of Francis's mission to the sultan 'qui assiégeait Damiette' (sic) and who shows respect for the saint, is at p. 334. A partial reproduction of this text is found in Maxime Alexandre (ed.), *Romantiques allemands*, i (Paris: Pléiade, 1963), 1546–52. On this text, see Reblin, *Freund und Feind*, 159–61.

30. Reblin, *Freund und Feind*, 178–83.

31. Ibid. 195–7.

32. Jules Michelet, *Histoire de la France: Le Moyen Age* (Paris: Laffont, 1981; 1st publ. 1879), 360.

CHAPTER 13

1. Sabino De Sandoli, *The Peaceful Liberation of the Holy Places in the Fourteenth Century: The Third Return of the Frankish or Latin Clergy to the Custody and Service of the Holy Places through Official Negotiations in 1333* (Cairo: Franciscan Center of Christian Oriental Studies, 1990; online at: http://www.christusrex.org/www2/liberation/II-10a.html); Golubovich, iv. 1–12; Augustino Arce, 'De origine Custodiae Terrae Sanctae', *Acta Ordinis Fratrum Minorum*, 83 (1964), 182–205; Heinrich Fürst, *Die Custodie des Heiligen Landes: Die Mission der Franziskaner imi Heiligen Land und im Vorderen Orient* (Munich: Kommissariat für das Heilige Land, 1981); Kaspar Elm, 'La custodia di Terra Santa: Franziskanisches Ordensleben in der tradition der lateinischen Kirche palästinas', in *I Franciscani nel trecento: Atti del XIV convegno internatzionale* (Perugia: Centro di Studi Francescani, 1988), 127–66.

2. See Setton (ed.), *History of the Crusades*, iii. 51–4; Tyerman, 'Marino Sanudo Torsello and the Lost Crusade', 64–5.

3. Burr, *Spiritual Franciscans*, 74.

4. Margaret Toynbee, *Saint Louis of Toulouse and the Process of Canonisation in the Fourteenth Century* (Manchester: MUP, 1929); Edith Pásztor, *Per la storia di San Ludovico d'Angiò (1274–1297)* (Rome: Istituto Palazzo Borromini, 1955).

5. Samantha Kelly, *The New Solomon: Robert of Naples (1309–1343) and Fourteenth-Century Kingship* (Leiden: Brill, 2003); Kelly, 'King Robert of Naples (1309–1343) and the Spiritual Franciscans', *Cristianesimo nella Storia*, 20 (1999), 41–80; Isabelle Heullant-Donat, 'En amont de l'Observance: Les lettres de Sancia, reine de Naples, aux Chapitres généraux et leur transmission dans l'historiographie du XIVe siècle', in F. Meyer and L. Viallet (eds.), *Identités franciscaines à l'âge des réformes* (Clermont-Ferrand: Presses Universitaires Blaise-Pascal, 2005), 73–99.

6. Julian Gardner, 'Saint Louis of Toulouse, Robert of Anjou and Simone Martini', *Zeitschrift für Kunstgeschichte*, 39 (1976), 12–33.

7. See Ch. 8 above.

8. See Ch. 11 above.

9. Golubovich, iv. 40.

10. Kelly, *New Solomon*, 82–6.

11. Ronald Musto, 'Queen Sancia of Naples (1266–1345) and the Spiritual Franciscans', in J. Kirshner and S. Wemple (eds.), *Women of the Medieval World* (Oxford: Clarendon, 1985), 179–214; Roberto Paciocco, 'Angioni e "spirituali": I differenti piani cronologici e tematici di un problema', *L'État angevin: Pousee, culture et société XIIIe et XIVe siècle* (Rome: Istituto Storico Italiano per il Medio Evo, 1998), 253–87.

12. *Chronicon XXIV Generalium* (cited by Golubovich, iv. 9–10): 'Anno Domini MCCCXXXIII idem Generalis (Geraldus Odonis) … misit multos fratres de Provincia Aquitaniae et de aliis partibus Ordinis ad convertendum … Armenos Armeniae et alios infideles … De quibus frater Rogerius Garini dictae Provinciae ad Terram Sanctam pergens, obtinuit a Soldano Aegypti locum sacrum Montis Sion, ubi fuit illud coenaculum magnum stratum … In quo locum fratrum conventum aedificavit; et ex tunc ibi et in Sancto Sepulcro fratres nostri habitaverunt usque in hodierum diem.' Cited by Sandoli, *Peaceful Liberation*.

13. The sultan communicated these ideas to Dominican friar and pontifical legate Pierre de La Palu in 1331, according to the anonymous Franciscan author of the *Chronicon de Lanercost* (Golubovich, iii. 359–67, esp. 363–4); Sandoli, *Peaceful Liberation*.

14. Kelly, *New Solomon*, 212; on Marino Sanudo, see Ch. 11 above.

15. Golubovich, iv. 59–73.

16. Ibid. 24–31 (text cited p. 27). Golubovich notes (pp. 21–4) that Giacomo da Verona, Augustinian canon, went to the Holy Land in 1335; he speaks of the presence of 'Franks' in Bethlehem, but does not say they were Franciscans. He describes the Cenacle as a pile of ruins, which suggests that the Franciscans had not yet taken possession of the site. On Ludolf von Sudheim, see Anne Simon, 'Of Smelly Seas and Ashen Apples: Two German Pilgrims' View of the East', in Allen (ed.), *Eastward Bound* (Manchester: MUP, 2004), 196–220.

17. Niccolò da Poggibonsi, *Libro d'Oltramare*, ed. Alberto Bacchi Della Lega and B. Bagatti (Jerusalem: Tipografia dei Francescani, 1945), 25–8; Golubovich, v. 1–24.

18. Ibid. 64; for Mt Sion, see pp. 9–10.

19. Ibid. 141.

20. Golubovich, v. 83–7. See Gioacchino Francesco D'Andrea, 'Il regno di Napoli e la custodia di Terra Santa', in Michele Piccirillo (ed.), *La Custodia di Terra Santa e l'Europa: I rapporti politici e l'attvità culturale dei Francescani in Medio Oriente* (Rome: Veltro, 1983), 37–70.

21. Golubovich, iv. 45–9. Some authors imagine that the friars received fabulous sums of money, up to 250 000 ducats per year, which is highly implausible. For an introduction to the history of the Franciscan custody of the Holy

Land and its artistic and cultural aspects, see the catalogue *In Terra Santa: Dalla crociata alla custodia dei Luoghi Santi* (Florence: Aftificio Skira, 2000).

22. Béatrice Dansette, 'Relation inedite d'un pèlerinage effectué en 1486', in *AFH* 72 (1979), 106–33 and 330–428 (here 335, 349).

23. Angelo Clareno, *Historia* (ed. Rossini), 78–83; *Liber chronicarum* (ed. Boccali), 164–75; see Ch. 8 above.

24. *Actus Beati Francisci et sociorum eius*, c. 27; see Ch. 9 above.

25. 'Cum ista campana Sanctus Franciscus populum ad predicationem convocabat et cum istis baculis percutiendo silentium ein *[sic]* ynponebat. Iovannes Nicholuti de Senis me fecit.' Golubovich, i. 81–2; Roberto Rusconi (ed.), *Francesco d'Assisi: Storia e arte* (Milan: Electra, 1982), 185.

26. 'S. Francesco…piglio uno cornetto da luy con doy bachette per securità.' See Ch. 11 above.

27. Wadding, *Annales minorum* ad an. 1235, cited by Golubovich, i. 82.

28. Golubovich, i. 71–6.

29. Ibid. 77–80.

30. Ibid. v. 1–369, cites the testimony of many Franciscans and pilgrims. On the role of the Franciscans in the organization of pilgrimages and the hosting of pilgrims, see Dansette, 'Relation inedite'.

31. Bertrandon de la Broquière, *Voyage d'Outremer*, ed. Charles Shefer (Paris: Ernest Leroux, 1892), 11, 12, 25, 27, 40.

32. See Rosalyn Voaden, 'Travels with Margery: Pilgrimage in Context', in Allen (ed.), *Eastward Bound* (Manchester: MUP, 2004), 177–95; Elka Weber, 'Sharing the Sites: Medieval Jewish Travelers to the Land of Israel', ibid. 35–52 (here 47); Simon, 'Of Smelly Seas', 211. Jewish traveller Meshram de Volterra, in narrating his travels of 1481, mentions Franciscans as proprietors of the tomb of David.

33. Golubovich, v. 242.

34. Ibid. 282–99. Isabelle Heullant-Donat, 'Les Martyrs franciscains de Jérusalem (1391), entre mémoire et manipulation', in Damien Coulon *et al.* (eds.), *Chemins d'Outre-Mer: Études d'histoire sur la Méditerrannée médiévale offertes à Michel Balard* (2 vols. Paris: Publications de la Sorbonne, 2004), ii. 439–59.

35. Louis de Rochechouart, *Journal de voyage à Jérusalem*, ed. C. Couderc, *Revue de l'orient latin*, 1 (1893), 1–107; French tr. Béatrice Dansette in *Croisades et Pèlerinages: Récits, chroniques et voyages en Terre Sainte XIIᵉ–XVᵉ siècle* (Paris: Laffont, 1997), 1124–67. On the anonymous text of 1486, see Dansette's edn., 'Relation inedite'; see her modern French tr. in *Croisades et Pèlerinages*, 1168–1225.

36. Nompar de Caumont, *Voyage d'Outre Mer en Jérusalem par le Seigneur de Caumont*, ed. le Marquis de la Grange (Paris, 1858); *Le Voyatge d'Oultremer en Jherusalem de Nompar, seigneur de Caumont*, ed. Peter Noble (Oxford: Basil Blackwell, 1975), 35–6; partial tr. Dansette in *Croisades et Pèlerinages*, 1057–1123 (here 1083–4).

37. The first eight Latin kings of Jerusalem were buried there; their tombs could be seen there until 1808. See Adrian Boas, *Jerusalem in the Time of the Crusades: Society, Landscape and Art in the Holy City under Frankish Rule* (London: Routledge, 2001), 180.

38. Louis Deshayes de Courmenin, *Voiage de Levant: Fait par le commandement du Roy en l'année 1621* (Paris: A. Taupinard, 1624; republ. Paris: Hachette, 1976), 355–6; text available at http://www.Gallica.fr.

39. Golubovich, iv. 184–93.

40. Bernardin Collin, 'La Francia e la Custodia di Terra Santa', in Piccirillo (ed.), *La Custodia*, 71–82.

41. Here I follow Golubovich (iv. 88–183), who demonstrates this convincingly, even though he is polemical and partisan (the Greeks, for him are 'eterodossi').

42. Cited ibid. iv. 214.

43. For examples from 14th-cent. Italy, see Louise Bourdua, *The Franciscans and Art Patronage in Late Medieval Italy* (Cambridge, CUP, 2004), 16–17.

44. Franciscus Quaresmius, *Historica theologica et moralis Terrae Sanctae elucidatio*, ed. Cypriano de Tarvisio (2 vols. Venice: Typis Antonellianis, 1880), esp. i. 115–27. 'Ad quid, quaeso, voluit Deus servum suum aspicere et perambulare terram a suis posteris postea obtinendam, nisi ut ipse intellegeret, ipsum accipere illius pro posteris suis possessionem?' (p. 118).

45. Mariano Morone da Maleo, *Terra Santa nuovamente illustrata* (2 vols. Piacenza, 1669–70).

46. 'che se bene le Chroniche noste ciò non dicano, si deue però suporre, non douendosi credere, che un Santo si diuoto, & inclinato alla pellegrinatione, trascurasse la maggior parte di tutte, passondoui da vicino.' Ibid. ii. 217–23 (passage cited 217). He again affirms that Francis himself took possession of the site and founded the convent of the Cenacle (p. 378); we find the same claim ibid. i. 17, 72, 187–8.

47. Juan de Calahorra, *Chrónica de la provincia de Syria y tierra santa de Gerusalen, contiene los progressos que en ella ha hecho la religión seráfica, desde el ano 1219 hasta el de 1632* (Madrid: Juan García Infançón, 1684). Juan de Calahorra was an Observant from the province of Burgos and an administrator in the province of Syria; he died in 1684. An Italian tr. was published ten years after the Spanish original: *Historia chronologica della provincia de Siria e Terra santa di Gerusalemme, dove nostro Salvatore operó le maraviglie della redenzione*, tr. Angelico da Milano (Venice, 1694). On this author, see A. Van den Wyngaert, 'Calahorra', *DHGE* xi. 333.

48. Francisco Jesús María de San Juan del Puerto, *Patrimonio seraphico de Tierra Santa: Fundado por Christo Nuestro Redentor con su preciosa sangre, prometido por su Magestad à N.P.S. Francisco para sì, y para sus hijos, adquirido por el mismo santo, heredado y posseìdo por sus hijos de la regular observancia, y conservado hasta el tiempo presente* (Madrid: Impr. de la Causa de V.M. María de Jesús de Agreda, 1724).

49. Calahorra takes inspiration from Quaresmius, *Historica theologica et moralis Terrae Sanctae elucidatio*, 148–9. Cf. Calahorra, *Chrónica*, 24–9; Morone da Maleo, *Terra Santa nuovamente illustrata*, 218; Del Puerto, *Patrimonio seraphico*, 31–4.

50. See Ch. 12 above.

51. Chateaubriand, *Itinéraire de Paris à Jérusalem*, in *Œuvres romanesques et voyages* (2 vols. Paris: Pléiade, 1969), ii. 1100; English tr. Frederic Shoberl, *Travels to Jerusalem and the Holy Land: Through Egypt* (London: H. Colburn, 1835), 130.

52. Chateaubriand, *Travels to Jerusalem*, 128–9.

53. Chateaubriand, *Mémoires d'outre-tombe*, ed. Maurice Levaillant (Paris: Flammarion, 1949–50), ii. 239; he refers to 'mon patron St. François' at iii. 410; he summarizes canto XI of Dante's *Paradiso* at iii. 552.

54. Chateaubriand, *Mémoires d'outre-tombe*, iv. 483.

55. See Elizabeth Siberry, *The New Crusaders: Images of the Crusades in the Nineteenth and Early Twentieth Centuries* (Aldershot: Ashgate, 2000), 66, 71–2.

56. L'Abbé Grand, *La Terre Sainte et les lieux illustrés par les Apôtres: Vues pittoresques d'après Turner, Harding et autres artistes célèbres. Histoire, description, mœurs actuelles* (new edn. Paris: Librairie d'Education, 1868; 1st edn. 1837), 38–9.

57. See David Goldfrank, *The Origins of the Crimean War* (London: Longman, 1994), 75–94; on the Franciscan custody in the second half of the 19th cent., see Giuseppe Buffon, *Les Franciscains en Terre Sainte (1869–1889): Religion et politique, une recherche institutionnelle* (Paris: Cerf, 2005).

58. Marcellino da Civezza, *Storia universale delle missioni francescane* (11 vols. Rome: Tipografia Tiberina, 1857–95).

59. Ibid. i. 43–4.

60. Ibid. i. 45.

61. See e.g. John Locke, *Second Treatise of Government* (1690), ch. 5, 'Of Property'.

62. Civezza, *Storia universale*, i. 55.

63. Ibid. 59.

64. Ibid. 78.

65. 'François d'Assise', in *La Grande Encyclopédie* (31 vols. Paris: H. Lamirault & cie., 1886–1902), xviii (1893), 44–9 (here 45).

66. Alphonse Couret, *Les Légendes du Saint Sépulcre* (Paris: Maison de la Bonne presse, 1894), 112–18; See Ferdinando Diotallevi, 'S. Francesco nei suoi viaggi e nel possesso dei Luoghi Santi', *L'Italia Francescana: Nel settimo centenario della morte di S. Francesco* (Assisi: Tip. Porziuncola, 1927), 274–93.

67. Patrick Ryan, 'The Roots of Muslim Anger', *America*, 185(17), 26 Nov. 2001.

68. Edward Said, *Orientalism* (New York: Random House, 1978).

69. Corbin, *La Saincte Franciade*, 285–7; see Ch. 12 above.

70. See Ch. 12 above.

71. Siberry, *New Crusaders*, 74.

72. On Michaud, see Jean Richard, 'De Jean-Baptiste Mailly à Joseph-François Michaud: Un moment de l'historiographie des croisades (1774–1841)', *Crusades,* 1 (2002), 1–12; Christopher Tyerman, *Fighting for Christendom: Holy War and the Crusades* (Oxford: OUP, 2004), 200–4; Siberry, *New Crusaders*; Adam Knobler, 'Saint Louis and French Political Culture', in Leslie J. Workman and Kathleen Verduin (eds.), *Medievalism in Europe II* (Studies in Medievalism, 8; Cambridge: CUP, 1996), 156–74; Kim Munholland, 'Michaud's History of the Crusades and the French Crusade in Algeria under Louis Philippe', in *The Popularization of Images: Visual Culture under the July Monarchy* (Princeton: PUP, 1994), 113–65.

73. Joseph-François Michaud, *Histoire des Croisades* (2nd edn. Paris: Ponthier, 1826), i. 466–7; English tr. W. Robson, *Michaud's History of the Crusades* (London: Routledge, 1852), i. 224–8.

74. *Michaud's History of the Crusades,* i. 264.

75. Ibid. ii. 245–6.

76. Ibid. ii. 246.

77. See Claire Constans *et al., Les Salles des croisades: Château de Versailles* (Doussard: Ed. du Gui, 2002).

78. Jean-Joseph-François Poujoulat and Joseph-François Michaud, *Abrégé de l'histoire des croisades, à l'usage de la jeunesse* (Paris : Ducollet, 1838), p. xvi. See Siberry, *New Crusaders,* 82.

79. Cited by Knobler, 'St Louis', 163.

80. Michaud, *Histoire des croisades, illustrée de 100 grandes compositions par Gustave Doré* (2 vols. Paris: Furne, Jouvet & Cie, 1877), pl. 50, i. 402. The engravings are reproduced in *Doré's Illustrations of the Crusades* (Mineola, NY: Dover Publications, 1997). On Doré, see Philippe Kaenel, *Le Métier d'illustrateur, 1830–1880: Rodolphe Töpffer, J.-J. Grandville, Gustave Doré* (Paris: Messene, 1996), 234–304; see Introduction above.

81. Andrea Giovannelli, *La Santa sede e la Palestina: La Custodia di Terra Santa tra la fine dell'impero ottomano e la guerra dei sei giorni* (Rome: Edizioni Studium: 2000), 14.

82. Girolamo Golubovich, *Serie chronologica dei reverendissimi superiori di Terra Santa, ossia dei provinciali custodi e presidenti della medisima* (Jerusalem: Tipografia del convento di San Salvatore, 1898).

83. Benoît XV, *Inclytum Fratrum* (4 Oct. 1918), in *Acta Apostolica Sedis,* 10 (1918), 437, cited by Giulio Basetti-Sani, 'San Francesco è incorso nella scomunica? Una bolla di Onorio III ed il supposto pellegrinaggio del Santo a Gerusalemme', *Archivum Franciscanum, Historicum* 65 (1972), 3–19.

84. Paolo Gaidano was born on 28 Dec. 1861 in Poirino, near Turin; he died in Turin in 1917. See E. Benzeit, *Dictionnaire des peintres, sculpteurs, dessinateurs et graveurs* (Paris: Gründ, 1999), v. 804.

85. Arnoldo Zocchi was born in Florence on 20 Sept. 1862 and died in Rome on 17 July 1940 (see Benzeit, *Dictionnaire,* x. 914). For the context of architecture

in Cairo in this period, see Mohamed Scharabi, *Kairo: Stadt und Architektur im Zeitalter des europäischen Kolonialismus* (Tübingen: Verlag Ernst Wasmuth, 1989); Scharabi does not mention St Joseph.

86. *San Francisco de Asis: Ilustraciones de José Benlliure y comentarios del padre Antonio Torró* (Valencia: Administración de la Tercera orden, 1926). On this artist, see Victoria Bonet Solves, *José Benlliure Gil: El oficio de pintor* (Valencia: Ayuntamiento de Valencia, 1998), esp. 130–2.

87. Ferdinando Diotallevi, 'S. Francesco nei suoi viaggi e nel possesso dei Luoghi Santi', *L'Italia Francescana: Nel settimo centenario della morte di S. Francesco* (Assisi: Tipografia Porziuncola, 1927), 274–93.

88. Ibid. 293.

89. Bernard d'Andermatt, *Saint François d'Assise* (2 vols. Paris: Œuvre de Saint François d'Assise, 1901), ii. 39.

90. Sabatier, *Vie de Saint François d'Assise*, 263.

91. Martiniano Roncaglia, *Saint Francis of Assisi and the Middle East* (Cairo: Franciscan Center of Oriental Studies, 1957), 29.

92. Ibid. 4.

93. Ibid. 20.

94. Ibid. 21.

95. Basetti-Sani, 'San Francesco è incorso nella scomunica?'

96. Franco Cardini, 'Nella presenza del Soldan superba: Bernardo, Francesco, Bonaventura e il superamento spirituale dell'idea di crociata', *Studi Francescani*, 71 (1974), 199–250.

97. Alain Absire, *Le Pauvre d'Orient* (Paris: Presses de la Renaissance, 2000), 247–51.

98. G. K. Chesterton, *St. Francis of Assisi* (London: Hodder & Stoughton, 1924 and 1958), 146–7.

99. Muriel Jaeger, *Experimental Lives: From Cato to George Sand* (London: G. Bell, 1932), 76–7.

100. D'Andermatt, *Saint François d'Assise*, ii. 33.

101. Valerie Martin, *Salvation: Scenes from the Life of St. Francis* (New York: Knopf, 2001), 134.

102. Ibid. 146.

CHAPTER 14

1. The letters between Louis Massignon and Mary Kahil are published in Jacques Keryell, (ed.), *L'Hospitalité sacrée* (Paris: Nouvelle Cité, 1987). See Pierre Rocalve, *Louis Massignon et l'Islam* (Damascus: Institut Français de Damas, 1993); Guy Harpigny, *Islam et Christianisme selon Louis Massignon* (Louvain la Neuve: Presses de l'Université Catholique de Louvain, 1981); *Louis Massignon et le dialogue des cultures* (Paris: Cerf, 1996) (see in particular the contributions of Jacques Berque and François Angelier); Massignon,

'Mystique musulmane et mystique chrétienne au moyen âge', *Opera minora*, ii (Beirut: Dar al-Maaref, 1963 and 1972), 470–84.

2. Jean Jacques Waardenburg, *Islam dans le miroir de l'Occident; comment quelques orientalistes occidentaux se sont penchés sur l'Islam et se sont formé une image de cette religion* (3rd edn. Paris, Mouton, 1969); Said, *Orientalism*, 263–74.

3. See Chs. 2 and 3 above.

4. Louis Massignon, *La Passion de Husayn Ibn Mansûr Hallâj, martyr mystique de l'Islam exécuté à Bagdad le 26 mars 922: Étude d'histoire religieuse* (4 vols. Paris: Gallimard, 1975), i. 600; see EI[2], 'mubâhala'.

5. Massignon, 'La Mubâhala de Médine et l'hyperdulie de Fatima', in *Opera minora*, i. 550–72.

6. Massignon, *La Passion*, ii. 337–8; Massignon, 'Mystique musulmane', 482–4.

7. *L'Hospitalité sacrée*, 61–2.

8. Ibid. 186. On his reunion with Mary Kahil and the establishment of the *Badaliya* foundation, see Christian Destremau and Jean Moncelon, *Massignon* (Paris: Plon, 1994), 244–9.

9. Massignon, *L'Hégire d'Ismaël* (Tours, 1935); repr. in Massignon, *Les Trois Prières d'Abraham* (Paris: Cerf, 1997), 59–118.

10. Massignon, 'al-Badaliya': *Statuts* repr. in *L'Hospitalité sacrée*, 373–8. For a description of this text and of Massignon's annual letters to the members of the foundation, see Harpigny, *Islam et Christianisme*, 174–91; Giulio Basetti-Sani, *Louis Massignon orientalista cristiano* (Milan: Vita e pensiero, 1971); English tr., *Louis Massignon (1883–1962), Christian Ecumenist, Prophet of Inter-Religious Reconciliation* (Chicago: Franciscan Herald Press, 1974), 93–4.

11. Denise Barrat, 'Témoignage sur un témoin', in Jacques Keryell (ed.), *Louis Massignon au cœur de notre temps* (Paris: Karthala, 1999), 23–8 (citation 25).

12. Massignon, 'Cinquième mystère douloureux', in *Opera minora*, iii. 844.

13. Basetti-Sani, *Louis Massignon orientalista cristiano*.

14. Basetti-Sani, *Il Corano nella luce di Cristo: Saggio per una reinterpretazione cristiana del libro sacro dell'Islam* (Bologna: EMI, 1972); English tr. *The Koran in the Light of Christ: A Christian Interpretation of the Sacred Book of Islam* (Chicago: Franciscan Herald Press, 1977).

15. Basetti-Sani, *Gesù Cristo nascosto nel Corano* (San Pietro in Cariano: Il segno, 1994).

16. Basetti-Sani, *Mohammed et Saint François* (Ottawa: Commissariat de Terre-Sainte, 1959).

17. Basetti-Sani, *Koran in the Light of Christ*, 32–4.

18. Basetti-Sani, *Per un dialogo cristiano-musulmano: Mohammed, Damietta et La Verna* (Milan: Vita e pensiero, 1969); *L'Islam e Francesco d'Assisi: La missione profetica per il dialogo* (Florence: La nuova Italia, 1975).

19. Francis de Beer, 'Saint François et l'Islam', *Concilium*, 169 (1981), 23–36 (citations 30–1).

20. Isaac Vázquez Janeiro, 'I francescani e il dialogo con gli ebrei e saraceni nei secoli XIII–XV', *Antonianum*, 65 (1990), 533–49 (here 534).

21. Cornelio Del Zotto, 'Il dialogo universale di Francesco d'Assisi: Pratica di pacificazione', *Antonianum*, 65 (1990), 495–532 (citations 522–4).

22. Michael Robson, *St Francis of Assisi: The Legend and the Life* (New York: Geoffrey Chapman, 1997), 237.

23. 'There are signs to suggest that Francis had initially absorbed many of the contemporary assumptions about society and the world order, although this evidence comes from biographers whose understanding of the saint was found to be limited. The process of conversion, however, opened new perspectives for Francis and enabled him to take a more objective view of the norms and beliefs prevailing in medieval society.' Robson, *St Francis*, 236.

24. J. Hoeberichts, *Franciscus en de Islam* (Assen: Van Gorcum, 1994); English tr., *Francis and Islam* (Quincy, Ill.: Franciscan Press, 1997), 5.

25. Kathleen Warren, *Daring to Cross the Threshold: Francis of Assisi Encounters Sultan Malek al-Kamil* (Rochester, NY: Sisters of St Francis, 2003), 36.

26. Del Zotto, 'Il dialogo universale di Francesco d'Assisi'.

27. Warren, *Daring to Cross the Threshold*, 42 n. 28.

28. For Romain Rolland (1866–1944), Gandhi is 'le petit saint François de l'Inde'. François Mauriac (1885–1970) makes the same comparison. See Vorreux, *François dans les lettres françaises*, 496 and 502.

29. Gwenolé Jeusset, *Rencontre sur l'Autre Rive: François d'Assise et les Musulmans* (Paris: Éditions Franciscaines, 1996).

30. Friedrich Böhringer, *Die Kirche Christi und ihre Zeugen, oder Die Kirchengeschichte in Biographien* (24 vols. 2nd edn. Stuttgart, 1860–79), xvi. 498, cited by Reblin, *Freund und Feind*, 180–1.

31. See Ch. 13.

32. Nikos Kazantzakis, *God's Pauper: St. Francis of Assisi*, tr. P. A. Bien (Oxford: Bruno Cassirer, 1962).

33. Julian Mitchell, *Francis* (London: Amber Lane Press, 1984).

34. Maruxa Vilalta, *Francisco de Asís, Obra en 14 cuadros* (Mexico: Fondo de Cultura Económica, 1993), 55–9.

35. 'Francis's ideal was fundamentally at odds with that of the crusaders.' Morris Bishop, *Saint Francis of Assisi* (Boston: Little, Brown & Co., 1974), 121. 'Francis is never quoted thereafter as recalling his Mideastern experiences. This silence may or may not be significant. It may be due to his unwillingness to remember a time filled with disillusion, failure, and shame before men and God' (131).

36. Henri Queffélec, *François d'Assise, le Jongleur de Dieu* (Paris: Calmann-Lévy, 1982), 228.

37. Absire, *Le Pauvre d'Orient*.

38. Steven Runciman, *History of the Crusades*, iii. *The Kingdom of Acre and the Later Crusades* (Cambridge: CUP, 1954; London: Penguin, 1965), 159–60.

39. 'San Francesco d'Assisi si oppose alla militanza cristiana propria del movimento delle crociate e come la sua missione in Oriente possa essere meglio considerata l'inizio della ricerca di una alternativa di pace. ...l'opposizione alle crociate serviva a promuovere l'alternativa missionaria che si sviluppò durante il periodo della vita del santo e scaturì direttamente dai suoi ideali.' James Powell, 'Francesco d'Assisi e la quinta crociata: Una missione di pace', *Schede Medievali*, 4 (1983), 68–77 (here 69). We find roughly the same perspective in Powell, *Anatomy*, 158–9, 187, and more recently in Powell, 'St. Francis of Assisi's Way of Peace', *Medieval Encounters*, 13 (2007), 271–80.

40. See Sean Edward Kinsella, ' "The Lord Give Your Peace" ': The Preaching of Peace in the Writings and Early Lives of St. Francis of Assisi', *Mediaevistik*, 16 (2003), 51–99. In this article the Egyptian mission is not mentioned.

41. Frugoni, *Francesco e l'invenzione delle stimmate*, 3.

42. Ibid. 368. She later speaks of 'la comprensione dell'altro che Francesco anche in questo caso dimostra' (392 n. 50).

43. Ibid. 407. Frugoni, *Vita di un uomo: Francesco d'Assisi* (Turin: Einaudi, 1995).

44. Francesco Gabrieli, 'San Francesco e l'Oriente islamico', *Espansione del francescanesimo tra Occidente e Oriente nel secolo XIII: Atti del VI Convegno internazionale di studi francescani* (Assisi, 1979), 108–22 (esp. 116–18). Frugoni, *Vita di un uomo*. Other authors follow Massignon's interpretation of the trial by fire; see the novelized version of Henri Queffélec, *François d'Assise, le Jongleur de Dieu*, 214–30. For a testimony of an Arab author astonished by the spectacle of judicial ordeals (a duel and a trial by water) practised by the Franks of Jerusalem, see Usâma ibn Munqidh, *An Arab-Syrian Gentleman and Warrior in the Period of the Crusades: Memoirs of Usāmah ibn-Munqidh*, tr. Philip K. Hitti (New York: Columbia University Press, 1929 and 2000), 167–9.

45. Frugoni, 'Analisi delle singole scene (note strorico-iconografiche)', in Zanardi, *Il cantiere di Giotto*, 62–382 (here 174).

46. Daniel, *Franciscan Concept of Mission*, 41–7.

47. Franco Cardini, 'Nella presenza del Soldan superba: Bernardo, Francesco, Bonaventura e il superamento spirituale dell'idea di crociata', *Studi Francescani*, 71 (1974), 199–250. See also his *Francesco d'Assisi* (Milan: Mondadori, 1989), 179–208. See Ch. 13 above.

48. Kaspar Elm, 'Franz von Assisi: Bußpredigt oder Heidenmission?', *Espansione del francescanesimo tra Occidente e Oriente nel secolo XIII: Atti del VI Convegno internazionale di studi francescani* (Assisi, 1979), 69–103.

49. Benjamin Kedar, *Crusade and Mission: European Approaches to the Muslims* (Princeton: PUP, 1984), 129–31.

50. Bert Roest, 'Medieval Franciscan Mission: History and Concept', in Wout Van Bekkum and Paul Cobb (eds.), *Strategies of Medieval Community Identity: Judaism, Christianity and Islam* (Leuven: Peeters, 2004), 137–61.

51. Idries Shah, *The Sufis* (New York: Doubleday, 1964).

52. Ibid. 232.

53. Idries Shah, *The Sufis* 233.

54. James Cowan, *Francis: A Saint's Way* (Liguori, Mo.: Liguori/Triumph, 2001), 106.

55. Francisco Jesús María de San Juan del Puerto, *Patrimonio seraphico de Tierra Santa*; see Ch. 13 above.

56. Julien Green, *Frère François* (Paris: Seuil, 1983); tr. Peter Heinegg as *God's Fool: The Life and Times of Francis of Assisi* (San Francisco: Harper & Row, 1985).

57. Absire, *Le Pauvre d'Orient*, 329–39.

58. Carlo Carretto, *Io Francesco* (Assisi: Citadella, 1980); English tr., *I, Francis* (Maryknoll, NY: Orbis Books, 1982).

59. Albert Jacquard, *Le Souci des Pauvres: L'Héritage de François d'Assise* (Paris: Calmann-Lévy, 1996), 14.

60. Ibid. 11.

61. 'Le sommet interreligieux d'Assise de Jean-Paul II: L'homme européen est-il capable de se relever de l'abîme?', *Le Monde,* 12 Jan. 1993. See also Henri Tincq, 'Alors que les musulmans ont répondu à l'invitation du pape, les orthodoxes ont boudé le sommet interreligieux d'Assise', *Le Monde,* 12 Jan. 1993.

62. Anton Rotzetter, 'Francis of Assisi: A Bridge to Islam', *Concilum,* 2 (1999), 107–15. The same author elsewhere affirms that Francis visited the sultan, 'nello spirito della Fraternità', opened the way to contemporary dialogue between religions; he affirms that Francis in Damietta showed that he was against all forms of armed violence (Rotzetter, *Impulse für eine Friedensstrategie bei Franz von Assisi: Theologische Einordnung und Aktualisierung* (Bonn: Missionszentrale der Franziskaner, 1983); Italian tr., *Per una strategia di pace secondo Francesco d'Assisi: Inquadramento teologico ed attualizzazione* (Rome: Conferenza intaliana superiori provinciali cappuccini, n.d.), 22, 45).

63. Vázquez Janeiro, 'I francescani e il dialogo', 540.

64. Robson, *St Francis,* 237–8.

65. See Jeusset, *Rencontre sur l'autre rive,* 205–11.

66. Plan for Franciscan Living, *Let us Seek the Lord: A Year of Prayer for the 800th Anniversary of St. Francis's Birth* (Pulaski, Wis.: Franciscan Publishers, 1982), part 11, July 1981, 'Damietta: Prayer for Peace and Justice'.

67. Peggy Schultz, review of Donald Spoto, *The Reluctant Saint: Life of St. Francis of Assisi*, in the *Catholic Herald,* 27 Nov. 2003. She also claims that the fifth crusade was the last one.

68. See Henri Tincq, 'Le Premier Coup de crosse de Benoît XVI vise les Franciscains d'Assise et leurs forums politiques', *Le Monde,* 24 Nov. 2005, p. 4. The report of the chicken-sacrifice may well be apocryphal; it is found in Vittorio Messori, 'Questo Pontefice così "guerriero" è lo stesso di Assisi', *Corriere della Sera,* 4 Feb. 2002, p. 5; Interview with Vittorio Messori, 'Ma ad

Assisi "sacrificavano" anche i polli', *La Stampa*, 21 Nov. 2005. Franciscans of Assisi deny that this took place.

69. Jacques Dupuis, *Toward a Christian Theology of Religious Pluralism* (Maryknoll, NY: Orbis Books, 1997).

70. Ibid. 104.

71. Ibid. 105.

72. Interview with Vittorio Messori, 'Ma ad Assisi'. See Tincq, 'Le Premier Coup de crosse'.

73. Patrick Ryan, 'The Roots of Muslim Anger', *America*, 185(17), 26 Nov. 2001.

74. Text found on the Vatican website, http://www.vatican.va/news_services/ press/sinodo/documents/bollettino_20_x-ordinaria-2001/02_inglese/b08_ 02.html

75. Tiziano Terzani, *Letters against the War*, English tr. David Gibbons at http:// www.tizianoterzani.com/TT_letterenglish.pdf

76. Ibid.

77. http://www.healingamongnations.org/Programs/assisi.htm

78. http://www.vatican.va/holy_father/john_paul_ii/speeches/2002/january/ documents/hf_jp-ii_spe_20020124_discorso-assisi_en.html

79. Henri Tincq, 'L'"Esprit d'Assise" invoqué contre les fanatismes', *Le Monde*, 25 Jan. 2002. Henri Tincq, 'Le Sommet interreligieux d'Assise contre la guerre "au nom de Dieu"', *Le Monde,* 26 Jan. 2002. Tincq, 'L'"Esprit d'Assise"'; see another article in *Le Monde* on the same day, 'Jamais plus la violence! Jamais plus le terrorisme!'

80. Cardinal Joseph Ratzinger, 'The Splendor of the Peace of Francis', *30 Days in the Church and in the World*, 20/1 (Jan. 2002).

81. Ibid.

82. Thomas Cahill, 'The Peaceful Crusader', *New York Times*, 25 Dec. 2006.

83. The artist's commentary comes from http://www.trinitystores.com/?browse =&alpha=F.

EPILOGUE

1. 'Les polémiques anciennes organisaient à leur insu la recherche scientifique', Michel de Certeau, *Écrire l'histoire* (Paris: Gallimard, 1975 and 2002), 58.

2. 'La mémoire est un absolu et l'histoire ne connait que le relatif', Pierre Nora, *Les Lieux de Mémoire* (Paris: Gallimard, 1997), i. 25.

Index